Heart Vitamins
One Year of Daily Prescriptions for
Understanding and Knowing the Heart of God
Volume One

"Let him who boasts boast about this:
that he understands and knows Me…"
Jeremiah 9:24

Written and Compiled
by Bryan L. Herde

To all the writers and compilers of superb devotional classics
throughout the years, including:

My Utmost for His Highest by Oswald Chambers
Morning and Evening by Charles H. Spurgeon
Streams in the Desert by Mrs. Charles E. Cowman

among others.

The Lord has for generations used these devotionals to encourage and
challenge disciples of Jesus Christ through profound insights gained
by the experience of difficult lives.

Published June 2018

Sovereign Grip Communications

Copyright© 2018 Sovereign Grip Communications

www.sovereigngrip.com

Contributing Authors

I am immensely grateful to the following individuals whose work is contained within this book. Their unique, Holy Spirit-empowered sermons, devotionals, essays and writings are ageless and so very relevant for our time. They are listed in the order of their birth years. If you would like to know a bit more about them, I have included short biographies of each of them at the end of this book, placed in alphabetical order.

Please Note: *All of the writings of those whose excerpts I use are taken from books published prior to 1923. Anything older than 1923 is declared to be part of the "public domain" and can be used without restriction.*

Thomas Watson
François Fénelon
George Whitefield
Edward Payson
George Müller
George H. Bowen
John Ross Macduff
John Ker
Henry Robert Reynolds
Andrew Murray
Catherine Booth
Joseph Parker
Hannah Whitall Smith
Major-General Charles George Gordon
Phillips Brooks
Alexander Whyte
James Russell Miller
George Matheson
A.B. Simpson
David James Burrell
Henry Drummond
Samuel Dickey (S.D.) Gordon
John Henry Jowett
John Daniel Jones
George Herbert Morrison

Introduction

I know the feverish motions of our time, the restlessness of fruitless desire, the disturbing forebodings of anxiety, the busyness of the devil, the sleepless and perspiring activity of Mammon [the devil of covetousness], the rush to be rich, the race to be happy, the craving for sensation, the immense momentum and speed characterizing every interest in our varied life, and added to all, the impulsive and rapid shedding of ancient forms and garments, and the re-clothing of the thoughts of men in modern and more congenial attire.

The excerpt you just read was written over 100 years ago by John Henry Jowett, who lived 1863-1923. But these few sentences sound like a description of today, don't they?

In a world drowning in information, crazed by stress, gripped with fear, and becoming more and more self-centered, each of us needs to take some time to learn from those who have gone before us. We have brothers and sisters in Jesus Christ who, in their own way and time, felt what we feel, struggled with what we struggle with, and hoped for what we hope for—a life that is pleasing to God and fulfills His deepest desires and plans for us, in us and through us.

If you take just a little bit of time each day to read a few hundred words from some of these "ancient" saints, you will be amazed at the depth of wisdom that is just as relevant for us today—maybe even more so—than it was for them in their own time. Because the writings in this book are the result of the filling and flowing of the Holy Spirit, what is presented in these pages is absolutely timeless.

That is why I have compiled this daily devotional in the manner I have. Every few days you will see that I have taken the liberty of inserting one of my own writings for you to consider. I am deeply humbled to be in the mix with my brothers and sisters in Christ who have gone to be with the Lord over the past 400 years and whose own writings I have included in this devotional.

I have found these women and men to be deep, profound, timeless, full of the Holy Spirit, and persons who enjoyed an intimate relationship with God through knowing and understanding Christ and the Bible.

January 3 through May 16 are excerpts from a larger collection of essays and sermons I compiled called *Travelers on the Ancient Paths: Ageless Wisdom for an Anxious World*. These excerpts are mixed in with chapters from one of my books entitled *In the Stream, Volume One: Being a Disciple of Jesus Christ*. The rest of the year entails an eclectic mix of twenty-plus authors, plus some more of my writings that are new, including poems, as well as a few chapters from my other books, *Against the Stream* and *In the Stream, Volume Two: Living in the Flow of God*.

I am convinced that this book will be a powerful resource that the Lord will use to help bring you into spiritual maturity and intimate oneness with Himself. Each of the daily prescriptions will feed your soul and strengthen your heart. How these daily doses impact you will be up to our Great Physician for how He will take you into knowing and understanding Him, His heart, His purposes, His ways, His time and His processes for shaping and conforming you into the likeness of Jesus Christ (Romans 8:28-29).

May the Lord be pleased to use this book to encourage, to strengthen, to challenge, to convict, and to nourish your heart throughout the coming days, months and years of your life.

Why Reading the Ancients is Vital

This is what the Lord says: "Stand at the crossroads and look; ask for the ancient paths, ask where the good way is, and walk in it, and you will find rest for your souls."
Jeremiah 6:16

What has been will be again; what has been will be done again; there is nothing new under the sun.
Ecclesiastes 1:9

Why is spending time with writers that have long since gone to be with the Lord so important? Simply because they existed in a time that was far less frenzied than our own. Time was spent in Scripture, with the writing of others who preceded them, and time just being quiet and still. Certainly, this was not completely true for everyone during those times, but it is absolutely true for those whose excerpts are included in this devotional. These men and women plumbed the depths of what it meant to be in relationship with God. And by God's grace and generosity, many of them were able to articulate with clarity, with passion, and with power what they learned. It is a fallacy to believe that just because we have advanced technologies, or expanded scientific knowledge, or deeper psychological understanding, that we have more wisdom. Increased knowledge is no guarantee of possessing deeper wisdom. We can learn much from these "travelers on the ancient paths."

When it comes to the spiritual life of a Christian, we absolutely must remember that we are walking a path that is not new or better now than in the past, or in any way an improvement over the lessons learned and the wisdom gained by those who preceded us in time. Just read these words by George Morrison who lived 1866-1928:

> I think we shall all agree that in the life of our modern city there is recognizable the note of haste. One has only to watch one of our crowded streets to detect the pressure at the back of life. Life is more urgent than it used to be, the quietness of an older day is passing. The stream had still and shaded stretches in it once, but today it hurries forward very swiftly. Now it is notable that with that greater haste there is found, without any question, a lesser

faith. There is a certain shrinking of the faculty of faith in the organism of our complex life. I am no pessimist, and I trust that none of you are. Life, for all its sorrow, is too real, too deep, too rich, to write that name of failure on its brow. But the most cheerful optimist cannot be blind to this, that faith, and reverence which is the child of faith, are not conspicuous in our modern city; and the singular thing is, that with that decline of faith we should have witnessed the increase of hurry. Did you ever think that these features were connected? The Bible affirms it in the clearest manner. You say that the absence of restfulness in modern life springs from the fiercer struggle for existence. But the Bible goes a great deal deeper than that: the want of rest is rooted in want of trust. Depend upon it, he that believes not is always in danger of feverish impatience. Depend upon it, that to the end of time, he that believes shall not make haste.

The following excerpt is by John Henry Jowett who lived 1863-1923. His advice is both timely and highly applicable.

How, then, can we become "lovers of God"? First of all, we must consort with the God we desire to love. We must bring our minds to bear upon Him. Love is not born where there has been no communion. There must be association and fellowship. And, in the second place, we must consort with them that are lovers already. It is well that this should be through personal interaction, if such happy privilege comes our way. But if this immediate fellowship be denied us, let us seek their company through the blessed communion of books.

This devotional series is one of the ways you can "consort with those that are lovers already" and do so "through the blessed communion of books." The men and women whose material is represented in this devotional series are all individuals who struggled, who battled with sin, and who are people that totally gave themselves to know and understand God—no matter what it cost!

I have been led through an adventurous life by God, one full of uncertainties, as well as incredible possibilities. In order to better understand this journey, I have been voraciously reading a wealth of writings from pastors, missionaries, writers, preachers, teachers and philosophers who have struggled with learning to distrust self and, in absolute surrender, to trust God. Perhaps we can call them "mystics." My initial foray into the world of Christian mystics began when the Lord launched me into the process of learning what *dying to self* means, what *waiting on God* means, what *absolute surrender* means, what *an undivided heart* means, and what *abiding in Christ* really encompasses.

When using the term "Christian mystics," I will, of course offend some and confuse others. But I am in good company. A.W. Tozer (prominent American pastor, 1897-1963) had the same difficulty. Tozer explains that a "mystic" is one who partakes in the "personal spiritual experience" that saints of Biblical and post-Biblical times enjoyed. He is speaking of "the evangelical mystic who has been brought by the gospel into intimate fellowship with the Godhead."

So how does the mystic differ from other Christians? Tozer answers:

> The mystic experiences his faith down in the depths of his sentiment being while the other does not. He exists in a world of spiritual reality. He is quietly, deeply, and sometimes almost ecstatically aware of the Presence of God in his own nature and in the world around him. His religious experience is sometimes elemental, as old as time and the creation. It is immediate acquaintance with God by union with the Eternal Son. It is to know that which passes knowledge. (Tozer's comments are excerpted from a devotional on *www.immoderate.wordpress.com*).

I am certainly not in perfect agreement with all of the various positions that the many authors in this book held on every Christian doctrine, philosophy or experience. However, the Christian mystics I have selected meet that most basic quality that was true of each of them: they burned with a passion for a deep, intimate, unfiltered and unfettered relationship with God—a synchronizing of hearts and minds with His. God's grace and love cover a multitude of sins! May this journey you are about to undertake over this next year help lead you to a deeper intimacy with God as you "ask for the ancient paths, ask where the good way is, and walk in it, and you will find rest for your souls."

Editor's Note

Because this book is primarily comprised of excerpts from much larger texts, you will routinely notice the insertion of *** in the flow of the page. This signifies that substantial portions have been eliminated prior to the next set of statements.

Sometimes you will encounter [ ] which means that text has been added in order to clarify a name, location or term.

Additionally, in order to ease the flow of each day's reading, I have taken the liberty of modernizing the language to some degree. It will still be apparent that most of the material predates 21st-century American English, and that's the way it should be. But in consideration of my contemporary readers, I've tried to make the flow as smooth as possible. For example, where the King James Bible is quoted, I've replaced the obvious antiquated words like, "Thee," "Thou," "Ye," etc. with "you" and "yours." This is also true for when words of this type appear in the writers' own texts. I've retained most of the older punctuation where it doesn't obscure the meaning. Also, there are a number of terms used by the authors that were words that are not part of common language anymore, like "languor" (day dream), "sacerdotal" (clerical), "aggrandizement" (self-promotion, boasting), etc. So I have substituted modern synonyms where appropriate.

Please Note: Almost all of the writers in this book come from eras where the term "man," or words similar thereto, were used in the general sense of all humankind. I have chosen to keep this literary convention.

And one more very important thing to note: In my effort to make all the contributions of each of the authors fit onto one page for each day, and for that day's content to have an impact as a "stand alone" entry, I've deleted various phrases, or statements but do not show you where those omissions occurred. I have done this in an effort to make the reading as smooth and fluid as possible while working with the material each author provides.

Heart Vitamins

January 1

Food for the Inner Man (Part 1 of 2)
by George Müller

The first great and primary business to which I ought to attend every day is to have *my soul happy in the Lord.* The first thing to be concerned about was not how much I might serve the Lord, or how I might glorify the Lord, but how I might get my soul into a happy state, and how my inner man might be nourished. For I might seek to set the truth before the unconverted, or I might seek to benefit believers, or I might seek to behave myself as it becomes a child of God in this world; and yet, not being happy myself in the Lord, and not being nourished and strengthened in my inner man day by day, all this might not be accomplished in a right spirit.

Before this time my practice had been, at least for ten years previously, as a habitual thing, to give myself to prayer after having dressed in the morning. Now I saw that the most important thing I had to do was to give myself to the reading of the Word of God, and to meditation on it, so that my heart may be comforted, encouraged, warned, reproved, and instructed; and that then, while meditating, my heart might be brought into experiential fellowship with the Lord. I began therefore to meditate on the New Testament, from the beginning, early in the morning. The first thing I did, after having asked in a few words the Lord's blessing upon His precious Word, was to begin to meditate on the Word of God; searching, as it were, into every verse, to get blessings out of it; not for the sake of the public ministry of the Word; not for the sake of preaching on what I had meditated upon; but for the sake of obtaining food for my own soul. The result I have found to be almost invariably this, that after a very few minutes my soul has been led to confession, or to thanksgiving, or to intercession, or to supplication; so that though I did not, as it were, give myself to prayer but to meditation, yet it turned almost immediately more or less into prayer.

Subsequently, when I have been for a while making confession, or intercession, or supplication, or have given thanks, I go on to the next words or verse, turning all, as I go on into prayer for myself or others, as the Word may lead to it; but still continually keeping before me that food for my own soul is the object of my meditation.

January 2

Food for the Inner Man (Part 2 of 2)
by George Müller

The difference between my former practice and my present one is this: Formerly, when I rose I began to pray as soon as possible and generally spent all my time until breakfast in prayer, or almost all the time. In all events I almost always began with prayer. But what was the result? I often spent a quarter of an hour, or even an hour on my knees before being conscious to myself of having derived comfort, encouragement, humbling of soul, etc.; and often after having suffered much from the wandering of my mind for the first ten minutes, or a quarter of an hour, or even half an hour, I only then began really to pray. I scarcely ever suffer now in this way. For my heart being nourished by the truth, being brought into experiential fellowship with God, I speak to my Father, and to my Friend (vile though I am, and unworthy of it!) about the things that He has brought before me in His precious Word.

It often now astonishes me that I did not see this sooner. In no book did I ever read about it. No public ministry ever brought the matter before me. No private discussion with a brother stirred me up to this matter. And yet now, since God has taught me this point, it is as plain to me as anything that the first thing the child of God has to do morning by morning is to obtain food for his inner man. As the outward man is not fit for work for any length of time, except that we take food, and as this is one of the first things we do in the morning, so it should be with the inner man. Now what is the food for the inner man: not prayer, but the Word of God, and here again not the simple reading of the Word of God, so that it only passes through our minds just as water runs through a pipe, but considering what we read, meditating on it, and applying it to our hearts.

By the blessing of God I credit to this mode the help and strength which I have had from God to pass in peace through deeper trials in various ways than I ever had before. How different when the soul is refreshed and made happy early in the morning, from what it is when, without spiritual preparation, the service, the trials and the temptations of the day come upon one!

January 3

That You May Know (Part 1 of 2)
by Hannah Whitall Smith

*These things have I written unto you that believe on the name of the
Son of God; that you may know that you have eternal life, and that
you may believe on the name of the Son of God.*
1 John 5:13

One of the most common sense principles in everyday life is a clear
knowledge of one's earthly position and one's earthly possessions. And
nothing is plainer in the Bible than that we were meant to have this
knowledge in our religious life as well. Uncertainties are fatal to all true
progress, and are utterly destructive of comfort or peace. And yet it has
somehow become the fashion among Christians to encourage uncertainty
in the spiritual life as being an indication of the truest form of godliness.
There is a great deal of longing and hoping among Christians, but there is
not much knowing. And yet the whole Bible was written for the purpose of
making us know. The object of a revelation is to reveal. If nothing has been
revealed to us by the Bible beyond longings and hopes, it has failed in its
purpose for us.

But I fear a large proportion of God's children never get beyond these
hopes and longings. "I hope my sins will be forgiven some day;" "I hope I
may be favored to reach heaven at last;" "I hope God loves me;" "I hope
Christ died for me." These are samples of the style of much Christian
testimony in the present day. Indeed, I have even known Christians who
could never get further than to say, "I hope that I have a hope." If this
word were used in the sense that the Bible always uses it, that is, in the
sense of firm expectation, it might be all right; but in the use of it which I
have described, there is so great an element of doubt that it does not
amount to a Bible hope at all. We need sometimes to bring our words out
into the light of common sense to see what we really do mean by them, and
I am afraid that in very many cases we should find that the word "hope"
would mean, being interpreted, the word "doubt."

January 4

That You May Know (Part 2 of 2)
by Hannah Whitall Smith

*These things have I written unto you that believe on the name of the
Son of God; that you may know that you have eternal life, and that
you may believe on the name of the Son of God.*
1 John 5:13

The vital question, then, is how we can come to know. Our foundation text tells us, "These things are written that we may know." We must believe the things that are written in the "record" God has given us of His Son. Then we will know. For believing is the same as knowing, where the person we believe is absolutely trustworthy. There are human beings whose word is so absolutely trustworthy that we would believe them even almost against the testimony of our own senses; and surely God's word can be no less trustworthy.

***

Most people do not accept God's testimony as really being final, but look for some feeling or emotion of their own to validate its truth. "I could believe such and such things to be true, if I could only feel that they were." In earthly matters we never are so foolish as to make facts depend upon our feelings; but in religious matters a great many seem to think this is the right way. How we ever came to think so, I cannot imagine; for a little exercise of common sense would tell us that facts can never in any area depend upon feelings, but feelings must always in all things depend upon facts. The divine order is always first to get your facts; then to put faith in those facts; and then, as a natural result, the feelings will follow appropriately with the facts. This order is always followed in earthly things by every sane person. But curiously enough in religious matters a great many people, otherwise very sensible, reverse this order, and put feelings first, then faith in those feelings, and come to the facts last, looking upon these facts, one would suppose, as the result of their feelings.

***

The day of knowledge will dawn for us when we come to the point of implicitly believing God!

January 5

Lovers of God
by John Henry Jowett

When I turn to the New Testament no definition of love is given. Everywhere there are signs of love's presence, and she is always engaged in elevating and beautifying service. Her works are evident, but the worker herself is elusive. Where she moves there is indescribable energy; there are powerful ministries of purity, and diverse experiences are drilled to a common and generous end. Everywhere wildernesses become gardens, and deserts are rejoicing and blossoming as the rose. But one thing is said, and said very clearly, and it is this—the way to love our fellows is by becoming lovers of God. "The first of all commandments is, You shall love the Lord your God." Everywhere this is taught—love for God is the secret of a large, generous, and receptive humanity. How, then, can we become "lovers of God"?

First of all, we must consort with the God we desire to love. We must bring our minds to bear upon Him. Love is not born where there has been no communion. There must be association and fellowship. We must recover something of the ministry of solitude. We must make space to contemplate the glory of the Lord, and especially those characteristics of the Divine life which work to constrain our souls into strong and tender devotion.

***

And, in the second place, we must consort with them that are lovers already. It is well that this should be through personal interaction, if such happy privilege comes our way. But if this immediate fellowship be denied us, let us seek their company through the blessed communion of books.

***

Let me mention a third method by which we shall be helped to become lovers of God. I think we ought to sing the songs of the great lovers [of God], songs that will create and nurse kindred dispositions in ourselves. The ministry of the lovers' songs is not fully appreciated in the Christian life or they would more frequently be upon our lips.

January 6

Contact But Not Communion
by John Henry Jowett

There is a soul in touch with truth, but not free; in touch with life, but not alive; in touch with God, but not sharing the nature of God. God is near, but the soul does no business. Hands touch, but they do not clasp in holy covenant. There is contact, but no communion [referring not to the sacrament, but to intimacy].

***

Take note of how the Word of the Lord applies to the secret exercises of worship. When we meet together for public communion God is near, how near we cannot express. We cannot help but touch Him. We are brushing against Him in every moment of the sacred hour. I say we cannot help the contact, but we can refuse the communion. There may be interest but no reverence. There may be graceful postures, but no worthy honor. When we bow to pray there may be touch, but no grip. In the feast of the holy sacrament we may handle the bread, and so touch the very hem of His garment, and yet there may be no sacred union. We may go away from the service in the assumption that we have had communion when we have only been in contact with the Lord.

***

In all our customary circumstances the holy Lord is near. We cannot help but touch Him; do we commune with Him? In the sacrament of the common meal, the Lord is with us at the table. The common meal may be graceless, thankless, Godless, with no enrichment or suggestion of things which are Divine. He is lovingly concerned about our daily toil, and He would hearten and enlighten the worker by the strength and comforts of His grace. The Lord is near, but not in the soul.

***

This alienation can be ended by the exercise of our own choice of will. The will to commune means that communion has begun. When I kneel in sincerity I am opening the door to the heavenly guest: "If any man will open the door I will come in and eat with him and he with Me." That is the promise of the Master; it has never been revoked; it has never been unredeemed. There is no unwillingness on the part of the Lord; the unwillingness rests with us.

January 7

The Commitment of a Disciple
by Bryan L. Herde

"If…"
Matthew 16:24; Luke 9:23, 14:26

Why Almighty God would allow His born-again ones, His saved ones, to *choose* whether they will become one of His disciples is a mystery of love, grace and mercy that is beyond our ability to comprehend. There is a lot of controversy currently raging within Christendom about whether a person is really born again if he or she is not a disciple. While I understand the concern, I don't agree with the debate.

Jesus used the word "must" when talking about being born again with Nicodemus in John 3:7. However, when He is describing the cost of becoming His disciple in Luke 14, He begins with the word "if." "Must" versus "if." Certainly, Jesus made no mistake in choosing His words. He meant that eternal life is only possible when a person is born again. But He did not link His "must" for being born again with a mandatory "yes" in response to His invitation to become a disciple. "If." How much risk there is on the part of Eternal Love that He would dare use such a simple and yet discretionary word!

The gulf between the "must" of John 3 and the "if" of Luke 14 can only be spanned by God Himself. I believe that this is where the activity of Philippians 1:6 really starts applying: "Being confident of this, that He who began a good work in you will carry it on to completion until the day of Jesus Christ." Once you have agreed with the "must" and believed on Jesus Christ as the sole source for your salvation from sin and hell, then immediately the Holy Spirit begins wooing you to respond affirmatively to the "if" of becoming Christ's disciple.

Though this wooing begins the moment you are born again, it is a sad fact that the call and cost of being a disciple of Jesus, as He stated it, is seldom preached or taught in America's churches.

January 8

He Spoke to Them of the Father (Part 1 of 2)
by Hannah Whitall Smith

All the discomfort and unrest of the religious life of so many of God's children come, I feel sure, from this very thing, that they do not understand that God is actually and truly their Father. They think of Him as a stern Judge, or a severe Taskmaster, or at best as an unapproachable dignitary, seated on a far-off throne, dispensing exacting laws for a frightened and trembling world; and in their terror lest they should fail to meet His requirements, they hardly know which way to turn. But of a God who is a Father, tender, and loving, and full of compassion, a God who, like a father, will be on their side against the whole universe, they have no conception.

I am not afraid to say that discomfort and unrest are impossible to the souls that come to know that God is their real and actual Father.

***

Never, never must we think of God in any other way than as "our Father." All other attributes with which we endow Him in our conceptions must be based upon and limited by this one of "our Father." What a good father could not do, God, who is our Father, cannot do either; and what a good father ought to do, God, who is our Father, is absolutely sure to do. In our Lord's last prayer in John 17, He says that He has declared to us the name of the Father in order that we may discover the wonderful fact that the Father loves us *as* He loved His Son. Now, which one of us really believes this? Do any of us believe that it is an actual, tangible fact, that God loves us as much as He loved Christ? If we believed this to be actually the case, could we, by any possibility, ever have an anxious or rebellious thought again? Would we not be absolutely and utterly sure always under every conceivable circumstance that the divine Father, who loves us just as much as He loved His only begotten Son, our Lord Jesus Christ, would of course care for us in the best possible way, and could not tell us so emphatically not to be anxious or troubled about anything, for He knew His Father and knew that it was safe to trust Him utterly.

January 9

He Spoke to Them of the Father (Part 2 of 2)
by Hannah Whitall Smith

If God is our Father, the only thing we can do with doubts, and fears, and anxious thoughts is to cast them behind our backs forever, and have nothing more to do with them ever again. We *can* do this. We can give up our doubts just as we would urge a drunkard to give up his drink. We can pledge against doubting. And if once we see that our doubts are an actual sin against God, and imply a question of His trustworthiness, we will be eager to do it. We may have cherished our doubts before now because perhaps we have thought they were a part of our religion, and an agreeable attitude of soul in one so unworthy; but if we now see that God is in very truth our Father, we will reject every doubt with horror, as being a libel on our Father's love and our Father's care.

***

No wonder we are told to cast all our care upon Him, for He cares for us. He cares for us; of course He does. It is His business, as a Father, to do so. He would not be a good Father if He did not. All He asks of us is to let Him know when we need anything, and then leave the supplying of that need to Him; and He assures us that if we do this the "peace of God that passes all understanding shall keep our hearts and minds." The children of a good, human father are at peace because they trust in their father's care; but the children of the heavenly Father too often have no peace because they are afraid to trust in His care. They make their requests known to Him perhaps, but that is all they do. It is a sort of religious form they feel it necessary to go through. But as to supposing that He really will care for them, no such idea seems to cross their minds; and they go on carrying their cares and burdens on their own shoulders, exactly as if they had no Father in Heaven, and had never asked him to care for them.

***

"If you had known me," says Christ, "you should have known my Father also; and from this point forward you know him, and have seen him." The thing for us to do then is to make up our minds that from this point forward we will receive His testimony, and will "know the Father."

January 10

Humility: The Glory of the Creature
by Andrew Murray

They shall cast their crowns before the throne, so saying: "Worthy are You, our Lord and our God, to receive the glory, and the honor and the power: for You did create all things, and because of Your will they are, and were created."
Revelation 4:11

In our ordinary religious teaching, being a sinner has been too exclusively put in the foreground, so that some have even gone to the extreme of saying that we must keep sinning if we are indeed to keep humble. Others again have thought that the strength of self-condemnation is the secret of humility. And the Christian life has suffered loss, where believers have not been distinctly guided to see that, even in our relation as creatures, nothing is more natural and beautiful and blessed than to be nothing, that God may be all; or where it has not been made clear that it is not sin that humbles most, but grace, and that it is the soul, led through its sinfulness to be occupied with God in His wonderful glory as God, as Creator and Redeemer, that will truly take the lowest place before Him.

***

The life God bestows is imparted not once for all, but each moment continuously, by the unceasing operation of His mighty power. Humility, the place of entire dependence on God, is, from the very nature of things, the first duty and the highest virtue of the creature, and the root of every virtue.

***

Humility is the only soil in which the graces take root; the lack of humility is the sufficient explanation of every defect and failure. Humility is not so much a grace or virtue along with others; it is the root of all, because it alone takes the right attitude before God, and allows Him as God to do all. Let us feel that nothing but a very determined and persevering waiting on God and Christ will discover how lacking we are in the grace of humility, and how impotent we are to obtain what we seek.

January 11

The Attitude of a Disciple (Part 1 of 3)
by Bryan L. Herde

*Do nothing out of selfish ambition or vain conceit, but in humility consider others better
than yourselves. Each of you should look not only to your own interests,
but also to the interests of others.*
Philippians 2:3-4

The work accomplished and the life lived by Jesus Christ was only possible because He "made Himself nothing" (Philippians 2:7a). Humility was absolute. There was no ego, no "me first" attitude, no "what's in it for me" considerations, nor were there ambitious personal agendas in the life of Jesus. He came to allow the fullness of the Godhead to dwell in Him and allow God to do all and be all. In order for disciples of Jesus Christ to bear much fruit, humility must be pervasive. Humility is like a glass jar: the purer the glass, the more clearly one can see through it to what is inside it. And what the world wants—even when it doesn't know it—is to see Jesus. Through the clarity of humility, Jesus is evident and tangible to others in us.

According to Andrew Murray in his book *Humility*, "Humility, the place of entire dependence upon God, is, from the very nature of things, the first duty and the highest virtue of man. It is the root of every virtue." Humility enables disciples to:
- Pray wholeheartedly
- Wait patiently
- Worship powerfully
- Relate lovingly
- Think correctly
- Do rightly

When Paul said, "Your attitude should be the same as that of Christ Jesus," he wasn't just suggesting that humbling ourselves was a good idea; the Lord was using him to communicate the absolute necessity of humility. Pride, the enemy of humility, was the original sin in the Garden of Eden because it was the initial sin of Satan. Pride is by far the most damaging of sins in the life of the church and the life of a disciple.

January 12

The Attitude of a Disciple (Part 2 of 3)
by Bryan L. Herde

Do nothing out of selfish ambition or vain conceit, but in humility consider others better than yourselves. Each of you should look not only to your own interests, but also to the interests of others.
Philippians 2:3-4

Pride is sterile soil in which no Godlike virtues can take root. Pride is the cancer that eats away at the church and continues to weaken it all too readily. Pride is the pest that eats away at the branches sprouting from the Vine that is Jesus.

True humility is best defined as giving up total control of ourselves to the Lord. It seems to me that our fear associated with giving up control weakens and disables faith more than any other. We by nature fear the unknown. I personally struggle with the fear that the unknown will always be negative, not positive. We fear what may or may not happen if we relinquish control over our lives to One who more than likely will not orchestrate our lives to our trouble-avoidance satisfaction, or work things out along our ideal timelines, or do things the way we believe would be best—either for ourselves or for others.

There is a contemporary Christian music group called Casting Crowns who sings an insightful song entitled "In the Middle." One of the phrases from that song that addresses this issue is, "How close can I come to my surrender without losing all control?" In our minds, we believe that we would be happiest if we could blend an appropriate mix of our goals and God's desires into a suitable combination that would ensure our happiness and result in as little pain and suffering as possible.

Beyond the "Big Three" areas of suffering—relationships, health and finances—we would also like to escape the suffering of not knowing how long something is going to last, how difficult the process is going to be, and what the result will be.

January 13

The Attitude of a Disciple (Part 3 of 3)
by Bryan L. Herde

*Do nothing out of selfish ambition or vain conceit, but in humility consider others better
than yourselves. Each of you should look not only to your own interests,
but also to the interests of others.*
Philippians 2:3-4

Over the past several years, I have been in numerous discussions where we
were addressing certain decisions or perspectives. One question was almost
always asked, "What does or will that (result) look like?" Faith is most often
hampered because we cannot predict the future. If we could, we wouldn't
need faith. Certainly, we have promises in the Bible that tell us "all things
work together for good" (Romans 8:28), "God will supply all our needs
according to His riches in Christ Jesus" (Philippians 4:19), etc. But what the
Lord never explains to us is how He will do it, precisely when He will do it
or, to be quite honest, whether or not we will like the process He chooses.

Just like bearing fruit, humbling ourselves is not something we can do.
Rather it is something we yield ourselves to having done in us and to us.
Our hearts possess too much pride for humility to be a self-generated
attitude. For example, I know for a fact that I have too many times been
proud of my humility; proud of when I've allowed others to walk over me;
proud of when I've humbled myself to serve others; and have used my
moments of humility as bargaining tools when asking the Lord to act on my
behalf. Conscious humility is most likely fleshly humility, not a quality of
Jesus.

Going back to the initial illustration of humility being like pure glass, it is
important to remember that glass is made from sand ("He remembers that
we are dust," Psalms 103:14) that is transformed into glass through the
intense heat of a furnace. The only way we become humble is through the
"fiery trials" the Lord engineers in our lives in order for the glory of Christ
to be revealed in us (1 Peter 4:12-19). Humility becomes our prized garment
as the contrary will of our flesh is burned away through difficulties,
hardships and persecution.

January 14

Reality and Mystery (Part 1 of 2)
by John Henry Jowett

"The wind blows where it will, and you hear the sound thereof, but cannot tell where it comes and where it goes; and so is everyone that is born of the Spirit."
John 3:8

Jesus told disquieted Nicodemus that there are momentous happenings in the world of the Spirit, and their reality is not in the least degree impaired by the absence of a rationale. We can be sure of the wind even though we cannot explain it. We can be sure of spiritual realities even though reason limp and loiter on the road. In a word, we can have experience long before we have explanation. We can have spiritual reality before intellectual clarity. We can have life before light. We can be sure of the wind even when reason has not put its mysteries into chains.

Now this is not a trivializing of the intellect. We do not devalue things by placing them in their appointed rank and order. I do not disparage the alphabet when I say that a child can talk long before he knows that the alphabet exists. It is just a matter of grade, and order and succession. And when it is said that in the realm of the Spirit we can have happenings which are impressive before they are expressive, that life can have association with realities before intellect has made her survey and begun to offer explanations, we are only proclaiming the divine order, and we are saying that the loitering intellect does not impoverish my assurance because of its delay.

***

When we direct our minds to the supreme spiritual realities we are inclined to argue that things are unreal unless the intellect can unravel their secrets and present them in brilliant understanding. We argue as though intellect were everything. We speak as if we have no other power of comprehension. But we have many powers. We have higher-sense perceptions which give us mystic sight, and taste, and touch. That was the Master's teaching to Nicodemus. He told him he could have assurance of spiritual reality long before he had powers of understanding.

January 15

Reality and Mystery (Part 2 of 2)
by John Henry Jowett

"The wind blows where it will, and you hear the sound thereof, but cannot tell where it comes and where it goes; and so is everyone that is born of the Spirit."
John 3:8

Let us take the counsels of the Master to another mystery, the mystery of divine companionship. And what is that? It is enshrined in the promise of the Master, "I am with you all the days." Here is a Friend who is always on the road. What kind of a road? Every sort of road. Through the green pastures and by the still waters! By the steep and rugged paths of righteousness! Through the valley of the shadow of death! Through landscapes crimson with the rose of Sharon! Through the trackless desert where the carrion eagle screams! Along the shining way to the marriage altar! Along the dripping way to the grave! The Friend is on every road. And that Presence is to millions of people a wonderful reality. They have the impressive sense of a strong and chivalrous companion. "But warm, sweet, tender, even yet a present help is He." And there are some souls whose sense of fellowship with the Lord is so intimate that they feel that the removal of the thinnest veil would bring Him face to face. He brings them counsel. When the roads are rocky He bathes their bleeding feet. He imparts unto them strength for fine ventures. He gives them courage when the horizon is gloomy with the menace of the cross. "I will not leave you nor forsake you."

***

Give high place to your instincts, your intuitions, your affections, your faith, your hope. Follow the path of the noblest assumption. Fling yourself in the way of your faith, and follow it with the strength of a consecrated venture. Offer your life to the Savior-hood and the governance of Christ. Do it as a sacred act of dedication, do it as a simple act of will. Let it be as an act in which you solemnly surrender your life to the highest. And you shall surely hear the wind that blows where it will.

January 16

What Think You of Christ? (Part 1 of 2)
by Alexander Whyte

"What think you of Christ?"
Matthew 22:42

What think you of Christ? That is the question of all questions. No other question so important and so pressing as that question has ever been put to the mind, and to the heart, and to the conscience of man. There is no other possible question that so taxes and so tests the whole soul of every man as just this question—what he thinks of Christ.

***

One sad, and not small class among us, is composed of those men and women who simply never think of Christ at all.

***

But happily, there is another class of men and women among us who are the exact opposite of that. They are but a small class, it is to be feared, in any congregation, and yet, who can tell? They may be more in number than anyone would believe. Few or many, this noble class is composed of those men and women among us who in their heart of hearts are continually thinking of Christ.

***

But, with all their happy experiences of Christ, even the best of believers too much forget to think of Him, when they are suddenly surprised with some unforeseen temptation, or heavy trial, or sharp cross, or sore hurt, or great loss. But the root of the matter is in them all the time. And they soon recover their feet, and say to Christ: "Whom have I, and whom need I, but You alone?"

The very best of believers will have seasons of the most terrible depression, and desolation, and despair. But the sun shines out, and they are themselves again. That is to say—Christ is Himself to them again. Ups and downs like these go on with the best of believers, all through their life on earth. That is to say, into the glory of Christ: according to His all-prevailing prayer in their behalf, "Father, I desire that those whom You have given Me will be with Me where I am."

January 17

What Think You of Christ? (Part 2 of 2)
by Alexander Whyte

"What think you of Christ?"
Matthew 22:42

It is what you think of yourself that will always decide what you think of Him. Tell me what you think of yourself, and I will undertake to tell you what and how much you think of Christ. Just as, tell me what and how much and how often you think of Christ, and I will already know to a certainty what you think of yourself.

***

Jesus Christ, the Son of God, is ten thousand things to God, and man, and angels: ten thousand things on earth and in heaven, in time and in eternity, in grace and in glory; but, first and foremost, to you and to me today, He is our Savior from our sins.

***

Now let us go over and tell to ourselves, and to one another, some of the things that have helped us most to our best thoughts concerning Christ:
- What is it in Christ that you most admire?
- What is it in Him that most moves your heart?
- What is it in Him that makes your heart sing within you?
- To what incident in His recorded life on earth do you like best to return?
- What miracle of His do you always ask to be repeated in you?
- What mighty work of His do you pray urgently, persistently to have worked over again in your son or in your daughter or yourself?
- What parable of His do you esteem to be His gem and His masterpiece?
- What secret prayer of yours has He so openly and so wonderfully answered?
- What blessing do you possess at this moment that you got from Him when you asked Him for it?

January 18

Lose to Find (Part 1 of 2)
by John Henry Jowett

"He that finds his life shall lose it; and he that loses his life for My sake shall find it."
Matthew 10:39

I am amazed at the almost bold directness of the program. There is no hiding of the sharp blade, no softening of the shadow, no gilding of the cross. The hostilities bristle in naked obviousness. Every garden is a prospective battlefield; "I am not come to send peace, but a sword." The choice of the Christ involves a perpetual challenge to war.

***

Let us proclaim the methods of the Lord. It is not by silence, but by expression that we win: "Whoever shall confess Me before men." It is not by drifting, but by endurance that we win; "He that endures to the end shall be saved." It is not by self-promotion but by self-sacrifice that we win: "He that loses his life for My sake shall find it." This is the secret of Jesus; life is sustained and enriched by expression, by endurance, and by sacrifice.

***

It is not by the policy of self-importance that we can find the secrets of an enduring progress. Life is not enriched by selfishness, but by sacrifice. Life becomes fruitful only when it becomes sacrificial. This is true concerning our influence upon one another. It seems ordained that life has to attain a certain fervor of sacrifice before it can become contagious and multiply itself throughout the race. On the cold planes of calculation and selfishness life is unimpressive, and its products leave the general life unmoved.

***

I say, therefore, that the spirit of sacrifice enriches self while yet it fertilizes others. Our giving is our getting. "With what measure you give, it shall be measured to you again."

***

Here, then, are the gates to a rich and roomy individual life; not silence, but expression; not drifting, but endurance; not self-seeking, but sacrifice; for "he that finds his life shall lose it, but he that loses his life for My sake shall find it."

January 19

Lose to Find (Part 2 of 2)
by John Henry Jowett

"He that finds his life shall lose it; and he that loses his life for My sake shall find it."
Matthew 10:39

By the methods of the world the Church will never gain her life. Life gained in such conditions is miserably deceptive. The vitality is only apparent. The growth is sickly swelling. The finding is only a losing. The Church that would grow rich must externalize and invest its treasure. The Church that would live must die. If she would have her Olivet of enriched communion, she must seek it by the way of Golgotha and the Cross. If she would gain, she must lose. She must be a missionary Church, working out her salvation by the ministries of expression, endurance, and sacrifice.

***

We discover while we evangelize. Our torch emits new flame while we light the lamps of others. We get while we give. "He that finds his life shall lose it; he that loses his life for My sake shall find it."

***

When the church is easeful she loses the power to redeem.

***

When the church's life is lived on the plane of ease, and comfort, and bloodless service, she has no power to fertilize the dry and barren places of the earth. When the Church becomes sacrificial, she becomes impressive. The sacrificial things in history are the influential things today. It is the men and the women who give away their being, the bleeding folk, who are our present inheritance.

***

The finders have lost. The apparent losers are at the winning post! The sacrificial are the triumphant. "They loved not their lives unto the death, and they overcame by the blood of the Lamb." A sacrificial Church would speedily conquer the world! "He that finds his life shall lose it; and he that loses his life for My sake shall find it."

January 20

The Investment of a Disciple (Part 1 of 3)
by Bryan L. Herde

Therefore, I urge you, brothers and sisters, in view of God's mercy, to offer your bodies as a living sacrifice, holy and pleasing to God—this is your true and proper worship. Do not conform to the pattern of this world, but be transformed by the renewing of your mind. Then you will be able to test and approve what God's will is—His good, pleasing and perfect will.
Romans 12:1-2

Sacrifice for the sake of sacrifice is not what is being urged; it is a *living* sacrifice that God wants. A living sacrifice is something that, though it is dead, lives. That is why Paul could say in Galatians 2:20, "I am crucified with Christ." He died in Christ on the cross. Obviously, none of us were there physically [including Paul] but, by God's grace, we were there spiritually. And since we are indeed spiritual beings, then that is the substantive reality about which Paul is talking.

But then Paul goes on to say, "nevertheless I live." He is still alive physically though the physical body no longer has power. Its power—sin—was crucified and no longer has dominion over us who are saved.

So if Christ is our personal Savior, we were indeed, in God's reality, put to death in Christ when He died on the cross. That is why we no longer need to fear death and judgment, because the judgment for our sins was carried out against Jesus and we were in Him when that happened. We have passed from death to life. We are alive forevermore because we died with Him and we also live with Him because we were raised from the dead in Him.

Then Paul said in Galatians 2:20, "yet not I, but Christ lives in me." So it is not our life that lives in our hearts but that of Jesus. Jesus was the first living sacrifice because all other sacrifices before Him died and did not come back to life. Only Jesus shed His blood, "the Lamb that was slain," and was raised to life and seated at the right hand of God the Father.

January 21

The Investment of a Disciple (Part 2 of 3)
by Bryan L. Herde

Therefore, I urge you, brothers and sisters, in view of God's mercy, to offer your bodies as a living sacrifice, holy and pleasing to God—this is your true and proper worship. Do not conform to the pattern of this world, but be transformed by the renewing of your mind. Then you will be able to test and approve what God's will is—His good, pleasing and perfect will.
Romans 12:1-2

"The life which I now live in the flesh, I live by the faith of the Son of God." It is His faith that lives in us, is powerful and almighty, capable of moving mountains and overcoming the most fearsome threats. That is why we are urged to surrender our bodies as living sacrifices so that the life and faith of Jesus may have their full freedom to do what He wants done, how He wants to do it, when He wants to do it and where He wants to do it. Our responsibility is to yield; Jesus' responsibility is to do all the work He commanded. What liberty and freedom! No man or woman can possibly do everything God commanded us to do. But Jesus can!

Yield. Surrender. Let Jesus live through you and you will see the marvel of a life that abides and rests in His wondrous power, a life that pleases God in every way at all times. It isn't your job to undertake to do what only Jesus can do through the perfect faith He produces in us. Declare yourself dead to sin, for you are, whether you feel like it or not. Now declare yourself dead to yourself and enjoy the abundant life He has promised when you walk through life as a "living sacrifice, holy, and pleasing to God." Then you will see God's perfect will completed through you because you *are* His will. Total surrender. This is what Jesus asks, in light of our security in Him. That means that I give up all rights to myself, to my decision-making, to my relationships, to my ambitions, to my agendas, to my self-fulfillment, to my possessions, to my desires; in other words, *everything!* Why would I want to hold onto anything, considering that all I have and will have, now and forever, is not really mine anyway? How do we respond to a love that is that complete? Through surrendering our all to Jesus.

January 22

The Investment of a Disciple (Part 3 of 3)
by Bryan L. Herde

*Large crowds were traveling with Jesus, and turning to them He said: "If anyone comes to Me and does not hate his father and mother, his wife and children, his brothers and sisters—yes, even his own life—he **cannot** be My disciple. And anyone who does not carry his cross and follow Me **cannot** be My disciple. In the same way, any of you who does not give up everything he has **cannot** be My disciple.*
Luke 14:26-27, 33 (emphasis added)

What I find most striking in these verses are the three uses of the word "cannot." "Cannot," as used here, means exactly what it says: *cannot!* A person who wants to be a disciple cannot be a disciple unless he or she gives up everything for Jesus. There is no middle ground! You either hold onto nothing or you hold onto everything. There are no partial possibilities here. That runs contrary to so much of what is taught in our churches today. The number of self-fulfillment, leadership, health, wealth, happiness, do-good and feel-good books, sermons and publications contain nothing of total surrender. It seems that we would gladly receive the gifts of God without any notion of real gratitude. We are incurably selfish, wanting the gifts, the power, the blessings and the favor of God—yet without giving the one thing He asks of us.

He doesn't want our prayers, our giving, our service, our praises—He wants us! He wants our hearts to desire Him, not just what He has to offer, but Him (Isaiah 29:13). The passage quoted above finds Jesus asking us if we really love Him. Isn't that at the heart of His statements about hating, giving up, carrying your own cross and following Him? Isn't He really asking us to love Him more than anything?

His requirement is quite alarming and our failure to comply results in one of the most difficult uses of the word "cannot." If we don't surrender all, then we are not His disciples. We may be saved and rescued from the flames of hell, from the pit of darkness and the grip of the enemy, but we are not His disciples.

January 23

Carnal or Spiritual?
by Andrew Murray

And Peter went out and wept bitterly.
Luke 22:62

These words indicate the turning point in the life of Peter—a crisis. There is often a question about the life of holiness. Do you grow into it? Or do you come into it by a crisis suddenly? Peter has been growing for three years under the training of Christ, but he had grown terribly downward, for the end of his growing was, he denied Jesus. And then there came a crisis. After the crisis he was a changed man, and then he began to grow aright. We must indeed grow in grace, but before we can grow in grace we must be put right. If a man is a babe in Christ and has a little of the Holy Spirit and a great deal of the flesh, he is called *carnal,* for the flesh is his chief mark. If he gives way, as the Corinthians did, to strife, temper, division, and envy, he is a carnal Christian. He is a Christian, but a carnal one. But if he gives himself over entirely to the Holy Spirit so that He (the Holy Spirit) can deliver from the temper, the envy, and the strife, by breathing a heavenly disposition; and can mortify the deeds of the body; then God's Word calls him a "spiritual" man, a true spiritual Christian.

***

The message that I want to bring to you is this: That the great majority of Christians, alas, are not spiritual men, and that they may become spiritual men by the grace of God. I want to come to all who are perhaps hungering and longing for the better life, and asking what is wrong that you are without it, to point out that what is wrong is just one thing—*allowing the flesh to rule in you, and trusting in the power of the flesh to make you good.*

***

The Holy Spirit had changed Peter. He could not understand what Christ taught him. It was impossible before the death of Christ; but on the day of Pentecost how he is able to expound the word of God as a spiritual man! I tell you, beloved, when the Holy Ghost comes upon a man he becomes a spiritual man, and instead of denying his Lord he denies himself.

January 24

Counsel to Christians (Part 1 of 2)
by George Müller

That I may know Him...
Philippians 3:7

The question arises naturally: What is it that the Apostle particularly desires in our text, "That I may know Him?" That he might know the Blessed One in all His loveliness, in all His beauty, just as the saints finally will see the King in His beauty, will know Him in all His loveliness, in all His characters, so as every one of His saints will know Him in the glory finally, so, while the Apostle was yet in the body, while yet in weakness, while yet Satan was not bound, and himself not in the glory, he desired more and more intimately to become acquainted with the precious adorable Lord Jesus Christ in all His loveliness, so that the joy and the blessedness of the glory in the world to come might, in a great measure, already be realized by him while he was yet in the body.

***

Therefore, the great point is to be able to treat the Lord Jesus Christ as a bosom friend, to be able to go to Him and say "My precious Lord, speak to me the word in season," when we are weary. While passing through this valley of tears, in the middle of trial and difficulty, in the middle of labor and sadness, in the middle of severe temptation, in the middle of conflict of greater or lesser degree, again, and again, and again, the child of God, who desires to walk in the ways of the Lord, will find himself spiritually worn. Now then go to the precious Lord and say, "My Lord, speak to me the word in season, for I am weary."

***

Thus becoming increasingly acquainted with the Lord Jesus Christ, we should finally get into the state to which we find reference made in Psalm 9:10, "They that know Your name will put their trust in You."

And therefore we say, knowing Him they confide in Him, they trust in His power, they trust in His love, they trust in His wisdom, they trust in Him at all times and under all circumstances.

January 25

Counsel to Christians (Part 2 of 2)
by George Müller

That I may know Him…
Philippians 3:7

As the redeemed of the Lord, it is proper for us to continually keep before us the fact that our own salvation is not the ultimate end, but the glory of God. This we have never to lose sight of; and in order that we may do our part as witnesses for God in this world, it is necessary that we should not be conformed to the world, but transformed. Without this it is entirely impossible to be witnesses for God in a right way. We may think we do this and we do another thing to the glory of God, and yet just only in so far as we are not conformed to this world, but are transformed, are we truly witnesses for God.

***

Should there be anyone among us with whom it is a question whether half the heart or three-fourths of the heart are given to the Lord, or whether the whole heart has been given to the Lord, then let me urge such, my beloved brethren in Christ, not to be satisfied until they come to this, that the whole heart is given to the Lord, so that we can stand before the Lord and say, "My Father, You know all things; You know that Your poor child is feeble and weak, but You know also that my heart is given to You: You have my heart."

***

In this one thing we must be honest, that there does not remain to ourselves a part of the heart; He will have the whole heart. He says, "My son, give Me your heart," not "part of your heart." Nor does He say, "My son, give me a little of your money;" but He says, "Give me your heart," and He will accept nothing in place of the heart. When the heart is really given to the Lord, then the purse is given to Him also; then the profession and business are given to Him also; then our houses and lands belong to Him also; and all we have and are belongs to the Lord. At this we should aim, and with nothing short of it should we be satisfied.

January 26

Out of and Into
by Andrew Murray

And He brought us out from there, that He might bring us in,
to give us the land which He swore to our Fathers.
Deuteronomy 6:23

So in the life of the believer, there are ordinarily two steps quite separate from each other: bringing him out of sin and the world; and bringing him into a state of complete rest afterward.

***

How glorious was the rest of Canaan after all the wanderings in the wilderness! And so is it with the Christian who reaches the better promised Canaan of rest, when he comes to leave all his charge with the Lord Jesus— his responsibilities, anxieties, and worry; his only work being to hand the keeping of his soul into the hand of Jesus every day and hour, and the Lord can keep, and give the victory over every enemy. Jesus has undertaken not only to cleanse our sin, and bring us to heaven, but also to keep us in our daily life.

I ask again: Are you hungering to get free from sin and its power? Anyone longing to get complete victory over his temper, his pride, and all his evil inclinations? Anyone longing to walk in the full sunshine of God's loving favor?

***

Are you willing to give up your sins, to walk with God continually, to submit yourself wholly to the will of God, and have no will of your own apart from His will? Are you going to live a perfect life? What is this perfection? A state in which your hearts will be set on perfect integrity without any reserve, and your will wholly subservient to God's will.

***

How does God lead us in? By leading us in a very definite act, namely, that of committing ourselves wholly to Him: entrusting ourselves to Him, that He may bring us into the land of rest, and keep us in.

January 27

The Heart of a Disciple (Part 1 of 4)
by Bryan L. Herde

Give me an undivided heart, that I may fear Your name.
Psalm 86:11b

An undivided heart. Wouldn't that be a marvelous thing to have? No more erratic behaviors, no more doubts, no more fears, no more self-centeredness! Only one person has ever enjoyed that while living upon this planet, and that is Jesus.

Yet here we have David, a man after God's own heart (Acts 13:22), asking for that very thing. And if we are to be true disciples of Jesus Christ, then we should not only desire it, but we should be courageous enough to ask for the Lord to give us an undivided heart as well. But it is the asking and receiving, and then having God start working on us and in us that may cause us to stay just short of such a request.

And that is why I used the word "courageous." It does take courage, stamina and resolve to endure what is required to have an undivided heart worked in us by God. An undivided heart is not something that we can do ourselves. That is why David asked for it from God. How do we know that we can't do this?

- "The heart is deceitful above all things, and desperately wicked: who can know it? I the Lord search the heart..." (Jeremiah 17:9-10a)
- "For it is from within, out of a person's heart, that evil thoughts come: sexual immorality, theft, murder, adultery, greed, malice, deceit, lewdness, envy, slander, arrogance and folly. All these evils come from inside and defile a person" (Mark 7:21-23).

But God is capable:
- "God, who knows the heart" (Acts 15:8a)
- "[God] knows the secrets of the heart" (Psalms 44:21b).
- "[God] who searches our hearts knows the mind of the Spirit" (Romans 8:27)

January 28

The Heart of a Disciple (Part 2 of 4)
by Bryan L. Herde

Give me an undivided heart, that I may fear Your name.
Psalm 86:11b

The Lord Himself is the King of Hearts, and lives in our hearts according to His promises:

- "If anyone loves Me, he will obey My teaching. My Father will love him, and We will come to him and make Our home with him" (John 14:23).
- "And I will ask the Father, and He will give you another Counselor to help you and be with you forever—the Spirit of truth. The world cannot accept Him, because it neither sees Him nor knows Him. But you know Him, for He lives with you and will be in you" (John 14:16-17).
- "I have made You known to them, and will continue to make You known in order that the love You have for Me may be in them and that I Myself may be in them" (John 17:26).

In addition to all this, we know that the Lord asked us to love Him with all of our hearts, as He states in Matthew 22:36-40:

- "'Love the Lord your God with *all* your heart and with all your soul and with all your mind.' This is the first and greatest commandment. And the second is like it: 'Love your neighbor as yourself.' All the Law and the Prophets hang on these two commandments" (emphasis added).

A whole heart without divided loyalties is God's desire for each of us. He can and will work that in us. That is, in essence, what growing mature in the Lord actually means. Gaining an undivided heart is the process of growing in the Lord, of becoming a mature Christian who lives by faith and trust in God alone. It is the desire that the Lord implants in us from His own heart that creates in us the hunger for Him alone, that compels us to yield ourselves to His working so that we, too, may have a heart whose divisions of loyalty are always being undone, and a heart that is being brought into submission to God's all-encompassing and all-filling abundance.

January 29

The Heart of a Disciple (Part 3 of 4)
by Bryan L. Herde

Give me an undivided heart, that I may fear Your name.
Psalm 86:11b

Listen to these words of David that express his heart's comprehension of the vastness and nearness of God:

> Where can I go from Your Spirit? Where can I flee from Your presence? If I go up to the heavens, You are there; if I make my bed in the depths, You are there. If I rise on the wings of the dawn, if I settle on the far side of the sea, even there Your hand will guide me, Your right hand will hold me fast. If I say, "Surely the darkness will hide me and the light become night around me," even the darkness will not be dark to You; the night will shine like the day, for darkness is as light to You. For You created my inmost being; You knit me together in my mother's womb. I praise You because I am fearfully and wonderfully made; Your works are wonderful, I know that full well. My frame was not hidden from You when I was made in the secret place, when I was woven together in the depths of the earth. Your eyes saw my unformed body; all the days ordained for me were written in Your book before one of them came to be. How precious to me are Your thoughts, God! How vast is the sum of them! Were I to count them, they would outnumber the grains of sand—when I awake, I am still with You (Psalm 139:7-18).

This is not the expression of a man who does not want this all-seeing, all-being God in his life—far from it! No, David is delighting in the comprehensive, pervasive and expansive reality of God. David delights in this truth about God! That is why David could also say in Psalms 37:4, "Delight yourself in the Lord and He will give you the desires of your heart." The great blessing imbedded in this verse is that it is God who implants the desires that He then fulfills. And because He lives in our hearts, He is not sending those desires across space and time to enter into our hearts: they are desires that simply emanate from Him within us.

January 30

The Heart of a Disciple (Part 4 of 4)
by Bryan L. Herde

Give me an undivided heart, that I may fear Your name.
Psalm 86:11b

An undivided heart is the resulting reality of the "in-ness" that Jesus prayed for in John 17:20-21:

> "My prayer is not for them alone. I pray also for those who will believe in Me through their message, that all of them may be one, Father, just as You are in Me and I am in You. May they also be in Us so that the world may believe that You have sent Me."

Ultimately, an undivided heart is the desire of God *for us* that He alone can work *in us*. All He asks is that we yield to His desire so that our will can be conformed to His will. And that, my brothers and sisters, is how an undivided heart can become a reality for each of us. "Yet, O Lord, You are our Father. We are the clay, You are the Potter; we are all the work of Your hands" (Isaiah 64:8). This is the essence of the transformational process that Paul describes in 2 Corinthians 4:6-12:

> For God, Who said, "Let light shine out of darkness," made His light shine in our hearts to give us the light of the knowledge of God's glory displayed in the face of Christ. But we have this treasure in jars of clay to show that this all-surpassing power is from God and not from us. We are hard pressed on every side, but not crushed; perplexed, but not in despair; persecuted, but not abandoned; struck down, but not destroyed. We always carry around in our body the death of Jesus, so that the life of Jesus may also be revealed in our body. For we who are alive are always being given over to death for Jesus' sake, so that His life may also be revealed in our mortal body.

And that my friends, is the ever-present reality of a heart that is growing and achieving, by God's craftsmanship, a unity, a wholeness, an undividedness that more and more permits the light of Christ to radiate from within us. We do this so that Jesus' very own life may be revealed to this world in any and every way He chooses.

January 31

God's Side and Man's Side
by Hannah Whitall Smith

I would just say that man's part is to trust and God's part is to work; and it can be seen at a glance how contrastive these two parts are, and yet not necessarily contradictory. I mean this: There is a certain work to be accomplished. We are to be delivered from the power of sin, and are to be made perfect in every good work to do the will of God. "Beholding as in a glass the glory of the Lord," we are to be actually "changed into the same image from glory to glory, even as by the Spirit of the Lord." We are to be transformed by the renewing of our minds, that we may prove what is that good and acceptable and perfect will of God. A real work is to be wrought in us and upon us. Besetting sins are to be conquered. Evil habits are to be overcome. Wrong dispositions and feelings are to be rooted out, and holy tempers and emotions are to be cultivated. A positive transformation is to take place. So at least the Bible teaches. Now somebody must do this. Either we must do it for ourselves, or another must do it for us. We have most of us tried to do it for ourselves at first, and have grievously failed; then we discover from the Scriptures and from our own experience that it is a work we are utterly unable to do for ourselves, but that the Lord Jesus Christ has come on purpose to do it, and that He will do it for all who put themselves wholly into His hand, and trust Him to do it.

Now under these circumstances, what is the part of the believer, and what is the part of the Lord? Plainly the believer can do nothing but trust; while the Lord, in whom he trusts, actually does the work entrusted to Him.

***

Sanctification is both a sudden step of faith, and also a gradual process of works. It is a step as far as we are concerned; it is a process as to God's part. By a step of faith we get into Christ; by a process we are made to grow up unto Him in all things. By a step of faith we put ourselves into the hands of the Divine Potter; by a gradual process He makes us into a vessel for His own honor, suitable for His use, and prepared for every good work.

February 1

You Are the Branches (Part 1 of 2)
by Andrew Murray

"I am the vine; you are the branches"
John 15:5a

Everything depends on our being right ourselves in Christ. If I want good apples, I must have a good apple tree; and if I care for the health of the apple tree, the apple tree will give me good apples. And it is just so with our Christian life and work. *If our life with Christ be right,* all will come right. There may be the need of instruction and suggestion and help and training in the different departments of the work; all that has value. But in the long run, the greatest essential is to have the full life in Christ—in other words, to have Christ in us, working through us. I know how much there often is to disturb us, or to cause anxious questionings; but the Master has such a blessing for every one of us, and such perfect peace and rest, and such joy and strength, if we can only come into, and be kept in, the right attitude toward Him.

***

What a simple thing it is to be a branch, the branch of a tree, or the branch of a vine! The branch grows out of the vine, or out of the tree, and there it lives and grows, and in due time, bears fruit. It has no responsibility except just to receive from the root and stem sap and nourishment. And if we only by the Holy Spirit knew our relationship to Jesus Christ, our work would be changed into the brightest and most heavenly thing upon earth.

***

Workers, here is your first lesson: learn to be nothing, learn to be helpless. The man who has got something is not absolutely dependent; but the man who has got nothing is absolutely dependent. Absolute dependence upon God is the secret of all power in work. The branch has nothing but what it gets from the vine, and you and I can have nothing but what we get from Jesus. No one who learns to rest upon the living Christ can become slothful, for the closer your contact with Christ the more of the Spirit of His zeal and love will be borne in upon you.

32

February 2

You Are the Branches (Part 2 of 2)
by Andrew Murray

"I am the vine; you are the branches"
John 15:5a

Everything depends on our being right ourselves in Christ. *If our life with Christ be right,* all will come right. The greatest essential is to have the full life in Christ—in other words, to have Christ in us, working through us. I know how much there often is to disturb us, or to cause anxious questionings; but the Master has such a blessing for every one of us, and such perfect peace and rest, and such joy and strength, if we can only come into, and be kept in the right attitude toward Him.

***

In the first place, it is a life of absolute dependence. The branch has nothing; it just depends upon the vine for everything. *Absolute dependence* is one of the most solemn and precious of thoughts. If I can learn every moment of the day to depend upon God, everything will come right. You will get the higher life if you depend absolutely upon God.

***

If I am something, then God is not everything; but when I become *nothing,* God can become *all,* and the everlasting God in Christ can reveal Himself fully. That is the higher life. We need to become nothing. Oh, become nothing in deep reality, and, as a worker, study only one thing—to become poorer and lower and more helpless, that Christ may work all in you.

***

Learn to be nothing, learn to be helpless. The man who has got something is not absolutely dependent; but the man who has got nothing is absolutely dependent. Absolute dependence upon God is the secret of all power in work. The branch has nothing but what it gets from the vine, and you and I can have nothing but what we get from Jesus.

***

Take your place every day at the feet of Jesus, in the blessed peace and rest that come from the knowledge—I have no care, my cares are His! I have no fear, He cares for all my fears.

February 3

The Position of a Disciple (Part 1 of 4)
by Bryan L. Herde

"I am the true vine, and My Father is the gardener. Every branch in Me that does not bear fruit He takes away, and every branch that does bear fruit He prunes, that it may bear more fruit...Abide in Me, and I in you. As the branch cannot bear fruit by itself, unless it abides in the vine, neither can you, unless you abide in Me. I am the vine; you are the branches. Whoever abides in Me and I in him, he it is that bears much fruit, for apart from Me you can do nothing."
John 15:1-5

Abiding in the Vine. This is our position which encompasses our life, our fruitfulness and our total effectiveness—a simple teaching that is not really well understood by many. I believe that there are four reasons why abiding is such a difficult truth to comprehend and apply:
1. It is understood by faith, by the heart, not by the head;
2. It is inherent in human nature to not do something until a person fully understands what it means, what it requires and what it will look like when put into practice;
3. In 21st-century America, productivity—measurable and manageable—has become the mantra of both our society and our churches; and
4. Contemporary role models are virtually nonexistent.

The primary objection to abiding is the fear of being lazy. I have heard it said more than once, "God can't steer a parked car." Well, that just doesn't seem right to me. As far as I recall in all of Scripture, the only thing God can't do is sin! But "steer a parked car"? Less than a thought on His part and that is done. Remember, He is the One who merely spoke and all creation came into being. Now, I certainly do understand why someone would make that comment. It is the fear of being thought of by God or others as being lazy: just sitting still and waiting for something to happen. My friends, that is not abiding. Abiding, true abiding, is extremely hard work because it is not natural—it is supernatural!

February 4

The Position of a Disciple (Part 2 of 4)
by Bryan L. Herde

"I am the true vine, and My Father is the gardener. Every branch in Me that does not bear fruit He takes away, and every branch that does bear fruit He prunes, that it may bear more fruit...Abide in Me, and I in you. As the branch cannot bear fruit by itself, unless it abides in the vine, neither can you, unless you abide in Me. I am the vine; you are the branches. Whoever abides in Me and I in him, he it is that bears much fruit, for apart from Me you can do nothing."
John 15:1-5

When it comes to this essential discipline of really abiding in Christ, there *has* to be the willingness to take a risk of sitting *too* still, or waiting *too* long. But if your fear of others' opinions—or even self's—is allowed to have control, then how will you ever learn to discern when to sit still and do nothing versus when to act in the flow of God and by His initiative? "Active abiding" requires a commitment to run the risk of embarrassment or shame. In fact, in true abiding, you are simultaneously *passively active* and *actively passive*. And this is a discipline that is learned through experience, not through mental gymnastics or frenzied activity. David expressed these same concerns:

> To you, O Lord, I lift up my soul; in You I trust, O my God. Do not let me be put to shame, nor let my enemies triumph over me. No one whose hope is in You will ever be put to shame...Guard my life and rescue me; let me not be put to shame, for I take refuge in You (Psalm 25:1-3a, 20).

Jesus learned and synchronized Himself so completely with His Father that He made these very bold statements:

> "I tell you the truth, the Son can do nothing by Himself; He does only what He sees His Father doing. Because whatever the Father does the Son also does" (John 5:19).

> "By Myself I can do nothing...for I seek not to please Myself but Him who sent Me" (John 5:30).

February 5

The Position of a Disciple (Part 3 of 4)
by Bryan L. Herde

"I am the true vine, and My Father is the gardener. Every branch in Me that does not bear fruit He takes away, and every branch that does bear fruit He prunes, that it may bear more fruit....Abide in Me, and I in you. As the branch cannot bear fruit by itself, unless it abides in the vine, neither can you, unless you abide in Me. I am the vine; you are the branches. Whoever abides in Me and I in him, he it is that bears much fruit, for apart from Me you can do nothing."
John 15:1-5

Another objection against abiding is the sense of obligation and duty that demands that we are constantly active in fulfilling the commands of Jesus. In the Sermon on the Mount, Jesus gave more than 20 commands for His followers. Fulfilling them is impossible if you set out in a determined fashion to undertake them. They are accomplished by faith through the working of the Holy Spirit in you. Without Jesus you can do nothing (John 15:5b), and that is especially true in obeying His commands.

Also, we wrongly believe that we must be constantly active, in a measurable sense, in order to be truly obedient. If Jesus were to come to Earth today again as a child, I can almost guarantee that we would take that twelve-year old wonder child and put Him on an international speaking tour. We would never have expected Him to astound the leaders of the synagogue at the age of 12, and then disappear into obscurity for the next 18 years. We would cry out that all that time was wasted. Yet it pleased God to have Jesus remain anonymous for 90% of His life here on earth. That is a modality we do not understand, believe in or put into practice. We believe that we have received His orders through His Word and that we then must spend the rest of our lives scurrying around trying to do a work *for* the Lord that pleases Him. We know nothing of abiding in Him and allowing Him to do all that He commanded to be done. He is not a God who gives us orders, then sits back to see how we do and only occasionally intervenes when we desperately seek His help.

February 6

The Position of a Disciple (Part 4 of 4)
by Bryan L. Herde

"I am the true vine, and My Father is the gardener. Every branch in Me that does not bear fruit He takes away, and every branch that does bear fruit He prunes, that it may bear more fruit...Abide in Me, and I in you. As the branch cannot bear fruit by itself, unless it abides in the vine, neither can you, unless you abide in Me. I am the vine; you are the branches. Whoever abides in Me and I in him, he it is that bears much fruit, for apart from Me you can do nothing."
John 15:1-5

When Jesus said, "without Me you can do nothing," He meant that *with* Him we can do everything (Philippians 4:13). See the contrast—"nothing" versus "everything"—that is the difference between a disciple and a believer who is not a disciple. Disciples will allow Christ to do through them all the things He wants done. A believer tries to mimic Christ instead of allowing Him to do the work. The truth of abiding has a dependence methodology at its very core.

What does a branch do? It grows out of the vine, not by its own energy but by that of the vine. It is the sap flowing from the roots through the vine into the branch that gives the branch life. It is also the nourishment flowing from the vine that courses through the branch that enables fruit to grow. And all of this is under the caretaking oversight and work of our Master Gardener—God the Father.

As a branch of the true Vine, we can do nothing without the Vine. Yet if we allow the Gardener and the Vine to work together, then they are responsible for both the quantity and the quality of the fruit that is produced. Without the joint working of the Gardener and the Vine, we can do nothing. We have no life without the Vine and we would never be able to bear much fruit without the caretaking work of the Gardener. We are totally dependent upon God for every aspect of our lives.

February 7

The Changed Life (Part 1 of 4)
by Henry Drummond

We all with unveiled face reflecting as a mirror the glory of the Lord are transformed into the same image from glory to glory even as from the Lord the Spirit.
2 Corinthians 3:18

The change we have been striving after is not to be produced by any more striving after. It is to be wrought upon us by the molding of hands beyond our own. As the branch ascends, and the bud bursts, and the fruit reddens under the cooperation of influences from the outside air, so man rises to the higher stature under invisible pressures from without. The radical defect of all our former methods of sanctification was the attempt to generate from within that which can only be wrought upon us from without. Every man's character remains as it is, or continues in the direction in which it is going, until it is compelled *by outside pressure* to change that state. Our failure has been the failure to put ourselves in the way of the pressures. There is clay, and there is a Potter; we have tried to get the clay to mold the clay.

***

We all reflecting as a mirror the character of Christ are transformed into the same Image from character to character—from a poor character to a better one, from a better one to one a little better still, from that to one still more complete, until by slow degrees the Perfect Image is attained. Here the solution of the problem of sanctification is compressed into a sentence: Reflect the character of Christ and you will become like Christ.

***

The influences we meet are not simply held for a moment on the polished surface and thrown off again into space. Each is retained where first it fell, and stored up in the soul forever. The Apostle Paul sees that character is a thing built up by slow degrees; that it is hourly changing for better or for worse according to the images which flit across it.

It is the Law of Influence that *we become like those whom we habitually admire.* Through all the range of literature, of history, and biography this law presides. Men are all mosaics of other men.

***

February 8

The Changed Life (Part 2 of 4)
by Henry Drummond

We all with unveiled face reflecting as a mirror the glory of the Lord are transformed into the same image from glory to glory even as from the Lord the Spirit.
2 Corinthians 3:18

Since we are what we are by the impacts of those who surround us, those who surround themselves with the highest will be those who change into the highest. There are some men and some women in whose company we are always at our best. While with them we cannot think mean thoughts or speak ungenerous words. Their mere presence is elevation, purification, sanctity. All the best stops in our nature are drawn out by their interaction, and we find music in our souls that was never there before. Suppose even *that* influence prolonged through a month, a year, a lifetime, and what could not life become?

***

How can modern men today make Christ, the absent Christ, their most constant companion still? The answer is that Friendship is a spiritual thing. It is independent of Matter, or Space, or Time. That which I love in my friend is not that which I see. What influences me in my friend is not his body but his spirit.

***

Our companionship with Him, like all true companionship, is a spiritual communion. All friendship, all love, human and Divine, is purely spiritual. It was after He was risen that He influenced even the disciples most. Hence in reflecting the character of Christ it is no real obstacle that we may never have been in visible contact with Himself. There lived once a young girl whose perfect grace of character was the wonder of those who knew her. She wore on her neck a gold locket which no one was ever allowed to open. One day, in a moment of unusual confidence, one of her companions was allowed to open it and learn its secret. She saw these words: "Whom having not seen, I love" [1 Peter 1:8]. That was the secret of her beautiful life. She had been changed into the Same Image. Now this is not imitation, but a much deeper thing. For the difference in the process, as well as in the result, may be as great as that between a photograph secured by the infallible pencil of the sun, and the rude outline from a schoolboy's chalk.

February 9

The Changed Life (Part 3 of 4)
by Henry Drummond

We all with unveiled face reflecting as a mirror the glory of the Lord are transformed into the same image from glory to glory even as from the Lord the Spirit.
2 Corinthians 3:18

Imitation is mechanical, reflection organic. The one is occasional, the other habitual. In the one case, man comes to God and imitates Him; in the other, God comes to man and imprints Himself upon him. It is quite true that there is an imitation of Christ which amounts to reflection.

Be more under His influence than under any other influence. Ten minutes spent in His society every day, yes, two minutes if it be face to face, and heart to heart, will make the whole day different. Every character has an inward spring, let Christ be it. Every action has a keynote, let Christ set it. Your soul today is not at the ordinary angle. "Things which are not seen" are visible. For a few short hours you live the Eternal Life. The eternal life, the life of faith, is simply the life of the higher vision. Faith is an attitude—a mirror set at the right angle.

***

When tomorrow is over, and in the evening you review it, you will wonder how you did it. You will not be conscious that you strove for anything, or imitated anything, or crucified anything. You will be conscious of Christ; that He was with you, that without compulsion you were yet compelled, that without force, or noise, or proclamation, the revolution was accomplished. You do not congratulate yourself as one who has done a mighty deed, or achieved a personal success, or stored up a fund of "Christian experience" to ensure the same result again. What you are conscious of is "the glory of the Lord." And what the world is conscious of, if the result be a true one, is also "the glory of the Lord." In looking at a mirror one does not see the mirror, or think of it, but only of what it reflects. For a mirror never calls attention to itself except when there are flaws in it.

February 10

The Changed Life (Part 4 of 4)
by Henry Drummond

We all with unveiled face reflecting as a mirror the glory of the Lord are transformed into the same image from glory to glory even as from the Lord the Spirit.
2 Corinthians 3:18

Men always look for a mystery when one talks of sanctification; some mystery apart from that which must ever be mysterious wherever the Spirit works. It is thought some peculiar secret lies behind it, some hidden experience which only the initiated know. Thousands of persons go to church every Sunday hoping to solve this mystery. At meetings, at conferences, many a time they have reached what they thought was the very brink of it, but somehow no further revelation came. Poring over religious books, how often were they not within a paragraph of it; the next page, the next sentence, would reveal all, and they would be borne on a flowing tide forever. But nothing happened. The next sentence and the next page were read, and still it eluded them; and though the promise of its coming kept faithfully up to the end, the last chapter found them still pursuing. Why did nothing happen? Because there was nothing to happen—nothing of the kind they were looking for. Why did it elude them? Because there was no "it." When shall we learn that the pursuit of holiness is simply the pursuit of Christ? When shall we substitute for the "it" of a fictitious aspiration, the approach to a Living Friend? Purity is in character and not in moods; Divinity in our own plain calm humanity, and in no mystic rapture of the soul.

***

Do not think that nothing is happening because you do not see yourself grow, or hear the whirr of the machinery. All great things grow noiselessly.

***

Foundations which have to bear the weight of an eternal life must be surely laid. Character is to wear forever; who will wonder or grudge that it cannot be developed in a day? To await the growing of a soul, nevertheless, is an almost Divine act of faith.

February 11

The Corn [Grain] of Wheat (Part 1 of 2)
by Alexander Whyte

Jesus answered them, saying, "The hour is come, that the Son of Man should be glorified. Verily, verily, I say unto you, Except a corn [grain] of wheat falls into the ground and dies, it abides alone: but if it dies, it brings forth much fruit"
John 12:20-33

It is a proverb among us that though death may have been long looked for, yet, when it actually comes, it always comes suddenly. Death takes the best prepared men by surprise. And this too sudden message from those Greek proselytes took our Lord by surprise; for it brought Him too sharply, and too suddenly, face to face with His Cross.

He had long been ready for it; He had long been laboring to make His disciples ready for it; but when the full fruits of it were thus suddenly demanded of Him, He reeled under the blow, and took some time to recover Himself. He felt that the cup was, at that moment, too suddenly thrust into His hand; and the Cross too suddenly laid upon His shoulders. "The hour is come then," He said, more to Himself than to anyone else.

And during that "hour," between the beginning of it and the end of it, He knew that He had to finish a work, the bare thought of which at that moment threw Him back upon all the faith, all the obedience, all the strength and all the resolution that even He could command. He had been inclined to set forth some of the things of the Kingdom of Heaven to His disciples in parables; and, at that weak and over-weighted moment, He took up this powerful parable and laid it on His own heart to calm and subdue and strengthen it. It was far more to commit and confirm Himself at that heart-sinking moment than to instruct or console His disciples that He said in their hearing and presence: "Except a [grain] of wheat falls into the ground and dies, it abides alone: but if it dies, it brings forth much fruit."

February 12

The Corn [Grain] of Wheat (Part 2 of 2)
by Alexander Whyte

*Jesus answered them, saying, "The hour is come, that the Son of Man should be glorified.
Verily, verily, I say unto you, Except a corn [grain] of wheat falls into the ground and
dies, it abides alone: but if it dies, it brings forth much fruit"*
John 12:20-33

Ah, my brethren, even to Jesus Christ, preaching was one thing and
practice another. Rapture of soul in contemplation of heavenly truth and
eternal life is one thing; and the upward path of the Cross is another. But
here again He sinks back into the body until He feels the thick darkness
closing around it, and the nails and the spear crashing through it. The cup
still stands before Him with the undrunk curse filling it. And again His
"true body and His reasonable soul," His affectionate and passionate soul,
shrank and trembled and was troubled.

It is out of instances like this that the Apostle generalizes the heart-
comforting character he gives to Christ as our great High Priest. "He was in
all points tempted like as we are." For after all our earlier temptations have
fallen off us, after our first fierce passions are all burnt to dross and dust
under our feet, a new and more deadly approach of temptations attack us:
temptations to rebellion and bitterness against God and man; to envy and
ill-will, to gloom and grumbling of soul, a settled stubbornness to accept
and do and go through with the holy will of God. "Now is our soul
troubled" at poverty; now at bereavement; now at bodily infirmity; now at
some thorn in our flesh, or some shift in our circumstances; now at
approaching age, and now at near and inevitable death. But then, so was
our Lord. "Yet," blessed be His name, "without sin." Let all the afflicted
people of God take this true comfort that it is only human nature to be
troubled in soul under the pressure of temptation and affliction. And that it
only becomes sin when affliction is nursed and brooded over and held close
to an unbroken heart. Let it never be passed by or for one moment
forgotten by any troubled soul that our Savior was and is a Man of like
passions and like affections with ourselves.

February 13

The Hallmarks of a Disciple (Part 1 of 5)
by Bryan L. Herde

To the Jews who had believed Him, Jesus said, "If you hold to My teaching, you really are My disciples. Then you will know the truth, and the truth will set you free."
John 8:31-32

"A new command I give you: Love one another. As I have loved you, so you must love one another. By this all men will know that you are My disciples."
John 13:34-35

"This is to My Father's glory, that you bear much fruit, showing yourselves to be My disciples."
John 15:8

These three statements by Jesus are the clearest in terms of outlining what is expected of a disciple. Condensed, Jesus says:
1. Hold to my teaching
2. Love one another
3. Bear much fruit

Hold to My Teaching
Hold is the opposite of "let go." What He is talking about here is belief, obedience, loyalty, commitment, continuance, perseverance and longevity. In John 6:29, Jesus said, "The work of God is this: to believe in the One He sent." Wholehearted belief in Jesus is the first level of being a disciple. Without a heart absolutely committed to Jesus, love is erratic and fickle, and bearing fruit is occasional and inconsistent.

Some of the most compelling qualities of Jesus were His consistency in His obedience to His Father, His purpose, and His patience in waiting for His appointed time. He expects the same of us. Selflessness in submission to the prominence of Jesus is a rare and marvelous hallmark of a disciple.

February 14

The Hallmarks of a Disciple (Part 2 of 5)
by Bryan L. Herde

It is critical to remember that without Jesus we can do nothing. And this includes holding to His teaching. Every time we read or hear one of God's commandments, our response needs to be, "Lord, make this true in my life," rather than, "I will obey this command." Self-determined obedience and adherence to our Lord's teaching will always fail. But if we abandon ourselves to the complete control of the Lord, then we allow Him to take full responsibility for accomplishing the task. He never asks us to do anything He will not do in us and through us if we will allow Him to have free rein in our lives.

I invite you to lay yourself before the Lord and offer up to Him everything you believe. Ask Him to sort through it all and retain what He wants, remove what needs to go, and implant new understanding as He desires. He alone can shake out the shakable so that which is unshakable will remain (Hebrews 12:25-28). Believe me, there is no way any of you knows what is really in your heart (Psalm 44:21; Jeremiah 17:9-10) and what filters exist between you and the Lord. The work in our hearts is the exclusive responsibility of the Lord and no one else—including you.

Love One Another
"A new command I give you: Love one another. As I have loved you, so you must love one another. By this all men will know that you are My disciples."
John 13:34-35

Love is wrapped up in humility, sacrifice, compassion, honesty and time invested. Love is something that flows from a Person; it is not something one does. Abiding in Jesus allows the "sap" of His essence—first and foremost being love—to flow through us into the hearts and lives of others. Jesus loved us because that is who He is. We are to love others because that is who we are. A life fully yielded to the Lord surrenders itself to the One who is love in order for love to flow consistently and abundantly.

February 15

The Hallmarks of a Disciple (Part 3 of 5)
by Bryan L. Herde

"A new command I give you: Love one another. As I have loved you, so you must love one another. By this all men will know that you are My disciples."
John 13:34-35

In the early stages of becoming a disciple, love is very difficult and full of self. But, over time, the Holy Spirit purifies our motives, changes our perspective, fills us with Himself and moves us with the compassion, mercy and love of God to give ourselves to others. In the beginning, it is hard. But with maturity, it becomes less conscious and more of who we really are. We find ourselves loving others without having to force it.

A few years ago, I was asked by a missionary friend of mine to visit an older gentleman who had moved to Denver to receive care for lung cancer. The Lord had arranged my work schedule to be free of client obligations so I had a lot of time on my hands. When I first met this gentleman, I felt like I was just doing my duty. But as he very quickly became much sicker and was moved into hospice care, I found myself spending a lot of time with him and his wife. Something began to live in me that was not normal for me. In fact, it seemed that I watched Another love and care for Karl through me. I realized that the Holy Spirit was loving Karl through me. I watched myself wipe his fevered brow, watched my hands feed him, listened to my voice sing with him and read Scripture to him. I knew that for this time, I genuinely loved this man whom I had only known for a few weeks. When he died, that great compassion went away and I returned to "normal." I know that I experienced the fruit of the Spirit—love—flowing through me for this man. It lasted as long as it was needed and then it was gone, at least in the fullness I had known it for a time. When a life is surrendered to the Lord, then He works a greater love for others than we could ever imitate or manufacture. The residual benefit for me is that I learned that I, like Paul, can "become all things to all men." I can move in and out of lives and allow the Lord to be who He wants to be to each person as long as I allow Him the freedom to flow and change as He desires.

February 16

The Hallmarks of a Disciple (Part 4 of 5)
by Bryan L. Herde

"This is to My Father's glory, that you bear much fruit,
showing yourselves to be My disciples."
John 15:8

Bear Much Fruit

It is an ill system which measures spiritual success by external standards. Let me give you a practical example: Back in 2003, I heard an interview with Bill Bright, the founder of Campus Crusade, while he was on his death bed. That interview led me to experience some interaction with the Lord that centered around "success" as Christ defines it. I saw myself standing behind Bill Bright as we were in line meeting Jesus and giving an account of our lives. Bill Bright was greeted by millions of people who were saved as a result of the work of Campus Crusade. Then it was my turn. I looked at the few who were waiting to greet me and then I looked at Jesus and showed Him my empty hands. Jesus' response staggered me: "Didn't I ask you to give me your life and your all? You did that. That is all I wanted you to do. I accomplished My will in and through your life. Well done, good and faithful servant."

Right then I understood that I am totally incapable of measuring the "much fruit" that the Master Gardener takes responsibility for cultivating and the Vine for producing. I cannot possibly measure what only God can measure. I yield and I trust and I wait for Him to fulfill His will and achieve His results. This also lies at the very core of Proverbs 3:5, "Trust in the Lord with all your heart and lean not on your own understanding." This is a comprehensive truth that applies to our entire relationship with the Lord. We relate to Him with our hearts first and foremost. That is where He lives and the realm in which He operates (Luke 6:45).

Bearing "much fruit" is beyond our capacity to measure. Since the Master Gardener is the One in charge, who do we think we are that we can determine what is successful and what isn't?

The Hallmarks of a Disciple (Part 5 of 5)
by Bryan L. Herde

"This is to My Father's glory, that you bear much fruit,
showing yourselves to be My disciples."
John 15:8

Another good example of immeasurable fruit is the lives of the men who died in Ecuador back in the 1950's, a small group of five missionaries led by Jim Elliot and Nate Saint. The "much fruit" of their lives was not realized during their lifetimes. It was their deaths while they were in their 20's that spawned a huge missionary movement from the U.S. that continues to impact the world to this day.

Much the same could be said of Jesus Christ. It was absolutely necessary for Him to come and die. While He was on this planet, His actual "fruit" was relatively small when laid against the enormity of humankind and the world. But the "much fruit" of His life has and is yet being borne through the lives of the people who have been, are and will yet be His Body—the Church. The impact of His life while on the earth was small—the impact of His life since that time is impossible for us to measure. But our Heavenly Father, the Master Gardener, knows every grape that has ever been produced by the Vine through the branches—of that you can be absolutely confident!

One other element of bearing "much fruit" is the necessary process of pruning. John 15:2b states "Every branch that does bear fruit He prunes so that it will be even more fruitful." Pay particular attention to the fact that pruning happens to the branch that is already bearing fruit. This is not what we want to hear, nor, sadly, is it what is being taught today in our nation's churches. The Master Gardener alone knows how to use every means under Heaven to accomplish the pruning we branches need in order to bear "much fruit." This includes trouble, testing, trials, pain, suffering and hardship. James 1:2-4 also speaks loudly on this subject. The purpose of our trials is so that we may be "mature and complete, not lacking anything." Through perseverance and patience—in the face of adversity—we will be pruned so that we too may bear much fruit.

February 18

The Extent and Reasonableness of Self-Denial (Part 1 of 2)
by George Whitefield

And He said unto them all, "If any man will come after Me, let him deny himself."
Luke 9:23

We must not lean to our own understanding, being wise in our own eyes, and prudent in our own sight; but we must submit our short-sighted reason to the light of divine revelation. There are mysteries in religion, which are above, though not contrary to, our natural reason; and therefore we shall never become Christians unless we call down imaginations, "and every high thing that exalts itself against the knowledge of God, and bring into captivity every thought to the obedience of Christ." We must, with all humility and reverence, embrace the truths revealed to us in the holy scriptures; for thus only can we become truly wise, even "wise unto salvation." It was a matter of our blessed Lord's thanksgiving to his heavenly father, that he had "hidden these things from the wise and prudent, and had revealed them unto babes." And in this respect we must also "be converted and become as little children," teachable, and willing to follow the Lamb into whatsoever mysteries he shall be pleased to lead us; and believe and practice all divine truths, not because we can demonstrate them, but because God, "who cannot lie," has revealed them to us.

***

We must deny ourselves in our understandings, so must we deny, or, as it might be more properly stated, renounce our wills; that is, we must make our own wills no rule of action, but "whether we eat or drink, or whatsoever we do, we must do all (not merely to please ourselves but) to the glory of God."

***

A prudent Christian therefore, will consider not only what is lawful, but what is expedient also; not so much what degrees of self-denial best suit his inclinations here, but what will most effectively break his will, and fit him for greater degrees of glory hereafter.

February 19

The Extent and Reasonableness of Self-Denial (Part 2 of 2)
by George Whitefield

And He said unto them all, "If any man will come after Me, let him deny himself."
Luke 9:23

Were we indeed in a state of innocence, and had we, like Adam before his fall, the divine image fully stamped upon our souls, we then should have no need of self-denial; but since we are fallen, sickly, disordered, self-righteous creatures, we must necessarily deny ourselves (and count it our privilege to do so) before we can follow Jesus Christ to glory. To reject such a beneficial practice on account of the difficulty accompanying it at first, is much too like the stubbornness of an unreasonable sick child, who is disgusted and refuses the potion handed out to it by a skillful physician or a tender parent, because it has an unpleasant taste.

***

And if we are unwilling to deny ourselves, and come after Jesus Christ in order to be cured, it is a sign we are not conscious of the wretchedness of our state, and that we are not truly made whole.

***

Meditate frequently on the life of our blessed Lord and Master Jesus Christ. Follow him from his cradle to the cross, and see what a self-denying life he led! And shall not we drink of the cup that he drank of, and be baptized with the baptism that he was baptized with? Or do we think that Jesus Christ did and suffered everything in order to have us excused and exempted from sufferings? No, far be it from any sincere Christian to judge after this manner, for St. Peter tells us, "He suffered for us, leaving us an example that we should follow his steps." Had Christ, indeed, like those that sat in Moses' chair, laid heavy burdens of self-denial upon us (supposing they were heavy, which they are not) and refused to touch them himself with one of his fingers, we might have had some reason to complain. But since he has not asked to do anything except what he first put in practice himself, you are inexcusable, O disciple, whoever you are, who would be above your persecuted self-denying master.

February 20

Ishmael and Isaac: The Death of Self (Part 1 of 2)
by Albert B. Simpson

...not I, but Christ...
Galatians 2:20

This is the lesson of Isaac's offering and Paul's experience. "I have been crucified with Christ," that is the death of sin; "nevertheless I live," that is the new life in the power of His resurrection; "Yet not I, but Christ lives in me," that is the offering of Isaac, the deliverance from self, and the substitution of Christ Himself for even the new self, a substitution so complete that even the faith by which this life is maintained is no longer our self-sustained confidence but the very "faith of the Son of God who loved me and gave Himself for me," that is, instead of me, and as my Substitute.

***

It is necessary that our will be wholly renounced and God's will invariably accepted instead, and then we can put into it all the strength and force of our being, and will it even as God wills it, and because He wills it. In short, it is an exchanged will.

***

The sanctified heart is not a self-constituted engine of power, but is just a set of wheels and pulleys that are absolutely dependent upon the great central engine whose force is necessary continually to move them. It is just a capacity to hold God; just a vessel to be filled with His goodness, held and used by His hand; just a possibility of which He, in His abiding life is constantly the energizing power and driving force.

***

Vanity only seeks the praise of others but pride disdains the opinions of others and rests back in the complacent consciousness of its own excellency. Whatever its phase may be, the root and principle is the same. It is irreverent self, sitting on the throne of God, and claiming the honor and glory that belong to Him alone.

February 21

Ishmael and Isaac: The Death of Self (Part 2 of 2)
by Albert B. Simpson

...not I, but Christ...
Galatians 2:20

Self leads to every other sin and brings back the whole power of the carnal nature. For while self alone attempts to keep the heart [pure], it finds sin and Satan too strong. A self-perfection is not possible for any man. There must be more than "I" before there can be victory.

***

Any soul that becomes self-constituted or occupied with its own virtues, and tries to be independent of Jesus, either as the source of its strength or the supreme end of its being, will fall under the power of Satan and share his awful descent.

***

The very secret of Christian cooperation and happy church life is "forbearing one another in love," endeavoring to keep the unity of the Spirit in the bond of peace, "in honor preferring one another." God often has to let self have its way until it cures us effectively by showing us the misery and failure which it brings. This is the only good there is in our own struggling, that it shows us the vanity of the struggle and prepares us more quickly to surrender to God.

***

It is Christ Himself who lives inside and who is big enough to crowd out and keep out the little "I." There is no other that can truly lift and keep the heart above the power of self but Jesus, the Mighty Lord, the stronger than the strong man armed, who takes away his armor wherein he trusted and spoils all his goods and then takes forever the heart that has given him its goods. Blessed Christ! He is able not only for sin, sorrow and sickness, but He is able for you and me—able so to be our very life, that moment by moment we shall be conscious that He in us fills us with Himself and conquers the self that ruled before. The more you try to fight a self-thought the more it clings to you. The moment you turn away from it and look to Him, He fills all the consciousness and disperses everything with His own presence. Let us abide in Him and we shall find there is nothing else to do.

February 22

Taking Up the Cross (Part 1 of 2)
by Hannah Whitall Smith

Then said Jesus unto His disciples, "If any man will come after Me, let him deny himself, and take up his cross, and follow Me. For whoever will save his life shall lose it; and whoever will lose his life for My sake shall find it."
Matthew 16:24-25

The only use of the cross is to put to death, not to keep alive. It may be a suffering death, but still it is sooner or later death. All through the Bible the meaning of the cross is simply and always death. In most cases this is obvious to everyone; and why we have chosen to give it a different meaning in its mystical sense, and make it mean not death, but living in misery, would be hard to explain. When, therefore, our Lord told His disciples that they could not be His disciples unless they took up the cross, He could not have meant that they were to find it hard to do His will; but He was, I believe, simply expressing in figurative language the fact that they were to be made partakers of His death and resurrection, by having their old man crucified with Him, and by living only in their new man, or, in other words, in the resurrection life of the Spirit.

***

To crucify means to put to death, not to keep alive in misery. But so hidden has the whole subject become to the children of God, that I believe a great many feel as if they were crucifying self when they are simply seating self on a pinnacle, and are tormenting it and making it miserable. Man will undergo the most painful self-sacrifices, and call it "taking up the cross," and will find great satisfaction in it; and all the time will fail to understand that the true cross consists in counting the flesh, or the "old man," as an utterly worthless thing, fit only to be put to death. There is a subtle enjoyment in torturing the outward self, if only the interior self-life may be fed thereby. A man will make himself a religious ascetic, if it is only self that does it, so that self can share in the glory. The flesh of man likes to have some credit; it cannot bear to be counted as dead and therefore ignored; and in all religions of legalism it has a chance. This explains, I am sure, why there is so much legality among Christians.

February 23

Taking Up the Cross (Part 2 of 2)
by Hannah Whitall Smith

Then said Jesus unto His disciples, "If any man will come after Me, let him deny himself,
and take up his cross, and follow Me. For whoever will save his life shall lose it; and
whoever will lose his life for My sake shall find it."
Matthew 16:24-25

I fear there are a great many Christians who look upon the Christian life, as
I in my childish ignorance looked upon grown-up life. I thought that
grown-up people wanted to play as much as I did, but that there was a law
forbidding it after a certain age; and I pitied with all my heart everybody
who had passed that age, which, somehow, I fixed in my mind at fifteen,
and dreaded beyond measure the time when I should reach that age myself,
and should have to "take up the cross" that awaited me there. In the same
way I believe many Christians think religion means always to give up the
things they love, and to do the things they hate; and they call this "taking up
the cross," and actually think God enjoys this "grudging" service. To my
mind, grudging service is no more acceptable to God from us than it would
be to us from one another; and such an idea of the "cross" as this, seems to
me a very poor and low substitute for the glorious truth of our death with
Christ, and our resurrection into the triumphant spiritual life hid with Christ
in God.

***

That part of us which is born of God, the spiritual man in us, cannot sin,
because it is holy in its very nature or essence. If we sin, therefore, it must
be because we have permitted what is in us which is born of the flesh to
have some life; and have submitted ourselves, i.e., our personality, more or
less to its control. And not only would I say this concerning sin, but I
would also say it concerning that shrinking from and dislike of God's will
which so many Christians think constitutes the cross. The spiritual man in
us cannot dislike God's will, for in the very nature of things that which is
born of God must love the will of God. That which shrinks and suffers
must be the self-life; and the self-life we are commanded to crucify and
deny (Mark 8:34-35).

February 24

The Passion of a Disciple (Part 1 of 8)
by Bryan L. Herde

I want to know Christ and the power of His resurrection and the fellowship of sharing in His sufferings, becoming like Him in His death, and so, somehow, to attain to the resurrection from the dead…All of us who are mature should take such a view of things.
Philippians 3:10-11, 15a

I believe that there are four components to a disciple's passion, as taught by the Lord through Paul in this passage:
1. To know Christ
2. To know the power of His resurrection
3. To have the fellowship of sharing in His sufferings
4. To become like Him in His death

Know Christ
What does it mean to "know" someone? It is obviously much more than just knowing *about* them. It is greater than just being acquainted *with* them. And it is more than knowing people who know them. Knowing someone, as it is intended to be interpreted here, is knowing:
- What motivates them;
- What they like
- What they dislike;
- What is most important to them;
- What their passions are;
- What makes them happy;
- What makes them sad;
- Who their friends are;
- Where their interests lie;
- What their agenda is;
- What they desire from me;
- That they want to be with me;
- That they accept me; and
- That they love me.

February 25

The Passion of a Disciple (Part 2 of 8)
by Bryan L. Herde

I want to know Christ and the power of His resurrection and the fellowship of sharing in His sufferings, becoming like Him in His death, and so, somehow, to attain to the resurrection from the dead...All of us who are mature should take such a view of things.
Philippians 3:10-11, 15a

I believe that knowing is imbedded in the concept of identification with someone. In the case of our oneness with Jesus Christ, wouldn't it be awesome for someone to say of us, "When I'm with him or her, I feel the very presence of Jesus"? If people who "want to see Jesus" were able to meet Him in me, then wouldn't that be a strong affirmation of my knowing Him and knowing Him well? The essence here is not that I am able to quote chapter and verse, parse my Biblical verbs, trump every argument with great apologetics, or explain every bit of prophecy. Rather, what is important is what Jesus did with the two men on the road to Emmaus: "And beginning with Moses and all the Prophets, Jesus explained to them what was said in all the Scriptures concerning Himself" (Luke 24:27). The result says it all: "They asked each other, 'Were not our hearts burning within us while He talked with us on the road and opened the Scriptures to us?'" (Luke 24:32). It was Christ revealing Himself throughout Scripture. That is to be our work as well. We present others with a Person who is everything they need, not just a belief system to which they must adhere.

When Paul spoke of knowing Christ in Philippians 3, I have no doubt that this is what he meant. He wasn't relying upon his training in the Scriptures as an intellectual, a Pharisee, a teacher of the Law. He wanted desperately to know Jesus Christ better. Read his words from the *Amplified Bible* version of Philippians 3:10a:

> For my determined purpose is that I may know Him, that I may progressively become more deeply and intimately acquainted with Him, perceiving and recognizing and understanding the wonders of His Person more strongly and more clearly...

February 26

The Passion of a Disciple (Part 3 of 8)
by Bryan L. Herde

I want to know Christ and the power of His resurrection and the fellowship of sharing in His sufferings, becoming like Him in His death, and so, somehow, to attain to the resurrection from the dead...All of us who are mature should take such a view of things.
Philippians 3:10-11, 15a

Paul was talking about seeing the Living God, especially Jesus Christ, the Messiah, throughout all of Scripture and then living in and through His life. He passionately wanted the fullness of oneness, not knowledge. This should not only be an admonition to have the same passion as Paul, but also a dire warning not to settle for anything less.

Sadly, I have known pastors and teachers in America's churches who are masters of Biblical knowledge, analyzing and dissecting every word, every phrase, unequalled in knowing what the Bible says, but sorely lacking an intimate, interactive and dynamic relationship with Jesus Christ Himself. They tickle our ears for a while but leave our hearts malnourished and starving for more. The yearning of our hearts for intimate oneness is not nourished, cultivated or directed to the only One who satisfies.

Please get this, if nothing else: Don't be like the Pharisees, who believed that knowing God's Word either substituted for knowing Him or, worse yet, was just as good. That is exactly what Jesus admonished them for in John 5:39, "You diligently study the Scriptures because you think that by them you possess eternal life. These are the Scriptures that testify about Me, yet you refuse to come to Me to have life." When Jesus said in John 14:6 that He is "the way, the truth and the life," He wasn't just talking about our initial salvation experience, He was talking about living, believing and following Him forever. As a disciple of Jesus Christ, my primary passion must be the Lord Himself, and nothing less. All other efforts are dung, manure and trash by comparison to the awesome reality of oneness with Him (Philippians 3:8-9). May I never be satisfied with anything less, no matter what!

February 27

The Passion of a Disciple (Part 4 of 8)
by Bryan L. Herde

I want to know Christ and the power of His resurrection and the fellowship of sharing in His sufferings, becoming like Him in His death, and so, somehow, to attain to the resurrection from the dead...All of us who are mature should take such a view of things.
Philippians 3:10-11, 15a

Power of the Resurrection

Next in line to define my heart's and life's passion is knowing the power of Jesus' resurrection. Again, note Paul's words from the *Amplified Bible* in Philippians 3:10b: "And in that I may in that same way come to know the power outflowing from His resurrection which it exerts over believers..."

What exactly is that power flowing from the resurrection of Jesus Christ? That power resulted in numerous benefits that directly and eternally impact us every moment of every day:

- We are sealed by the Holy Spirit, who lives in us as a security deposit of our salvation (Ephesians 4:30).
- Because of His resurrection, we, too, will be resurrected (1 Thessalonians 4:15-17).
- We are forever secure from judgment, death and punishment (1 John 4:15-18).
- We are perpetually holy and righteous before God (1 Corinthians 1:30).
- We are adopted as God's children, becoming joint heirs with Christ, etc. (Romans 8:14-17).
- We wrestle with spiritual enemies, but they are already defeated (Ephesians 6:12; Colossians 2:15).
- We will dwell with the Lord forever (John 14:1-3).
- The Lord will have victory and dominion over all who oppose Him (1 Corinthians 15:24).
- We are granted power with God through prayer in Jesus' name and according to His will (John 14:13-14).

February 28

The Passion of a Disciple (Part 5 of 8)
by Bryan L. Herde

I want to know Christ and the power of His resurrection and the fellowship of sharing in His sufferings, becoming like Him in His death, and so, somehow, to attain to the resurrection from the dead…All of us who are mature should take such a view of things.
Philippians 3:10-11, 15a

Fellowship of His Sufferings
The third component of a disciple's passion based upon these verses in Philippians is "the fellowship of sharing in His sufferings."

Some years ago, I sat in a church service where the pastor was teaching using this same passage (Philippians 3:7-16) as his text. He did a fair job with the first two points (knowing Christ and the power of His resurrection) but he completely skipped this third part about suffering. In his version of theology, a true, faithful Christian would never suffer if they really lived by faith. Not only is that wrong, it goes completely against the grain of what Paul said he wanted and that was to share in Christ's sufferings, not avoid them!

And why did Paul want to share in the sufferings? Because Jesus said in Matthew 10:38, "Anyone who does not take his cross and follow Me is not worthy of Me." If there is anything Paul wanted, he wanted to be counted worthy of Jesus, no matter what it cost him. As we know from Scripture, Paul went through many types of suffering. He endured stonings, beatings, rejection, shipwrecks, hunger, thirst, loneliness and other pains. There are many of our brothers and sisters who have and even now are suffering like Paul through great physical traumas. Until Jesus comes, this will always be true. The world hated Jesus, and it hates those who are His as well.

If the Lord leads you into suffering and allows it to come upon you, you must embrace it, count it all joy and rejoice that you can participate in the sufferings of Jesus Christ. For He has chosen this trial as the best thing that can happen in your life at this time.

(For a Leap Year, February 29 reading, go to page 366)

March 1

The Passion of a Disciple (Part 6 of 8)
by Bryan L. Herde

I want to know Christ and the power of His resurrection and the fellowship of sharing in His sufferings, becoming like Him in His death, and so, somehow, to attain to the resurrection from the dead…All of us who are mature should take such a view of things.
Philippians 3:10-11, 15a

Suffering in the life of a saint accomplishes many things:
- It kills the flesh so that Christ in us may shine all the more brightly (Ephesians 5:8-14).
- It increases our patience, which is indispensable to having strong faith (James 1:2-4).
- It is used by God to bring encouragement and boldness to others (Philippians 1:14).
- God has oftentimes used the blood of martyrs to stimulate movements of workers into the work of foreign missions (e.g., the death of the five American men striving to evangelize the Auca tribe in Ecuador in 1956).
- It enables us to comfort others who are suffering in the same way we were comforted during our sufferings (2 Corinthians 1:3-7).
- Believers grow in their faith, as all of their false beliefs, expectations and perceptions are shown to be of the flesh, not of Him (1 Peter 1:6-9).

Only God Himself knows the full reasons and purposes for the suffering endured by His children. Rest assured, Jesus meant it absolutely when He said, "In this world you will have trouble. But take heart, I have overcome the world" (John 16:33).

Like Him in His Death
We will never be able to replicate precisely the death of Jesus Christ. He alone became sin for the whole of creation; He alone was both fully God and fully man, who freely gave His life as a substitute for us, undergoing the full wrath of God against sin; and His blood alone saves us. Obviously, Paul intended a likeness in some other way.

March 2

The Passion of a Disciple (Part 7 of 8)
by Bryan L. Herde

I want to know Christ and the power of His resurrection and the fellowship of sharing in His sufferings, becoming like Him in His death, and so, somehow, to attain to the resurrection from the dead…All of us who are mature should take such a view of things.
Philippians 3:10-11, 15a

So what are the ways we can become like Jesus in His death? I believe that they are many, of which the following five are primary:
1. Living with a will completely yielded to God;
2. Accepting everything as being the will of the Father for us;
3. Being used mightily or insignificantly, or consumed, or destroyed according to the Father's choosing;
4. Trusting God no matter what; and
5. Knowing that I am loved even when it doesn't feel or look like it.

I believe that the last 24 hours of Christ's earthly life show us each of these and that they are what He wants for us. For instance:
1. **A completely yielded will** as evidenced by Jesus' prayer in the garden of Gethsemane: "Yet not as I will, but as You will" (Matthew 26:39b). We certainly have the right to express our desires, our hopes and our wishes in prayer, but as disciples of Jesus Christ, we *always* defer to the will of our Heavenly Father.
2. **Accepting everything** as evidenced when Jesus was arrested in the garden and Peter used his sword to "defend" Jesus. Jesus' response was: "Do you think that I cannot call on My Father, and He will at once put at My disposal more than twelve legions of angels? But how then would the Scriptures be fulfilled that say it must happen this way?" (Matthew 26:53-54). If Jesus chose to accept the Father's will for Him in this situation when He had the right and the ability to call in a rescue, how much more willing should we be to accept the Father's will so that His plans for us might be fulfilled?

March 3

The Passion of a Disciple (Part 8 of 8)
by Bryan L. Herde

I want to know Christ and the power of His resurrection and the fellowship of sharing in His sufferings, becoming like Him in His death, and so, somehow, to attain to the resurrection from the dead…All of us who are mature should take such a view of things.
Philippians 3:10-11, 15a

There are additional ways that we can become like Jesus in His death:

3. **Being used/destroyed** as evidenced by the conversation with Pilate when Pilate said: "Don't you realize I have power either to free you or to crucify you?" Jesus answered, "You would have no power over Me if it were not given to you from above" (John 19:11). Even though it appears that men or circumstances or anything else are positioned to destroy us, they have no power unless permitted or enabled by our Father in Heaven.

4. **Trusting God** as evidenced by Jesus when He cried out on the cross: "My God, My God, why have you forsaken Me?" (Matthew 27:46). And then moments later He called out with a loud voice, "Father, into Your hands I commit My spirit" and died (Luke 23:46). Yes, there will be times when we feel deep within ourselves that our God has abandoned us, but He has promised that will never happen to us (Hebrews 13:5). After crying out in anguish, He then proclaimed His ruthless trust in His Father in ruthless circumstances by committing His spirit to the Father.

5. **Love** as evidenced by Jesus in His wonderful prayer in John 17:26: "I have made You known to them [believers], and will continue to make You known in order that the love You have for Me may be in them and that I Myself may be in them." Even knowing what was coming, love was the undergirding, overwhelming and permeating truth about what was happening. Even in the most severe set of circumstances, love was working. We must never forget that!

Becoming like Jesus in His death is, again, not a thing we can make happen—it is a work that God and God alone can do. It is His delight to make Paul's passion our own passion. For before anyone else, it was the passion of Jesus as a disciple of His Father.

March 4

Crucified with Christ
by Alexander Whyte

I am crucified with Christ: nevertheless I live; yet not I, but Christ lives in me: and the
life which I now live in the flesh I live by the faith of the Son of God,
Who loved me, and gave Himself for me.
Galatians 2:20

Martin Luther, commenting on this very text, says:

> Paul speaks not here of crucifying by imitation or example, for to
> follow the example of Christ is also to be crucified with Him. This
> crucifying is not that of which Peter speaks, that Christ left us an
> example that we should follow in his steps. But Paul speaks here of
> that high crucifying, whereby sin, and the devil, and death are
> crucified in Christ, and not in me. Here Christ does it alone by
> Himself. But I, believing in Christ, am by faith also crucified with
> Christ, so that sin, and death, and the devil, are all crucified and
> dead unto me.

***

"The law never loved me, nor gave a hair of its head for me. Even when I
obeyed it above many my equals in my own nation, all the time it never
loved me. And then, when I, in its least commandment, inadvertently and
unconsciously broke it, it turned upon me with its bowels of brass and its
flaming sword. But, O the depth of the grace of God! I see now that the
Son of God loved me even when I was dead in trespasses and sins; and I
now love Him because He first loved me. I love Him now, and He knows
it; but He loved me first: He was beforehand with His love. It was His part
and privilege to love me first. He was the Son and He loved me, and
revealed to me the age and the depth and the strength of His love, and by
all that He carried my heart captive, and keeps it captive in a willing, a holy,
and an everlasting captivity. Me! Yes, me! Me—He loved me," says Paul.

Christ loved him, loved Paul himself—yes, Paul himself. For the time being
Paul takes the whole of Christ's love to himself, the whole of Christ's heart,
the whole of His Cross, the whole of His atoning death, the whole of His
blood, and the whole of His Righteousness.

March 5

Difficulties Concerning the Will (Part 1 of 2)
by Hannah Whitall Smith

The common thought is that this life hid with Christ in God is to be lived in the emotions, and consequently all the attention of the soul is directed towards them, and as they are satisfactory or otherwise, the soul rests or is troubled. Now the truth is that this life is not to be lived in the emotions at all, but in the will, and therefore the varying states of emotion do not in the least disturb or affect the reality of the life, if only the will is kept steadfastly abiding in its center, God's will.

To make this plain, I must enlarge a little. Fénelon says somewhere that "pure religion resides in the will alone." By this he means that, as the will is the governing power in the man's nature, if the will is set straight, all the rest of the nature must come into harmony.

***

For the decisions of our will are often so directly opposed to the decisions of our emotions, that, if we are in the habit of considering our emotions as the test, we shall be very apt to feel like hypocrites in declaring those things to be real which our will alone has decided. But the moment we see that the will is king, we shall utterly disregard anything that cries against it, and shall claim as real its decisions, let the emotions rebel as they may.

***

The secret lies just here: our will, which is the spring of all our actions, is in our natural state under the control of self, and self has been working it in us to our utter ruin and misery. Now God says, "Yield yourselves up unto Me, as those that are alive from the dead, and I will work in you to will and to do my good pleasure" [Philippians 2:13]. And the moment we yield ourselves, He of course takes possession of us, and does work in us "that which is well pleasing in His sight through Jesus Christ," giving us the mind that was in Christ, and transforming us into His image (see Romans 12:1-2).

Cease to consider your emotions, for they are only the servants; and regard simply your will, which is the real king in your being. Is that given up to God? Is that put into His hands?

March 6

Difficulties Concerning the Will (Part 2 of 2)
by Hannah Whitall Smith

Does your will decide to believe? Does your will choose to obey? If this is the case, then you are in the Lord's hands, and you decide to believe, and you choose to obey; for your will is yourself. And the thing is done. The transaction with God is as real, where only your will acts, as when every emotion coincides. It does not seem as real to you; but in God's sight it is as real. And when you have got hold of this secret, and have discovered that you need not attend to your emotions, but simply to the state of your will, all the Scripture commands—to yield yourself to God, to present yourself a living sacrifice to Him, to abide in Christ, to walk in the light, to die to self—become possible to you; for you are conscious that, in all these, your will can act, and can take God's side: whereas, if it had been your emotions that must do it, you would sink down in despair, knowing them to be utterly uncontrollable.

When, then, this feeling of unreality or hypocrisy comes, do not be troubled by it. It is only in your emotions, and is not worth a moment's thought. Only see to it that your will is in God's hands; that your inward self is abandoned to His working; that your choice, your decision, is on His side; and there leave it.

Remember, then, that the real thing in your experience is what your will decides, and not the verdict of your emotions; and that you are far more in danger of hypocrisy and untruth in yielding to the assertions of your feelings, than in holding fast to the decision of your will. So that, if your will is on God's side, you are no hypocrite at this moment in claiming as your own the blessed reality of belonging altogether to Him, even though your emotions may all declare the contrary.

I am convinced that, throughout the Bible, the expressions concerning the "heart" do not mean the emotions, that which we now understand by the word "heart"; but they mean the will, the personality of the man, the man's own central self; and that the object of God's dealings with man is that this "I" may be yielded up to Him, and this central life abandoned to His entire control. It is not the feelings of the man God wants, but the man himself.

March 7

The Focus of a Disciple (Part 1 of 2)
by Bryan L. Herde

He shall not be afraid of evil news: his heart is fixed, trusting in the Lord.
Psalm 112:7

So we fix our eyes not on what is seen, but on what is unseen. For what is seen is temporary, but what is unseen is eternal.
2 Corinthians 4:18

As a branch of the Vine that is Jesus Christ, our primary responsibility is to fix our all upon the connection to the Vine and not upon the fruit. Imagine yourself as a branch that grows out of a grapevine. Your eyes, your heart, your mind, your all should constantly be turned toward the Vine itself, and not the other direction—towards the extension of your own branch to see one of three things:

1. How well the fruit-bearing is progressing;
2. How you compare to the other branches in the vineyard; and
3. What the Master Gardener is or isn't doing to feed you, water you and protect you.

By continually focusing upon the Vine, you are fixed upon the source of all the Life you will ever need for the results the Master Gardener desires. Why? Because the Vine has finished the work, and your job, as a branch, is to believe in the completed work of the Vine. What does it mean to "fix" our eyes and our thoughts upon Jesus? If I were to fix something to the wall I would nail it or screw it to the wall. In other words, that object I fixed is not going anywhere; it is there to stay. That is what is meant by the use of the word here. When we fix our eyes and our thoughts upon Jesus they are put there to stay. Certainly, it seems that we tend to lift our eyes to Jesus and focus our thoughts upon Him only when things are going badly, but that is not being "fixed" upon Him. Focus can be temporary or momentary, like when the Israelites looked at the bronze snake on the pole that was created by Moses (Numbers 21:6-9). They would be healed, but they didn't fix, with permanence, their eyes upon the cross. It was a temporary act.

March 8

The Focus of a Disciple (Part 2 of 2)
by Bryan L. Herde

He shall not be afraid of evil news: his heart is fixed, trusting in the Lord.
Psalm 112:7

So we fix our eyes not on what is seen, but on what is unseen. For what is seen is temporary, but what is unseen is eternal.
2 Corinthians 4:18

All too often, we gaze temporarily or long enough for our trouble to resolve and then we turn back to our own ways and processes, at least until the next crisis. That is not being in a place where we have fixed ourselves upon Jesus. The question is often asked, "Just how does one fix their eyes and thoughts upon Jesus?" Well, you can't do it if you didn't offer yourselves as a living sacrifice (Romans 12:1) and give up everything you have to Him (Luke 14:33). Why not? Because you are the one trying to fix yourself upon Jesus; He is the only One that can do it right and do it well in you and for you.

Fixing yourself upon Jesus is a state to which you yield yourself to be placed and kept there by God Himself. You must abandon yourself to the Lord for Him to do this work in you and for you. But you must want Him to do it. And trust me, He will take your willingness to do this and keep working it in you, even when you may want to quit. That is the very essence of Philippians 1:6, "being confident of this, that He who began a good work in you will carry it on to completion until the day of Jesus Christ."

For us as believers, it all begins and ends with our hearts. If my heart is fixed—stable, secure, trusting—then how I react to events, circumstances, relationships, hardships, persecutions and the like should ultimately do nothing to shake the solidity of my heart's focus upon the Lord. The eyes that Paul refers to in Ephesians 1:18 are the "eyes of your heart." That is an interesting phrase, but it fits so perfectly with those expressed by David in the verse from the Psalm quoted above. A heart that is fixed will quite naturally have its "eyes" fixed where and upon Whom they should be.

March 9

The Divine Ability
by John Henry Jowett

Now unto Him that is able to do exceeding abundantly above all that we ask or think, according to the power that works in us, unto Him be glory in the Church by Christ Jesus throughout all ages, world without end. Amen.
Ephesians 3:20-21

"Now unto Him that is able to do." There is something so quiet, so easy, so tremendous in the content of this word "do." It is not the noisy, unmistakable doings of a manufacturer; it is suggestive of an easy creation.

***

"Exceeding abundantly." Here Paul coins a Greek word for his own peculiar use. There was no superlative at hand which could describe his sense of the overwhelming ability of God, and so he just constructed a word of his own, the intensity of which can only be suggested in our English phrase "exceeding abundantly." The power flows up, and out, and over! It is a spring, and therefore incalculable.

***

"Above all we ask." The ability of God is beyond our prayers, beyond our largest prayers! What I have asked for is nothing compared to the ability of my God to give. I have asked for a cupful, and the ocean remains! "Or think." Then His ability is beyond even our imagination! Let us stretch our imaginations to the utmost! Let us seek to realize some of the promised splendors that are ours in Christ.

***

When all our workings and all our thinkings are put together, and piled one upon another, like some stupendous Alpine height, the ability of our God towers above all, reaching away into the mists of the immeasurable.

***

Before God can "do," my will must be operative. Our wills, however weak, must be on the side of God. You can will yourself onto your knees. You can will yourself to pray. You can do more than that, you can take the initial steps in obedience.

March 10

Faith: The Measure of Blessings (Part 1 of 2)
by Henry Robert Reynolds

"Great is your faith: be it done unto you even as you will."
Matthew 15:28

While faith occupies a most conspicuous place in the New Testament, as the instrument by which men become united to God, and are prepared and qualified to receive the light and peace of the gospel, we must be upon our guard against drawing too much conclusion from the analogical lessons of our Lord's miracles. The method of Divine mercy varies in each case. When our Lord, in the royalty of His love, spoke to the dull, cold ear of death, there is no hint that the child of the centurion, or that the widow's son, or that the spirit of Lazarus was stirred into faith by the person or claims of Jesus. In these and other instances, Christ declared Himself independent of any human condition whatever on the part of the recipient, yet, in a multitude of other cases, He did regard faith, moral surrender to His will, profound recognition of His claims as the channel of His noblest gifts, and as the measure of the kind and degree of blessing which He was able to impart. "If you can do anything," is the language of the father of the epileptic child. In our Lord's reply, He seemed to reproach the half-faith which made so feeble a draw upon the almightiness of God, and cried, "If you can believe...all things are possible." He could not do many mighty works, because of the unbelief of His own people.

***

Faith in the nature and promises of God's greatest self-manifestation appears the normal method for the bestowment of Divine blessing. Faith on sufficient evidence, moral acceptance in the character and claims of the living Christ, is the prime condition of life itself. Faith is the capacity for blessedness and the condition of power. It is the eye by which we see heavenly beauty, the hand with which we grasp exhaustless treasure, the ear into which falls the melody and harmony of truth, the faculty for tasting the sweetness of the Divine mercy, of complying with the mastery and supremacy of the Divine will, and the power by which we take hold of God and abandon self to the ends of the kingdom of God.

March 11

Faith: The Measure of Blessings (Part 2 of 2)
by Henry Robert Reynolds

"Great is your faith: be it done unto you even as you will."
Matthew 15:28

Knowledge, love, faith, prayer, service—what strange powers they possess! They are linked with each other as heat, motion, electricity, light are related to each other, and they have a tendency to produce one another. There must be some initial knowledge to believe and to love; but just in proportion to the simplicity of your faith and the reality of your love is your knowledge deepened. When this higher knowledge breaks upon you, then your faith becomes a full assurance, an invincible and real agreement; then love burns more fervently and flashes a higher enthusiasm for holy service, and demands self-abandonment. If faith be great and strong, it becomes a *prophecy*, a seeing of the invisible, a knowledge of what the will of the Lord is. Your hand takes hold of the Lord's hand; His strength is made perfect in your weakness. The expression of your faith is two-fold. It takes the form of prayer and service, of intimate communication with God and a consecrated life. The highest conception of prayer is revealed to us in the intercession of Jesus.

***

Further, it is just in proportion as your own hearts and minds rise up into the heart and will of your Lord, that *your* persistent prayer also becomes a prophecy of God's ways, an anticipation of what *He* will do.

You are let into the secret of His heart; you know that the answer of love is near, and that the Lord Jesus will triumph. There is no apparent limit to His grace. Ask what you will, and it shall be given; seek what you intensely desire, since He gave you the desire, and you shall find. Press Him hard with what faith tells you is undoubtedly in harmony with His will, and you will have the answer of peace. Certainly, if God hears the prayer of man at all, either the wishes of man prevail over the decrees of God, or the desires of man must have been purified and lifted up into the purposes of the Eternal.

March 12

The Fruit of a Disciple (Part 1 of 4)
by Bryan L. Herde

But the fruit of the Spirit is love, joy, peace, patience, kindness, goodness, faithfulness, gentleness and self-control. Against such things there is no law.
Galatians 5:22

It seems to me that the church has long focused upon a more worldly definition of what is meant by "fruit." We have typically defined it as something measurable, quantifiable and numbers-related: converts, baptisms, churches, works, ministries, services, etc. But the only definition I've been able to find in Scripture is a definition rooted in qualities and character—things not so easily measured. I'm not saying that quantifiable definitions are completely irrelevant. Nonetheless, if we focus foremost upon the qualities of fruitfulness, then the quantifiable elements consequently will be right. Our surety is in the Lord's faithfulness to His measuring standards, not ours. For we "live by faith, not by sight" (2 Corinthians 5:7).

Since the fruit we are to bear is manifested via the person of the Holy Spirit, let's look at some real life examples of the Spirit's fruit that were exhibited in the life of Christ:

- **Love**—Upon meeting and interacting with the rich young ruler who rejected Jesus: "Jesus looked at him and loved him" (Mark 10:21).
- **Joy**—After the return of the seventy two that Jesus sent out at the beginning of Luke 10: "At that time Jesus, full of joy through the Holy Spirit, said, 'I praise you, Father, Lord of heaven and earth, because you have hidden these things from the wise and learned, and revealed them to little children. Yes, Father, for this was Your good pleasure'" (Luke 10:21).
- **Peace**—Jesus being rejected at Nazareth: "All the people in the synagogue were furious when they heard this. They got up, drove Jesus out of the town, and took Him to the brow of the hill on which the town was built, in order to throw Him down the cliff. But He walked right through the crowd and went on His way" (Luke 4:28-30).

March 13

The Fruit of a Disciple (Part 2 of 4)
by Bryan L. Herde

But the fruit of the Spirit is love, joy, peace, patience, kindness, goodness, faithfulness, gentleness and self-control. Against such things there is no law.
Galatians 5:22

Here are some more examples of the fruit of the Spirit in Jesus' life:

- **Patience**—After His brothers came to Him and urged Him to show Himself in Judea: "Therefore Jesus told them, 'The right time for Me has not yet come; for you any time is right...for Me the right time has not yet come'" (John 7:6-8).
- **Kindness**—Feeding the four thousand: "Jesus called His disciples to Him and said, 'I have compassion for these people; they have already been with Me three days and have nothing to eat. I do not want to send them away hungry, or they may collapse on the way'" (Matthew 15:32).
- **Goodness**—When the woman caught in adultery was brought to Jesus: "But Jesus bent down and started to write on the ground with His finger. When they kept questioning Him, He straightened up and said to them, 'If any of you is without sin, let him be the first to throw a stone at her.' Again He stooped down and wrote on the ground. At this, those who heard began to go away one at a time, the older ones first, until only Jesus was left, with the woman still standing there. Jesus straightened up and asked her, 'Woman, where are they? Has no one condemned you?' 'No one, sir,' she said. 'Then neither do I condemn you,' Jesus declared. 'Go now and leave your life of sin'" (John 8:6-11).
- **Faithfulness**—After healing an invalid on the Sabbath and in response to the Jews' accusations. "Jesus gave them this answer: 'I tell you the truth, the Son can do nothing by Himself; He can only do what He sees His Father doing, because whatever the Father does the Son also does. By Myself I can do nothing; I judge only as I hear, and My judgment is just, for I seek not to please Myself but Him who sent Me'" (John 5:19, 30).

March 14

The Fruit of a Disciple (Part 3 of 4)
by Bryan L. Herde

But the fruit of the Spirit is love, joy, peace, patience, kindness, goodness, faithfulness, gentleness and self-control. Against such things there is no law.
Galatians 5:22

Here are some final examples of the fruit of the Spirit in Jesus' life:

- **Gentleness**—The crucifixion: "Near the cross of Jesus stood His mother, His mother's sister, Mary the wife of Clopas, and Mary Magdalene. When Jesus saw His mother there, and the disciple whom He loved standing nearby, He said to His mother, 'Dear woman, here is your son,' and to the disciple, 'Here is your mother.' From that time on, this disciple took her into his home" (John 19:25-27).

- **Self-control**—Jesus being arrested in the Garden of Gethsemane: "Put your sword back in its place," Jesus said to Peter, "for all who draw the sword will die by the sword. Do you think I cannot call upon my Father, and He will at once put at My disposal more than twelve legions of angels? But how then would the Scriptures be fulfilled that say it must happen this way?" (Matthew 26:52-54).

Undoubtedly, you may have instances from Jesus' life that you believe better illustrate the fruit of the Spirit, but these are the ones that have captured me. Even while I was looking up each of the above quoted texts, I was deeply moved by the nothingness of Jesus in yielding Himself to the will of the Father. It isn't natural for any man to be as fruitful as Jesus was during His short life on our planet. It is utter foolishness on the part of any person—especially a believer and disciple of Jesus Christ—to read Scripture and then to determine to execute what it says. Many, many thousands of people far better than we are have tried and they all failed. In fact, two of the world's greatest missionaries, Adoniram Judson (American missionary to Burma in the early 1800's) and Hudson Taylor (English missionary to China in the mid-1800's) were examples of men who determined to live Godly lives and do a great work for the Lord. Both "hit the wall" and as a result discovered what they and others have called "the exchanged life."

March 15

The Fruit of a Disciple (Part 4 of 4)
by Bryan L. Herde

But the fruit of the Spirit is love, joy, peace, patience, kindness, goodness, faithfulness, gentleness and self-control. Against such things there is no law.
Galatians 5:22

The "exchanged life" is a life that begins where self-effort ends, and we absolutely abandon ourselves to the working of the Holy Spirit in and through us to live the life we are commanded to live. When Jesus made the statement in John 5:30, "For I seek not to please Myself but Him who sent Me," He established the exact condition by which much fruit is produced through us. It is complete and comprehensive nothingness that God requires of us, nothing more and nothing less.

It is our weakness that we must embrace, not our strengths (2 Corinthians 12:7-10). God isn't working to strengthen our weaknesses, He wants to be the strength that flows *through* our weakness. He doesn't make us strong, He *is* our strength. As long as we are continually working to rid ourselves of weakness and make ourselves strong, we are opposed to the working of the Holy Spirit. John the Baptist made the most powerful statement when it comes to our life's reality, "Jesus must increase, I must decrease" (John 3:30).

Brothers and sisters, if you don't get anything else out of this book, please get this: God doesn't want our abilities, He wants our *inabilities*. He doesn't want our strengths, He wants our *weaknesses*.

Only the Holy Spirit can produce the fruit our Father, the Master Gardener, wants. We can't imitate it and we can't generate it—it is altogether heavenly. It is the life of Another coursing through us that produces all the fruit. We are only branches through which the fruit appears, produces an aroma as it ripens, and is then harvested in the season of the Lord's choosing for distribution to others. We abide in the Producer of Fruit—the Vine, Jesus Christ—through the indwelling of the Holy Spirit. In every way, it is His fruit, not ours.

March 16

To the Half-Hearted
by George H. Morrison

Whatsoever you do, do it heartily, as to the Lord.
Colossians 3:23

I should like to say, by way of caution, that true enthusiasm is not a noisy thing. Whenever we think of an enthusiastic crowd, we think of uproar, tumult, wild excitement. And I grant you that in the life of congregated thousands, touched into unity by some great emotion, there seems to be some call for loud expression. But just as there is a sorrow that lies too deep for tears, there is an enthusiasm far too deep for words; and the intense purpose of the whole-hearted man is never noisy. When the children of Israel, defeated by the Philistines, sent for the ark of God into the camp, do you remember how, when the ark appeared, they shouted until the earth rang and tore open? Yet spite of that outburst of emotion they were defeated, and the ark of God was captured. But Jesus, in the enthusiasm of His kingly heart, set His face steadfastly to go to Jerusalem; and yet He would not strive nor cry nor lift up His voice in the streets. The noisiest are generally shallow. There is a certain silence, as of an under-purpose, wherever a man is working heartily.

***

I want you to note how Paul lays his hand on the real secret of all the large enthusiasms. He centers his appeal upon a person. Had Paul been writing in some quiet academy, the text, I dare say, might have read like this, 'Whatsoever you do, do it heartily, for that is the road to nobility of character'; or 'Whatsoever you do, do it heartily, for the best work is always done that way.' Paul wrote for the masses. Paul wrote for the great world. And he knew that nothing abstract, nothing cold, would ever inspire the enthusiasm of thousands. A cause must be concentrated in some powerful name, it must live in the flesh and blood of personality, if the hearts of the many are ever to be stirred, and the lives of the many are ever to be won. So Paul, with the true instinct of universal genius, gathered all abstract arguments for zeal into the living argument of Jesus. And whatsoever you do, do it heartily, as what? as to the Lord.

March 17

The Law of Faith (Part 1 of 2)
by Hannah Whitall Smith

Where is boasting then? It is excluded. By what law? Of works?
No: but by the law of faith.
Romans 3:27

The law which lies behind the fact is, of course, the really potent thing. The fact of gravitation was a great discovery, but it would not have revolutionized the world as it has without the further discovery of its laws. Until these laws were discovered, the mighty force hidden in the fact of gravitation was comparatively worthless. It could not be applied.

But what we need is to get at the practical, common-sense, everyday laws of the spiritual life, that we may use them in our daily battle with the world.

***

"And the Lord said, 'If you had faith as a grain of mustard seed, you might say unto this sycamore tree, Be plucked up by the root, and be planted in the sea; and it should obey you'" (Luke 17:6). I believe myself that Christ was here telling us of a mighty, irresistible, spiritual law that is inherent in the nature of God, and that is shared, according to our measure, by everyone who is begotten of God and is a partaker of His divine nature. Just as gravitation is a law of matter, inherent in matter, and absolutely unerring and not stopping in its working, so is faith a law of spirit, inherent in spirit, and equally unerring and not stopping in its working.

When Christ says, therefore, that "nothing shall be impossible" to faith, He is not stating a marvelous fact only, but He is revealing a tremendous law. We know that all things are possible to God, and here our Lord tells us that all things are possible to us also, if we only believe. No assertion could be more distinct or unmistakable. The great thing for us, therefore, is to discover the law by which faith works, in order that we may know how to exercise this tremendous spiritual force, that is declared by our Lord to be our birthright, as being children of God, and partakers of His nature.

March 18

The Law of Faith (Part 2 of 2)
by Hannah Whitall Smith

Where is boasting then? It is excluded. By what law? Of works?
No: but by the law of faith.
Romans 3:27

The "law of faith" appears, therefore, to consist simply in two things, namely, a conviction of God's will, and a perfect confidence that that will must necessarily be accomplished. There are two passages that seem to me to set forth very clearly and definitely the working of this law:

And this is the confidence that we have in Him, that, if we ask anything according to His will, He hears us: and if we know that He hears us, whatever we ask, we know that we have the petitions that we desired of Him (1 John 5:14-15).

And Jesus answering said unto them, "Have faith in God. For truly I say unto you, That whoever shall say unto this mountain, Be removed, and be cast into the sea; and shall not doubt in his heart, but shall believe that those things which he says shall come to pass; he shall have whatsoever he says. Therefore I say unto you, Whatever things you desire, when you pray, believe that you receive them, and you shall have them" (Mark 11:22-24).

***

God disregards all appearances, but, calling "those things which are not as though they are," He creates them by that very calling. How much of this creative power of faith we His children share, I am not prepared to say, but that we are called to share far more of it than we have ever yet laid hold of, I feel very sure. There are, I am convinced, many "mountains" in our lives and experiences, which might be overcome, had we only the courage of faith to say to them, "Be you removed," accompanied with a calm assurance that they must surely go. The difficulty is that we neither "say" the word of faith, nor "pray" the prayer of faith. We say generally the word of doubt, and pray the prayer of experiment, and then we wonder why our faith and our prayers are so ineffectual.

March 19

The Leisure of Faith
by George H. Morrison

He that believes shall not make haste.
Isaiah 28:16

It is impossible that a true Christian should be a sluggard. Such new conceptions of life have dawned on him; duty, and service, and the building up of character, are so expanded when God has touched the soul, that as with the stirring music of the trumpet we are called to redeem the time because the days are evil. But the man who hastes never redeems the time. You never redeem anything by hurrying up.

And it is of that impatience, so closely akin to fickleness—and an age of hurry is extraordinarily fickle—it is of that impatience which knows no inward quietness, and which robs life of its music and its pace, that the prophet is speaking here. He that believes shall run and not be weary. He that believes shall press toward the mark. He that believes—God to his tardy feet has promised to lend the swiftness of the deer. But spite of that—no, because of that—he that believes shall not make haste.

I like to apply our text to hasty judgments. He that believes shall not make haste to judge. It is amazing how rashly and how recklessly we pass severe judgments on each other. There is nothing harder than suspense of judgment in our daily interactions with men and women. Even the kindliest are in danger of prejudging, and those who are not kindly do so constantly. Now do you see how we are to escape that sin? Do you observe the secret of suspended judgment? It is not a matter of caution after all—he that believes shall not make haste to judge. In all belittling there is a lack of faith.

***

In all God's dealings with the human race, and in all God's dealings with the human soul, there is purpose, urgency, infinite persistence; but I think no man will detect hurry there.

March 20

Why All Things Work Together for Good (Part 1 of 2)
by Thomas Watson

The grand reason why all things work for good is the near and dear interest which God has in His people. The Lord has made a covenant with them. "They shall be my people, and I will be their God" (Jeremiah 32:38). By virtue of this compact, all things do, and must work, for good to them. "I am God, even your God" (Psalm 1:7). This word, 'Your God,' is the sweetest word in the Bible, it implies the best relations; and it is impossible there should be these relations between God and His people, and everything not work for their good.

***

If all things work for good, therefore learn that there is sovereign control. Things do not work of themselves, but God sets them working for good. God is the great Disposer of all events and issues, He sets everything working. "His kingdom rules over all" (Psalm 103:19). It is meant of His providential kingdom. Things in the world are not governed by second causes, by the counsels of men, by the stars and planets, but by divine control. There are three things in sovereign control: God's foreknowing, God's determining, and God's directing all things to their periods and events. Whatever things do work in the world, God sets them to working.

***

How much good comes to the saints by affliction! When they are pounded and broken, they send forth their sweetest smell. Affliction is a bitter root, but it bears sweet fruit. "It yields the peaceable fruits of righteousness" (Hebrews 12:11). Affliction is the highway to heaven; though it be rocky and thorny, yet it is the best way. Poverty shall starve our sins; sickness shall make grace more helpful (2 Corinthians 4:16). Rebuke shall cause "the Spirit of God and of glory to rest upon us" (1 Peter 4:14). Death shall stop the bottle of tears, and open the gate of Paradise. No man did ever come off a loser by his acquaintance with God. By this, good shall come unto you, abundance of good, the sweet essences of grace, the hidden manna, yes, everything shall work for good. Oh, then get acquaintance with God, merge with His interest.

March 21

Why All Things Work Together for Good (Part 2 of 2)
by Thomas Watson

God works strangely. He brings order out of confusion, harmony out of discord. He frequently makes use of unjust men to do that which is just. "He is wise in heart" (Job 9:4). He can reap His glory out of men's fury (Psalm 76:10). Either the wicked shall not do the hurt that they intend, or they shall do the good which they do not intend. God often helps when there is least hope, and saves His people in that way which they think will destroy. He made use of the high priest's malice and Judas' treason to redeem the world. Through indiscreet passion, we are apt to find fault with things that happen; which is as if an illiterate man should criticize philosophy, or a blind man find fault with the work in a landscape painting. "Vain man would be wise" (Job 11:12). Silly animals will be challenging sovereign control, and calling the wisdom of God to the bar of reason. God's ways are "past finding out" (Romans 11:33). They are rather to be admired than understood. There is never a divine action of God, but what it has either a mercy or a wonder in it. How stupendous and infinite is that wisdom, that makes the most adverse circumstances work for the good of His children!

Learn how little cause we have then to be discontented at outward trials and emergencies! What? Discontented at that which shall do us good? All things shall work for good. There are no sins God's people are more subject to than unbelief and impatience. They are ready either to faint through unbelief, or to fret through impatience. When men fly out against God by discontent and impatience it is a sign they do not believe this text. Discontent is an ungrateful sin, because we have more mercies than afflictions; and it is an irrational sin, because afflictions work for good. Discontent is a sin which puts sin upon sin. "Fret not yourself to do evil" (Psalm 37:8). He that frets will be ready to do evil; fretting Jonah was sinning Jonah (Jonah 4:9). The devil blows the coals of passion and discontent, and then warms himself at the fire. Oh, let us not nourish this angry viper in our breast. Shall we be discontented at that which works for our good? So the Lord may bruise us by afflictions, but it is to enrich us. These afflictions work for us a weight of glory, and shall we be discontented?

March 22

Is God in Everything?
by Hannah Whitall Smith

One of the greatest obstacles to living unwaveringly this life of entire surrender is the difficulty of seeing God in everything. People say, "I can easily submit to things which come from God; but I cannot submit to man, and most of my trials and crosses come through human instrumentality." Or they say, "It is all well enough to talk of trusting; but when I commit a matter to God, man is sure to come in and disarrange it all; and while I have no difficulty in trusting God, I do see serious difficulties in the way of trusting men."

This is no imaginary trouble, but it is of vital importance, and if it cannot be met, it does really make the life of faith an impossible and visionary theory. For nearly everything in life comes to us through human instrumentalities, and most of our trials are the result of somebody's failure, or ignorance, or carelessness, or sin. We know God cannot be the author of these things, and yet unless He is the agent in the matter, how can we say to Him about it, "Your will be done"?

Besides, what good is there in trusting our affairs to God, if, after all, man is to be allowed to come in and disarrange them; and how is it possible to live by faith, if human agencies, in whom it would be wrong and foolish to trust, are to have a predominant influence in molding our lives?

Moreover, things in which we can see God's hand always have a sweetness in them which consoles while it wounds. But the trials inflicted by man are full of bitterness.

What is needed, then, is to see God in everything, and to receive everything directly from His hands, with no intervention of second causes. And it is just to this that we must be brought, before we can know an abiding experience of entire abandonment and perfect trust. Our abandonment must be to God, not to man, and our trust must be in Him, not in any arm of flesh, or we shall fail at the first trial.

March 23

The Refusals of Christ
by George H. Morrison

Jesus sometimes refused to work a miracle. It was in the desert where our Lord was tempted, and Satan came to Him when He was hungry, and he said, "If you are the Son of God, command that these stones be made bread." Yet never a stone became a loaf that day. "Man shall not live by bread alone, but by every word that proceeds out of the mouth of God." Christ's ministry was to be rich in miracle, and He began by refusing to perform one. And do you see the meaning of that refusal? It was our Lord refusing for His own use the powers that God had given Him for others. It was for others Jesus Christ was here. He came, not to be ministered unto, but to minister.

***

Jesus sometimes refused to answer prayer. We read of the Gadarene demoniac. But it is not only a lesson in the power of Jesus, it is a lesson in the art of prayer. For the devils prayed, 'Lord, let us enter the swine,' and the devils got the permission that they craved. And the Gadarenes prayed Jesus to depart, and by the morning Jesus had left their country. But the demoniac, cured, clothed, in his right mind, prayed Christ that he might follow Him and serve Him, and that was the only prayer that Christ refused. "Go home to your friends," said Christ, "and tell them how much the Lord has done for you." And do you catch the meaning of that refusal? There was an infinite pity for poor dead Gadara in it. I dare say it almost broke the demoniac's heart. It would have been so exquisitely sweet to follow Christ. But men are saved to serve, not to enjoy, and service like charity begins at home.

***

O brethren, try to realize tonight the peerless faithfulness of Jesus Christ, from the hour when He refused to turn the stones to bread until the moment when He refused the vinegar upon the cross. If Christ has never won you by His calls, shall He not win you now by His refusals? For every rejection of that man of Nazareth was in the service of a fallen world. He pleased not Himself. You must be hard to please if He does not please you. "Lord, I believe! Help my unbelief!"

March 24

The Delays of Love (Part 1 of 2)
by John Daniel Jones

When therefore He heard that he was sick, He remained at that time two days in the place where He was. Then after this He said to the disciples, "Let us go into Judah."
John 11:6-7

Did you ever know a *therefore* so strange as that? Because He loved Martha, and her sister, and Lazarus, *therefore* He stayed away from them when they most needed His help. Because He loved Martha, and her sister, and Lazarus, *therefore* when they sent an urgent message begging him to hurry to them, for two days He took no notice of their request. Because He loved Martha, and her sister, and Lazarus, *therefore* He did nothing to avert the threatening trouble and actually left them to bear it alone.

***

But, staggering and amazing though this *therefore* is, there is a perfect wealth of comfort and good hope in it. For what is its message but this: that there may be love in our delays and disappointments and crushing sorrows? "Your love," says one of our hymns, "has many a lighted path no mortal eye can trace." So it has. It takes strange roads at times. It takes us through trouble and loss, through griefs multiplied and long delays. We are tempted often to say, "An enemy has done this." No, it is love's road!

***

The Lord allows delay and disappointment and sorrow to visit us, not *although* He loves us, but *because* He loves us. The very things that make us think sometimes that God has forgotten us may be the proofs of His love. Because He loves us, *therefore* He weakens our strength in the way. Because He loves us, *therefore* He lets all His waves and billows go over us. Because He loves us, *therefore* when we cry to Him to save those we loved dearer than life, He makes no sign but lets them die. Because the Father loves us, *therefore* He chastens us. This *therefore*, if we but took it to our hearts, contains in it a great and glorious Gospel.

March 25

The Delays of Love (Part 2 of 2)
by John Daniel Jones

When therefore He heard that he was sick, He remained at that time two days in the place where He was. Then after this He said to the disciples, "Let us go into Judah."
John 11:6-7

Now Jesus loved Martha, and her sister, and Lazarus. And no risks in the world could prevent Him from hurrying to their help in their great sorrow and bereavement. "After this He said to His disciples, 'Let us go into Judaea again.'" And this was not the greatest risk that Christ's love compelled Him to take. Think of the risk He took for you and me. While He was yet in His glory with the Father He loved us. He loved us when we were in our lost estate. He loved us while we were strangers and aliens from God. And because of His love for us He left His home in heaven for this world of ours. There were risks of misunderstanding, of rejection, of hatred, of death. He knew them before He came. But His love for us was so deep and strong that He took them all. Love compelled Him to risk everything, even life itself, in order to save us. "The Son of God loved me," says Paul, "and gave Himself up for me." The Son of God loved and took the risk of the Cross.

***

We profess to love Christ; has our love ever made us risk anything for Him? I get concerned sometimes about the fact that there is so little that is adventurous and risky about our religion. We are cautious and careful people. Our religion never gets us into trouble. We keep so discreetly silent about our religion that we run no risk even of the scorn and laughter of the world. It gives us an easy time, no doubt, but our religion is not particularly effective. There is one maxim of Nietzsche's which the Church of Christ must learn if she is to regain power. It is this: "Live dangerously." The Church must be willing to take risks. Christian people must be willing to take risks. When we are ready to risk ease and comfort and popularity because of our love for Christ, things will begin to move. Is our love of that sacrificial kind? Christ risked everything for us; are we risking anything for Him?

March 26

The Patience of a Disciple (Part 1 of 6)
by Bryan L. Herde

Wait for the Lord; be strong and take heart and wait for the Lord.
Psalm 27:14

Be still before the Lord and wait patiently for Him...
Psalm 37:7a

There are three qualities of patience that I would like to examine. They are:
1. Waiting
2. Perseverance
3. Endurance

All three words are used of differing types of patience throughout scripture. The Old Testament is riddled with the word "wait;" the New Testament with the words "perseverance" and "endurance." Without a doubt, churches in hostile areas around the world know much about learning to persevere and endure for the name of Jesus. Even though the American Church is not yet undergoing overt persecution or hardship requiring great amounts of perseverance and endurance due to open attacks, she needs to learn how to wait now. Only the Lord knows when persecution and suffering requiring great perseverance and endurance will come.

For the American Church, the downside to having plenty is that we can't really seem to justify the need to wait for anything. But, oh, how the Church suffers because of her self-reliance, impatience and pride!

True waiting means that we learn to want God's best—His way and in His time—no matter what. It is a surrendering of one's self to the control of Another. This is why humility is so important. True waiting allows you to get in sync with God—to have yourself aligned with His heart and with His mind. This is a work you yield yourself to for Him to accomplish, as it is beyond your capacity to achieve.

March 27

The Patience of a Disciple (Part 2 of 6)
by Bryan L. Herde

Wait for the Lord; be strong and take heart and wait for the Lord.
Psalm 27:14

Be still before the Lord and wait patiently for Him...
Psalm 37:7a

Willingly giving up control is critical to growing as a disciple. In fact, when Jesus said, "In the same way, any of you who does not give up everything he has cannot be My disciple" (Luke 14:33), He meant that our determination and desire to control, outline agendas, make plans, fulfill desires, put forth efforts—in fact, *everything*—must be given to Him in order for us to be counted as one of His disciples.

More often than not, I am asked the question, "Surely, by waiting you don't mean that you just sit around and do nothing?" My answer is always the same, "Waiting for instructions and/or waiting for supplies are the hardest things you will ever do, and I don't consider something that hard to be doing nothing." Of all the disciplines of our faith, waiting is the most contrary to our natural impulses, our cultural pressures, our churches' philosophies of mission and ministry, and our personal understanding and beliefs about what it means to be a Christian. We have convinced ourselves that the most important thing is to be busy doing good. We have come to believe that our purpose, our mission, our success are determined by the wake we leave in life that can be measured, understood and documented. We have allowed the non-Biblical statement by Ben Franklin, "God helps them that help themselves," to become more imperative for us than the Word itself. Whenever I was around other Christian leaders or workers and someone asked me what I am doing with my life, my first response was always to answer with a list of the organizations with which I was participating, or the extent of my writings, or my self-assessment of my effectiveness in the lives of others. Instead I should have answered like David did in 1 Chronicles 17:16, "Who am I, O Lord God...that you have brought me this far?"

March 28

The Patience of a Disciple (Part 3 of 6)
by Bryan L. Herde

Wait for the Lord; be strong and take heart and wait for the Lord.
Psalm 27:14

Be still before the Lord and wait patiently for Him…
Psalm 37:7a

Instead of trying to make myself out to be something, I should only declare who the Lord has made me and what He is yet making me. My validation as a Christian is not to be based upon my spiritual-productivity resume, but upon Christ alone. Isn't this the very essence of what Jesus reproved the Ephesians for in Revelation 2:4 when He told them to repent because they lost their first love?

As of the moment of this writing, I am going to make my answer this: "I have been called by the Lord to give up all rights to myself and all control over my entire existence. I don't know where I'm going and I don't know what He is doing in and through me. But I know Who I am following and I trust that He will fulfill the desires of His heart when and how He pleases." May I be faithful to make this statement (or words along these lines), rather than a list of my activities.

Waiting upon the Lord will cause you to lose all confidence in yourself, in your own intellect, in your own powers and in your own ability to do anything that you think would please the Lord. If the Lord doesn't initiate and lead you in all areas of your life, nothing will be done that will endure. Waiting teaches you to leave *all*, and I mean *everything*, in His hands and in His care. It is a slow but thorough process. Learning to wait upon the Lord will enable a person to be supernaturally reshaped and prepared for the inevitable tests of perseverance and endurance. I do believe, however, that you can persevere and endure to some degree with very little true waiting upon the Lord. The strength of a person's will, of determination and sometimes stubbornness can enable these actions. True waiting is something else entirely.

March 29

The Patience of a Disciple (Part 4 of 6)
by Bryan L. Herde

Wait for the Lord; be strong and take heart and wait for the Lord.
Psalm 27:14

Be still before the Lord and wait patiently for Him...
Psalm 37:7a

True biblical waiting is dependent upon one's helplessness—voluntary or involuntary—as the Lord sovereignly decrees. I say "voluntary" because I believe that when we encounter a statement of how a believer is to act, we should take that to the Lord and offer ourselves to Him and ask Him to make this true in our lives. Instead, what we typically do is take a command and then determine how we can best fulfill that command, while sometimes asking for God's help. The result is almost always frustration and failure. Why? Because we set out to do something we cannot do.

If we had, however, taken the command and ourselves to the Lord and then waited upon Him to work that truth in and through us, we would discover that it will become as natural to us as breathing. Only God knows what the process will be and how long the process will take. We must wait for Him to do all. "Without Me, you can do nothing."

The qualities of patience called "perseverance" and "endurance" have long been associated with suffering, typically, the more classic types: injustice, persecution, deprivation, illness, etc. There are many places, people and individuals around the world and here in the U.S. where and in whom these types of suffering exist. The call to persevere and endure were exhortations given by the Lord through Paul, Peter and James to the Christians who were suffering all kinds of persecution and hardship throughout the first century. These same exhortations apply to all believers today.

March 30

The Patience of a Disciple (Part 5 of 6)
by Bryan L. Herde

Wait for the Lord; be strong and take heart and wait for the Lord.
Psalm 27:14

Be still before the Lord and wait patiently for Him...
Psalm 37:7a

There is, however, a call to persevere and endure in a way that is little discussed, taught or understood in 21st-century America, and that is the suffering that comes when a disciple of Jesus surrenders their all to Jesus Christ. This is one area in which I believe that our Lord Jesus Christ suffered constantly. As you read through the Gospel accounts, notice how many times Jesus says, "My time has not yet come." Here is the God-Man of all time who had perfect humanness and total deity all in one body. He had the privilege of rank and authority to execute His will at any time, anywhere and any way He chose. However, as we are plainly told in Philippians chapter 2, He set all that aside and made Himself nothing. In John chapter 5 Jesus even goes so far as to say that "By Myself I can do nothing" and "I do nothing to please Myself." What we see modeled in the life of Jesus is not simply a perfect life that sets a standard and a model for our lives, but much, much more. He perfected an attitude that precedes all His actions—that of absolute surrender of Himself to the will of Another.

In truth, the bumper sticker slogan that says, "What Would Jesus Do?" actually places the cart far ahead of the horse. All that Jesus did flowed out of who He was in relationship to the Father, not what He had predetermined to do. And because of this, He was not in control of His life's circumstances, His life's fulfillment, His life's activities, His life's teaching, or His life's purpose. Jesus' purpose was to allow the Father to fulfill *His* purpose in and through Him. Jesus perfectly modeled a life where self-determination did not exist. He lived for the joy and fulfillment of His Father, not for Himself.

March 31

The Patience of a Disciple (Part 6 of 6)
by Bryan L. Herde

Wait for the Lord; be strong and take heart and wait for the Lord.
Psalm 27:14

Be still before the Lord and wait patiently for Him...
Psalm 37:7a

Having become nothing, so that He would do nothing on His own, He then calls us to live a life of nothingness, just like He did. And yet we see in His life the most that anyone could do or ever has done in a little over three years' time. But it required a life without rights to itself, without control of timing, without control through self-determination, or self-provision, or self-protection, or self-promotion, and without accessing the full resources of Heaven to serve His own interests. He yielded Himself to God because He loved God with all His being, and He loved all others as He loved Himself.

That same life is available for us as well. But we must desire Him to make us nothing so that He can be all He desires and is willing to be in us.

Once a person has handed over their will to Jesus Christ, then one must wait, persevere and endure the processes our loving Father knows we need for Christ to be completed in us, so that Jesus Christ, through the Holy Spirit, may be free to do all that is in the Father's heart to do. This is denying oneself and carrying one's cross. Death to self is a process that requires staggering amounts of waiting, persevering and enduring. There is no formula, there is no pre-known timeline, and there is no way you can do it yourself. You must give all and leave all in the hands of our God to do what only the Sovereign, Almighty, Loving and Gracious God can do.

A life so yielded will certainly hear, "Well done, good and faithful servant."

April 1

Resurrected, Not Raised
by A.B. Simpson

Resurrected with my Risen Savior,
Seated with Him at His own right hand;
This the glorious message Easter brings me.
This the place in which by faith I stand.

Men would have you rise to higher levels,
But they leave you on the human plane.
We must have a heavenly Resurrection;
We must die with Christ and rise again.

Once there lived another man within me,
Child of earth and slave of Satan he;
But I nailed him to the Cross of Jesus,
And that man is nothing now to me.

Now Another Man is living in me,
And I count His blessed life as mine;
I have died with Him to all my own life;
I have risen to all His life Divine.

Oh, it is so sweet to die with Jesus!
And by death be free from self and sin.
Oh, it is so sweet to live with Jesus!
As He lives the death-born life within.

April 2

Love's Wastefulness
by George H. Morrison

To what purpose is this waste?
Matthew 26:8

There is a wasteful spending that is supremely selfish. There is a lavish giving that is disowned in heaven, because the giver is always thinking of himself. But God suspends the pettier economies, and will not tolerate a single murmur, when He detects the wastefulness of love. It is the nature of love to give. It is love's way to forget self and lavish everything. And Mary's [of Bethany] way was love's way when she broke the box and poured the ointment on the feet of Christ. And being love's way, it was God's way too. And so we reach the truth that I am anxious to press home on your hearts. If God be Love, and if a careless expenditure like that of Mary is the very essence of all love, then in the handiwork of God we shall detect a seeming wastefulness. I scan the works of the Almighty, and everywhere I see the marks of wisdom. I look abroad, and the great universe assures me of His power. But God is more than wisdom or than power. God is Love. And I can never rest until I have found the traces of that love in all I know and all I see of God. Here, then, is one of love's sure tokens. It is a royal expenditure, a lavish and self-forgetful waste.

***

Do you really believe that the whole world is being saved today? Are there not multitudes for whom life's tragedy is just the "might have been"? And souls unnumbered, here and everywhere, galloping down to the mist and mire. And there was room within the heart of Christ for all! And there was cleansing in the Savior's death for everyone! O waste! Waste! Waste! And to what purpose is that wasted agony? And why should Jesus suffer and die for all, if all were never to accept His love? Ah, Mary, why did you break the alabaster box and pour the precious ointment upon Christ? That wastefulness was just the Savior's spirit that brought Him to the cross and to the grave. Love gives and lavishes and dies, for it is love. Love never asks how little can I do; it always asks how much. There is a magnificent extravagance in love, whether the love of Mary or the love of God.

April 3

To the Disheartened
by George H. Morrison

Why are you cast down, O my soul?
Psalm 42:5

It is one source of the eternal freshness of the psalms that they tell the story of a struggling soul. They open a window on to that battlefield with which no other battle can be compared—the moral struggle of the individual with himself.

***

Now as we read that story of the psalmist's struggle, one of the first things to notice is just the likeness of that battle to our own. Ages have passed, and everything is different, since the shepherd-king poured out his heart in melody. And yet his failures and his hopes are so like yours, he might have been shepherding and reigning yesterday. We are so apt to think we fight alone. We are so prone to think there never was a life so weak, so ragged, so full of a dull gnawing, as ours. We are so ready to believe that we have suffered more than any heart that ever loved and lost. And then God opens up the heart of David, and we see its failures and we hear its cries, and the sense of loneliness at least is gone. He prayed as you have prayed. He fell as you have fallen. He rose and started again as you have done. He was disheartened, and so are we.

***

Never pass judgments in your disheartened hours. It is part of the conduct of an honest soul never to take the verdict of its melancholy. The hours come when everything seems wrong. And all that we do, and all that we are, seems worthless. And by a strange and subtle trick of darkness, it is just then we set to judge ourselves. Suspend all judgment when you are disheartened. Tear into fragments the verdict of your melancholy. Wait until the sunshine comes, wait until the light of the face of God comes, then judge—you cannot judge without the light. But in your darkness, steady yourself on God and act. Disheartenment is the wise man's time for striking out. It is only the fool's time for summing up.

April 4

A Suasive [Urging] to Contentment (Part 1 of 5)
by Thomas Watson

We are exhorted to labor for contentment; this is that which beautifies and decorates a Christian, and as a spiritual embroidery, does set him off in the eyes of the world. But it seems I hear some bitterly complaining, and saying to me, "Alas! How is it possible to be contented? The Lord has made 'my chain heavy;' he has cast me into a very sad condition." Every sin labors either to hide itself under some mask; or, if it cannot be concealed, then to vindicate itself by some excuse. This sin of discontent I find very witty in its excuses, which I shall first reveal, and then make a reply. We must lay it down as a rule that discontent is a sin, so that all the pretenses and excuses with which it labors to justify itself are but the painting and dressing of a prostitute.

***

A thief may take away all the money that I have about me, but not my land; even more a Christian has a title to the land of promise.

***

Be content; if God dams up our outward comforts, it is so that the stream of our love may run faster another way.

***

Another may have more property than you, but more worry; more riches, less rest; more revenues, but with all the more occasions of expense; he has a greater inheritance, yet perhaps God does not give "him power to eat thereof" (Ecclesiastes 6:2); he has the control of his estate, not the use; he holds more but enjoys less; in a word, you have less gold than he has, and perhaps less guilt.

***

Remember in every loss there is only a suffering, but in every discontent there is a sin, and one sin is worse than a thousand sufferings. What! Because some of my revenues are gone, shall I part with some of my righteousness? Shall my faith and patience go, too? Because I do not possess an estate, shall I not therefore possess my own spirit? O learn to be content.

April 5

A Suasive [Urging] to Contentment (Part 2 of 5)
by Thomas Watson

"My child is rebellious." Though to see him undutiful is your grief, yet not always do you see your own sin. Has a parent given the child not only the milk of the breast but "the sincere milk of the word?" Have you seasoned his tender years with religious education? You can do no more; parents can only work knowledge, God must work grace; they can only lay the wood together, it is God who must make it burn; a parent can only be a guide to show his child the way to heaven, the Spirit of God must be a magnet to draw his heart into that way. So, is a parent put in God's place to give grace? Who can help it, if a child, having the light of conscience, Scripture, education—these three torches in his hand—yet runs willfully into the deep ponds of sin? Weep for your child, pray for him; but do not sin for him by discontent.

***

It is sad, when a friend proves to be like a brook in summer (Job 6:15). The traveler being parched with heat, comes to the brook, hoping to refresh himself, but the brook is dried up, yet be content. You are not alone, others of the saints have been betrayed by friends; and when they have leaned upon them, they have been as a foot out of joint. This was true for David; "it was not an enemy that disappointed me, but it was you, O man, my equal, my guide, and my acquaintance; we took sweet counsel together" (Psalm 55:12-14); and in the case of Christ, he was betrayed by a friend: and why should we think it strange to have the same measure dealt out to us as Jesus Christ had? "The servant is not above his master."

***

You have a friend in heaven who will never fail you; "there is a friend," said Solomon, "that sticks closer than a brother" (Proverbs 18:24); such a friend is God; he is very studious and inquisitive on our behalf; he debates with himself, consulting and projecting how he may do us good; he is the best friend which may give contentment in the middle of all discourtesies of friends.

April 6

A Suasive [Urging] to Contentment (Part 3 of 5)
by Thomas Watson

Jesus Christ was content to be reproached by us; he despised the shame of the cross (Hebrews 12:2). It may amaze us to think that he who was God could endure to be spit upon, to be crowned with thorns, in a kind of mockery; and when he was ready to bow his head upon the cross, to have the Jews in scorn shake their heads and say, "he saved others, himself he cannot save." The shame of the cross was as much as the blood of the cross; his name was crucified before his body. The sharp arrows of accusation that the world shot at Christ went deeper into his heart than the spear; his suffering was so humiliating, that it seemed as if the sun blushed to behold it, it withdrew its bright beams, and masked itself with a cloud (and well it might when the Sun of Righteousness was in an eclipse); all this abuse and reproach did the God of glory endure, or rather disregard, for us. O then let us be content to have our names degraded for Christ; let not an insult lie at our heart, but let us bind it as a crown about our head! Alas, what is an insult? This is but small shot; then how will men stand at the mouth of a cannon? These who are discontented at an insult will be offended at an imprisonment.

***

If you are a child of God, you must look for disrespect. A believer is in the world, but not of the world; we are here in a pilgrim condition, out of our own country, therefore we must not look for the respect and praise of the world; it is sufficient that we shall have honor in our own country (Hebrews 13:14). It is dangerous to be the world's favorite.

***

Your sufferings are not so great as your sins: put these two in the balance, and see which weighs heaviest; where sin lies heavy, sufferings lie light. A carnal soul makes more of his sufferings, and less of his sins; he looks upon one at the large end of the perspective, but upon the other at the little end of the perspective. The carnal heart cries out, "take away the frogs" (Exodus 8:8): but a gracious heart cries out, "take away the iniquity" (2 Samuel 24:10). The one says, never has anyone suffered as I have done; but the other says, never has one sinned as I have done (Micah 7:7-9).

April 7

A Suasive [Urging] to Contentment (Part 4 of 5)
by Thomas Watson

To see the wicked flourish is a matter rather of pity than envy; it is all the heaven they will have; "woe to you that are rich, for you have received your comfort" (Luke 6:24). From here David made it his solemn prayer, "deliver me from the wicked, from men of the world, which have their portion in this life, and whose belly you fill with your hidden treasure" (Psalm 17:15). The word (I believe) is David's prayer; from men of the world, which have their portion in this life, "good Lord, deliver me." When the wicked have eaten of their dainty dishes, there comes in a sad reckoning which will spoil all. The world is first musical and then tragic; if you would have a man fry and blaze in hell, let him have enough of the fat of the earth. The times are full of heresy and ungodliness, and this is what troubles me. This excuse consists of two branches:

Branch 1—The times are full of *heresy*. This is indeed sad; when the devil cannot by violence destroy the church, he endeavors to poison it; when he cannot with Samson's foxtails set the corn on fire [Judges 15:3-5], then he sows weeds; as he labors to destroy the peace of the church by [false] visions, so the truth of it is destroyed by error; we may cry out that we live in times wherein there is a channel open to all unique opinions, and every man's opinion is his Bible. Well, this may make us mourn, but let us not murmur through discontent.

Branch 2—The second branch of the excuse that discontent makes is the *irreverence* of the times; I live and converse among the ungodly: "O that I had wings like a dove, for then would I fly away and be at rest" (Psalm 55:6). It is indeed sad to be mixed with the wicked. David beheld "transgressors and was grieved." Lot was vexed, worn out with the unclean lifestyles of the wicked; he made the sins of Sodom spears to pierce his own soul. We ought, if there is any spark of divine love in us, to be very sensible of the sins of others, and to have our hearts bleed for them; yet let us not break forth into mourning and discontent, knowing that God in his sovereign control has permitted it, and surely not without some reasons.

April 8

A Suasive [Urging] to Contentment (Part 5 of 5)
by Thomas Watson

Grace is beyond spiritual gifts; you compare your grace with another's gifts. There is a vast difference: grace without gifts is infinitely better than gifts without grace. In religion, the vital things are best: gifts are a more external and common work of the Spirit, which is apt to happen to backsliders; grace is a more distinguishing work, and is a jewel hung only upon the elect. Have you the seed of God, the holy anointing? Be content.

***

You say: You cannot speak with fluency as others do...a purified heart is better than a silver tongue.

***

Be not discontented, for God does usually proportion a man's parts to the place to which he calls him; some are set in a higher sphere and function, their place requires more parts and abilities; but the most inferior member is useful in its place, and shall have a power delegated for the discharge of its particular office.

***

God has always grown religion by sufferings. The foundation of the church has been laid in blood, and these optimistic showers have ever made it more fruitful. Cain put the knife to Abel's throat, and ever since the church's veins had bled: but she is like the vine, which by bleeding grows, and like the palm tree, which the more weight is laid upon it, the higher it rises. The holiness and patience of the saints, under their persecutions, have added much to the growth of religion.

***

That sorrow for sin which drives us away from God is not without sin, for there is more despair in it than true regret; the soul has so many tears in its eyes that it cannot see Christ. Sorrow, as sorrow, does not save, as if to make Christ out of our tears, but is useful as it prepares the soul, making sin repellant, and Christ precious.

April 9

Pax Vobiscum [Peace Be With You] (Part 1 of 3)
by Henry Drummond

"Come unto Me all you that are weary and heavy-laden and I will give you rest. Take My yoke upon you and learn of Me, for I am meek and humble in heart, and you shall find rest unto your souls. For My yoke is easy and My burden light."
Matthew 11:28-30

This lack of connection between the great words of religion and everyday life has bewildered and discouraged all of us. Christianity possesses the noblest words in the language; its literature overflows with terms expressive of the greatest and happiest moods which can fill the soul of man. Rest, Joy, Peace, Faith, Love, Light—these words occur with such consistency in hymns and prayers that an observer might think they formed the basis of Christian experience. But on coming to close contact with the actual life of most of us, how surely would he be disenchanted. I do not think we ourselves are aware how much our religious life is made up of phrases; how much of what we call Christian experience is only a dialect of the Churches, a mere religious phraseology with almost nothing behind it in what we really feel and know. For some of us, indeed, the Christian experiences seem further away than when we took the first steps in the Christian life. That life has not opened out as we had hoped; we do not regret our religion, but we are disappointed with it.

***

I am quite sure that the difficulty does not lie in the fact that men are not in earnest. This is simply not the fact. All around us Christians are wearing themselves out trying to be better.

***

Rest, that is to say, is not a thing that can be given, but a thing to be *acquired*. It comes not by an act, but by a process. It is not to be found in a happy hour, as one finds a treasure; but slowly, as one finds knowledge. It could indeed be no more found in a moment than could knowledge.

April 10

Pax Vobiscum [Peace Be With You] (Part 2 of 3)
by Henry Drummond

"Come unto Me all you that are weary and heavy-laden and I will give you rest. Take My yoke upon you and learn of Me, for I am meek and humble in heart, and you shall find rest unto your souls. For My yoke is easy and My burden light."
Matthew 11:28-30

Wounded vanity, disappointed hopes, unsatisfied selfishness—these are the old, vulgar, universal sources of man's unrest. Now it is obvious why Christ pointed out that the two chief objects for achievement are the exact opposites of these. To Meekness and Lowliness these things simply do not exist. They cure stress by making it impossible. These remedies do not trifle with surface symptoms; they strike at once at removing the causes. The ceaseless irritation of a self-centered life can be removed at once by learning Meekness and Lowliness of heart [humility]. He who learns them is forever resistant to it. He lives from then on a charmed life. Christianity is a fine inoculation, a transfusion of healthy blood into an anemic or poisoned soul.

***

He who is without expectation cannot fret if nothing comes to him. It is self-evident that these things are so. The lowly man and the meek man are really above all other men, above all other things. They dominate the world because they do not care for it. The miser does not possess gold, gold possesses him. But the meek possess it. "The meek" said Christ, "inherit the earth." They do not buy it; they do not conquer it; but they inherit it.

***

This is what Christianity is for—to teach men the Art of Life—and its whole curriculum lies in one phrase: "Learn of Me." Unlike most education, this is almost purely personal, it is not to be had from books or lectures or creeds or doctrines. It is a study from life. Christ never said much in mere words about the Christian graces. He lived them, He was them. Yet we do not merely copy Him. We learn His art by living with Him, like the old apprentices with their masters.

April 11

Pax Vobiscum [Peace Be With You] (Part 3 of 3)
by Henry Drummond

"Come unto Me all you that are weary and heavy-laden and I will give you rest. Take My yoke upon you and learn of Me, for I am meek and humble in heart, and you shall find rest unto your souls. For My yoke is easy and My burden light."
Matthew 11:28-30

There is no suggestion here that religion will exempt any man from bearing burdens. That would be to exempt him from living, since it is life itself that is the burden. What Christianity does propose is to make it tolerable. Christ's yoke is simply His secret for the alleviation of human life, His prescription for the best and happiest method of living. Men harness themselves to the work and stress of the world in clumsy and unnatural ways. A rough, ill-fitted collar at best, they make its strain and friction past enduring, by placing it where the neck is most sensitive; and by mere continuous irritation this sensitivity increases until the whole nature is raw and sore.

***

It is the beautiful work of Christianity everywhere to adjust the burden of life to those who bear it, and them to it. It has a perfectly miraculous gift of healing. Without doing any damage to human nature it sets it right with life, harmonizing it with all surrounding things, and restoring those who are worn-out with the fatigue and dust of the world to a new grace of living.

***

Then the Christian experiences are our own making? In the same sense in which grapes are our own making, and no more. All fruits grow—whether they grow in the soil or in the soul; whether they are the fruits of the wild grape or of the True Vine. No man can make things grow. He can get them to grow by arranging all the circumstances and fulfilling all the conditions. But the growing is done by God. Causes and effects are eternal arrangements, set in the constitution of the world; fixed beyond man's ordering. What man can do is to place himself in the midst of a chain of sequences. Thus he can get things to grow: thus he himself can grow. But the grower is the Spirit of God.

April 12

The Stillness of a Disciple (Part 1 of 3)
by Bryan L. Herde

Stand in awe, and sin not: commune with your heart upon your bed, and be still.
Psalm 4:4 (KJV)

Be still, and know that I am God...
Psalm 46:10 (KJV)

I have discovered the following statement attributed to St. Jerome to be incredibly profound and highly applicable to the life of a disciple:

> "Hold you still." And this is the hardest precept that is given to man; to such a degree that the most difficult principle of action sinks into nothing when compared with this command to inaction. [Written about the phrase, "Be still before the Lord" from Psalm 37:7.]

Stillness is *not* a quality that the Lord gives His disciples via a once-for-all dose. No, it is a quality emanating from His *own* patience, goodness, faithfulness, mercy, trustworthiness and love.

Stillness is Jesus refusing the self-deliverance of which He was capable (Matthew 26:53).

Stillness is Jesus standing before His accusers and saying nothing (Matthew 27:12-14).

Stillness is Jesus walking down the road carrying His cross and being able to look at others who were weeping for Him, addressing them with powerful and eternal truths spoken through His own misery (Luke 23:27-31).

Stillness is Jesus hanging on His cross and asking for forgiveness for those who were crucifying Him (Luke 23:34).

Stillness is a quality that is forged through the fiery trials that purify our faith (1 Peter 1:6-7).

April 13

The Stillness of a Disciple (Part 2 of 3)
by Bryan L. Herde

Stand in awe, and sin not: commune with your heart upon your bed, and be still.
Psalm 4:4 (KJV)

Be still, and know that I am God...
Psalm 46:10 (KJV)

Stillness is the inner confidence, the quietness of heart that result from believing God, knowing Him, understanding Him and trusting Him to be in constant and total control of you, your circumstances, your environment and, in fact, all things at all times in every way. Life surrounding both Jesus and Paul certainly was not quiet. It was comprised of chaos, persecution, frenzy, injustice, pain, crying, anger, evil and suffering. But their hearts were steadfastly still, immovable and confident in spite of all the "noise" enveloping them.

I once envisioned myself being in a room inside my heart with Christ that had a glass ceiling overhead. The space where we were together was quiet, calm and still, while overhead it was chaotic. This is the inner stillness to which I am referring. In a way most miraculous, God is able to work in us a stillness that is solely of Him and a quietness that is at the very heart of who He is. Just imagine for a moment the amount of information God processes every second of created time:
- There are likely trillions of stars in the universe all in constant movement and change, and God knows every detail about every one of them everywhere all the time;
- Jesus told us that God feeds the birds of the air (estimated to be 200-400 billion in number!) and clothes the grass of the field (Matthew 6:25-34);
- Jesus told us that God has numbered every hair on our heads (Matthew 10:30) and there are over seven billion heads roaming our planet right now!

Yet there is a stillness of God, and in God, that exists even in the very center of all His activity and responsibility.

April 14

The Stillness of a Disciple (Part 3 of 3)
by Bryan L. Herde

Stand in awe, and sin not: commune with your heart upon your bed, and be still.
Psalm 4:4 (KJV)

Be still, and know that I am God...
Psalm 46:10 (KJV)

In addition to all the activity of God mentioned in yesterday's devotional, He is living in each believer's heart and working constantly to conform each of us into the likeness of Christ by utilizing all the events, people, circumstances—everything—to bring about that transformation; and on top of that, He is directing the invisible war going on with His enemies and ours (Ephesians 6:12).

In spite of all God's infinite busyness, He is the One who called for us to "be still, and know that I am God." He is the One who revealed Himself to Elijah via a whisper instead of a display of power (1 Kings 19:12-13). And God is the One who chose for our redemption to be accomplished through the death of one man upon a cross that He didn't deserve, as the means whereby Satan's rule was overthrown, the power of sin was destroyed, and the keys of both death and hell came into Christ's possession.

We believe this by faith but cannot fully understand intellectually how it is that God is infinitely and intimately engaged in His whole creation, at both the atomic and universal level, while remaining one hundred percent involved in every detail of our own lives.

In light of that, what can we say? Nothing. It is time for us to be silent and to simply abide in His presence. We have the ability, by a decision of our own wills, to bring ourselves before Him, and ask Him to calm us and quiet us so that we may be still before Him. He has commanded it, and He certainly deserves that level of attention and respect.

April 15

Things That Cannot Be Shaken (Part 1 of 2)
by Hannah Whitall Smith

And this word, Yet once more, signifies the removing of those things that are shaken, as of things that are made, that those things which cannot be shaken may remain.
Hebrews 12:27

If love sees those it loves going wrong, it must, because of its very love, do what it can to save them; and the love that fails to do this is only selfishness. Therefore, just because of His unfathomable love, the God of love, when He sees His children resting their souls on things that can be shaken, must necessarily remove those things from their lives in order that they may be driven to rest only on the things that cannot be shaken; and this process of removing is sometimes very hard.

***

Many a religious experience that has seemed fair enough when all was going well in life has trembled and fallen when trials have come, because its foundations have been insecure. It is therefore of vital importance to each one of us to see to it that our religious life is built upon "things that cannot be shaken."

***

The apostle tells us that the things that are shaken are the "things that are made"; that is, the things that are manufactured by our own efforts, feelings that we cultivate, doctrines that we develop, good works that we perform. It is not that these things are bad things in themselves. It is only when the soul begins to rest on them instead of upon the Lord that He is compelled to "shake" us from off them.

***

Sometimes the dependence is upon good feelings or pious emotions, and the soul has to be deprived of these before it can learn to depend only upon God. Sometimes it is upon "sound doctrine" that the dependence is placed, and the man feels himself to be occupying a secure position, because his views are so correct, and his doctrines are so well-established; and then the Lord is obliged to shake his doctrines, and to plunge him, it may be, into confusion and darkness as to his views.

April 16

Things That Cannot Be Shaken (Part 2 of 2)
by Hannah Whitall Smith

And this word, Yet once more, signifies the removing of those things that are shaken, as of things that are made, that those things which cannot be shaken may remain.
Hebrews 12:27

We, like Abraham, are looking for a city which has foundations whose builder and maker is God, and therefore we too shall need to be emptied from vessel to vessel. But we do not realize this, and when the overturnings and shakings come, we are in despair and think we shall never reach the city that has foundations at all. But it is these very shakings that make it possible for us to reach it. The psalmist learned this, and after all the shakings and emptying of his eventful life, he cried: "My soul, wait only upon God; for my expectation is from him. He only is my rock and my salvation: he is my defense; I shall not be moved. In God is my salvation and my glory: the rock of my strength and my refuge is in God" [Psalm 62:5-7].

***

At last God was everything to him; and then he found that God was enough. And it is the same with us. When everything in our lives and experience is shaken that can be shaken, and only that which cannot be shaken remains, we are brought to see that God only is our rock and our foundation, and we learn to have our expectation from Him alone.

***

"Because we are receiving a kingdom that cannot be moved, let us have grace by which we may serve God acceptably with reverence and godly fear; for our God is a consuming fire" [Hebrews 12:29]. A great many people are afraid of the consuming fire of God, but that is only because they do not understand what it is. It is the fire of God's love that must in the very nature of things consume everything that can harm His people; and if our hearts are set on being what the love of God would have us be, His fire is something we shall not be afraid of, but shall warmly welcome.

April 17

Suffering According to the Will of God
by Andrew Murray

*Since you are partakers of Christ's sufferings, rejoice. For that reason, let them also that
suffer according to the will of God commit their souls
in well-doing unto a faithful Creator.*
1 Peter 4:13, 19

Nothing can come to us without the will of God. What is done may be
most contrary to the will of God, and the doer most guilty in His sight—
that it is done to us, that we suffer by it, is God's will. And the first duty of
the child of God is not to look at the man who does it, to seek revenge on
him, or be delivered from his hands, but to recognize and bow beneath it as
the Father's will.

That one thought—it is the Father's will—changes our feelings towards it,
enables us to accept it as a blessing, changes it from evil into good. In all
suffering let the first thought be to see the Father's hand, and count on the
Father's help. Then no circumstance whatever can for one moment take us
out of the blessed will of God.

***

Men may learn from us what the power of Grace is, to soften and to
strengthen; what the reality is of the heavenly life and joy that enables us to
bear all loss; and what the blessing is of the service of the Divine Master,
who can make His own path of suffering so attractive and so blessed to His
followers. And it is in well-doing we can commit our souls unto a faithful
Creator.

***

We can only suffer for Him as He lives in us. The attempt to do or bear the
will of God correctly, as long as we are living on a different level from that
on which Christ lived, must be failure. It is only where the whole-hearted
surrender to live and die for the will of God, as Jesus did, possesses the soul
that the mighty power of His Love, and Grace, and Spirit can do their
wonders in the life.

April 18

Persecution: Every Christian's Lot (Part 1 of 2)
by George Whitefield

Those who live godly in Christ may not so much be said to live, as Christ to live in them: He is their Alpha and Omega, their first and last, their beginning and end. They are led by his Spirit, as a child is led by the hand of its father; and are willing to follow the Lamb wherever he leads them. They hear, know, and obey his voice. Their affections are set on things above; their hopes are full of immortality; their citizenship is in heaven. Being born again of God, they habitually live to, and daily walk with, God. They are pure in heart; and, from a principle of faith in Christ, are holy in all manner of conversation and godliness. This is to "live godly in Christ Jesus;" and from here we may easily learn why it is that so few suffer persecution. Because so few people live godly in Christ Jesus. You may live formally in Christ, you may take care of outward duties; you may live morally in Christ, you may (as they term it) do no one harm, and thereby avoid persecution; but they "that will live godly in Christ Jesus shall suffer persecution."

***

It is a great breach of the sixth commandment to slander anyone; but to speak evil of and slander the disciples of Christ, merely because they are his disciples, must be highly provoking in the sight of God; and such who are guilty of it (without repentance) will find that Jesus Christ will call them to account, and punish them for all their ungodly and hard speeches in a lake of fire and brimstone. This shall be their portion to drink. It would be impossible to enumerate in what various shapes persecution has appeared. It is a many-headed monster, cruel as the grave, insatiable as hell; and, what is worse, it generally appears under the cloak of religion. But, cruel, insatiable, and horrid as it is, they that live godly in Christ Jesus must expect to suffer and encounter it in all its forms.

***

Wicked men hate God, and therefore cannot help but hate those who are like him: they hate to be reformed, and therefore must hate and persecute those who, by contrary behavior, testify that their deeds are evil.

April 19

Persecution: Every Christian's Lot (Part 2 of 2)
by George Whitefield

But though all Christians are not really called to suffer every kind of persecution, yet all Christians are liable thereto; and undoubtedly some may live in more peaceful times of the church than others, yet all Christians, in all ages, will find by their own experience that, whether they act in a private or public capacity, they must, in some degree or other, suffer persecution.

***

Remember you cannot reconcile two irreconcilable differences, God and Mammon, the friendship of this world with the favor of God. Know you not who has told you that "the friendship with this world is hostility with God?" If therefore you are in friendship with the world, in spite of all your deceptive pretenses to godliness, you are hostile with God: you are simply heart-hypocrites; and, "What is the hope of the hypocrite, when God shall take away his soul?" Let the words of the text sound an alarm in your ears; O let them sink deep into your hearts; "Yes, and all that will live godly in Christ Jesus, shall suffer persecution."

***

In nothing be terrified by your adversaries: on their part Christ is evil spoken of; on your part he is glorified. Be not ashamed of your glory, since others can glory in their shame. Think it not strange concerning the fiery trial with which you are or may be tried. The Devil rages, knowing that he has but a short time to reign. He or his agents have no more power than what is given them from above: God sets their boundaries, which they cannot pass; and the very hairs of your head are all numbered. Fear not; no one shall set upon you to hurt you without your heavenly Father's knowledge.

***

Jesus Christ came into the world to save sinners, even persecutors, the worst of sinners: his righteousness is sufficient for them; his Spirit is able to purify and change their hearts. He once converted Saul: may the same God magnify his power, in converting all those who are causing the godly in Christ Jesus to suffer persecution!

April 20

Unweariedness in Well-Doing (Part 1 of 2)
by Henry Robert Reynolds

Let us not be weary in well-doing; for in due season we shall reap, if we do not give up.
Galatians 6:9

It is probable that we may have become suddenly aware of our own weakness and incompetence to do that which we had undertaken to do. Such a revelation is painful enough, and whether we are right or wrong in our judgment, it requires great patience and courage to govern our conduct rightly. Under this bitter conclusion the most prudent man is often in practical despair; the most Christian disciple is tempted by hopeless thoughts to wish everything to be different from what it is, and to murmur not only against his own lot, but against the sovereign control and laws of God. Physical disease, moral weakness, natural indecision of character may have aggravated all these occasional trials of our courage and temper, but they have not declared us innocent. They were Divine testings which were intended to allure us to virtue and effort: we have, alas, made them temptations to sin; for at such times the demon of laziness has seized on us, has cramped our efforts, and bound us hand and foot with his cruel chains.

We have found it hard even to think and resolve; we have permitted this evil spirit to surround us with a network of silly excuses and to withdraw the weak blood from our feeble circulation. We have thrown the blame of our inactivity on everything rather than on the true cause, and have given up in the middle of our way from sheer lack of spiritual vigor. Ever attempting to predict definite results, we have attained nothing. Forgetting the great laws to which we are subjected, we have been hindered rather than aided by them. Wasting our strength in a combat with the irreversible laws and forces of nature, instead of trying to uncover and utilize them, we have at length become weary and helpless, and have imagined ourselves the butt of the universe and the scorn of heaven.

April 21

Unweariedness in Well-Doing (Part 2 of 2)
by Henry Robert Reynolds

Let us not be weary in well-doing; for in due season we shall reap, if we do not give up.
Galatians 6:9

If we contemplate the great power of evil, if we try to realize its presence, to separate it in thought from the world which it defiles and seeks to ruin, we are appalled by its ceaseless efforts to accomplish its deadly purpose. The pleasures that evil poisons, the infected banquets which it spreads, the troops it can deploy at its bidding, the infinity of objects it can measure for its own miserable purpose, assure us that the spirit and the designer of the whole is unbeatable in his energy, and vast in his resources. We know not "the evil that there is on the earth." It is difficult to estimate adequately the malice and diversity of the mechanisms at the disposal of the prince of this world. He seeks to pervert all human affections into lusts, to transform the machinery by which man has with wondrous creativity contrived to conserve strength, into the artillery with which he deals destruction on his victim. He debases and prostitutes all the resources of civilization, all the conclusions of science, to the service of human passion and selfishness.

***

We must remember that Christ Himself lives and works within the Christian by the power of His Spirit. His divine and exhaustless energy did not come to an end upon the Cross. From that time forward the Eternal Word no longer graced to be incarnate in one solitary human soul, but to be the divine life of a multitude whom no man can number. He began from that point forward a diviner, more energetic operation. You by faith are crucified with Him; nevertheless you live, yet it is not you, but Christ who lives in you. Christ is formed within you, He will cooperate with every holy desire that you feel; He will invigorate every effort of every member of His body. By laziness, or forgetfulness of this genuine characteristic of the Christian, you may quench the Spirit of your Master, and resist the Life of God, which is always striving for expression through your life.

April 22

Without Me You Can Do Nothing (Part 1 of 2)
by Hannah Whitall Smith

"Without Me you can do nothing."
John 15:5b

"There it is," I said to myself, "Jesus himself said so, that apart from Him we have no real life of any kind, whether we call it temporal or spiritual, and therefore, all living or doing that is without Him is of such a nature that God, who sees into the realities of things, calls it 'nothing.'" And then the question forced itself upon me as to whether any soul really believed this statement to be true; or, if believing it theoretically, whether anyone made it practical in their daily walk and life. And I saw, as in a flash almost, that the real secret of divine union lay quite as much in this practical aspect of it as in any interior revealings or experiences. For if I do nothing, literally nothing, apart from Christ, I am of course united to Him in a continual oneness that cannot be questioned or denied; while if I live a large part of my daily life and perform a large part of my daily work apart from Him, I have no real union, no matter how exalted and delightful my emotions concerning it may be."

***

If we are one with Him, then of course in the very nature of things we can do nothing without Him. For that which is one cannot act as being two. And if I therefore do anything without Christ, then I am not one with Him in that thing, and like a branch severed from the vine I am withered and worthless. It is as if the branch should recognize its connection with and dependence upon the vine for most of its growth, and fruit-bearing, and climbing, but should feel a capacity in itself to grow and climb over a certain fence or around the trunk of a certain tree, and should therefore sever its connection with the vine for this part of its living. Of course if that was to be attempted, an independent life would wither and die in the very nature of things. And just so it is with us who are branches of Christ the true vine. No independent action, whether small or great, is possible to us without withering and death, any more than by the branch of the natural vine.

April 23

Without Me You Can Do Nothing (Part 2 of 2)
by Hannah Whitall Smith

"Without Me you can do nothing."
John 15:5b

An old spiritual writer says something to this effect, that in order to become a saint it is not always necessary to change our works, but only to put an internal purpose towards God in them all; that we must begin to do for His glory and in His strength that which before we did for self and in self's capacity; which means, after all, just what our Lord meant when He said, "Without me you can do nothing." There is another side of this truth also which is full of comfort, and which the Psalmist develops in the verses I have quoted. "It is vain," he says, "to rise up early, to sit up late, to eat the bread of sorrows." Or, in other words, "What is the use of all this worry and strain? For the work will after all amount to nothing unless God is in it, and if He is in it, what folly to fret or be burdened, since He of course, by the very fact of His presence, assumes the care and responsibility of it all." Ah, it is vain indeed, and I would that all God's children knew it!

***

Let us believe, then, that without Him we can literally do nothing. We must believe it, for it is true. But let us recognize its truth, and act on it from this time forward. Let us make a hearty denial of all living apart from Christ, and let us begin from this moment to acknowledge Him in all our ways, and do everything, whatever we do, as service to Him and for His glory, depending upon Him alone for wisdom, and strength, and sweetness, and patience, and everything else that is necessary for the right accomplishment of all our living. If, then, you would know, beloved reader, the internal divine union fulfilled in your soul, begin from this very day to put it outwardly in practice as I have suggested. Offer each moment of your living and each act of your doing to God, and say to Him continually, "Lord, I am doing this in You and for Your glory. You are my strength, and my wisdom, and my all-sufficient supply for every need. I depend only upon You." Refuse utterly to live for a single moment or to perform a single act apart from Him. Persist in this until it becomes the established habit of your soul. And sooner or later you shall surely know the longings of your soul satisfied in the abiding presence of Christ, your indwelling Life.

April 24

The Legacy of a Disciple (Part 1 of 3)
by Bryan L. Herde

"My prayer is not for them alone. I pray also for those who will believe in Me through
their message, that all of them may be one, Father,
just as You are in Me and I am in You."
John 17:20

The legacy we inherit from those who have obeyed the Lord in making us
His disciples is the exact same legacy we should leave behind after our time
on Earth is through. To be used by Him to cultivate trust in the Lord, to
know Him intimately, to enjoy Him fully and to stimulate and guide others
to do the same is the highest calling, privilege and duty of any man or
woman. And what is even more wonderful is that that is all He asks of us.
By so doing, we have fulfilled His greatest commands: "Jesus replied, 'Love
the Lord your God with all your heart and with all your soul and with all
your mind.' This is the first and greatest commandment. And the second is
like it: 'Love your neighbor as yourself'" (Matthew 22:37-39). I believe that
there are three stages in every maturing Christian's life when it comes to
their individual role in making disciples of Jesus Christ:

1. Absolute surrender of one's own life to the Lord once for all and
   then a moment-by-moment, day-by-day re-affirmation of the same;
2. Refusal to give up, or turn back, or settle for the status quo—not
   pulling up short; and
3. Trusting that the Lord will bring someone to you who wants to be
   mentored, and then walking with them through the first two stages.

The struggle that disciple-makers have is that they see the need and even
the potential for someone to step into the stream of becoming a disciple of
Jesus. The problem is that person may not be ready. That is why disciplers
need to intercede for others and then wait upon the Lord to initiate the
desire in their hearts to be discipled. Without fail, those whom I have been
privileged to disciple are those who came to me and asked me to mentor
them.

April 25

The Legacy of a Disciple (Part 2 of 3)
by Bryan L. Herde

"My prayer is not for them alone. I pray also for those who will believe in Me through their message, that all of them may be one, Father, just as You are in Me and I am in You."
John 17:20

The first question for the Church is, "How do we make disciples?" Colossians 1 and 2 outline what I believe the Lord intended the process to entail. There are several key actions listed here for disciple-makers:
1. Praying unceasingly for present and future disciples
2. Presenting the Word of God in its fullness
3. Proclaiming Jesus Christ
4. Admonishing and teaching with all wisdom
5. Cultivating maturity
6. Struggling to do so through the energy of Jesus

The final goal is to present mature disciples to Jesus ("To this end I labor…" Colossians 1:29). I believe that one particular passage in Scripture contains the very essence of what disciple-makers cultivate in the hearts of new believers, as well as mature believers who need revival. The passage is Luke 24:13-35, especially verse 32: "They asked each other, 'Were not our hearts burning within us while [Jesus] talked with us on the road and opened the Scriptures to us?'"

Disciples' hearts burn when they have the Scriptures opened up to them as they begin to grow in their intimacy with a Person—God Almighty, rather than just growing in their knowledge of the Bible. The two disciples on the road to Emmaus had the Person of all creation revealed to them. They were not just being shown some new doctrine, or essential teaching, or Bible study method. No, it was the Living Word (John 1:1-18) coming alive in their hearts. Old texts were being given new meaning by the Lord to move these men into a more intimate relationship with Jesus Christ.

April 26

The Legacy of a Disciple (Part 3 of 3)
by Bryan L. Herde

"My prayer is not for them alone. I pray also for those who will believe in Me through their message, that all of them may be one, Father, just as You are in Me and I am in You."
John 17:20

As disciple-makers, we are charged by Christ to make disciples of Him, not of anything else. We of all people must be all the more abandoned to the Lord in order to ensure that we are not creating followers of a system, or of personalities, or of a program, or of a methodology, or even of a particular set of doctrines or practices. No, we show men and women Jesus—living in us and alive in His Word. Those who begin as "our" disciples must, as soon as possible, transfer all their loyalty, affection and wills to their Master, Jesus Christ. Our role then becomes one of being their friends and companions as we all walk together through the journey of life and growing intimacy with the Lord.

Our efforts need to be focused upon making disciples who are (Colossians 2:2-4):
1. Encouraged in heart
2. Lovingly united with all believers
3. Full of the riches of complete understanding
4. Resistant to deceit
5. Enjoying an intimate relationship with the Trinity

The word "make" obviously communicates a process. But what I find most interesting is that all of the above should happen simultaneously rather than progressively. The list, as shown, is not to be a successive process for making disciples, but it rather highlights those things that should be happening at all times within every church and every individual. The goals themselves are also not progressive but rather should be inherent qualities of all mature disciples.

April 27

The Ministry of Rest
by John Henry Jowett

And He said unto them, "Come you yourselves apart into a desert place, and rest a while": for there were many coming and going, and they had no leisure so much as to eat.
Mark 6:31

This is not the speech of an old man, but of quite a young man, barely thirty-three years of age, and who is burdened with the superlative ministry of the redemption of the human race. All the arrangements of His public life are made on the assumption of its briefness. And yet He made time for rest! Sometimes we allow the sacredness of our labor to tempt us to regard rest as laziness and relaxation as waste. True rest is the minister of progress. The hour of seclusion enriches the public service.

***

And to us, as to the disciples, the call comes from the Redeemer Himself: "Come you yourselves apart into a desert place, and rest a while." Now what will these deliberately arranged times of spiritual rest do for the stunned and distracted soul? In the first place, they will help us to realize the reality of the invisible, the immediacy of "things not seen." I know that if we were spiritual experts this fine perception would be experienced everywhere. But the possibility in publicity is conditioned by experiences in private. If we are to have a real sense of God in the crowd it must be by discipline in secret. When the pressure of external circumstances is relaxed, and we are alone, the veil of the temple is torn open, and we are in the holy of holies, and we know ourselves to be in the presence of God. If we practice that Presence in the special moment it will abide with us through the hour. In the middle of life's moving affairs we see life fragmentarily and not entirely. We see items, but we are blind to their relationships. We see facts, but we do not discern their far-reaching issue and destiny. We are often ill-informed as to the true size of a thing which looms large in the immediate moment. There are many feverish and threatening crises which would dwindle into harmless proportions if only we saw them in calm detachment.

April 28

The Disciples' Rest (Part 1 of 2)
by John Henry Jowett

"Come unto Me all you that labor and are heavy laden and I will give you rest. Take My yoke upon you and learn of Me, for I am meek and humble in heart, and you shall find rest unto your souls."
Matthew 11:28-29

It is not a work, but a fruit; not the product of organization, but the sure and silent issue of a relationship. "Come unto Me...and I will give you rest." But even the gift of rest does not disclose its contents in a day. It is an immediate gift, but it is also a continuous discovery. "Learn of Me...and you shall find rest." Part of "the things which God has prepared for them that love Him" lie in this wealthy gift of rest, and it is one of the frequent and delightful surprises of grace that we should repeatedly come upon new and unexpected veins of ore in this deep mine of "the peace of God which passes all understanding." I say that the rest of the Lord is an immediate gift and a perpetual discovery.

***

I know the feverish motions of our time, the restlessness of fruitless desire, the disturbing feelings of anxiety, the busyness of the devil, the sleepless and perspiring activity of Mammon [friendship with the world], the rush to be rich, the race to be happy, the craving for sensation, the immense momentum and speed characterizing every interest in our varied life, and added to all, the hastened discarding of ancient forms and garments, and the re-clothing of the thoughts of men in modern and more congenial attire. I do not wonder at the restlessness of the world, but I stand amazed at the restlessness of the Savior's Church! We are encountering restlessness by restlessness, and on many sides we are suffering defeat. The antagonist ought to be of quite another order. The challengers must be restfulness versus rest, and the odds will be overwhelmingly on our side. We must distinguish between slothful passivity and active restfulness. I am not pleading for weakening ease, but for enabling and inspiring rest. Ease is an opiate; rest is a stimulant, say, rather a nourishment. Ease is the enemy of strength; rest is its hidden resource.

April 29

The Disciples' Rest (Part 2 of 2)
by John Henry Jowett

"Come unto Me all you that labor and are heavy laden and I will give you rest. Take My yoke upon you and learn of Me, for I am meek and humble in heart, and you shall find rest unto your souls."
Matthew 11:28-29

The man who is sure and restful in the conscious companionship of his Lord has about him the strainlessness and inevitableness of the ocean tide, and gives off invigorating influence like God's fresh and wondrous sea.

***

Think of our resources in grace. You cannot turn to any of the epistles of the great Apostle without feeling how immense and immediate is his conception of his help-meets in grace. Grace runs through all his arguments. It is allied with all his counsel. It bathes all his ethical ideals. It flows like a river close by the highway of his life, winding with all his windings, and remaining in inseparable companionship. Grace was to Paul an all-enveloping atmosphere, a defensive and oxygenating air, which invigorated and nourished his own spirit, and wasted and consumed his foes. "The abundant grace!" "The riches of the grace!" "The exceeding riches of His grace!" can never recall Paul's conception of grace without thinking of broad, full rivers when the snows have melted on the heights. And, brethren, these glorious resources of grace are ours, our allies in the work, and the pace, and the conflict of our times. Don't you think that if she obtained them, the Church would lose her wrinkles and her strain, and would move in the strength and the assurance of a glorious rest? Devilry does not have the unimpeded run of the field. The swaggering adversary runs up against Almighty God, and all his feverish schemes are turned aside. It is marvelous to watch the terrific twist given to circumstances by the compulsion of an unseen and mysterious hand. "The things that happened unto me have turned out rather unto the progress of the Gospel." How can a man with that persuasion be shaken with panic? How can he fight and labor in any spirit but the restful optimism of a triumphant hope?

April 30

Rest in the Lord (Part 1 of 2)
by Henry Robert Reynolds

Rest in the Lord, and wait patiently for Him.
Psalm 37:7

It was more difficult for David to do this than for us to do it. He had more at stake, and less to help him; he had all the mysteries which harass us, and many more peculiar to his age and to the dispensation under which he lived. That which we look back upon as prophecy fulfilled, as supernatural anticipation of better days, was, as it passed through his mind, only a hope and an aspiration. For him there was very little light thrown around the darkness of the grave; it was a pit of destruction and forgetfulness, haunted by strange fears. He was surrounded by enemies, and often well-nigh crushed by misfortune. He found it harder than we do to sever earthly disasters from Divine inflictions; and yet he could use this inspiring language, and summon his brothers to rest in Jehovah, and wait patiently for Him.

My most anxious task as a preacher of the gospel has always been to create the uneasiness and distress which could find its only true comfort in the everlasting righteousness, power, and love of God—to awaken that distrust of self which can only be soothed by taking possession of the grace and promise of God. Yet, when we look more deeply into this matter we shall find that the laziness resulting from self-indulgence and worldliness, the indifference and self-confidence from which we seek to awake the slumbering conscience, and the sloth from which the Church has need ever to be aroused, are all opposed to "resting in God," and "waiting patiently for Him." Moreover, it seems to me that there are now everywhere many symptoms of overwrought excitement, of cynical effort, of perilous assumption, of discontented inquiry, of restless searching after the impossible, of an arrogant hurrying of God, which render this gentle reprimand especially timely; and I am sure that there are few Christians who do not find every day of their lives abundant need for the consolation which the words of this verse administer.

May 1

Rest in the Lord (Part 2 of 2)
by Henry Robert Reynolds

Rest in the Lord, and wait patiently for Him.
Psalm 37:7

There is not only that kind of spontaneous inevitable inactivity by which the powers of mind, heart, and spirit are renovated for fresh exertion, but there is that voluntary rest, which is to some extent within our own power; which is the sign of vigor rather than of weakness, of strong determination rather than of over-taxed effort, of untiring patience rather than of relaxed energy. It is this kind of repose which puts the rein on passion, curbs the eagerness of the one who seeks after honor, pleasure, or knowledge, holds us back when we might otherwise rush into danger, and helps us to wait without anxiety for the unfolding of the future. It is this which teaches us to discharge the duty of today, not striving to hurry the development of the seeds that have been sown, nor to tear apart the half-expanded leaves, nor pluck the unripe fruit; but to stand still and wait for the unfolding of God's purposes; for the revelation of a design in our handiwork, which—like the logic that underlies the operations of instinct—is not our design, nor our purpose, nor our logic, but the unknowable purpose of the Supreme God. This rest of conscious strength is closely associated with every Christian grace, and is as necessary to our success in the conflicts of the divine life as it is to the culture of our higher nature. Neither faith, nor hope, nor love can be maintained within us without the *rest* of faith, the *rest* of hope, and the *rest* of love.

***

The future life must be wrapped in obscurity. If we knew much more about it we might find it still more difficult to wait, but the victory that we gain by faith is a victory of waiting patiently for the Lord's own triumph over all the obstacles which unbelief and sin have put even in His way. The senses may provoke our impatience, the flesh may sting us into angry shamefulness, the devil may accuse and attempt to deceive us, but by resting in the Lord we shall gain the victory. The world of ambition, of business, of Christless joys, of perishable attractions, and deceptive treasures, may never leave us unmolested, but "this is the victory that overcomes the world, even our faith."

May 2

Waiting Upon the Lord (Part 1 of 2)
by Henry Robert Reynolds

They that wait upon the Lord shall renew their strength; they shall mount up with wings as eagles; they shall run, and not be weary; they shall walk, and not faint.
Isaiah 40:31

If we listen to Isaiah's triumphant discovery, we find it is enriched and deepened and made rich in sound in many a word of Him who is the Word incarnate. "Wait upon the Lord" finds its answer in "Come unto Me, and I will give you rest."

***

There are not fewer than twenty different words in the Hebrew and Greek Scriptures which are all translated by one English word "wait," and this simple fact shows us how the prophetic and troubled souls of God-taught men have strained and writhed to express the thought that was in them. I think they may be reduced to three fundamental ideas: *silence, hope*, and *eager expectancy*. The prophets call on their souls to *wait silently and patiently*, to *wait hopefully*, and to *wait expectantly*, for the Lord.

***

When we can thoroughly trust in the living God the mystery is read, the deepest shadow is accepted, the horror of great darkness is felt to be the hollow of the hand of Him who dwells in the thick clouds. This kind of waiting upon the Lord is closely related to the abandonment of self which reconciliation with God insures at the beginning of our spiritual life, and is often much needed when new uncertainties arise to our faith which the mere reason cannot solve and which no experience can adequately meet. There are moments of fierce trial for mature Christians, when certain formulas seem to have vanished, some flowers and fruits of grace seem to be sucked out and squeezed of all sweetness, and some phrase sanctified by long usage appears to have lost its power and even its meaning. These discoveries are like looking into the burning fiery furnace, and the best form of our waiting upon the Lord is to be still, and know that God is God.

May 3

Waiting Upon the Lord (Part 2 of 2)
by Henry Robert Reynolds

They that wait upon the Lord shall renew their strength; they shall mount up with wings as eagles; they shall run, and not be weary; they shall walk, and not faint.
Isaiah 40:31

Because we are reconciled to God we find ourselves in the stress of a new contest. Hope is born in the heart of the weaned child. We see a goal to be pursued and an end to be secured beyond the simple fact of our reconciliation. We find ourselves in the middle of a plunging onward movement. What seemed like *stillness* is the active balancing of mighty forces, is the balance of the parts of our nature in their rushing race. The reconciliation reveals other forces and adverse ones, principalities and powers which must be subdued under us, which are against us, but which we must more than conquer—no, which we must transform into our allies.

Being reconciled by the death of the Son of God, we are much more to be saved by His life. We are saved by cherishing a sacred desire. What we see, we do not hope for. But many things are invisible. We gaze still through a glass darkly; and we hope on and look upwards. So it comes to pass that much which Holy Scripture describes as waiting upon God, is a Divine longing. God gives us these desires after Himself.

***

Noble work is done by those who know that God's love to the world cannot be a failure. Because they *see*, they toil. Because they expect great things *from* God, they do great things *for* God. Disappointment, dark clouds, angry storms of human hate; nakedness, peril, and sword, are powerless to crush those who are persuaded that nothing can separate them from the love of God. The despairing pessimism of our day is the result of agnosticism, is the cloud which rolls up from the "sunless gulfs of doubt." Those who wait upon the Lord are not dismayed by the past history, nor confounded by the present condition of the world.

May 4

Waiting Patiently
by Andrew Murray

Rest in the Lord, and wait patiently for Him.
Psalm 37:7

"In patience possess your souls." "You have need of patience." "Let patience have its perfect work, that you may be perfect and entire." Such words of the Holy Spirit show us what an important element patience is in the Christian life and character. And nowhere is there a better place for cultivating or displaying it than in waiting on God. There we discover how impatient we are, and what our impatience means. We confess at times that we are impatient with men and circumstances that hinder us or with ourselves and our slow progress in the Christian life. If we truly set ourselves to wait upon God, we shall find that it is with Him we are impatient, because He does not at once, or as soon as we could wish, do our bidding. It is in waiting upon God that our eyes are opened to believe in His wise and sovereign will, and to see that the sooner and the more completely we yield absolutely to it, the more surely His blessing can come to us.

***

We have as little power to increase or strengthen our spiritual life as we had to originate it. All the exercises of the spiritual life, our reading and praying, our willing and doing, have their very great value. But they can go no farther than this—that they point the way and prepare us in humility to look to and to depend alone upon God Himself, and in patience to wait His good time and mercy. The waiting is to teach us our absolute dependence upon God's mighty working, and to make us in perfect patience place ourselves at His disposal. They that wait on the Lord shall inherit the land; the promised land and its blessing. The heirs must wait; they can afford to wait.

***

Give God His glory by resting in Him, by trusting him fully, by waiting patiently for Him. This patience honors Him greatly; it leaves Him, as God on the throne, to do His work; it yields self wholly into His hands. It lets God be God.

May 5

Who Waits On Us
by Andrew Murray

Those that wait upon the Lord, they shall inherit the land.
Psalm 37:9

If you ask, how is it, if He waits to be gracious, that even after I come and wait upon Him, He does not give the help I seek, but waits on longer and longer? There is a double answer. The one is this: God is a wise gardener, who "waits for the precious fruit of the earth, and has long patience for it." He cannot gather the fruit until it is ripe. He knows when we are spiritually ready to receive the blessing to our profit and His glory. Waiting in the sunshine of His love is what will ripen the soul for His blessing. Waiting under the cloud of trial that breaks in showers of blessing is as needful. Be assured that if God waits longer than you could wish, it is only to make the blessing doubly precious. God waited four thousand years, until the fullness of time, before He sent His Son; our times are in His hands; He will avenge His elect speedily; He will make haste for our help, and not delay one hour too long.

***

The giver is more than the gift; God is more than the blessing. And our being kept waiting on Him is the only way for our learning to find our life and joy in Himself. Oh, if God's children only knew what a glorious God they have, and what a privilege it is to be linked in fellowship with Himself, then they would rejoice in Him, even when He keeps them waiting. They would learn to understand better than ever: "Therefore will the Lord wait, that He may be gracious unto you." His waiting will be the highest proof of His graciousness.

***

Yes, it is blessed when a waiting soul and a waiting God meet each other. God cannot do His work without His and our waiting His time. Let waiting be our work, as it is His. And if His waiting is nothing but goodness and graciousness, let ours be nothing but rejoicing in that goodness, and a confident expectancy of that grace.

May 6

Where Our Greatest Battles Are Fought (Part 1 of 2)
by John Henry Jowett

Men ought always to pray and not to give up.
Luke 18:1

The guiding word may mean that men are always to pray and never to give up in prayer. Or it may mean that men ought always to pray and they would never give up even when opposing forces rear themselves like awful mountain ranges between them and their goal. It is probable that both interpretations are equally true and that both are included in the Master's mind and purpose. For the chief matter is this: the heavy emphasis which Jesus Christ puts upon the ministry of prayer as a predominant means of grace. "Men ought *always* to pray."

***

There are times when I would come to the King, burdened with intercessions, and I would spread the world of my necessities before the favor of His grace. I am coming to a King, but I am coming to more than a King. I am coming to a Father, and Fatherhood is larger than Kinghood, just as home is larger than a throne. A king may have gifts at his disposal, he may have honors and benefits and offices to grant to his subjects; but fatherhood moves in a circle of intimacies and shared secrets, even in the matchless commerce of truth and grace and love. When prayer turns into this marvelous realm it is not so much as a petitioner, laden with requests, as much as a wondering child walking in the revealing companionship of the Father in heaven.

***

Prayer is not always petition, sometimes it is just communion. It is the exquisite ministries of friendship. It is the delicate passage of intimacies; it is the fellowship of the Holy Ghost.

***

There is a very vital part of prayer which can do without the vehicle of words. We can escape from the burden of the limitation of words. So there are times in prayer when I long to escape from the ministries of words, and to have wordless fellowship in the Presence of God.

May 7

Where Our Greatest Battles Are Fought (Part 2 of 2)
by John Henry Jowett

Men ought always to pray and not to give up.
Luke 18:1

It is in the field of prayer that life's critical battles are lost or won. We must conquer all our circumstances there. We must first of all bring them there. We must examine them there. We must master them there. In prayer we bring our spiritual enemies into the Presence of God and we fight them there. Have you tried that? Or have you been satisfied to meet and fight your foes in the open spaces of the world? If I am like John Bunyan's pilgrim, and encounter Apollyon [Satan] on the exposed road, and begin to combat there I shall be sadly beaten, and he will leave me bruised and broken by the way. My resource is to get him immediately onto the field of prayer and engage him there.

***

When we fight the world and the flesh and the devil on the battleground of prayer, we have a certain victory. Let us bring our evil thoughts on to the field of prayer. Let us drag our mean judgments on to the field of prayer. Let us drive our dishonorable purpose on to the same field, and our insane prejudices, and our malicious practices, and our controlling passions. Let us fight them on our own battleground and slay them there. Men ought always to bring their evil struggles and aggravations into the Presence of God. Force them into God's holy place and there fight and slay them. Men ought always to pray, and they will not give up in the heaviest day. And on the same field of prayer we must bring our troubles, for we get on to the top of them in the holy place. It very frequently happens that many of our troubles lose their fictitious stature when we bring them into the Presence of the eternal God. They shrink when we set them in a large place. It is almost amusing how little things appear big when they are set in confined and narrow spaces. Put them in a bigger field and they lose their alarming size. And there is many an anxiety that looks gigantic until we set it in the holy field of prayer in the Presence of the Lord.

May 8

The Power of a Disciple (Part 1 of 4)
by Bryan L. Herde

The prayer of a righteous man is powerful and effective.
James 5:16b

This is the confidence we have in approaching God: that if we ask anything according to His will, He hears us. And if we know that He hears us—whatever we ask—we know that we have what we asked of Him.
1 John 5:14-15

A disciple who has given up everything he or she is and has to Jesus, who is being made humble by the Lord, who is willing to learn to wait for the Lord in everything, is a disciple who realizes the power of prayer. Prayer is communicating with God the Father through the Holy Spirit in the name of Jesus Christ by making requests, claiming promises, expecting action, waiting for the right time, recognizing the ways of the Lord, and realizing the fullness of His plans and purposes for you and for those for whom you pray. Prayer is not simply throwing requests in God's direction and hoping things happen the way you want them to unfold. Powerful praying is rooted in substance and evidence...in other words, in faith.

One of the great misunderstandings about prayer is its tendency to be cloaked in formality. By formality, I don't mean "high church" or public prayers or recitations from the prayer books of old. I'm referring to the formalizing of prayer we do on a personal basis.

Most of the time when we talk about a Christian's prayers, we mean a specific time of prayer, such as before meals, in the morning during a "quiet time" or personal devotion, or in the evening when we lie down to sleep. In no way do I intend to discount or replace the specific times of prayer we all should have. Those are vital as well. We should however look at prayer as a lifelong and intimate conversation, a constant and uninterrupted flow of communication with the Trinity.

May 9

The Power of a Disciple (Part 2 of 4)
by Bryan L. Herde

The prayer of a righteous man is powerful and effective.
James 5:16b

This is the confidence we have in approaching God: that if we ask anything according to His will, He hears us. And if we know that He hears us—whatever we ask—we know that we have what we asked of Him.
1 John 5:14-15

As I have visited with others, I am amazed at the number of us who process our feelings, fears, concerns, hopes, desires and intentions within the context of our own thinking *before* we voice them to God. Certainly, God already knows what is going on inside our heads. But I am convinced that in order to benefit from the oneness that Jesus prayed for in John 17, the Lord wants to be engaged in all of our issues *before* we commit them to Him in "formal" prayer. In that context, that changes our very definition of prayer.

Rather than analyzing all our potential prayer requests *before* we voice them to God, what would it be like if we analyzed them *with* Him instead of announcing them *to* Him? If I treated my communications with my wife the way most of us treat the Lord with our requests, I would not have a high-quality, intimate and wonderful marriage. What works in a marriage is cooperative wrestling with issues, concerns and plans, not simply announcing one's final resolutions and asking that they be blessed.

Wouldn't you prefer that your child come to you at the very beginning of an issue so that the two of you could talk it through together? Doesn't that vulnerability actually cultivate greater intimacy, trust and love? That is what our Father in Heaven desires as well.

***

Just as we so easily converse with others around us, we also should converse with our Lord and Savior just as freely and confidently.

May 10

The Power of a Disciple (Part 3 of 4)
by Bryan L. Herde

The prayer of a righteous man is powerful and effective.
James 5:16b

This is the confidence we have in approaching God: that if we ask anything according to His will, He hears us. And if we know that He hears us—whatever we ask—we know that we have what we asked of Him.
1 John 5:14-15

There are times where powerful, intentional and very specific intercession is needed. There are times where we need to be on our knees, our faces and/or fasting for spiritual breakthroughs, miracles and intervention. What makes those times more common, more accessible and more powerful in the life of a disciple is where the conversation with one's God and Father is already a constant flow back and forth. Then when a particular need arises, the petition falls into the flow of conversation—through oneness—with the vibrant relationship already existing. Otherwise, it's hard to "prime the pump" for connectivity and focus.

***

It is in that context that real prayer lives and functions. We don't have to wait until our "appointment" with the Lord. We should and must be visiting with Him all the time about everything. That is the prayer life of a disciple. It is marked by humility, constancy and, dare I say, comfort and acceptance. We need not plead for the Lord's attention. We have it all the time. We need not get ourselves ready to pray, we are always in the flow of praying.

In fact, it seems to me that the real privilege of prayer is our ability to abide in the constant stream of perpetual communication that is always in process among the Father, the Holy Spirit and the Son of God. Psalm 37:4 says that when we delight ourselves in the Lord, He will give us the desire of our hearts. That is the seedbed of our requests. Romans chapter 8 states that since we don't know what we should pray for, the Holy Spirit intercedes for us. That is the prayer that is flowing constantly for us in accordance with God's will.

May 11

The Power of a Disciple (Part 4 of 4)
by Bryan L. Herde

The prayer of a righteous man is powerful and effective.
James 5:16b

This is the confidence we have in approaching God: that if we ask anything according to His will, He hears us. And if we know that He hears us—whatever we ask—we know that we have what we asked of Him.
1 John 5:14-15

Oswald Chambers makes a radical statement in *My Utmost for His Highest*, "The disciple who abides in Jesus *is* the will of God, and what appears to be his free choices are actually God's foreordained decrees." So many of our prayers are rooted in the request to discern the will of God. Undoubtedly, that is important. But as disciples of Jesus who live and communicate in a constant flow with and in Him, we live as His will at all times, no matter what. Does that mean that we do not sin? Of course not. But we already know we have forgiveness appropriated by the blood of Jesus for us. As the Lord said through Paul in Romans 8:29, we are being "conformed to the likeness of His Son," and in Philippians 1:6, "He who began a good work in you will carry it on to completion until the day of Christ Jesus." We know that it is His commitment to us that is far greater than our puny efforts to stay committed to Him.

So many of our prayers are panic-stricken simply because we are not waiting upon the Lord, patiently and consistently communicating with Him about all things. Therefore, we find ourselves caught off guard, seemingly alone and highly vulnerable, as though not only we, but surely even the Lord, were surprised by the event or issue. Prayer is the flow of life, an interchange with our Creator, an intimate conversation with the Lover of our soul, and the incredible power of both a Best Friend and an Almighty God who is more than ready, willing and able to act on our behalf, come to our aid, help our friends and family, save the lost and dying, and bring honor and glory to His Name. All of these are the very essence of a powerful, effective and awesome oneness of a disciple and His Lord.

May 12

Silent Unto God
by John Henry Jowett

My soul, wait only upon God; for my expectation is from Him. He only is my rock and my salvation; He is my defense; I shall not be moved.
Psalm 62:5-6

In these three words the Psalmist expresses something of his thought of the all-enveloping and protecting presence of God. He is "my rock," "my salvation," "my defense." What, then, shall be the attitude of the soul towards this God? "My soul, wait only upon God." "Wait!" Or as the marginal rendering so beautifully gives it, "be silent unto God." We are to be in the presence of God with thoughts and feelings which are the opposite to those of false haste. The spirit of impatience is to be hushed and subdued. There is to be nothing of strong emotion or of hot temper. Loud grumblings are to be silenced. Our own protesting wills are to be restrained. The perilous heat is to be cooled. We are to linger before God in composure, in tranquility. We are to be unruffled. It is the unruffled surface of the pool that receives the reflected beauty of the skies. The reflection is clearest where the life is most calm.

***

Perhaps we are inclined to talk too much in communion with our God. If silent our spirits might be the more receptive. "One evening," says Frances Ridley Havergal, "after a relapse, I longed so much to be able to pray, but found I was too weak for the least effort of thought, and I only looked up and said, 'Lord Jesus, I am so tired,' and then He brought to my mind 'Rest in the Lord,' and its lovely marginal rendering, 'Be silent to the Lord,' and so I was just silent to Him, and He seemed to overflow me with perfect peace in the sense of His own perfect love."

***

Note how the Psalmist's confidence has grown by the exercise of contemplation. In the beginning of the Psalm his spirit was a little unsteady and uncertain. "I shall not be *greatly* moved." But now the qualifying adverb is gone, the uncertainty has vanished, and he says in unshaken confidence and trust, "I shall not be moved."

May 13

God Is Enough (Part 1 of 2)
by Hannah Whitall Smith

My soul wait only upon God, for my expectation is from Him. He only is my rock and my salvation; He is my defense; I shall not be moved. In God is my salvation, and my glory: the rock of my strength and my refuge is in God.
Psalm 62:5-7

The last and greatest lesson that the soul has to learn is the fact that God, and God alone, is enough for all its needs. This is the lesson that all His dealings with us are meant to teach; and this is the crowning discovery of our whole Christian life. *God is enough!* Christ has not been all we want. We have wanted a great many things besides Him. We have wanted fervent feelings about Him, or realizations of His presence with us, or an internal revelation of His love; or else we have demanded satisfactory systems of doctrine, or successful Christian work, or something of one sort or another, besides Himself, that will constitute a personal claim upon Him. Just Christ Himself, Christ alone, without the addition of any of our experiences concerning Him, has not been enough for us in spite of all our singing; and we do not even see how it is possible that He could be enough.

***

Your discomfort and unrest arise from your strenuous but useless efforts to get up some satisfactory basis of confidence within yourselves; such, for instance, as what you consider to be the proper feelings, or the right amount of intensity or earnestness, or at least, if nothing else, a sufficient degree of interest in spiritual matters. And because none of these things are ever satisfactory (and, I may tell you, never will be), it is impossible for your religious life to be anything but uncomfortable. But if we see that all our salvation from beginning to end depends on the Lord alone; and if we have learned that He is able and willing to do for us "exceeding abundantly above all we can ask or think," then peace and comfort cannot fail to reign supreme. Everything depends upon whether the Lord, in and of Himself, is enough for our salvation, or whether other things must be added on our part to make Him sufficient.

May 14

God Is Enough (Part 2 of 2)
by Hannah Whitall Smith

My soul wait only upon God, for my expectation is from Him. He only is my rock and my salvation; He is my defense; I shall not be moved. In God is my salvation, and my glory: the rock of my strength and my refuge is in God.
Psalm 62:5-7

As long as our attention is turned upon ourselves and our own experiences, just that long it is turned away from the Lord. This is plain common sense. We can only see the thing we look at, and while we are looking at ourselves, we simply cannot "behold God." It is not that He hides Himself; He is always there in full view of all who look unto Him; but if we are looking in another direction, we cannot expect to see Him. Before, it may be our eyes have been so fixed upon ourselves that all our internal questioning has been simply and only as rewarding our own condition. Is my love for God warm enough? Am I earnest enough? Are my feelings toward Him what they ought to be? Have I enough zeal? Do I feel my need as I should? And we have been miserable because we have never been able to answer these questions satisfactorily. Although we do not know it, it has been a mercy we never could answer them satisfactorily, for, if we had, the self in us would have been exalted, and we should have been filled with self-congratulation and pride.

How does God feel toward me? Is His love for me warm enough? Has He enough zeal? Does He feel my need deeply enough? Is He sufficiently earnest? Although these questions may seem irreverent to some, they simply embody the doubts and fears of a great many doubting hearts, and they only need to be asked in order to prove the fact that these doubts and fears are in themselves the real irreverence. We all know what would be the triumphant answers to such questions. No doubts could withstand their testimony; and the soul that asks and answers them honestly will be bound to a profound and absolute conviction that God is and must be enough.

May 15

The Reward of a Disciple
by Bryan L. Herde

Whatever you do, work at it with all your heart, as working for the Lord, not for men,
since you know that you will receive an inheritance from the Lord as a reward.
It is the Lord Christ you are serving.
Colossians 3:23-24

The reward of a disciple has so little to do with how well we performed our duty. It is rather how much we loved the Lord with all our hearts, souls, minds and bodies, and then how well we loved others. As a disciple, my all has been given completely to the Lord for Him to fulfill all His purposes and His desires in and through me. A life fully yielded to Him can't help but be one that climaxes in fulfilling the desires of our Heavenly Father's heart as well. The reason I make this point is to contrast a disciple's life with anything less than a vibrant relationship with the Lord. This is especially true of our tendency to develop and trust in fleshly systems, programs and methodologies devised by humans, rather than a complete abandonment of ourselves to the working of the Holy Spirit. As fallen persons, we tend to trust what we can control, what we can measure and what we can manage. The Holy Spirit is not someone who fits in boxes of our own creation. Certainly, the Holy Spirit can be grieved and limited by unbelief (Ephesians 4:30). We must be careful with any process which binds a checklist-driven duty to rewards and benefits. I believe that that is why the rewards mentioned by Scripture—other than the three crowns listed (James 1:12; 2 Timothy 8:8; 1 Peter 5:4)—are indefinite in their specifics. The real reward is a Person, not things.

***

There is a particular quality of our relationship with God that will never be the same as it can be now: getting to know intimately Someone who loves us infinitely while we are yet still sinful, still weak, still selfish, still faithless, still proud, still angry, still hurtful, still distrusting, still fearful, still anxious and still controlling. The joy that breaks through our own darkness and the darkness of others whom the Lord uses us to disciple is a pleasure not to be missed here and now. That is a reward one must not forget. And that is the life of being a disciple of Jesus Christ.

May 16

That God May Be All In All
by Andrew Murray

Then the end will come, when He [Christ] hands over the kingdom to God the Father after He has destroyed all dominion, authority and power. For He must reign until He has put all His enemies under His feet. The last enemy to be destroyed is death. For He "has put everything under His feet." Now when it says that "everything" has been put under Him, it is clear that this does not include God Himself, who put everything under Christ. When He has done this, then the Son Himself will be made subject to Him who put everything under Him, so that God may be all in all.
1 Corinthians 15:24-28

"That God may be all in all," I must not only allow Him to take His place, but secondly, I must accept His will in everything. I must accept His will in every sovereign action. Whether it be a Judas that betrays, or whether it be a Pilate in his indifference, who gives me up to the enemy; whatever the trouble, or temptation, or frustration, or worry that comes, I must see God in it, and accept it as God's will to me. Trouble of any sort that comes to me is God's will for me. It is not God's will that men should do the wrong, but it is God's will that they should be in circumstances of trial. There is never a trial that comes to us but it is God's will for us, and if we learn to see God in it, then we bid it welcome.

***

Have you learned to say, "There is never a trouble, and never a hurt by which my heart is touched or even pierced, but it comes from Jesus, and brings a message of love"? Will you not learn to say from today, "Welcome every trial, for it comes from God"? Oh, learn to accept God's will in everything! Come learn to say of every trial, without exception, "It is my Father who sent it. I accept it as His messenger," and nothing in earth or hell can separate you from God.

***

The deepest quietness has often been proved to be the inspiration for the highest action. It has been seen in the experience of many of God's saints, and it is just the experience we need—that in the quietness of surrender and faith, God's working has been made evident.

May 17

From July 4, 1876 Letter to His Sister (Part 1 of 4)
by General C.G. "Chinese" Gordon

Last night I thought over what we pray for, namely, direction in the earth's courses we should pursue; and I think, provided your request is made in sincerity and that you really wish to do His will and not your own, even if you do not daily renew that request, I believe it is granted, and it is lack of faith which prevents your enjoying the fruits. Therefore I think that all who have even once made that request in *sincerity* may rest comfortably, with the trust that all that happened that day is His will, let it be good or bad, or let it be according to our reason or not. This jewel will comfort me for a long time. Though in its aspect it seems fresh, it is not so; it is only the application of the fact and truth that *all things* are ruled by Him and that He inspires and answers our prayer; it is, as it were, a clearer view of the island from the ship; it existed before, but now a portion more of the fog or veil is swept away.

The way these truths fit into one another confirms my faith in them; if they differed, then I would fear; but as they are one and indivisible, I accept them at once. No doubt they may be for a time obscured, when one is carnal; the veil may come over them again, but it is only a temporary hiddenness. When a man abuses these truths, the veil over the whole of them falls at once, and he no longer believes them, and then can no longer abuse them, for he falls under the law's direct action.

We are all approaching at different intervals our great existence—God. He has explained Himself to us as the Truth, Love, Wisdom, and Almighty; we accept these attributes in the abstract, but do not believe them heartily, on account of *apparent* contradictions. We are as it were blind, and by degrees He opens our eyes and enables us by the use of severe troubles to know Him little by little. We may not at once sincerely accept His statements, but eventually He will show Himself, as He is, to each one of us.

May 18

From July 4, 1876 Letter to His Sister (Part 2 of 4)
by General C.G. "Chinese" Gordon

According to His pleasure, He reveals Himself in different degrees to different people, to some sooner, to some later. *To know Him* is the ultimate point of His vast design of creation, both of this and all worlds. Man from his birth beholds a veil before him which shrouds the Godhead. If his destiny is to be born in Christian lands, he has the attributes of the Godhead explained to him by the Word, both written and incarnated; but, though he may know by his intellect the truth of the Word, things are so contradictory in this life that the mystery still remains.

By suffering and trials the veil is torn, and according to the extent of that tear his mind accepts sincerely that which he before had accepted by his intellect. The tear in the veil may often present inconsistencies to him which disappear on new tears being made, and he at length sees a harmonious whole.

To the African the same shrouded Being reveals Himself, but we do not know in what manner; and perhaps the African could not tell himself; but it is the same Godhead and has the same attributes, whether known or unknown. Watch the conflict of the flesh and the Spirit in peace, for the result is certain. "Stand you still, and see the salvation of the Lord" (2 Chronicles 20:17). Every time the flesh is foiled by the Spirit, just as often is a tear made in the veil, and we know more of God. Every time the reverse takes place, that often does the veil fall again.

When the inevitable event—death—occurs, then the veil is torn altogether and no mystery remains. The flesh is finally vanquished by the Spirit, who is thus the conqueror of his life-long foe. I think the veil is thickened by the doctrines of men, and that to tear it is more difficult when these doctrines have been accepted and found inefficient. Had you not been permeated with them—had God not willed it in His wisdom—you would not have had such suffering in learning the truth.

May 19

From July 4, 1876 Letter to His Sister (Part 3 of 4)
by General C.G. "Chinese" Gordon

I believe when we begin life we are far more capable of accepting those truths than afterwards; when we have absorbed man's doctrine we must unlearn and then learn again; a child has only to learn. It is easier for a tax collector to accept those truths than a Pharisee. The Pharisee builds his house and uses man's doctrine; after a time he sees differently, and tries to dovetail his new views into his house. They will not fit in, and he says, "Why, I cannot pull down all my work and begin again!" So he forces them in, and still they will not fit; then he takes down a little, and then a little more, but it is no good; he finds the foundation is at fault, from there great trials and troubles, until at last he has to pull all down. When he has done all that—why, the miracle of a new house on the true foundation appears before him, in which work he has not had to make an effort. The tax collector has built and feels he can build nothing, but that all is done for him.

Why one should be a Pharisee and have all this toil and the other should be a tax collector and have none, is the mystery of God's rule. It is pain and grief to pull down a life's work and grub up even the foundations; but while you pull down each stone, God is building up your true house, so that in fact, while you are pulling down, you are in reality having your house built.

***

Men would make themselves a dwelling place for eternity out of their works in this world; we need not so trouble ourselves, for we have one already made; theirs is transitory and to be seen, ours is eternal and invisible.

One is God's work, the other is man's. In us are the two natures, both building houses of their experiences, the materials being widely different; one builds on sand, the other on the rock; each nature thinks the other a fool. The architect of one is the world and the doctrines of man, and the Architect of the other is God.

May 20

From July 4, 1876 Letter to His Sister (Part 4 of 4)
by General C.G. "Chinese" Gordon

I often think I should like to return and study these truths in quiet; but this is foolishness, for if I returned I might not know them. I feel sure that no study without trial is of value; life must be lived to learn these truths. I believe, if a man knows his Bible fairly and then goes forth into the world, God will show him His works. The Jews learned the Scripture by heart, and so I expect our Savior did; He therefore had no need to study it. He applied its teachings to life and its trials.

But to go back to the "house." We must think what our Savior meant by His type: a house is a place one returns to, where one is sheltered from storms, winds, and weather, where one keeps one's treasures, and where one looks for rest. The "religion" of a man is *his house*, built up of doctrines. He forms his idea of God and His working, and looks to that "religion" for shelter in all tribulation. When that "religion" or "house" is built of the doctrines of men, and when the builders try to *fit in* God's doctrine and cannot do so, they fall into a desperate state, and become atheistical and indifferent, give up all effort, so to say, and are, perhaps, at last driven into relinquishing their old ideas, pulling down the house they had built. You have often said, "Why is it there is so much effort, and yet no comfort?" Because that toil has been erected on a false foundation, namely, man's work, and not Christ's free grace—we would *do* something. This is the main obstacle, however we may blind ourselves. until we recognize futility, we are not on the true foundation, and everything we may build is therefore doomed to fall or fail us in the trials of life. Our buildings give us no shelter.

The following was added by Bryan L. Herde
My hope is built on nothing less than Jesus' blood and righteousness;
I dare not trust the sweetest frame, but wholly lean on Jesus' name.
On Christ, the solid Rock I stand, all other ground is sinking sand,
All other ground is sinking sand.

First verse of the hymn, *The Solid Rock*, lyrics by Edward Mote

May 21

Crosses
by François Fénelon

God is ingenious in making crosses for us. He makes them of iron and of lead, which are heavy in themselves. He makes them of straw which seems to weigh nothing, and which are less difficult to carry. He makes them of gold and of precious stones, which dazzle the spectators, which excite the envy of the public, but which crucify no less than the crosses which are most despised. He makes them of all the things which we like the best, and turns them to bitterness. It gives what we do not want, and takes away what we should like.

***

In this state there is hardly anything to be done. God does not need us to say many words to him, nor to think many thoughts. He sees our heart, and that is enough for him. He sees very well our suffering and our submission. We have only to repeat continuously to a person we love, "I love you with all my heart." It even often happens that we go a long time without thinking that we love him, and we love him no less during this period than in those in which we make to him the most tender declarations. True love rests in the depth of the heart. It is simple, peaceful and quiet. Often we deafen ourselves in multiplying conversations and reflections. This experience of love is felt only in a heated imagination.

***

It is he who sends even the grandeur with all its torments and its cursed gear. It is he who brings to birth within us the dryness, the impatience, the discouragement, to humiliate us by testings and to show us ourselves such as we are. It is he who does all. We have only to see him and to adore him in all.

We must not be at all in a hurry to obtain an artificial presence of God and of his truths. It is enough to live simply in this disposition of heart, to wish to be crucified; most of all a simple effortless life, which we renew every time that we are turned from it within by some memory, which is a kind of awakening of the heart.

May 22

Anxiety, Worry, Fretting and Fear:
The Most Frequent Fiery Darts of Satan
by Bryan L. Herde

In all circumstances take up the shield of faith, with which you can extinguish
***all** the flaming darts of the evil one...*
Ephesians 6:16 (ESV, emphasis added)

Jesus did not live, die and live again to make us better and stronger people. No! He came so that He might be our Life utterly and completely, inexhaustibly, without limit or measure! This is why He Himself so passionately desired to live in us (John 17:26). He finished the work so that He can live that completed work through us, if for no other reason than this: He already walked and talked and lived all the requirements of God to perfection! He knows what He is doing. He can, will, and desires to live His life in us and through us.

Are anxiety, worry, fretting and fear real? Absolutely. Can they do us harm? Certainly. But these sins are just that—sin. They are the natural DNA of our flesh, the world and Satan. But they only harm us if we allow them. In order for the shield of faith to be even more effectively used to protect us from eternal harm, it must be tried and tested. So the paradox is this: that which we wield to defend us (the shield of faith) is also that which in the defending is being perfected. Our faith must be attacked in order for it to grow. The fiery darts of anxiety, worry, fretting and fear must and will come. It is faith that quenches them, that keeps them from getting through to our hearts and minds—our vitals, our souls. Consequently, a weak faith will be attacked in order to make it stronger. The shield of faith does not become more powerful in the closet. No, we are in a constant state of battle and every moment of our lives the shield of faith, as well as all the other pieces of our armor, are to be worn and used, and all so we can simply stand our ground. Our Almighty God allows the enemy to attack our faith even though our enemy desires our destruction. But God knows and sets the limits to the attacks (1 Corinthians 10:13) so that we will be more reliant upon Christ, so that we can be like Christ in His humility, His dependence upon the Father, and His absolute submission to the will of the Father—no matter what!

May 23

Christ the Day-Dawn and the Rain
by John Ker

His going forth is prepared as the morning; and He shall come unto us as the rain.
Hosea 6:3

When our Savior came into the world it was silently and alone. All heaven was moved, and followed him down to the threshold, but few on earth knew it. One solitary star pointed to the humble birthplace, and sang hymns of it, heard only at night by the watching shepherds. He walked our world through years softly in the bitterness of his soul. He left where the common eye beheld but a humiliated sufferer, one of three on Golgotha, and men became aware that the Son of God had come and gone only when the clear light began to break in the eastern sky from that great work of his, and when the open gate of mercy was thrown back, with a cross before it, to call the lost and wandering home. And as it was with his descent into the world, so is it, in the general, with his entrance by his Spirit into the heart. There may be the thunder and the mighty rushing wind before it, the sovereign actions may be loud and violent, but the Spirit itself is like the rain. It moves from soul to soul among the rising generations, and there is no outward crisis to tell of the birth of souls.

The kingdom of heaven comes not with observation. And, even in times of revival more noticeable, for such times are promised and should be expected; yet even in such times, the Spirit's great work is not in the earthquake, or the mighty rushing wind, but in the still small voice. Unless it meets us there, in the secrecy of the soul, in the privacy of the prayer room, in rising to seek Christ at his grave, in the quiet resurrection morn, when the busy world and all the guards are asleep, unless it bring the soul into close and secret communion with Christ himself, it meets us not at all. In his gospel and his Spirit, Christ is moving through the great inner world which men too much neglect—the world of souls; and there in the solitude of the heart, alone with him, it must be ours to seek and find.

May 24

Apostolic Optimism (Part 1 of 2)
by John Henry Jowett

Rejoicing in hope.
Romans 12:12

Paul's mental and spiritual outlook comprehend a great army of positive forces laboring in the interests of the Kingdom of God. His conception of life was amazingly rich in friendly dynamics! I do not wonder that such a wealthy consciousness was creative of a triumphant optimism. Just glance at some of the apostle's assertions: "Christ lives in me!" "Christ lives in me!" He breathes through all my aspirations. He thinks through all my thinking. He wills through all my willing. He loves through all my loving. He travails in all my labors. He works within me "to will and to do His good pleasure." That is the primary faith of the hopeful life.

But see what follows in swift and immediate succession. "If Christ is in you, the spirit is life." "The spirit is life!" And therefore you find that in the apostle's thought dispositions are powers. They are not passive entities. They are positive forces vitalizing and energizing the common life of men. My brethren, I am persuaded there is a perilous leakage in this department of our thought.

We are not bold enough in our thinking concerning spiritual realities. We do not associate with every mode of the consecrated spirit the mighty energy of God. We too often eject from our practical calculations some of the strongest and most aggressive allies of the saintly life. Meekness is more than the absence of self-assertion; it is the manifestation of the mighty power of God. To the Apostle Paul love expressed more than a relationship. It was an energy productive of abundant labors. Faith was more than an attitude. It was an energy creative of mighty endeavor. Hope was more than a posture. It was an energy producing a most enduring patience. All these are dynamics, to be counted as active allies, cooperating in the ministry of the kingdom.

May 25

Apostolic Optimism (Part 2 of 2)
by John Henry Jowett

Rejoicing in hope.
Romans 12:12

The epistles abound in the recital of mystic ministries at work. The Holy Spirit works! Grace works! Faith works! Love works! Hope works! Prayer works! And there are other allies robed in less attractive garb. "Tribulation works!" "This light affliction works." "Godly sorrow works!" On every side of him the apostle conceives cooperative and friendly powers. "The mountain is full of horses and chariots of fire round about him." He exults in the consciousness of abounding resources.

He discovers the friends of God in things which find no place among the regular powers of the world. He finds God's raw material in the world's discarded waste. "Weak things," "contemptible things," "things that are despised," "things that are not," mere nothings; among these he discovers the operating agents of the mighty God. Is it any wonder that in this man, possessing such a wealthy consciousness of multiplied resources, the spirit of a cheery optimism should be enthroned? With what stout confidence he goes into the fight!

He never mentions the enemy timidly. He never seeks to underestimate his strength. No, again and again he catalogues all possible antagonisms in a spirit of buoyant and exuberant triumph. However numerous the enemy, however subtle and aggressive his devices, however towering and well-established the iniquity, however black the gathering clouds, so sensitive is the apostle to the wealthy resources of God that among it all he remains a sunny optimist, "rejoicing in hope," laboring in the spirit of a conqueror even when the world was exulting in his supposed discomfort and defeat.

May 26

Love Revealed: Meditations on John 13 (Part 1 of 2)
by George Bowen

He arose from supper and laid aside His garment; and took a towel and wrapped Himself. After that He poured water into a basin, and began to wash His disciples' feet, and to wipe them with a towel with which He was wrapped.
John 13:4-5

It is well to have conviction of sin—we cannot have it too deeply; we can scarcely take too dark a view of our own character; but humility, as a Christian grace, must ever draw the heart to Christ. There is nothing more worthless than the self-deceit which leads some to say, I am content to be an inferior Christian, and to be undistinguished by spiritual accomplishments; if I were a more devoted servant of the Lord, I might be lifted up with pride. That is to say, you are afraid you would lose your humility if you obtained more faith. Well, lose your humility; it will be no great loss.

If you really obtain a strong faith, you will have along with it a very different humility from that which you now have. Consider and confess. Your present humility is something most base, for it makes God a liar, saying it is not good for a man to love God with all his heart and soul; and further it says that he is not worthy that you should serve him devotedly. It tears almost all the pages out of the Bible, for almost every page of Scripture contains promises, invitations, commands, which your current version of humility nullifies.

A genuine humility will ever feel the need of the largest measures of grace, and will be perfected just in the degree in which that grace is given. Spiritual pride shows, not that there has been too much, but too little, of the operation of the Spirit. The only way to overcome it is to push ahead. The truly humble man will seek to be filled with all the fullness of God, knowing that when he is so filled there is not the slightest place for pride or for self.

May 27

Love Revealed: Meditations on John 13 (Part 2 of 2)
by George Bowen

He arose from supper and laid aside His garment; and took a towel and wrapped Himself. After that He poured water into a basin, and began to wash His disciples' feet, and to wipe them with a towel with which He was wrapped.
John 13:4-5

Peter had doubtless taken part in the dispute of the disciples as to which of them should be greatest—the very dispute which prompted our Lord to do what he was now doing. [Peter's] conduct in the after part of the evening showed plainly that he was far from being perfect in humility. It must be very offensive to God when we fail to give those proofs of humility which the occasion properly demands, and then insist that some unrequired thing done by us has the impression of that heavenly grace.

Some are deterred from communicating freely with God concerning this and that temporal affair which occupies their minds by the idea that it is beneath the dignity of God to take note of such matters. The only acceptable devotion is to let God reign in your heart. To partition off a part of your thought-world, and call it a holy of holies, and hang a thick curtain before it, and then surrender the outer court to Gentiles, this is no devotion. You may make God a prisoner and visit him at times in priestly garments, and then clothe yourself with the deep tone of reverence that marks your approaches to him. The disciples imagined that they were giving proof of an admirable respect for the person of Jesus when they refused to allow little children to be brought to him. They would cut him off from a portion of humanity that had for him a high attraction. Your minor cares Christ will not reject.

True Humility
by Bryan L. Herde

In my determination to get it right, as a proof of my own humility,
Would I have refused my Lord's actions, Him kneeling in front of me?
True humbleness is allowing God to do whatever His heart desires
No matter how odd, how unexpected, yielding to whatever He requires.

May 28

The Omnipresence of God (Part 1 of 2)
by Alexander Whyte

"Do not I fill heaven and earth?" says the Lord.
Jeremiah 23:24

The omnipresence of God is that glorious attribute of the Divine Nature on which we are to meditate today. And it will demand all our powers of meditation. God's omnipresence—that is to say, God's presence everywhere and wholly everywhere. God's presence with all His creatures of all kinds, and in all places of His realm. Give strength, then, to your understanding, and give wings to your imagination, and give holy fear to your heart, while we try to enter upon those great matters, "which eye has not seen, nor ear heard, neither have entered into the heart of man. But God has revealed them unto us by His Spirit."

When you try to do it, you cannot limit the presence of God to any one place on earth, or in heaven: no, nor to all places on earth and in heaven, taken together. Place, precinct, locality, situation—when you attempt it, you soon find how absolutely impossible it is to limit and restrict Almighty God in that way.

***

God is the true and only resident of both the physical and the spiritual universe. God is the ultimate analysis, and the innermost essence, and the deepest root, and the all-producing and the all-sustaining cause of all existence. The whole universality and immensity of all things, created and uncreated, is all one and the same mystery of Godliness.

All created things—the most firm and stable—would instantly stagger and reel back, and dissolve into their original nothingness and annihilation if Almighty God withheld His all-upholding hand from them for one moment, from a grain of sand on the seashore, up to all the endless systems of suns and stars in the heavens. "For, of Him, and through Him, and to Him, are all things."

May 29

The Omnipresence of God (Part 2 of 2)
by Alexander Whyte

"Do not I fill heaven and earth?" says the Lord.
Jeremiah 23:24

If anything could add to the awe and the wonder of God's glorious sustaining power, it would be this other incomparable truth—that He Who is everywhere is also *wholly* everywhere. Almighty God is wholly, and is continually, with every one of us in all the completeness, and in all the totality, of His Godhead.

Were we but able to receive it—we have our God, and the whole of our God, as much with us as if we had been Adam, new from the hand of God, and walking alone with the whole presence of God, among the trees of the garden.

***

But then, God is present and is wholly present only to him who believes that. Our belief does not indeed cause God to be; and our unbelief does not cause Him not to be.

Believe in God and in His presence with you, and His presence is immediately and wholly with you as it was with David in the Psalms, and with Jesus Christ in the Gospels, and with Paul in the Epistles. Have faith in God, and in your own souls.

***

Here is thought, infinitely the most magnificent; and observation the most inexhaustible; and experience, gathered out of God, and out of a man's own soul; out of all time, and yet to be gathered out of a coming eternity. Here is meditation, both the sweetest and the most strengthening. Here is the life of prayer on earth, and the life of praise in heaven. Here is the chief end of our creation and our redemption—God. "That they all may be one: as You, Father, are in Me, and I in You. I in them, and You in Me: and that the love wherewith You have loved Me may be in them, and I in them." How glorious is the practice of the Omnipresence of God!

May 30

The God of Salvation
by Andrew Murray

My soul waits upon God; from Him comes my salvation.
Psalm 62:1

If salvation indeed comes from God, and is entirely His work, just as our creation was, it follows, as a matter of course, that our first and highest duty is to wait on Him to do that work as pleases Him. Waiting becomes then the only way to the experience of a full salvation, the only way, truly, to know God as the God of our salvation. All the difficulties that are suggested as keeping us back from full salvation, have their cause in this one thing: the defective knowledge and practice of waiting upon God. All that the Church and its members need for the display of the mighty power of God in the world is the return to our true place, the place that belongs to us, both in creation and redemption, the place of absolute and unceasing dependence upon God. Let us strive to see what the elements are that make up this most blessed and necessary waiting upon God: it may help us to discover the reasons why this practice is so little cultivated, and to feel how infinitely desirable it is that the Church, that we ourselves, should at any price learn its blessed secret.

***

It is, then, because Christians do not know their relation to God of absolute poverty and helplessness, that they have no sense of the need for absolute and unceasing dependence, or the unspeakable blessedness of continual waiting on God. But when once a believer begins to see it, and consent to it, that he by the Holy Spirit must each moment receive what God each moment works, waiting on God becomes his brightest hope and joy. As he understands how God, as God, as Infinite Love, delights to impart His own nature to His child as fully as He can, how God is not weary of each moment taking charge of his life and strength, he wonders that he ever thought otherwise of God than as a God to be waited on all the day. God unceasingly giving and working; His child unceasingly waiting and receiving—this is the blessed life.

May 31

"It Is Finished" (Part 1 of 2)
by A.B. Davidson

This Son of man, thirty years of age or little more, dying in the bloom of manhood with such deep feeling of all that is lovely on earth, has no regret at leaving it. At first, indeed, the terrors of the death He had to die did overcome Him for a time, and the thought rose in His heart that, if it were only possible, He would stop short of entering the waters of that dark flood that now rolled close at His feet; and with great submissiveness He did in His agony approach His Father, risking the question whether it might not be possible to escape the cup that was now to be put into His hand—a thought that, perhaps, only the terrors of such an hour could have raised in His mind. But it was not possible, and He went forward with gladness and strength to that which was His Father's will. He has no regrets at leaving all that He loved on earth.

He has loved ones whom He is leaving; He has a mother, but He calmly provides for her. Bringing the beloved disciple and her together, He commends her to his care, calling her his mother and him her son; and this done, He says, "It is finished," and dies. And so, on the other hand, as there is no regret, there is no triumph. Even when, in the moment of His greatest weakness, still showing Himself to be the power of God unto salvation, and converting the dying thief, it is with no excitement, but a certain calmness, that He addresses him: "Today shall you be with Me in paradise." And there is the same calmness and faith in His words about Himself: "Father, into Your hands I commend My spirit."

How many of us could face death in this clear, calm way, with all our faculties about us, our hearts and consciences and memories all alive, and speaking out what is on them; and yet our memories able to draw up nothing from the past to terrify us, and our imaginations to conjure up nothing in the future to dismay us, knowing in whom we have believed? Oh, may we die the death of the righteous! And may our last end be like His! But to die His death, we must live His life.

June 1

"It Is Finished" (Part 2 of 2)
by A.B. Davidson

These words of Christ, "It is finished," cannot refer merely to His death agonies. They refer to the whole sorrows of His life. There is a depth about the words, and the sufferer speaks out from beneath a load of oppression that has lain on Him far longer than these hours upon the Cross. The sufferings of the Cross were perhaps, in some respects, less than those in the Garden; and those in the Garden were not alone. Often during His life, He would become strange-like to the bystanders, being carried away by other thoughts than the things about Him; and He retired, and wrestled on a mountain apart, and came back calm again. The words, "It is finished," refer to some deep lifelong oppression that lay on Him—that lay always on Him, though only now and then rising up so as to overmaster Him. What wondrous man is this that rises before us, so calm in death, so strange, and meek, and sorrowful when living? It is the man of sorrows; and when He says, "It is finished," He means that all this sorrow is over at last.

***

Whatever Christ came into the world for was finished. His work was not cut short by death. Death did not come on Him, as it comes on us, paralyzing us in the middle of our work, so that the tools fall from our hands, and we are changed and carried away. How many pieces of human work are thus forever interrupted, and hands that have acquired skill through a lifetime's exercised flexibility become rigid, and the work that was all but completed is postponed forever, and humanity fails to reap a portion of its destined harvest of beauty or of goodness! But death did not surprise Him, nor halt His work; it came to perfect Him, and to finish His work. All that is expressed in Christ's appearance—the coming near of God to men, the unveiling of the mysteries of our life, the reaching back to the hidden springs of all that God does—all this was sealed in Christ's death. "God has commended His love to us, in that while we were yet sinners Christ died for us." That He came to do, reached its end in His death; He made an end of sin, and brought in everlasting righteousness. He became obedient unto death, even the death of the Cross.

June 2

When Disappointment is Transformed Into Delight
by Bryan L. Herde

We do not want you to become lazy, but to imitate those who through faith
and patience inherit what has been promised.
Hebrews 6:11

Those of you who are caught in the confusion of not understanding why things are so hard, why there is so much pain, disappointment and suffering, and why you can't seem to get God to "fix" whatever struggles you want to end, please know this: Your faith, which is more precious than gold (1 Peter 1:7 KJV), must be refined by fire, for God said "without faith it is impossible to please God" (Hebrews 11:6). Also, "The testing of your faith develops patience, but let patience have its perfect effect that you may be perfect and entire, lacking nothing" (James 1:2-4).

It is through the hardship you are now enduring, or those hardships you have endured, and you will yet endure, that God is working to liberate your heart. He will not (and I pray for your sakes that He does not!) end your trial until He has completed the work He began that will truly set you free from sin, from self and from your love for the things of this world. Please know this: God is so focused upon your "forever" that your "now" is primarily the fuel He ignites and feeds the purifying flames of testing so that your faith—your absolute trust, reliance and belief in Him—will become as solid as the Rock of our salvation, and as enduring as the Alpha and Omega of our souls. "Delight yourself in the Lord and He will give you the desires of your heart" (Psalm 37:4). The Lord has placed in the hearts of each of His children a desire to be filled by Him to overflowing, filled with Him now, in preparation for seeing Him face to face forever.

Do not fight to free yourself from your trials. Rather, submit to His loving, sovereign choice for you at this moment and embrace this opportunity to share in the sufferings of Jesus Christ (Philippians 3:10) so that you, too, will learn and possess a heart of obedience that endures and perseveres, no matter what may come.

June 3

The Light of the Knowledge of the Glory of God (Part 1 of 2)
by Henry Robert Reynolds

The light, the illumination of the knowledge of the glory of God
in the face of Jesus Christ.
2 Corinthians 4:6

The light brighter than the sun which broke over the consciousness of St. Paul on his way to Damascus illumined every truth which he had already made his own. It reversed for him the highest wisdom of the past, and cancelled his inheritance in the privileges and pride of centuries. The knowledge of the glory of God in the face of Jesus Christ became so brilliant an illumination, threw such floods of light on deep problems, on obscure and unsuspected places of thought and of human experience, that he found himself in a new world, with new ideas of all things in heaven and earth, in time and eternity.

St. Paul was not alone in this matter. Every mind that has so far followed the apostle as to *know* God in *Christ,* has gone through a similar experience. The effect of the glare of light which thus illumines life differs with us all in accordance with our previous circumstances. The meteoric splendor which breaks upon some minds in the arrival of knowledge touching this supreme fact in the history of the world, has in some periods, so stimulated the understanding of mankind that those who saw it could do little else than try and systematize it, or endeavor to reduce the sublime synthesis to some form of creed.

During hundreds of years, men could not rest in the light. It awakened them so completely from their dreams that it might seem they had forgotten the power of the light itself in their restless efforts to fit it into their previous scheme of the universe.

June 4

The Light of the Knowledge of the Glory of God (Part 2 of 2)
by Henry Robert Reynolds

The light, the illumination of the knowledge of the glory of God
in the face of Jesus Christ.
2 Corinthians 4:6

New light meant new life. New life meant a strange power, and a peace which passed understanding. So that, while the philosophers and the councils were fighting about the way in which they could adequately express the relation of the Father and Son, and the relation of Jesus to both, hundreds, thousands were content to die for their Lord, and were bravely defying all the power of Roman courts, all the refinements of heathen malice, and all the cruelty of murderous mobs. They were following the Lamb wherever He led them, to prison and to death, and triumphing over both with songs of deliverance.

Sometimes the very same men who were most active in the intellectual endeavor to analyze the light were also able to bear with sublime and saintly patience the utmost cruelty of pagan hatred, and the desperate outbreaks of partisan intolerance. So through all the centuries, theological intensity has not always strangled, but rather stimulated, moral heroism and missionary enterprise.

Some special ages have been sharply characterized by the endeavor to criticize and refine theological forms; and others, again, by the tendency to ignore the intellectual side of Christianity, and even to abandon great truths for ethical enthusiasm, or for selfless or self-denying devotion.

Surely, my brethren, this light, this illumination of the knowledge of the glory of God in the face of the Christ is not to be simply gazed at with sharpened eyes of scientific or metaphysical sensitivity, but it is to be lived by; and we have not merely to look, but to live.

June 5

The Crown of Thorns (Part 1 of 4)
by George H. Morrison

And when they had braided a crown of thorns, they put it upon His head.
Matthew 27:29

Among all the sufferings which Christ had to endure in the last and terrible days of His humility, none has more deeply moved the heart of Christendom than His wearing of the crown of thorns. We have never felt the agony of nails, nor the cruel piercing of a Roman spear. And therefore we can but dimly realize the physical pain of such experiences. But in the torment of sharp and biting thorns we reach the commoner lot of our humanity. To us, who have never known the stab of wounds, the wound of a spear is but a faint imagining. It would take a soldier, gashed and bleeding on the field, to have fellowship with Jesus Christ in that. But in a world so thick with tangled briers, and thickest with them where man has had his dwelling, the crown of thorns is like a touch of brotherhood in a scene of lonely and exalted sorrow.

But there is something in that coronation that reaches deeper than any homely anguish. In Him was the very essence of humanity. In Him the race was gathered and united. In Him was every child who ever played and every woman who ever wept in secret. All human life was hidden in that form whose face was disfigured more than any man's; all joy that shares its secret with the stars; all passion that hears its echo in the winds. And Him they crowned—Him the representative—Him the embodiment of all mankind, and they crowned Him with a crown of thorns. And one of them stole out into the night and plucked the twigs from the garden of the palace. And he rejoiced in being a clever person, and he knew how his ready wit would be appreciated, and he never dreamed he was a bound messenger in the hand of an ordering and sovereign God. Here was a joke, and yet it was reality. Here was the coronation of mankind, and on its brow there was a thorny crown. And that is the deep and universal meaning of it, brought out by soldiers in their beastly sport, that on the brow of man there is a crown, yet always it is a crown of thorns.

June 6

The Crown of Thorns (Part 2 of 4)
by George H. Morrison

And when they had braided a crown of thorns, they put it upon His head.
Matthew 27:29

There is a passion in the heart to know, and man will know, though Paradise be lost. Loftier than any search for happiness, purer than any striving to be rich, more glorious than the pursuit of fame, that last imperfection of noble mind, the passion for knowledge in the human breast, tireless, unsubduable and unending. This passion for knowledge is more heated than the passion for social standing or power. It is this that animates the lonely student to shun delights and live laborious days. It is this that has penetrated to the icy pole, and forced its way across uncharted seas. It is this that has triumphed over persecution, and defied a world of dangers, and filled with luxury the home of poverty, and vanquished the cruel ravages of disease.

The greatest thing in all the world is loving.

The second greatest in all the world is learning. There is a joy in it, an acceleration of the heart, an exaltation of the personality. And yet this precious crown of knowledge—this circlet after the pattern on the Mount—is it not after all a crown of thorns? The more we know, the more we cannot know. The more we see, the more we cannot see.

Let a man be ignorant, and be content, and he may always have music in his prison. It is when he beats against the prison wall, and climbs upward to the barred window, that voices reach him which are full of pain, and faces whose secret he shall never read. Every expansion of knowledge has brought joy. Every expansion of knowledge has brought sorrow. It has enlightened and it has perplexed. It has unveiled and yet it has confused. It has made it harder to grasp the garments of God; to live in unquestioning and simple faith; to keep alive the wonder of the child who feels that the angels are not far away.

June 7

The Crown of Thorns (Part 3 of 4)
by George H. Morrison

And when they had braided a crown of thorns, they put it upon His head.
Matthew 27:29

A flood of light has been poured upon the Bible, until it is literally a new book today. For centuries the Bible stood alone, not to be questioned nor criticized. Every sentence was of equal value, as verbally inspired by the Almighty. And men accepted it without a doubt, and women pondered it in simple faith, and it was a garden where the Lord was walking, as in the cool of the day He walked in Paradise. And do I say it is not so today? God forbid that I should be so foolish. It is still, and will ever be, the Word of God, in a sense no other book can ever bear. And there is light in it still for every hour of shadow, and comfort for every day of grief, and all our hope for time and for eternity is rooted in the message of the Cross.

No truth can ever overturn the truth. No knowledge can discredit Him who knew. It is our solemn duty to the Lord Jesus Christ to cast His Word into the fires of criticism. And yet with all the knowledge which that has brought us, knowledge so wonderful and so undreamed of, what pain has visited a thousand hearts, what agony of doubt and of unrest! Some have been tempted to renounce the light, that they might cherish a simple faith again. Some have turned to the critics and have cried, "You have taken away my Lord, and I know not where you have laid Him." And all of us have had seasons of confusion, not knowing what to think or what to do: only knowing if we were false to facts, we never could be true to Jesus Christ. Do not repeat that proverb of the coward, "Where ignorance is bliss it is foolish to be wise." That is a wrong assumption, for in a sphere like this, ignorance never can be bliss. Rather believe that knowledge is our crown, and wear it as the diadem of God, and if it pierces and is a crown of thorns, the servant is not greater than his Lord.

June 8

The Crown of Thorns (Part 4 of 4)
by George H. Morrison

And when they had braided a crown of thorns, they put it upon His head.
Matthew 27:29

There is another crown. It is the fairest of them all—the crown of love. Without it, the brow is always bare, and the heart is always very cold and lonely. But the commonest dwelling is a palace with it, and there is sunshine in the dreariest day. It is not hidden in some guarded ornamental chest, far from the hands of the common people. It is not only above the bright blue sky that there's a crown for little children. There's a crown for them here, where they are loved today, and for their mothers who rejoice in motherhood, and for their fathers who have not been false to their promises.

Love is the crown of life, for God is love, and everything is a mockery without it. He that dwells in love dwells in God, and to be loveless forever and ever, that is hell. And yet this love which is the crown of life, the bliss of angels and the air of heaven, tell me, is it not a crown of thorns? I think of Jesus Christ who loved us so, and who was mocked and beaten and killed, who found in love the pathway to His joy and equally the pathway to His cross. Love has its triumph and it has its torture. Love has its paradise and has its pain. Love has its mountain of transfiguration, and its olive garden where the sweat is blood. Love is the secret of the sweetest song; love is the secret of the keenest suffering. Love is the very crown of life— and it is a crown of thorns. And they braided a crown of thorns and put it on His head. That is what God is doing with us all. And shall I tell you why He treats us so, and stabs us in our coronation? It is that, looking upon the brow of Christ, we may all feel we have a Brother there. It is that, watching His patience and His courage, we may be patient and courageous too. It is that we may lift our eyes to where the Lamb is standing at the throne, where there is no more pain; where there is no more curse; where the thorn has vanished from the crown forever.

June 9

God Himself Will Establish You in Him
by Andrew Murray

He which establishes us with you in Christ, is God.
2 Corinthians 1:21

These words of Paul teach us a much needed and most blessed truth—that just as our first being united with Christ was the work of Divine omnipotence, so too we may look to the Father, for being kept and being fixed more firmly in Him. "The Lord will perfect that which concerns me"—this expression of confidence should ever accompany the prayer, "Forsake not the work of Your own hands."

In all his longings and prayers to attain to a deeper and more perfect abiding in Christ, the believer must hold fast his confidence: "He which has begun a good work in you will perform it until the day of Jesus Christ." There is nothing that will so help to root and ground him in Christ as this faith: "He which establishes us in Christ is God."

How many there are who can testify that this faith is just what they need! They continually mourn over the erratic manner of their spiritual life. Sometimes there are hours and days of deep earnestness, and even of blessed experience of the grace of God. But how little is needed to spoil their peace, to bring a cloud over the soul! And then, how their faith is shaken! All efforts to regain their standing appear utterly fruitless; and neither solemn vows, nor watching and prayer, were effective to restore to them the peace they for a while had tasted. If only they could understand how their own efforts are the cause of their failure, because it is God alone who can establish us in Christ Jesus. They would see that just as in justification they had to cease from their own working, and to accept in faith the promise that God would give them life in Christ, so now, in the matter of their sanctification, their first need is *to cease from striving themselves to establish the connection with Christ more firmly, and to allow God to do it.*

June 10

Religious Uses of Memory (Part 1 of 2)
by George Morrison

"Remember the former things of old: I am God, and there is no one like me."
Isaiah 46:9

Of all the powers that God has given us, none is more wonderful than memory. There is a mystery in thought that leaps out to its object and annihilates space. There is a mystery in hope that rises unconquerable in the heart. Imagination is mysterious: so are desire and fear. But of all the powers God has given us, none is more wonderful than memory.

For what is memory? It is a twofold power. It is the power that gathers in the past, and crowds into some secret cabinet here the twenty thousand things that we have learned. And then it is the power that out of that crowded storehouse brings the things forth again, calls them to mind. Some languages have different words for these two acts. We have but one. And not a little confusion has arisen from our using the one word for both.

***

Now I will venture to assert that there is no religion which lays such an emphasis on memory as Christianity. It is the glory of Jesus that He pressed all powers into His service. Thought, hope, imagination, fear—He used them all. But He exalted memory in religious service as it had never been exalted by another teacher. And He recognized its moral character as it had never been recognized before.

What do we call Christ's sayings? We call them memorable words. And memorable words are not merely words that we remember: they are words so chosen, and so arranged and set, that they make an instant impression on the memory. The words of Jesus are like the seal upon the wax. Once stamped with these, memory will bear them to the end. Christ recognized the character of memory in making His words so memorable as that.

June 11

Religious Uses of Memory (Part 2 of 2)
by George Morrison

"Remember the former things of old: I am God, and there is no one like me."
Isaiah 46:9

And when we sit at the Lord's Supper, what do we hear? "This do in remembrance of me." There at the Holy Table: there at the very center of the Gospel: there in the richest hour of feast and fellowship, the dominant note is memory. It is not hope, though I am hopeful there. It is not knowledge. It is not even faith, though I believe—help my unbelief! It is, "This do in remembrance of me." It sets a crown upon the head of memory, that supper. It shows what Christ expected of it. It is more than a gift, more than an aptitude. It is a moral power. It is a religious force.

Did you ever think what a daring thing it was of Christ and Christianity to lay such an emphasis on memory? It is with the past that memory deals; and to enlist the memory in His service meant simply that Christ was not afraid to face the past.

It is the glory of Christianity that it has a message for your past: "Though your sins be as scarlet, they shall be white as snow. Though they be red like crimson, they shall be as wool." Only Christ could dare to exalt memory so. And it took Calvary, and pardon to the uttermost, and peace with God, to do it.

***

Perhaps you have thought it would be an easier thing to be a Christian if Jesus Christ were here. If only you heard His footsteps on the street, and had the touch of His hand upon your brow, it would be easier to be better than it is. O God be thanked that we are spared this trial.

I can look back now. I can appreciate in the light of memory. I can go to my room and close the door, and be alone with God and the Spirit of remembrance.

June 12

Mental Weariness
by George Matheson

Consider Him [Christ]...so that you will not be wearied and give up in your minds.
Hebrews 12:3

What a strange cure for mental weariness! There is prescribed an increase of thought, "*consider* Him." I should have expected an invitation to mental *rest*. When a man's *body* is weary, we send him to sleep. When a man's mind is weary, why do we not also prescribe rest? Because the weariness of the mind needs an opposite cure from the weariness of the body. The weariness of the body is cured by sleep; but the weariness of the mind can be cured only by stimulus. The cry to a tired body is, "Sleep on now, and take your rest"; the cry to a tired mind is, "Awake, you who sleeps, and arise from the dead." To all who labor in *spirit* Christ says, "Come unto me." He prescribes not a sedative, but a stimulus; not more sleep, but more waking. To the man of the weary *hand* He says, "Cast *your* cares upon Me"; but to the man of the weary heart he cries, "Take *My* yoke upon *you*."

Lord, it is *wings* I need for my weariness—love's wings. That which tires my heart is not its work, but its inaction. It will never cease to be tired until it can soar—soar to You. The burden and heat of my spiritual day is not its work, but its aimlessness; give me an aim, O Lord! Sometimes even the entrance of an earthly friend transforms my soul from tiredness into light; much more will You if You enter in. I want a new interest to heal my heart's weariness—someone to live for, someone to work for, someone to wait for, someone to long for. It is my lack of longing that makes my lack of strength; it is my listlessness that brings my lethargy. Create a new heart within me—an eager, beating, bounding heart, a heart vibrating in response to Your love! Let me feel the passion and the sorrow of life, of Your life! Let me be taken captive by Your beauty! Let me catch the spell of Your loveliness! Let me be thrilled at the sound of Your footsteps! Let me learn the rapture of hearing Your name! Let me experience the glow of excitement when the murmur runs round, "Jesus of Nazareth passes by!" Then will the weariness of the heart vanish, then shall the slowness of the spirit cease; for the liberty of flight is the Sabbath of the soul. Then we shall mount up with wings as eagles; we shall not give up or be weary.

June 13

The Invisible Antagonisms
by John Henry Jowett

*Which is why you must take unto you the whole armor of God, that you may be able to
withstand in the evil day, and having done all, to stand.*
Ephesians 6:13

"Put on the complete armor of God." Let us begin there. Our first need is
God. Without God we are beaten even before the fight begins. We have no
more likelihood of conquering our spiritual foes without God than this unaided hand of mine would be able to drive back the solid forces of our
nation's enemies. We must begin with God. In the tenth verse of this
chapter the apostle unfolds the primary secret of victory. "Be strong in the
Lord and in the power of His might." But that is a very imperfect
translation, laying too much emphasis upon the soldier and too little upon
his Lord. I greatly like the marginal rendering of the Revised Version [of the
Bible]: "Be made powerful in the Lord." Does not that word sound full of
promise for soldiers who are about to storm a difficult position? "Be made
powerful in the Lord." Let God make you powerful! Such power is not a
trophy of battle; it is the result of relationship. This power is not something
we have to win; it is something we have to receive. "Be made powerful in
the Lord!" And listen again: "You shall receive power when the Holy Spirit
is come upon you." That power, that vital endowment of strength, is the
gift of God, one of the ministries of the divine grace, and it is offered to
every soldier without money and without price. So is it true that our first
necessity in battle is to hurry away to the Lord to receive the gifts of the
soldier's strength.

But not only is there the critical need of God for our initial strength, but for
every piece of armor which may be necessary in the fight. Armor for
offense, and armor for defense; armor to meet every device and scheme
with which we may be attacked. I have to tell you that you will find every
piece of armor in the abundantly stocked and open and free armory of
God. And therefore do I say again that if we are to be triumphant over our
enemies, our first need is God.

June 14

Christ and the Intellect
by George Morrison

What is Christ's doctrine of the intellect—what are our Savior's ethics of the mind? We know how Christ has affected our emotional life, expanding our feelings into undreamed-of fullness. We know how He has changed the life of action, investing the lowliest drudgery with splendor. But what I want to try to find is not Christ's attitude to work or feeling. It is the attitude of Christ to thought—the way in which He viewed the intellect.

***

I want to say a word in passing about the greatest intellectual sin in Christ's eyes. What feature, think you, of the mental life was darkest and most guilty to our Lord? Was it ignorance? Think of Him on the cross, crying "Father, forgive them, they know not what they do." Was it doubt? Think of Him with Thomas: "Thomas, put your hand here and feel the wound!" Christ was not harsh and terrible with doubters. Christ had an infinite pity for the ignorant. It was not to be ignorant that damned a man. What damned him was to be unteachable. "Except you become as little children, you cannot even see the kingdom of God." The one condition of entrance to the best was to be childlike, teachable, receptive. And so conversely to be fixed and immovable—to have every window closed and gateway barred, was the one way to lose the breath of heaven, and to miss the gentle footsteps of the angels. It is not doubt that is faith's opposite. Doubt sometimes is just faith disguised. The opposite of faith is that finality which does not believe in larger truth tomorrow. Faith throws the shutters back—unbars the door—waits for new messengers across the hills. Faith is expectant, eager, childlike, buoyant. Its opposite is not doubt, but death.

***

Jesus has invigorated and steadied human intellect by bringing immortality to light. "Now we know in part," says the apostle, and the wisest can but bow the head to that. We cannot grasp the least in its entirety, nor can we complete the mystic circle here. "Then shall we know, even as we are known."

June 15

The Illimitable Love of God (Part 1 of 2)
by John Henry Jowett

Neither height nor depth…will be able to separate us from the
love of God that is in Christ Jesus our Lord.
Romans 8:39

What is the biggest thing on which the human mind can be challenged? In what can we most easily lose ourselves in the overwhelming sense of the immeasurable? There are the vast lone spaces of the starry regions, peopled with countless worlds, crossed by mysterious highways, with stars as the pilgrims, ever moving on their unknown journeyings. We can lose ourselves there. There is "the dark backward and abyss of time," opening door after door in ever-receding ages, back through twilight and dawn into the prehistoric darkness, where the inquisitive mind falters and grows weak. And we can lose ourselves there. There is the appalling wilderness of human need, beginning from my own life, with its taint of blood, its defect of faculty, its dreary gap in circumstance and condition, and repeated in every other life in every street, in every city and village and country throughout the inhabited world. And we can lose ourselves there.

And then there is the deadly, universal presence of human sin, in all its chameleon forms—well-dressed, ill-dressed, blazing in passion, mincing in vanity, and freezing in moral indifference and unbelief. But there is something more majestic than the heavens, more wonderful than the far, mysterious vistas of time, more pervasive than human need, and more abounding than human sin. The biggest thing with which the mind must cope is the infinite love of God; and all our sanctified powers, and all the ministries of holy fellowship, and all the explorations of eternity will never reach a limit in its unsearchable wealth. The biggest thing you and I will ever know is the love of God in Jesus Christ our Lord. "The height, and depth, and length, and breadth, and to know the love of God, which passes knowledge."

June 16

The Illimitable Love of God (Part 2 of 2)
by John Henry Jowett

Neither height nor depth…will be able to separate us from the love of God that is in Christ Jesus our Lord.
Romans 8:39

The force of love always depends upon its height. There is a type of love which has no strength because it has no height. It is a weak, sickly sentiment which just crawls about you. It is low, and therefore it has no stimulating force. It is mixed with earthly elements, and therefore it has no heavenly energy.

The more holy love is, the higher it is and the more filled it is with vitality. How, then, must it be with the love of God? Born in holiness, it has power enough to waken the dead. His love, so glorious in holiness, can raise to its own level, and lift us into "heavenly places in Christ Jesus." "They shall sit with Me on My throne."

***

God's love is deeper than sin. One night, when I was recently crossing the Atlantic, an officer of our boat told me that we had just passed over the spot where the Titanic went down. And I thought of all that life and wreckage beyond the power of man to recover and redeem. And I thought of the great bed of the deep sea, with all its held treasure, too far down for man to reach and restore. "Too far down!" And then I thought of all the human wreckage engulfed and sunk in oceanic depths of nameless sin. Too far gone! For what? Too far down! For what? Not too far down for the love of God! Listen to this: "He descended into hell," and He will descend again if you are there. "If I make my bed in hell, You are there." "Where sin flourished, grace did even more flourish." "He bore our sin"; then He got beneath it; down to it and beneath it; and there is no human wreckage, lying in the ooze of the deepest sea of wickedness, that His deep love cannot reach and redeem. What a Gospel! However far down, God's love can get beneath it!

June 17

The Larger Christ (Part 1 of 2)
by David James Burrell

"O woman, great is your faith: be it done unto you even as you will."
Matthew 15:21-28

Hear him: "It is not appropriate," Jesus says to her, "to take the children's bread and cast it to the dogs." Here is a distinct blow. I imagine Peter at this point turning to John with the remark, "It is just as I supposed; as the 'minister of the circumcision' he can have nothing to do with her. Were she a Jew, he would heal her daughter as a matter of course; but she is an outsider and an alien. He belongs to us."

What then? Woman's wit to the rescue! Mother's love to the rescue! Dawning hope to the rescue. A great philosophical debater this woman proves herself to be. "Yes, Lord, but even the dogs have the crumbs that fall from the children's table." What but love immeasurable could thus have moved a humble woman to measure swords with the Mighty One? And love conquers. He gives her the freedom of his treasure city. Hear his answer, "O woman, great is your faith; be it unto you even as you will." And her daughter was made whole from that very hour.

***

But this was not the only or largest of her blessings. She took with her a new thought of prayer, which was quite in line with the Master's teaching, "Men ought always to pray and not to give up." It is a lesson for all parents who have been pleading, years and years, for wayward sons and daughters. Pray on, pray on! In due season you shall reap if you do not give up. The Lord may delay his answer; but his promise is sure, "ask, and you shall receive; seek, and you shall find; knock, and it shall be opened unto you." The times and the seasons are indeed with him. He may put our faith to a painful trial; but he will not fail us. His orchard is full of trees, and all of them are fruit trees. We plead for apples, but we must wait until his apples are ripe. Our prayers are instant; "Now! Now!" we cry; but his answers are all dated with the fullness of time. Therefore, wait on the Lord; be of good courage, and he shall strengthen your heart.

June 18

The Larger Christ (Part 2 of 2)
by David James Burrell

"O woman, great is your faith: be it done unto you even as you will."
Matthew 15:21-28

The crowning blessing which this [Canaanite] woman received was a new conception of Christ. She had learned, at length, how the Vine grows over the wall. No longer could she think of Jesus as merely the Messiah of the Jews. No more could she appeal to him as one far off. She had made the acquaintance of "the larger Christ"; and so must we. Let us not suppose that the church has an exclusive right in him, since the incidental blessings of his grace fall even upon those who reject him. He is not a Christ for the wise or the respectable alone; no, behold him "eating with tax collectors and sinners." The drunkard and the prostitute are included in his mighty plan and purpose of salvation; and the same promise which comes to us is extended to them: "He that believes has everlasting life." He is not the Christ of Christendom exclusively, but of the regions beyond, as well; the regions that lie in darkness and the shadow of death. And woe be to us, to whom the Scriptures are entrusted, if we carry not his message, "Look unto me all you ends of the earth and be saved!"

***

Go, therefore, and evangelize all nations. There are numberless souls in "the regions beyond" waiting for the blessings that have made Christendom what it is. Why do we delay in the sheep pens listening to the bleating of our flocks, when the lost sheep of pagandom are out on the dark mountains? Go into the city slums and out into the highways and rural areas; follow the footsteps of the Master up into the coasts of Tyre and Sidon; seek the wandering to the uttermost parts of the earth! These are the marching orders of our Lord. He came from heaven to seek and save the lost, and to us he said, "As the Father has sent me into the world, so send I you." Oh, for an enlargement of heart to grasp the glorious gospel of the larger Christ! His blood flowed most freely in streams of salvation. There is blood enough in the fountain to wash away the whole world's sin. Tell it, O follower of Christ!

June 19

Conduct of Men Towards Their Maker (Part 1 of 2)
by Edward Payson

Mankind seems to consider God as a sort of outlaw, who has no rights; or, at least, as one whose rights may be disregarded and trampled on at pleasure. They acknowledge that promises made to each other ought to be fulfilled; but they violate, without hesitation, those promises which they often make to God, in an hour of seriousness, sickness, or affliction. They acknowledge that earthly rulers ought to be obeyed, but they seem to think that no obedience is due to the Sovereign Ruler of the universe. They acknowledge that children ought to love, honor, and submit to their parents; but they do not appear to think that either love, honor, or submission should be paid to our Father in heaven. They acknowledge that gratitude is due to human benefactors, and that to repay their favors with ingratitude is a proof of horrible wickedness; but they practically deny that any grateful return should be made to our heavenly Benefactor for his innumerable benefits, and seem to consider the wickedest ingratitude towards him as scarcely a sin.

When a son forsakes his father's house; when he refuses to comply with his entreaties to return; when he chooses to endure all the evils of poverty rather than return—we are ready to suspect that his father must be a very disagreeable, unlovely, or cruel character, since his own children cannot live with him. At least we shall think this unless we have a very bad opinion of the son. We must condemn one or the other. So, when God's own creatures, whom he has nourished and brought up as children, forsake him, and refuse to return or be reconciled, it gives other people cause to suspect that he must be a very cruel, unlovely being; and they must either conclude that he is so, or form a very bad opinion of us. Now sinners will not acknowledge that the fault is theirs; of course they throw all the blame upon their Creator, and represent him as such an unkind, cruel parent that his children cannot live with or please him. It is true that God has power to justify his own character, and to show the universe that the fault is wholly ours. But this is no thanks to us. The tendency of our conduct is still the same; it still tends to load his character with the worst shame and disgrace.

June 20

Conduct of Men Towards Their Maker (Part 2 of 2)
by Edward Payson

"Will a man rob God? Yet you have robbed Me." It is evident that you withhold your hearts from God; or, in other words, rob him of your affections, the very thing which he principally desires. And is this a small offense? Should a person rob you of the affection and esteem of the partner of your bosom, of your children, or your friends, would you not think it a great injury? Would it not in many instances be worse than robbing you of your property? And is it, then, a trivial offense for intelligent creatures to rob their Creator, Father and benefactor of that supreme place in their affections to which he has a most perfect right, and which he prizes above everything they possess? The world is, in some form or other, the great Diana [Roman goddess], the grand idol of all its inhabitants, so long as they continue in their natural sinful state. They bow down to it; they worship it; they spend and are spent for it; they educate their children in its service; their hearts, their minds, their memories, their imaginations, are full of it; their tongues speak of it; their hands grasp it; their feet pursue it. In a word, it is all in all to them, while they give scarcely a word, a look, or a thought to him who made and preserves them; and who is really all in all.

From the manner in which we habitually treat the Bible, we may learn what our feelings and dispositions are towards God; for as we treat the word of God, so should we treat God himself, if he were to come and reside among us, in a human form, as he once dwelt on earth in the form of his Son. The contents of Scripture are a perfect transcript of the divine mind. If, then, God should come to dwell among us, he would teach the same things that the Scriptures teach, and pronounce upon us the same sentence which they pronounce. We should therefore feel toward him as we now feel towards them. If we reverence, and love, and obey the Scriptures, then we should reverence, love and obey God. But if we dislike or disbelieve the Scriptures, if we seldom study them, or read them only with indifference and neglect, we treat God in the same manner. Never would he be a welcome guest in a family where his word is neglected.

June 21

Extracts from the Letters of General Gordon (Part 1 of 2)
by General C.G. "Chinese" Gordon

Boldly and humbly study the Scriptures. God's dwelling in us is the key to them; they are a sealed book as long as you do not realize this truth, which is sure and certain, whether you feel it or not. Look on all trials as inevitable; you cannot make one hair white or black. No circumstances or annoyances are preventable or accidental. It is hard for the flesh to thank God for trials, but it is our duty to do so. The blending of our will with His is the perfection of worship; no prayers, almsgiving, or church-going are as acceptable to Him. Die now, and you will never die ("You are dead, and your life is hid with Christ in God").

I am at present two men: the one violent, brutal, hard, and in every way despicable; the other would hurt no one. Torn by these conflicting factions, my only rest at times is in thinking over my union with God; there and there alone can I find peace. I have had many enjoyable things in the world's opinion, but there is nothing in any way to be compared to the study of God's word. How wonderfully it fits in with the various events of life! Examine all things through the microscope of His Scriptures, how He turns this and that event; how some are blinded for a time, and the very things they condemn are done by them; it is an analysis which nothing escapes, and which shows each man to be the same weak creature as his brother; ostriches we are, all of us, to ourselves, and generally to others. Poor, poor indeed is the religion of Christ, if it did not contain more than is generally accepted. Where is its comfort? Where is its support? It is a delightful thing to be a fatalist, not as that word is generally used, but to accept that, *when things happen* and *not* before, God has for some wise reason so ordained them: all things, not only the great things, but all the circumstances of life. That is what to me is meant by the words "you are dead." We have nothing further to do, when the scroll of events is unrolled, than to accept them as being for the best. With this belief all I can say is, that in the middle of troubles and worries no one can have peace until he thus stands firm upon his God—that gives a superhuman strength.

June 22

Extracts from the Letters of General Gordon (Part 2 of 2)
by General C.G. "Chinese" Gordon

You are aware I look on death as being life. The end of our term on earth is much to be desired, for at the best it is a groaning life. I do earnestly desire that I were "ripe"; but I suppose I am not, for here I stay and am well, while others are gathered. I believe we have no more pain in leaving the world than we had in entering it, yet, to the eye the body seems in pain; how odd also it is that for years we know nothing, though we live and give plenty of trouble. God's indwelling is all in all, the great secret. We all have to go through the same path, and nothing we can say will cause any change; the experience must be made for each by each. For my part I feel caged on this earth, for the Bible has such very comforting promises, which all fit in so beautifully, that one longs to move into the future.

The inspired Paul says, "Know you not that your body is the temple of the Holy Ghost?" God dwells in you. He speaks of the body being the temple in which the Holy Ghost was, and is, embodied. What a wonderful thing we cannot be joined to Christ except by the Holy Ghost! If He who is the bond of union is absent, there can be no union. "No man can say Jesus is Lord, but by the Holy Ghost."

If the Holy Ghost is embodied in us now, He must be embodied in us forever, for His absence would break our union with the Lord; so that in heaven God the Son is embodied, and God the Holy Ghost is embodied, yet there are not two, but one, for the Head, Christ, is one with the body, the Church. I speak of a great mystery—Christ and His Church (Ephesians 5:32). The master key of the Scriptures is our union with Christ, by God the Holy Ghost in us. That is the life by faith, for if you examine, you will find that faith is distinctly the Holy Ghost's living presence in us. Anyone, to whom God gives to be much with Him, cannot even suffer a regret at death. For what is death to a believer? It is a closer approach to Him, whom, even through the veil, he is ever with.

June 23

Doubt
by George Matheson

"They have taken away my Lord, and I know not where they have laid Him."
John 20:13

To whom were these words spoken? To the angels. What a strange audience! One would have said they were more fit for the ears of a society of skeptics. Do they not breathe a spirit of the deepest doubt—a despair of the very body of Christ? Why is the doubt, why is the despair addressed to the angels? Because all honest doubt is prayer, and is borne on high by heavenly messengers. To whom do I cry when I am in doubt? Not to man, surely. I may proclaim my disbelief to a large gathering of men; but, if I am honest, I am speaking only at them, not to them; my real listener is God. My cry is the cry to touch the print of the nails. It sounds, below, like a denial; but, above, it is interpreted as a supplication. Men on earth say, "he blasphemes"; but the angels in heaven exclaim, "Behold, he prays." My soul, are you troubled with the problems of the mind? Are you beating against the bars that shut you out from flight—the flight of prayer? No, but the beating is a part of your flight, a part of your prayer.

It may be that the doubt is your search for God; in truth it is God's search for you. Only through God can you learn the barrier to God. No man would feel imprisoned if he had not an experience of liberty. Why do the wings beat against the cage? If there were nothing seen outside of it, there would be no beating; the cage would be the universe. But when the "beyond" appears, you are frantic to be free. It is the sun that makes your shadow; it is the music that makes your silence; it is the power of flight that makes your chains known. Your sense of bondage is the vision of the beyond; it is God that makes you want God. Your cry is a prayer. It is not yet the prayer of faith, but it is the prayer for faith. It brings nothing in its hand but the sense of its emptiness; yet God shall take the hand and fill it with His own.

June 24

On God's Terribleness and Gentleness (Part 1 of 2)
by Joseph Parker

Self-sufficiency on the part of man is an offense to God; not only so, it is a frustration to man himself. All efforts at completeness and independence of strength end in shame. How infinite is our folly in seeking to remove, by our own power, the mountains and hills that bar our way! God says He will remove them for us; why should we turn away His mighty arm? He claims such work as His own; why should we meddle with it as if we could do it better than He? But some of us will meddle: we persist in seeking omnipotence in our own hands, and trying to reach the tone which winds and seas obey. We will do it.

The devil urges us, and we yield. He says, "Be your own God," and we snatch at the suggestion as a prize. He says, "This little mountain you might surely manage to remove;" and then we set to work with pickaxe and shovel, and lo, the mountain grows as we strike it! Still the devil says, "It stands to reason that you must be making some impression upon it; try again;" and we try again, and again we fail—the mountain does not know us, the rock resents our intrusion, and having wasted our strength, the devil laughs at our impotence, and tells us in bitter mockery that we shall do better next time! Yes! Next time—next time—and then next time—and then hell! God says to us, when we stand at the foot of great hills and mountains, "I will beat them into dust, I will scatter the dust to the winds; there shall be a level path for your feet, if you will just put your trust in me." Here He is beside us, in front of us, around us, to help, to lead, to bless us in every way, always at our right hand, always within reach of our prayer, always putting out His hand when we come to dangerous places. The most unpolished mind might dream of God's infinite majesty, but only the richest quality of heart could have discovered Him in the touch of gentleness and the service of coming down to our level. Their theology is, indeed, to some men a frightful ghost. They would be happier if they were atheists. Behold! Behold! I call you to a God whose very terribleness may be turned into an assurance of security, and whose love is infinite, unchanging, eternal!

June 25

On God's Terribleness and Gentleness (Part 2 of 2)
by Joseph Parker

Men of business! you whose barns are full, whose rivers overflow, on whose estates the sun has written "Prosperity," and into whose storehouses autumn has forced the richest of her golden harvest, hear me! Do you not know that these things are all gifts of God, and that He who gave them can also withdraw them? "I will destroy and devour at once—I will dry up all their herbs." He has right of way through our fields and orchards; our vineyards and olive groves are His, and He can blow upon them until they wither, and cause their blossom to go up like the dust. "I have seen the wicked in great power, and spreading himself like a green bay tree, yet he passed away, and lo, he was not: yes, I sought him, but he could not be found." Not a fiber of his root could be discovered! All gone—the great branches gone—the bark gone—the trunk gone—the root gone—and the very name had perished from the memory of men! It is poor prosperity that is not held by God's favor. Gold goes a little way if it is not sanctified by prayer and giving of thanks. Bread cannot satisfy, unless it be broken by God's hands. Our fields may look well at night, but in the morning they may have been trampled by an invisible destroyer. It is because of inevitable judgment that I call upon men to walk in the light of righteousness in all the transactions of life.

Children of God! you especially who are called to suffering and weakness and great unrest because of numerous failings, God offers you his hand. Are you blind? He says, I will lead the blind. Are you full of care? He says, Let me carry your burden. Are you in sorrow? He says. Call upon me in the day of trouble, and I will answer you. Is there a very steep road before you at this moment—in business, in your family, in your responsibilities? He says, I will level mountains and hills, and the rough places shall be made smooth. So you are not alone—not alone, for the Father is with you. He is with you as a Father, not to test your strength, but to increase it; not to make experiments upon you, but to magnify His grace in you by working out for you a wonderful redemption. Rest on God. His arm, not your own, must be your strength. Fear God, and no other fear shall ever trouble you.

June 26

The Mystery of Iniquity
by Phillips Brooks

The mystery of iniquity...
2 Thessalonians 2:7

The first thought around which the grand wonder of the atonement grows into shape is this thought of sin as a real live thing standing before us to be fought with, to be conquered, to be killed. Not of a mere moral weakness to be strengthened, or an intellectual emptiness to be filled, but of an enemy to be slain, a giant to be subdued. To meet that enemy, to slay that giant, Christ comes forth with his wonderful nature. He undertakes a distinct and dreadful struggle. The sacred conflict goes on between Christ and Satan, in a region apart from, above, and separate from man. We see its outward manifestation in the agony of the cross. We see, but do not comprehend even that. All the deeper battle goes on out of our sight. We know not how it turns out until the word of God comes to tell us that the victory is won by our Redeemer, and that Satan is trampled into death by the dying Christ. You see how true a mystery it is. We know nothing but the fact. That we know perfectly. That shining, splendid fact, that gracious, glorious fact; the fact of the Lord's victory and of Satan's fall stands forth so clear that none can doubt it. It takes its place as the one certain, central fact of hope. By it the living live, by it the dying die; in it the glorified rejoice forever. But who shall go behind the fact, and tell its method? Who shall say how, why, where, that all-availing victory was won? Only the divine and human Christ met the power of sin and conquered it; and every human being in that triumph of the One Great Humanity stood as a potential victor over his mighty and malicious foe.

O wondrous mystery! Who asks to know the way? Who does not take the glorious truth and fasten desperate hands upon it, and draw himself up by it into hope? Who will not stand content and let the clouds cover the awful mystery of his great Master's struggle, so long as out of the clouds he hears the assuring voice of God: "This is my beloved Son, in whom I am well pleased. Whoever comes unto me by him shall not perish, but shall have everlasting life."

June 27

God's Rest for Believers
by Bryan L. Herde

Anyone who enters God's rest also rests from his own work, just as God did from His.
Hebrews 4:10

Biblical rest is a perpetual state of trust: wills have been exchanged, obedience is subconscious, God's glory is the first consideration, and patient waiting is the new normal. We believe that when God says that we are to rest from our works, just as He rested from His, that He Himself will fulfill all the commandments and requirements He gave to us in His Word. Not only that, but because we have learned to slow down by becoming patient people, we are now able to observe and marvel at just how active the Lord is in building His Kingdom all around us. Whereas we previously thought that our responsibility was always to be intense, frenzied and hyperactive for Jesus, we, unknowingly, were actually "elbowing" God out of our lives. It is now, as we wait upon Him, that we have the awesome privilege of participating in His working that flows through us into this world and the lives of others all around us.

We cease from our works, but we experience more fulfillment than we have ever known before. Instead of striving to produce the proper fruit, we abide in Christ and He produces the fruit. Instead of jumping up to fill every need we hear about, we pray and wait for our Lord to direct us as He sees fit. Instead of creating a checklist of His commandments to execute, we yield ourselves to Him constantly and let Him fulfill all His commands through us—in His time, in His way and in His power.

We do not fear inactivity and lack of productivity. We know that we have no sovereign ability to measure our own results. We are simply and contentedly a tool in His hands for Him to use as He pleases. If Christ should choose that our purpose in life is to perform a single act, or we are taken throughout the world to preach the Gospel, then as King, Jesus alone has the right to decide the role and productivity level of His subjects.

June 28

How Christ Transcends the Law
by Catherine (Mrs. William) Booth

Which is why, my brethren, you also have become dead to the law by the body of Christ,
that you should belong to another, to him who is raised from the dead,
so that we should bring forth fruit unto God.
Romans 7:4

What God does for us through Jesus Christ outside of us is one thing, and what He does in us by Jesus Christ is another thing, but the two are simultaneous, or one so immediately succeeds the other, that we hardly discern the interval. Now, I say, I want power to enable me to meet that temptation which is coming on me tomorrow, as it came on me yesterday, and, if Jesus Christ pardons me, and leaves me under the reigning power of my old appetites, what has he done for me? I shall be down in the mud, and tomorrow night I shall be as condemned as ever. I want power. I want regeneration—as the Holy Spirit has put it. I want the *renewing* of the *spirit* of my mind. I want to be created anew in Christ Jesus; "made a new creature."

Now, this is where Jesus Christ transcends the Law. The Law could not renew the spirit of my mind. It could only show me what a guilty rebel I was. It could not put a better spirit in me. It could not extract the venom, but only show it to me, and make me writhe on account of it. But Jesus Christ comes and does this for me—He gives me power. How does He give it to me? *He unites me to Himself.* I am dead to the Law. He delivers me from the condemning power of the Law when He pardons me, and then He does not leave me there, but He "marries" me to Himself. He unites me "to another" husband, and then I attain power to bring forth fruit unto God. Under the Law's power, my old "husband," I could do nothing but agonize, wrestle, and desire. There was no power in me until Jesus Christ comes and unites me to Himself, then He gives me power to bring forth fruit unto God. It is by the *union of my soul with Him.* You say, "Explain it!" I cannot. We cannot explain it, but we know it.

June 29

Choked Channels
by S.D. Gordon

Do you know what kind of a Christian you are? There are at least three others that do. First of all there is Satan. He knows. Many of our church officers are skilled in gathering and compiling statistics, but they cannot hold a candle to Satan in this matter of exact information. He is the ablest of all statisticians, second only to one other. He keeps careful record of every one of us, and knows just how far we are interfering with his plans. He knows that some of us good, respectable people, as common reckoning goes, neither help God nor hinder Satan. Does that sound rather hard? But is it not true? He has no objection to such people being counted in as Christians. Indeed, he rather prefers to have it so. Their presence inside the church circle helps him mightily. He knows what kind of a Christian you are. Do you know?

Then there is the great outer circle of non-Christian people—they know. Hungry for something they have not and know not just what it is; with high ideals, though vague, of what a Christian life should be. And they look eagerly to us for what they have thought we had, and are so often keenly disappointed that our ideals, our life, is so much like others who profess nothing. And when here and there they meet persons whose acts are dominated by a pure, high spirit, whose faces reflect a sweet radiance among all circumstances, and whose lives send out a rare fragrance of gladness and kindliness and controlling peace, they are quick to recognize that, to them, intangible something that makes such people different. The world knows what kind of Christians we are. Do we know?

There is a third one watching us today with intense interest. The Lord Jesus! Sitting up yonder in glory, with the scar-marks of earth on face and form, looking eagerly down upon us who stand for Him in the world that crucified Him. He knows. I imagine Him saying, "There is that one down there whom I died for, who bears my name; if I had the control of that life what power I would gladly breathe in and out of it, but he is so absorbed in other things." The Master is thinking about you, studying your life, longing to carry out His plan if He could only get permission, and is sorely disappointed in many of us. He knows. Do you know?

June 30

All for Good (Part 1 of 2)
by John R. MacDuff

*And we know that all things work together for good to them that love God,
to them who are called according to His purpose.*
Romans 8:28

The Apostle here makes the glorious assertion that whatever happens to God's children—their joys, sorrows, comforts, crosses, losses—all are a part of a Divine plan and arrangement, whose beginning and result is for their good. There is nothing as challenging to belief as this. That bitter pang which tore up my hopes by the root! that unexpected heritage of poverty! that anguished sickbed! that crushing sorrow! how can I write "good" upon these? How can this broken heart ever endorse such a statement as that of the sacred writer?

Yes! but faith *should* do so; faith *can* do so. Paul would have uttered what no Roman Christian, or any other Christian, would have attributed, had he said "we see." But observe, his language is the statement of believing trust: "the confidence of things not seen" (Hebrews 11:1). He says, "we know." Behind that dark cloud he speaks with assured conviction of a shining face. At that loom, which the world calls "fate," with these tangled, confused, crooked threads, he could tell of a Divine Artist who holds the shuttle in His hand, and who understands (what the spectator often does not understand) that all is for good. Can Paul's Lord be really supervising and controlling all? So may have reasoned some unfaithful hearts at the very time when in his dungeon he was writing this clause in one of his letters: "I would not have you to be ignorant, brethren, that the things which have happened to me have happened for advancing the Gospel" (Philippians 1:12).

How wide is this assertion of the Apostle! He does not say, "We know that *some* things," or "*most* things," or "*joyous* things." But "*all* things." From the minutest to the most momentous; from the humblest event in daily provision to the great crisis-hours in grace. And all things "work"—they *are* working; not all things *have* worked, or *shall* work, but it is a present operation. And then all things "*work together*." It is a beautiful blending.

July 1

All for Good (Part 2 of 2)
by John R. MacDuff

And we know that all things work together for good to them that love God,
to them who are called according to His purpose.
Romans 8:28

Many different colors, in themselves raw and unsightly, are required in order to weave the harmonious pattern. Many separate tones and notes of music, even discords and dissonances, are required to make up the harmonious song of praise. Many separate wheels and joints are required to make the piece of machinery. Take a thread separately, or a note separately, or a wheel or a tooth of a wheel separately, and there may be neither use nor beauty discernible. But *complete* the web, *combine* the notes, *put together* the separate parts of steel and iron, and you see how perfect and symmetrical is the result. Here is the lesson for faith: "What I do," says God, "you know not now, but you shall know hereafter."

We must, meanwhile, take the bitter with the sweet. The Great Physician knows that all the ingredients in His dealings are for our good. He compounds them. He gives us the cup to drink; and "shall we not drink it?" God is said to make His chariot—What? Is it the sunshine? Is it the clusters of gleaming stars or radiant planets? No, it is the *clouds*. But that cloudy chariot has an axle of love. And though clouds and darkness are round about His throne, mercy and truth go continually before His face.

Beautifully says our countryman, the distinguished missionary and traveler, [David] Livingstone: "We who see such small segments of the mighty cycles of God's sovereign actions, often imagine some to be failures, which He does not. If we could see a larger arc of the great sovereign cycle, we might sometimes rejoice when we weep. But God does not give an account of any of His matters. We must just trust to His wisdom." Let us be assured of this, He has our best interests at heart. He has what is here called our *"good"* in view. It may not be, it will not be, the world's definition of good—riches, honors, glory, worldly prosperity. But it will be better. It is our *soul's* good, ripening the immortal part of us for glory.

July 2

The Voice of God's Silence
by George Matheson

And when the voice was past, Jesus was found alone.
Luke 9:36

There is a revelation in the silence. There are times when the voice of God dies upon the height, and there is no testimony from the mountain. We call, but it answers not; we question, but there is no reply. Yet there is a substitute; the voice of God is followed by the form of man. God hides himself that I may see my brother. It is a glorious descent. On the top of the mountain earth seems very small. Its crosses dwindle in the light of eternity. I am in danger of becoming unsympathetic to common pain. The cries of the weary are lost in the songs of the redeemed. Therefore, unexpectedly my Father comes to me in a chariot of silence. He veils Himself from my sight. He shuts the doors of the upper sanctuary. He throws a cloud over the former glory. He forces me to look down instead of up. He leads me from the crown to the cross; from the opened heaven to the imprisoned earth. He shows me Jesus alone without His entourage, without His pomp, without His kingdom—sinking with pale expression under the weight of human suffering. The silence of God reveals Man.

You who are beating in vain against the problems of eternity, turn aside and be free. God's silence is a voice. It forbids you to stand gazing up into heaven. It tells you that life is not ripe for the tabernacle on the hill. It calls you back from the mountain to the plain—from the Divine search to the human pity. It puts the veil of Moses on your face; it teaches you meekness by the absence of vision. Obey the silence of God. Go down to the Son of Man among the darkened heavens. Go down to watch with Him in His hour of humiliation. Go down to accompany Him in the agony of man for man. There shall be no loss to you in the silencing of the Father's voice, if only by doing it you shall find "Jesus alone."

July 3

The Vulnerable Heart of God
by Bryan L. Herde

God set Himself up for tremendous pain and hurt when He gave men and women the right to accept or reject His offer of salvation. God's unconditional love, poured into and through Jesus Christ, had one condition for His love to be fully received, and that was to believe in Jesus Christ alone for salvation. Only then was unconditional love enabled to continue its full flow for those who now know Him as their Heavenly Father.

Long before the Son of God came to Earth, God was revealing and communicating His great love, and inseparably, His vulnerability to possible rejection by those to whom He was incredibly gracious, kind, merciful, generous and loving.

I hear all the time that we seem to see two Gods in the Bible: the God of the Old Testament and the God of the New Testament. Nothing could be further from the truth.

God is not like us. He alone can be all of who He is simultaneously without diminishment or dominance by any one characteristic. That is why God is a righteous judge, a loving father, a gentle friend, and an all-powerful sovereign operating in any capacity, or all capacities at once, fully, without being distracted or rendered powerless or lessened by any other capacity. This is really impossible for us to fully grasp because we are so limited by our mortality and our sin. But God is without limitations.

That is why I can approach Him with any issue in my life, or the lives of others, or the events of the world, or anything and everything without restriction. He is always right and true in every way and at all times.

I love the fact that this God, the one and only God, can be so vulnerable, while never diminished in His greatness. And I love Him all the more for it!

July 4

Why I Believe the Bible: Its Completeness (Part 1 of 3)
by David James Burrell

The Bible is a comprehensive summary of all spiritual truth, as far as a knowledge of spiritual truth is necessary to our temporal and eternal well-being. It is so characterized by Paul in one of his letters to Timothy, where he says:

> Abide in the things which you have learned and have been assured of, knowing of whom you have learned them, and that from a babe you have known the Sacred Writings, which are able to make you wise unto salvation, through faith which is in Christ Jesus. Every Scripture inspired of God is profitable for teaching, for reproof, for correction, for instruction which is in righteousness; *that the man of God may be complete, furnished completely unto every good work* (2 Timothy 3:14-16, Revised Version).

It thus appears that, in the opinion of Paul at least, all spiritual truth, so far as it is needed for our guidance, is summarized in the Scriptures. This fact is worthy of emphasis in view of what is being said about "progressive revelation" [*The concept that the sections of the Bible that were written later contain a fuller revelation of God compared to earlier sections.* Taken from *Wikipedia*]. Do we affirm, then, that there is no such thing as progress in the understanding of truth? By no means! But we do insist that all progress in spiritual knowledge is within the confines of this Book; as John Robinson said, when bidding farewell to the Pilgrims who were embarking at Delft Haven: "I pray you to remember that new light will be ever breaking forth from the Word of God!" New light, ever; but no new Sun of Righteousness.

It is a singular fact that, despite the philosophical research of centuries, no truth within the sphere of spiritual things has ever been discovered beyond the boundaries of Scripture: by which it would appear that Scripture contains the ultimate and adequate sum total required for the supply of human need. There are no limitations in God but there is a definite limit to our knowledge of him.

July 5

Why I Believe the Bible: Its Completeness (Part 2 of 3)
by David James Burrell

As there is no new force in the material universe, though there is no end of new adjustments and applications of force, also as there are no new principles in the spiritual province, there are continually new interpretations and larger uses of them. The sun, which is our source of light and energy, is not changed to meet the demands of a progressive world though there are many "new things under the sun." The Bible, in the same manner, though closed and finally sealed long centuries ago, was divinely adjusted to the progress of all succeeding ages. The uninspired word "Finis" on the last page of the Bible is as true as though it were incorporated in it. The meaning of that word is that the revelation of truth contained therein is so comprehensive that there would never be need of an *addendum*. It stands like a challenge to the progress of the future, saying, "Replace me or supplement me if you can!"

The last words of the last chapter of the last portion of Scripture are significant: "I testify unto every man that hears the words of the prophecies (i.e., teachings) of this Book; If any man shall add unto them, God shall add unto him the plagues which are written in this Book; and if any man shall take away from the words of the Book of this prophecy, God shall take away his part from the tree of life and out of the holy city which are written in this Book." I am aware that those who deny the integrity of the Scriptures are in the habit of saying that the warning referred to was intended to apply only to that particular portion of Scripture which contains it, namely "the Book of the Revelation of John." But this does not help the situation, for two reasons: *first,* because it is not easy to understand the grounds upon which this limitation is based or how its originators discovered it; and *second,* because, even allowing the argument, they would probably be as reluctant (putting it mildly) to consent to the full inspiration and trustworthiness of John's account of his apocalyptic visions as of any other portion of the Book. The only escape from the dilemma on their part is to deny the singular truth of the Scriptures *in total:* which, frankly stated, is precisely what they do.

July 6

Why I Believe the Bible: Its Completeness (Part 3 of 3)
by David James Burrell

At this point attention is called to a fact which is difficult to explain on the part of those so-called "Biblical experts" who deny—and not infrequently ridicule—the absolute and inerrant inspiration of the original autographs of Scripture. The business of textual criticism is to purge all current versions of unwarranted changes and additions by careful and scholarly comparison with the earliest manuscripts, so as to arrive, as nearly as possible, at the original text.

But why so? If this Book is to be classed as "mere literature" and treated accordingly, why not seek for the latest instead of the first edition? The textbooks in use when we were children at school are all obsolete. Those that are now being studied by our boys and girls must presently be revised and "brought up to date." The last editions are required in every case. Why, then, should the first edition of the Scriptures be in such universal demand? Is not this a practical admission that the original manuscript of Scripture, if found, would prove to be the highest authority in spiritual things for this and every age? In other words, marvelous to tell, the Bible, written so many centuries ago, must have been intended to abide through all generations as an unalterable Book; and this because it is full and complete, measuring out to the entire race its supply for all moral needs from the beginning to the very end of time.

God's Word
by Bryan L. Herde

Eternal, inerrant, alive and dependable.
Relevant, insightful, worthy and applicable.
God-breathed, Spirit-filled, exceptional.
Faithful, powerful, intentional.
God's heart revealed, His will unveiled.
His desires unsealed, His plans prevailed.

July 7

Why I Believe the Bible: Its Trustworthiness (Part 1 of 3)
by David James Burrell

No claim of inerrancy is made for the King James version of the Scriptures, nor for any other of the countless versions current in the world today.

It is claimed, however, *first*, that the original manuscripts, as they left the hands of "holy men who wrote as they were moved by the Spirit of God," must have been free from error in the necessity of the case; and second, that the errors in existing copies are of such a character as to convince an unprejudiced mind that the originals were without a flaw.

Whether or not the assurance of such inerrancy in the original manuscripts is worthwhile is another question. There are those who say, "What matters it to us whether the writings on sheepskin scrolls which perished long centuries ago were flawless or not? We never saw them and have practically nothing to do with them." To whom we answer: *first*, our belief in their integrity has a vital bearing not only on our opinion of the truthfulness of God but also of the character of those who claimed to be moved by his Spirit in declaring his holy will. It is possible to believe that a man whose mother died before he set eyes upon her might be wholly indifferent as to the question whether she was a good woman or not, but most of us would feel differently about it.

Our *second* answer to the man who objects to the importance of believing in the integrity of the original manuscripts is that our view with respect to that matter cannot but influence our attitude toward the trustworthiness of current versions. A thirsty traveler will readily drink from a brook by the roadside if he can trace its flow upward to a clear fountain in the high hills. He knows that the slight impurities due to the wearing of its banks have not impaired its wholesomeness. If, on the other hand, he were uncertain as to whether its origin were in a spring or a cesspool he would hesitate until he found out.

July 8

Why I Believe the Bible: Its Trustworthiness (Part 2 of 3)
by David James Burrell

Our *third* answer to deniers of the Bible's inerrancy is that the discrepancies in current versions are of such a character as to furnish presumptive proof of the entire correctness of the originals. It would naturally be supposed that a book of such antiquity and of such complex composition would suffer all sorts of disastrous changes in coming down the ages. Think of the tens of thousands of hands through which it has passed; of the copies made by the ancient Scribes with infinite pains; of the numberless transcriptions by medieval monks in their lonely rooms; of the translations into half a thousand languages and dialects. What possibilities of error! For remember that all these transcribers and translators were fallible men. Think of the temptation on their part to insert their personal views in the body of the inspired text, or to eliminate what did not please them. Think what sort of a Bible we would have if these transcribers and translators had been like the "higher critics" of our time. Think of these possibilities, and then look at the Scriptures as they are in the current versions of today.

The marvel is not that there are variations and discrepancies here, but that they are so trivial and insignificant. They are indeed of such a character as to convince any candid mind that they had no place in the original manuscript but have crept into the text in the process of transmission along the ages. Remarkably, there is none that affects in the slightest degree the integrity of the doctrine and ethics of the Book. If the destructive critics are taken at their word the Bible is full of frightful errors; its prophecies have failed, its history is unhistorical, its science is unscientific and its chronicles are myths. It need scarcely be said that, so far from being a true statement of the case, not a single error has yet been indicated which cannot be most reasonably explained as either purely imaginary or unimportant. But here is a marvelous thing: these enemies of Scripture are themselves insistent with one voice, that the errors in the Bible which they so loudly exploit do not in any degree impair the integrity of its doctrinal system and ethical code!

July 9

Why I Believe the Bible: Its Trustworthiness (Part 3 of 3)
by David James Burrell

These things being so, we are justified in concluding that the inspired Book has in some manner been singularly safeguarded in its transmission along the centuries. The same gracious God who protected his secretaries—those "holy men who wrote as they were moved by his Spirit"—from all possibility of error in the original manuscript, has apparently by a special sovereign control so protected the "flying scroll" in its journey down to us, that transcribers and translators have left an "infallible rule of faith and practice" in the versions now current among men.

If it is to be urged again that we are not practically concerned with the original manuscript, inasmuch as no living man has ever seen it; we observe that a similar objection could be offered against Christ himself with equal force on precisely the same grounds. The objection proves either too little or too much.

No living man has ever seen the Incarnate Word of God. He lived only thirty-three years in this world of ours and then vanished from sight. The only knowledge that we have of him, apart from the Scriptures, is through his followers; for every Christian is, so to speak, a current version of the Incarnate Word. Christ, like the Bible, has suffered by transcription through the ages.

It is nevertheless of supreme importance that we should believe that Christ, as he once lived on earth, was the perfect Son of God. The very mistakes of believers, in their earnest yet inadequate efforts to copy his life and character, are evidences of his perfection. We are forever striving to get back to the original Christ; precisely as reverent students of the Scriptures seek, by both textual and historical criticism, to reach the "original text," that is, the "first edition" of the written Word of God.

July 10

Ill-Temper: The Elder Brother (Part 1 of 4)
by Henry Drummond

"He was angry, and would not go in."
Luke 15:28

The twelve disciples—one of them is a devil. Jesus upon the Cross, pure and regal—on either side a thief. And here, as conspicuously, in this fifteenth chapter of Luke, the most exquisite painting in the Bible touched off at the foot with the black thundercloud of the elder brother—perfect, as a mere dramatic situation. But this conjunction, of course, is more than artistic. Apart from its reference to the Pharisees, the association of these two characters—the prodigal and his brother—side by side has a deep moral significance. When we look into Sin, not in its theological aspects, but in its everyday clothes, we find that it divides itself into two kinds. We find that there are sins of the body and sins of character. Or more narrowly, sins of the passions, including all forms of lust and selfishness, and sins of temperament. The prodigal is the instance in the New Testament of sins of passion; the elder brother, of sins of temperament.

One would say, at a first glance, that it was the younger brother in this picture who was the thundercloud. It was he who had dimmed all the virtues, and covered himself and his home with shame. And men have always pointed to the runaway son in contrast with his domestic brother, as the type of all that is worst in human character. Possibly the estimate is wrong. Possibly the elder brother is the worse. We judge sins, as we judge most things, by their outward form. We arrange the vices of our neighbors according to a scale which society has silently adopted, placing the more fleshly and public at the foot, the slightly less fleshly higher up, and then by some strange process the scale becomes obliterated. *Coarser* and *finer* are but words of our own. The chances are, if anything, that the finer sins are the worse. The subtle and unseen sin, that sin in the part of the nature nearest to the spiritual, ought to be more degrading than any other.

July 11

Ill-Temper: The Elder Brother (Part 2 of 4)
by Henry Drummond

"He was angry, and would not go in."
Luke 15:28

One of the first things to startle us about sins of temperament, is their strange *compatibility with high moral character*. The prodigal's elder brother, without doubt, was a man of high principle. When his father divided unto them his living, he had the chance to sow his wild oats if he liked. Instead, like a dutiful son he chose his career: he would be his father's right hand, and cheer and comfort his declining years. So to the servants he became a pattern of tirelessness; to the neighbors an example of thrift and faithfulness. For association with lofty character is a painful circumstance of this deformity. And it suggests strange doubts as to the real virtue of much that is considered to be virtue and gets credit for the name. In reality we have no criteria for estimating the true worth of men who are depicted as models of all the virtues. Everything depends on motive. The virtues may be real or only apparent, even as the vices may be real though not apparent.

But it is an instance of misconception about the nature of sin that with most men this counts for nothing. Many of those who "sow to the flesh" regard their form of sin as trifling compared with the inconsistent and unchristian graces of those who profess to sow to the spirit. Many a man, for example, who thinks nothing of getting drunk would refuse to do an ungenerous deed or speak a belittling word. And, as already said, it is really a question whether or not he is right. One man sins high up in his nature, the other low down; and the drunken spendthrift, on the whole, may be a better man than the acid Christian. "Verily, I say unto you," said Jesus to the priests, "the tax collectors and the prostitutes go into the kingdom of God before you." The fact, then, that there are these two distinct sets of sins, and that few of us indulge in both, but most of us indulge in the one or the other, explains the compatibility of moral conduct with much unloveliness of character. Now it is this very association which makes sins of temperament appear so harmless.

July 12

Ill-Temper: The Elder Brother (Part 3 of 4)
by Henry Drummond

"He was angry, and would not go in."
Luke 15:28

***

The point at which temper interferes with the intellect is in all matters of judgment. A quick temper really incapacitates sound judgment. Decisions are generated at a white heat, without time to collect grounds or hear explanations. Then it takes a humbler spirit than most of us possess to reverse them when once they are made. No doubt the elder brother secretly believed himself a fool the moment after his back was turned on the door. But he had taken his stand; he had said "I will not go in," and neither his father's pleadings nor his own sense of the growing absurdity of the situation—think of the man standing outside his own door—were able to shake him. Giving in to temper betrays a man into immature judgment, that is quickly followed by an inappropriate action, and then having placed one's self in the position to have to defend that action (especially, after having made such a fuss about it)—this is the natural progression and subsequent result when the sin of temper overrides the intellect.

***

Self-disgust and humiliation may come at once, but a good deal else within has to wait until the spirit is tuned again. For instance, prayer must wait. A man cannot pray until the sourness is out of his soul. He must first forgive his brother who trespassed against him before he can go to God to have his own trespasses forgiven. Then look at the effect on the father, or on the guests, or even on the servants—that scene outside had cast its miserable gloom on the entire company. We drive men from Christ's door many times by our sorry performance. Until men can say of us, "They suffer long and are kind, they are not easily provoked, do not behave themselves rudely, bear all things, think no evil," we have no chance against the world. One repulsive Christian will drive away a score of prodigals. God's love for poor sinners is very wonderful, but God's patience with ill-natured saints is a deeper mystery.

July 13

Ill-Temper: The Elder Brother (Part 4 of 4)
by Henry Drummond

"He was angry, and would not go in."
Luke 15:28

The worst of the misery caused by bad temper is that it does no good. Nothing in the world causes such irritating, long-lasting, unnecessary and fruitless pain. And Christ's words, therefore, when He refers to the breach of the law of love, are most severe; "If any man offend one of these little ones," He says, "it were better for him that a millstone were hanged about his neck, and that he were cast into the depths of the sea." And however impossible it may be to realize that now, however we may condone it as a pardonable weakness or small infirmity, there is no greater sin. A sin against love is a sin against God, for God is love.

***

It is quite useless, by force of will, to seek to empty the angry passions out of our life. Who has not made a thousand resolutions in this direction, only to behold them with unutterable shame dashed to pieces with the first temptation? The soul is to be made sweet not by taking the acidic fluids out, but by putting something in—a great love, God's great love. This is to work a "chemical change" upon them, to renovate and regenerate them, to dissolve them in its own rich fragrant substance. If a man lets this into his life, his cure is complete; if not, it is hopeless.

***

There are many heavens in the world even now from which we all shut ourselves out by our own exclusiveness—heavens of friendship, of family life, of Christian work, of compassionate ministries to the poor and ignorant and distressed. Because of some personal irritation, some disapproval of methods, because the types of work or some of the workers are not exactly to our taste, we play the elder brother, we are angry and will not go in. This is the naked truth of it, we are simply angry and will not go in. And this generates, if we could see it, its own worst penalty; for there is no severer punishment than just to be left outside, perhaps, to grow old alone, unripe, loveless and unloved. We are angry and will not go in.

July 14

The Humanheartedness of Jesus
by James Russell Miller

The central fact in every true Christian life is a personal friendship with Jesus. Men were called to follow him, to leave all and cling to him, to believe on him, to trust him, to love him, to obey him; and the result was the transformation of their lives into his own beauty. That which alone makes one a Christian is being a friend of Jesus. Friendship transforms—all human friendship transforms. We become like those with whom we live in close, intimate relations. Life flows into life, heart and heart are knit together, spirits blend, and the two friends become one.

We have but little to give to Christ; yet it is a comfort to know that our friendship really is precious to him, and adds to his joy, poor and meager though its best may be—but he has infinite blessings to give to us. "I call you friends." No other gift he gives to us can equal in value the love and friendship of his heart. No good man's money is ever worth so much as his love. Certainly the greatest honor of this earth, greater than rank or station or wealth, is the friendship of Jesus Christ. And this honor is within the reach of everyone. "From now on I call you not servants…I have called you friends." "You are my friends, if you do whatsoever I command you."

The stories of the friendships of Jesus when he was on the earth should cause no one to sigh, "I wish that I had lived in those days, when Jesus lived among men, that I might have been his friend too, feeling the warmth of his love, my life enriched by contact with his, and my spirit quickened by his love and grace!" The friendships of Jesus, whose stories we read in the New Testament, are only patterns of friendships into which we may enter, if we are ready to accept what he offers, and to consecrate our life to faithfulness and love. The friendship of Jesus includes all other blessings for time and for eternity. "All things are yours, and you are Christ's." His friendship sanctifies all pure human bonds—no friendship is complete which is not woven of a threefold cord. If Christ is our friend, all life is made rich and beautiful to us.

July 15

Sweet Sadness: The Christian's Undercurrent (Part 1 of 3)
by Bryan L. Herde

If in this life only we have hope in Christ, we are of all men most miserable.
1 Corinthians 15:19 (KJV)

He is despised and rejected of men; a man of sorrows, and acquainted with grief;
and we hid as it were our faces from him; he was despised, and we esteemed him not.
Isaiah 53:3 (KJV)

Joyful suffering, contented lack, restful perseverance, sweet sadness. All of these are the paradoxes of the Christian life. Both halves of each couplet is absolutely true. And each couplet is even more powerful when it is lived and evidenced in the life of a disciple of Jesus Christ.

One of the most powerful, modern-day illustrations of these realities is toward the very end of the movie, *Lord of the Rings: Return of the King*. The remaining soldiers and people of Minis Tirith in Gondor are gathered together to crown Aragorn king of Gondor. The song sung by now King Aragorn is plaintive yet victorious. The recent memories of what it cost for good to triumph over evil are all too evident to everyone attending: missing family members, lost soldiers, the utter destruction of cities—scars not yet healed. To me, that is also the feeling of the Christian life. "Rejoice always" does not happen without a corresponding sense of balancing pain, loss and cost. I count it all joy because of what Christ endured: "Let us fix our eyes upon Jesus, the author and perfector of our faith, who for the joy set before Him endured the cross, scorning its shame, and sat down at the right hand of the throne of God" (Hebrews 12:2). The sweetness of our salvation was made real by the humbling, humiliating agony of a life lived in the flesh— by God—being constantly misunderstood, abused, persecuted and eventually crucified—all so we could have full and complete reconciliation with our Creator and Father. Sin made it necessary and the grievous cost of sin required the shedding of faultless blood for each of us. But hallelujah, He did it! He gladly endured the sadness for the sweetness of oneness made available to each of us by Him, in Him.

July 16

Sweet Sadness: The Christian's Undercurrent (Part 2 of 3)
by Bryan L. Herde

The crowd joined in the attack against Paul and Silas, and the magistrates ordered them to be stripped and beaten with rods. After they had been severely flogged, they were thrown into prison, and the jailer was commanded to guard them carefully. When he received these orders, he put them in the inner cell and fastened their feet in the stocks. About midnight Paul and Silas were praying and singing hymns to God, and the other prisoners were listening to them.
Acts 16:22-25

It is the joy before us that enables us to rejoice and be optimistic in this life. Joy is a fruit of the Holy Spirit and is certainly not based upon pleasant circumstances. One of the most oft-quoted verses is taken from 1 Peter 3:15, "Always be prepared to give an answer to everyone who asks you to give the reason for the hope that you have." But what is seldom noticed is the context surrounding that verse—suffering.

It is the sweetness of hope within a person that is suffering the sadness of being misunderstood or mistreated or suffering unjustly. Suffering quietly while radiating the hope of Christ is precisely the essence of sweet sadness. It is sweet sadness that enables us to obey God's commands to "count it all joy," "rejoice always," and "patiently endure" all the pain and suffering that this world and our enemy, Satan, hurls at the disciples of Jesus. We do this by faith, not by feeling.

When Paul and Silas were singing in prison after being stripped, beaten and placed in stocks, their circumstances and their feelings certainly were not joyful, but their hearts were. Sweetness is to be an unwavering condition of our hearts, while all the sadness possible is heaped upon our souls. We live in two worlds: one is sad, broken and fallen. The other is joyful, holy and perfect. We are both temporal and immortal. Therefore, we can and will be sweet and sad living together while abiding in this jar of clay.

July 17

Sweet Sadness: The Christian's Undercurrent (Part 3 of 3)
by Bryan L. Herde

"But I say unto you, Love your enemies, bless them that curse you, do good to them that hate you, and pray for them which despitefully use you, and persecute you; That you may be the children of your Father which is in heaven..."
Matthew 5:44 (KJV)

An inherent part of the sadness we are supposed to know is the love of God for all men and women under the sun. God so loved the world—all humanity—that Christ died for them. The fact that they don't yet "get it" and lash out by mocking or rejecting those of us who do is something that should break our hearts, and it is certainly breaking God's heart. Listen to the crying heart of God when He was dealing with the evil in the days of Noah: "The Lord was grieved that He had made man on the earth, and His heart was filled with pain" (Genesis 6:6).

We have the sweetness of salvation from the penalty of our own sins, and the sweetness of Christ living in our hearts. There is therefore an aroma that comes with this abiding reality: "For we are to God the aroma of Christ among those who are being saved and those who are perishing. To the one we are the smell of death; to the other, the fragrance of life. And who is equal to such a task?" (2 Corinthians 2:15-16).

We are made equal to that "task" because of who we are in Christ and who He is in us. So we will necessarily experience sweet sadness all of our days in this life. Because Christ is indeed raised from the dead, we of all people are *not* most miserable—far from it! Because we do, like Paul, "die daily" (1 Corinthians 15:31), yet we also simultaneously live abundantly (John 10:10).

Being an "aroma" of both life and death—dying daily while living abundantly—are sweet and sad paradoxes, but vibrant truth nonetheless.

July 18

Revelation Waiting Upon Capacity (Part 1 of 6)
by John Henry Jowett

"I have many things to say unto you, but you cannot bear them now."
John 16:12

The Master is speaking to His disciples in the upper room. The words are a fragment of the wonderful discourse recorded for our advantage in the fourteenth, fifteenth, sixteenth and seventeenth chapters of John. If one may make comparison among things, all of which are superlative, one would say that when we enter these chapters we are in passages distinctly revered and awe-inspiring. If one may liken the whole of the New Testament to a temple, then these chapters would be the Holy of Holies, a place where the sacred things are gathered together in overwhelming seriousness and power. In this place things are being said of indescribable tenderness and unimaginable grandeur. Their range takes away one's breath. On the one hand they touch human life, with all its frailties, as gently as the wings of a bee touch the stamens of a flower; and on the other hand they lay hold of divine and eternal privileges with the majestic air of a King entering the capital city of his realm. Christ lays one hand on human necessity, and its touch is as sensitive as the touch of a nurse, and with the other hand He quietly grasps the scepter of the universe, and He claims the glory of God. Such is the range of movement in this Holy Place, and my text reflects a little of that movement as the great Lover touches the needs of His disciples: "I have many things to say unto you, but you cannot bear them now."

***

In the Master's sentence "to bear" has the simple significance of "to carry" as, for instance, in the phrase: "A man bearing a pitcher of water." So that when the Master suggests that there are some things which they are not yet able to carry, He means that they have not yet the necessary capacity to lay hold of them and understand them. They lack the necessary grasp. They may be able to take hold of this portion of truth, or that portion of truth, but there are other portions which are quite beyond them. The word therefore suggests the contrast between the hands of a child and the hands of a full-grown man.

199

July 19

Revelation Waiting Upon Capacity (Part 2 of 6)
by John Henry Jowett

"I have many things to say unto you, but you cannot bear them now."
John 16:12

The revelation must wait until the necessary grasp is mature. Now this principle is operative in every field of learning, and in every realm of discernment. Revelation has to wait upon capacity, and it has to wait patiently until capacity is grown.

***

An art master may say to his pupil, "Art has many things to say to you, but you cannot carry them now!" There are delicacies of light and shade, there are dainty marriages of color, there are fairy secrets, there are subtle glories of which you have never dreamed! You can see a little way, but just beyond your range there is a world of beautiful mystery. And so the spirit of art has to wait until an eye has been acquired which can seize and carry the hidden glory. "Your eye has not seen!" "You cannot carry them now."

***

With every added power to the lens the invisible world loses a veil, and it displays a new range of its treasures. And so it is with the truth in Christ Jesus. So it is with the greatest secrets—the hidden knowledge of God and His grace, the mysteries of His will, His cloud-shrouded judgment, the tangle of His sovereign control—they are waiting for an eye, an ear, a requisite strength of holiness, the necessary purity of life. The treasures are even now assembled like the glories of the starry world: they are "the things which God has prepared for them that love Him," but they are veiled before our immaturity. There are many words of Christ which await the approach and touch of adequate capacity. What does our Lord and Master say about His words? This is what He says: "The words that I speak unto you, they are spirit and they are life." Mark the depth of the background which He gives to His words, "they are spirit, and they are life", and we feel them stretch back, and back, and back, like regions of untraveled and undiscovered country, back and back, losing themselves in misty and mysterious depth. "My words are spirit, and they are life!" They are like unplumbed seas, "the unsearchable riches of Christ."

July 20

Revelation Waiting Upon Capacity (Part 3 of 6)
by John Henry Jowett

"I have many things to say unto you, but you cannot bear them now."
John 16:12

Let us carefully note that if our Savior's words are spirit and life, then as we add to the clarity of our own spirit, and the purity of our own life, we are acquiring the necessary means of interpretation, and we can plumb an ever deeper depth in these unfathomed seas. And therefore His words wait for fuller interpretation, they are always waiting for the larger interpretation which is found through a larger life. "I have many things to say unto you, but you cannot bear them now."

Now we take a step further. If these are words of Jesus waiting for an interpreting capacity, may we not say the same about events? There are happenings in the life of Christ which may seem silent and mysterious as the Sphinx, but the silence is only the witness that the interpreting ear is absent. If only we had a finer ear these mystical happenings would reveal a voice, and the voice would unfold the secret things of God.

Events are always insignificant until they are met by the necessary power of discernment, and as that power becomes more and more mature the hidden secrets troop out of their hiding like the fabled princess who had been imprisoned in the gloomy wood. What about the happenings in Gethsemane? What is there in them—how little or how much? What about the awful happenings on the Cross? What is there in them—how little or how much? What about the mysteries of the empty grave? What have they to say to us—how little or how much? What about the mysteries of the Pentecostal morning? What do they say to us?

We cannot stand around these central sacred events of our world, yes, and of all worlds—we cannot stand around them like casual observers, with our hands in our pockets, and yet expect these events to tell us their secrets. Mere observation will take us nowhere.

July 21

Revelation Waiting Upon Capacity (Part 4 of 6)
by John Henry Jowett

"I have many things to say unto you, but you cannot bear them now."
John 16:12

For each and all of us the events are waiting for an interpreting capacity, and until that capacity is set before them they will look at us, with all the mysterious silence of the Sphinx. Well, then, how is this carrying capacity to be acquired? How is this discernment to be gained? Let us reverently consult the counsel of the Lord. The word of my text which expresses our incapacity is accompanied by a word of promise proclaiming how the incapacity may be removed. "I have many things to say unto you, but you cannot bear them now. But when He, the Spirit of Truth, is come, He shall guide you into all truth." In the Christian life our incapacity is to be teamed with a Guide, who is to be the minister of our spiritual expansion. Take note, we are not left to an impersonal director—that would be a guide post. We are not left with an impersonal code of laws—that would be a guide book. The promise is neither a *guide post* nor a *guide book,* but a *Guide.* He, the Spirit of Truth, shall guide you into all truth. And let no one limit the ministry of this Guide to the presentation of knowledge, and to the opening out of secrets as we walk with Him along the way. His guidance is not only to inform, but to inspire; it is to prepare and refine the aptitude as well as to present the truth. He enlarges our capacity, and we apprehend the waiting truth. He guides us into all truth.

And where does He train us? And what is the medium of His training? The common events of daily life. Our faculties are polished by the smaller issues, and we come to see the greater ones. Our powers are prepared in smaller spheres for explorations in larger ones. We have not two consciences, one for business and one for religion; we have only one, and the conscience is made more sensitive by the hourly faithfulness of common interaction. We have not two mental powers, one for secular affairs, and one for devotions; we have but one reason, and it is strengthened by the singleness of its quest through all the jungle of thickly competing interests which throng our daily life.

July 22

Revelation Waiting Upon Capacity (Part 5 of 6)
by John Henry Jowett

"I have many things to say unto you, but you cannot bear them now."
John 16:12

We have not two wills, one for the flesh and one for the spirit; we have only one will, and this will is invigorated by a thousand unwitnessed wrestlings on a thousand obscure fields. Our reason, and our conscience, and our will are prepared in these minor happenings, and they march up to the major happenings and to enlarged judgments.

The heart, which has been tried and proved in heartbreak, wanders into the garden of Gethsemane, and wonderingly finds that it has eyes for the darkness, and in the midnight gloom it begins to see. The love which has been trained by the Holy Spirit among the desolation of wasting experiences, goes and stands before the Cross, and the mystery begins to break in solemn and amazing glory. It is through the guided and inspired ministry of daily events that we therefore find the keys to larger interpretations of the word and life of our Lord. The event may be a sunny one, bright as the brightest morning; it may be a little child knocking at the door, God's love gift to our expectant hearts, and the little one brings the key to the very heart of God. Or the event may be a somber one, cold and black as a starless winter's night; it may be death knocking at our door, and the dark-robed presence is made to put into our hand the key of the grave. In all these ways reason is strengthened, and perception is refined, and with the increased capacity we are able to hear voices that once were silent, we are able to decipher the meaning of words that once had no significance; we begin to handle more of the keys of life and death. "I have many things to say unto you, but you cannot carry them now!" Yea, so it is; but when the great Guide has strengthened and purified our powers, then—"Master speak, Your servant hears!" And His will and His grace will unfold their treasures to the eternal enrichment of our souls.

July 23

Revelation Waiting Upon Capacity (Part 6 of 6)
by John Henry Jowett

"I have many things to say unto you, but you cannot bear them now."
John 16:12

Take note: this is to be the supreme work of the Guide. He is to prepare our powers for a progressive perception and understanding of our Lord and Savior Jesus Christ. "He shall glorify Me," says Jesus, "for He shall take of Mine and declare it unto you." Christ is to be more and more gloriously revealed to us through our refined discernments and the ministry of unique and unfamiliar events. Along the great road of time every age should succeed to a larger and richer interpretation of Christ.

This age in which we live should see Christ as He has never been seen before—in clearer vision of His truth, in new and broader applications of His will, and in the carrying of His fertilizing spirit to every desert waste in human life. How to know Christ, and how to convert the divine knowledge into human grace and loveliness, that is our perpetual problem; and this is the perpetual solution to the problem—"He shall guide you into all truth, for He shall take of Mine and shall declare it unto you."

We must not be afraid of new things. We must not be afraid of larger ways of looking at old things. We must not fear the new application of Christian truth to the new and complex necessities of our day.

There are two things we must pray for—vision and venture, and for these let us pray without ceasing. "Lord, that I may receive my sight." That is the secret of vision. "Your will be done on earth!" That is the spirit of venture. And vision and venture will translate themselves into venture and vision, and we shall go on from faith to faith, from strength to strength, and from glory to glory.

July 24

Paul's Love Song
by George Matheson

God forbid that I should glory, save in the cross of our Lord Jesus Christ, through whom the world is crucified unto me, and I unto the world.
Galatians 6:14

Can anything make the bearing of a cross glorious? Many things can make a cross endurable: patience can, pride can, despair itself can. But can anything make it a glory? I know of only one thing that can—love! It has been often said that love will go through fire and water for its object. But Paul says a great deal more than that. He says that love courts the fire and water. I think he is right. I believe the morning stage of all love is a craving for the cross. Peter is no abnormal specimen when he cries, "Ask me to come to You on the water!" He has been charged with the love of display; it was really the love of Jesus. All love, secular and sacred, begins with the cry for martyrdom. The earliest imagination in the heart of love is not that of a golden palace; it is that of a terrible battle in which it is fighting for its object's life and joy. Its morning picture is the den of lions; its opening fancy is the fiery furnace; its primitive desire is to brave the Sea of Galilee. Its birth-cry is the cry for denial.

My soul, your love for Jesus is but the continuation of love's natural morning! There are not two kinds of love. Your love for Jesus is the extending of the morning star. Have you considered this love song of Paul's? It is a love song to Jesus—the oldest in the world. Have you considered how alike it is to all pure songs of love? Listen to its music: "I should glory to be with You in the garden; I should delight to be near You on Your cross. Oh that Your wilderness were mine to share. Meet me in some spot where I can help You, in some hour when I can aid You! At the Garden gate where still You suffer, at the Bethany graveyard where still You weep, at Samaria's well where still You thirst, in Jerusalem's streets where still Your heart is broken—I would meet You there! Meet me in Your wards of sickness; meet me in Your vigils with the sad; meet me on Your road to the prodigal. My proudest height of glory will be the foot of Your Cross.

July 25

Excerpts From July 11-August 3, 1883 Letters to His Sister
(Part 1 of 4)
by General C.G. "Chinese" Gordon

I found six or seven sermons of [Charles H.] Spurgeon in the hotel, and read them. I like him; he is very earnest; he says: "I believe that not a worm is picked up by a bird without direct intervention of God, yet I believe entirely in man's free will; but I cannot and do not pretend to reconcile the two." He says he reads the paper to see what God is doing and what are His designs. I confess I have now much the same feeling; nothing shocks me but myself. I believe truly that the secret of work, and our defined duty, is the life in the Spirit, the constant desire, even if not completely fulfilled, to feel God's indwelling in us; it means, of course, the death of self, as if we loaned our bodies to God to work in; I think that is the true object of a godly life, and nothing else. God in the loaned body will work sufficiently and in due time, but there will be no fuss or worry. Before the fall, Adam was to care for the garden, not to labor with fatigue; and through Christ we regain this position of Adam. I am sure this will be a comfort to you, as it is to me; it is the sunset of life to realize this, or rather it is the dawn of the resurrection life.

Summed up, it is "all things are ruled by God in Christ;" all working for good, all working in love, our whole work is to be still in His hands and to keep our temples fit for His residence. That many will agree with us is not likely, for they must be passers through of tribulation; they must have had the experience derived from the failure of any other work to satisfy; and all carnal enjoyment of the world must have ceased. How few have reached or been given this! Can we wonder that we find no one who will meet us in these matters? "Be still and know that I am God," is "Let go." You know how often we are told we are saved by faith alone; most tracts, as well as the Bible, say that. Well, when we are brought to the sense of religion, what is the first thing we do? We rush off to prayer meetings, tract distributions, etc., etc.; and we torture ourselves to do all this. Yet "Be still" is the truth; all this fuss does good, i.e., it is turned to good, for we worry others, and we learn our own insufficiency. Yet if we did what God tells us, "Let go," what toils we should save ourselves!

July 26

Excerpts From July 11-August 3, 1883 Letters to His Sister
(Part 2 of 4)
by General C.G. "Chinese" Gordon

I quite look on this fussiness as coming from Satan's distorting truth. It comes from the flesh; the flesh feels it is important, self-sufficient, and must be a doer of great things. Many will say, "Have we not prophesied in Your name? and in Your name have cast out devils? and in Your name done many wonderful works?" to whom Christ will say, "I never knew you" (Matthew 7:22-23). The will of my Father is to be done, i.e., submitted to; that is our sanctification.

It is remarkable that the "Be still" is so clearly put in the Bible: Enter into rest; cease from these works. "It is a people that do err in their heart, and they have not known my ways: Unto whom I swore in my wrath that they should not enter into my rest" (Psalm 95:10-11).

If a portion of machinery were worked by any other life or driving force than the main one, there would be a jarring and inevitable clash; so it is with us. "Be still, let go."

"Except the Lord build the house, they labor in vain" (Psalm 127:1) shows that efforts are not productive of fruit: that is the reward of God. Look at a tree: it makes no effort, but fruit comes from its union with the root. I consider this view is a true gem; that by this abiding, by intercessory prayer, and by using every opportunity God gives us for comforting people we fulfill His will. With this there is no fuss, no hurrying.

It is one of the most difficult things to give comfort to a person in trouble; nothing but truth will benefit, and that truth must be delivered very gently, and little by little. The comforter must get into the same position as the person to be comforted; not in words only but in feelings. I have found this to be the case so very often, and have felt that when I do not sympathize with the grief of another, whatever I may say does not give comfort.

July 27

Excerpts From July 11-August 3, 1883 Letters to His Sister
(Part 3 of 4)
by General C.G. "Chinese" Gordon

In Him we reach to the end of the world; out of Him we are localized in Southampton or Jaffa. Reason supports this view: to be at the headquarters of a ruler, who by telegraph can communicate orders and even supervise their execution, is certainly a higher position than to be working in one's own way in a petty place. How much more does this apply to those who seek and obtain, by the cessation of their own work, the indwelling of the Lord of heaven and earth. I think many would like these thoughts, they are calming. I want forty years more to quiet me, but, God willing, it will come at last. One verse always comforted me: "The Lord will perfect that which concerns me" (Psalm 138:8); for a believer is always in the exact position he should be in. The tearing apart of the soul and body, which is made necessary by the death of the flesh, is a most painful operation, and a lingering one; all have to undergo it at one time or another in their pilgrimage, either now or at their death.

"Let go." "Be still," even if the mountains fall into the sea. There is death in the seeking of high posts on this earth for the purpose of what the world calls doing great things; the mightiest of men are flies on a wheel; a kind word to a street sweeper delights Christ in him, as much as it would delight Christ in a queen. I want you to look at accidents like that at Sunderland [stampede that killed 183 children] from God's point of view; we, each of us, as members of Him who is Lord of heaven and earth, are a party to His works, and submit to them; for a member cannot differ from its head. Any feeling of wishing this had happened rather than that, is the raising up of the head of a rebel. Continuing the subject of "Be still," we see how the fact of our being the temple of God is inseparable from quiet and rest; one cannot think that the temple should be full of noise and fuss, such as our bodies are in, when we get mixed up with much secular religious work. Those thoughts, which cause the fuss, are the money-changers and sellers of doves whom our Lord drove out of the Temple.

July 28

Excerpts From July 11-August 3, 1883 Letters to His Sister
(Part 4 of 4)
by General C.G. "Chinese" Gordon

What comforts me is the thought that we are being shaped here below into stones for the heavenly temple; that to be made like Him is the object of our earthly existence. He is the shaper and carpenter of the heavenly temple. He must work us into shape, our part is to be still in His hands; every irritation is a little chip; also we must not be in a hurry to go out of the quarry, for there is a certain place for each stone, and we must wait until the building is ready for that stone; it would disrupt the building, if we were inserted recklessly. This also is a comfort in respect to ambition, for the things of this world are only important as tools to shape us. One wishes one could always feel this. It is truly wonderful how very accurate the Scriptures are, but then they are divine.

I am sure of one thing, that we do lose the very sweetest times by rejecting willfully what God gives us, i.e., in avoiding people and disagreeable things. God says: I will preserve you from all evil; I will preserve your going out and your coming in from this time forth; there shall no evil befall you; and yet we refuse to believe this for even a second, and go on plotting and praying, praying for more communion with Him, and then, the moment He begins to work, we flee from Him. I want to realize this more than I do, it is evidently the reason of our deadness; there can be no confidence with distrust.

If we think we are bound to look after ourselves, if we think those strong expressions are only figurative or dependent on any particular frame of mind, they are useless to us. Until we take them in their strength, we shall crawl along all our days. What wonderful things the Spirit shows forth from the Scriptures, yet how few will study them! Thank God, I have got to consider that salvation is a free gift. Though clearly declared to be so in the Scripture, a full comprehension is not always given; when it is, the knowledge is a great relief.

July 29

Mystery (Part 1 of 5)
by George H. Morrison

Now I know in part.
1 Corinthians 13:12

It has ever been a mark of Christianity that it kept men alive to the mysteries around them. The souls that have drunk most deeply of the Christian doctrine are the souls who have most felt the mystery of life. You may gather up the Christian teaching in creeds, and it is vitally necessary that that should be done. But when everything is tabulated and reduced to a system, we are still haunted by a sense of the inexplicable—more is meant than meets the ear. I dare say a scientist could explain to me the causes of all the colors in a sunset. And yet in the blending glories of a sunset there is something that no man shall ever analyze. So men have gathered up and set in order the contents of the Christian revelation, but the great secrets have not ceased to baffle them.

And yet, perhaps, there never was a time in which the sense of mystery was less present than today. "We have not any mysteries today," said a French writer whom I came across lately. How far that dying out of the mysterious may be traced to the decline of living faith is a question that might be cause for much discussion. But there are other causes which I should like to point out.

One is the tyranny of facts under which we live. I suppose there was never a time in the world's history when there was such a craving for scientific truth. There is no man more apt to be blind to the great mysteries than the specialist, and this is preeminently the age of specialism. Tennyson is most wonderfully accurate in every reference he makes to nature, and in this, as in so many other points, he interprets the spirit of the age he lived in. Now no one will question the value of that spirit, nor the immense gains which it has won for us. I only suggest that an age with that dominant note is not likely to be haunted by the mystery of things.

July 30

Mystery (Part 2 of 5)
by George H. Morrison

Now I know in part.
1 Corinthians 13:12

This is an age of machinery, and there is little mystery in a machine. We are likely to grow dull to many wonders, when we take to calculating by *horse-power*. "So many hundred hands in this mill," says Charles Dickens in that powerful little story of his, *Hard Times*, "so many hundred horse steam power. It is known, to the force of a single pound-weight, what the engine will do. There is no mystery in it." And he means that when an age puts the emphasis not on man but on machinery, we are not likely to be troubled greatly by the strange sense of the inexplicable.

And then this is an age of travel. The world is explored into its darkest corners. We do not expect now, as men expected once, to hear of marvelous things from Africa or India. I love to turn the pages of Sir John Mandeville, that most amazing medieval wanderer. You had only to cross the sea with Sir John Mandeville, and you were in the middle of astounding mysteries at once. But the world is very different today. Its most distant countries have been mapped and photographed. Knowledge has come, and perhaps a little wisdom with it; but the older sense of the world's mystery has gone. "Ah me!" says our Scottish poet Alexander Smith, in his most delightful essay *On Vagabonds*, "what a world this was to live in two or three centuries ago, when it was getting itself discovered. Then were the Arabian Nights commonplace, enchantments a matter of course, and romance the most ordinary thing in the world. Then man was courting Nature, now he has married her. Every mystery is dispelled."

I think, then, that it is supremely important in these times that we should endeavor to keep alive the sense of mystery. And I am sure that the Lord Jesus Christ always meant it to have large room in His disciples' hearts.

July 31

Mystery (Part 3 of 5)
by George H. Morrison

Now I know in part.
1 Corinthians 13:12

Think of what our Lord meant by unbelief. "Why are you fearful, O you of little faith?" That was the one rebuke which He used to launch at His disciples, for there was nothing that grieved Christ more than lack of faith. And it was not lack of faith in any particular doctrines—it was not *that* which called out the rebuke of Christ. It was rather such a view of God's great universe as left no room for any mystery in it. Why are you fearful, O you of little faith? Is there nothing else abroad but storm and wind-driven clouds? Had they only felt the mystery of the Divine, touching and encircling even the angry waters, they had been less disquieted, out at sea. That was what Jesus meant by unbelief: not a mind that denies, but a spirit that disowns. A heart that will not recognize, among things seen, the power, the love, the mystery of God. You see, then, that the disciple of Christ must have a spirit that is alive to mystery.

And then you remember that other declaration: "Except you become as little children." You cannot even see the kingdom of God, unless within you is the heart of childhood, and all things are mysterious to the child. I do not think that any child would be much surprised if it met God out in the green fields. Flowers speak to them in voices we have lost, the night winds cry to them, the clouds are still populated countries. The fear of childhood is not the fear of cowardice; the fear of childhood is the fear of imagination. We should all fear the darkness as the child does, if we believed it was full of eyes and living things. Now Jesus wants no disciple to be childish: when we become men we put away childish things. But the childlike spirit that believes in possibilities, that hungers for a world behind the world, that cannot touch a flower or hear an echo but there comes some suggestion of things mystical, *that* spirit is the spirit of the Christian.

August 1

Mystery (Part 4 of 5)
by George H. Morrison

Now I know in part.
1 Corinthians 13:12

It is notable, too—I wish to impress this on you—that Jesus deepened the mystery of everything He touched. Things never become less mysterious, always more, when they have passed through the mind and heart of Jesus Christ. We think of Jesus as the great explainer, and we thank God for the rough places Christ has made plain. He has given an answer to a thousand problems. He has come like light into our human darkness. But Jesus never explained anything by lessening the mystery that clung to it. Jesus enlarged the mystery of things, intensified it, deepened it twentyfold. When He wished to make men understand a matter, He showed that there was more to be understood than they had dreamed.

Take one of His leading words like *life*, for instance. You say, and say rightly, that Christ explains life to you. You understand it better, and you can live it better, in the light that Jesus has cast upon its meaning. But when I think of what life meant in the old pagan world, how shallow it was, how sensuous and short, and when I compare that with the life that is in Christ, with its depth, its joy, its fullness, its infinite issues, I feel at once how the mystery of life is deepened in passing through the hands of Jesus Christ. Or take the thought of *death*. Christ has illumined death. It is when the heart is empty, and the grave is open, that we know the tenderness and power of Christian comfort. Christ has illumined death; but has He banished its mystery? He has taken away its sting, but deepened its mystery. There are moral bearings in it: it is the wages of sin. There are glorious hopes in it: the body shall be raised. There are dim suggestions in the very word, of eternal separations from love and joy and God. And all this mystery of light, and mystery of darkness, has been poured into the cup of death by Jesus Christ. Death has strange meanings for the humblest now that it had not for the wisest before Jesus came. Christ has intensified its mystery a thousand-fold.

August 2

Mystery (Part 5 of 5)
by George H. Morrison

Now I know in part.
1 Corinthians 13:12

Take the thought of *God*. You and I know God through the Lord Jesus Christ. All that we know of God from outward nature, and all that we gather from the world's long history is but the development of that revelation which is ours through the life and death of Jesus. Now tell me, is God less mysterious to us in the light of that revelation of Christ Jesus? "God without mystery is not good news." God was a Sovereign once, now He is Father, and there are more mysteries in Fatherhood than in Kingship. God was a God of power once; He is a God of love now; and all the power of all the thunderbolts of Jove [Roman god of weather] are not so mysterious as the slightest spark of love. Now, baffling comprehension, yet most real, we have a vision of Three in One and One in Three. Christ has intensified the mystery of God.

I trust that you see, then, how true it is, that Jesus deepened the mystery of things. And I trust that you begin to understand what the spirit of Christ longs to achieve in you. The Christian view is always the deepest view. The Lord who inspired it saw kingdoms in mustard seeds. There is more in the world, and in man, and in the Bible, than the best calculation can discover, if we would only see it through the eyes of Christ. It is then that a man becomes humble. Touched by a sense of mystery, he must be reverent. And it is then that he begins again to wonder; and when a man ceases to wonder, may God pity him! Do not be dogmatic. Do not be bigoted. The world is too mysterious for that. Expect surprises. Have an open eye. Believe that there are more things in heaven and earth than have been dreamed of in your philosophies. And then, when common actions are illuminated, and common lives flash into moral glories, when the mysteries of life, and love, and death, and God, so baffle us that we can only say with Paul "we know in part"—we shall be nearer the spirit of Jesus than we dreamed.

August 3

Knowing God (Part 1 of 4)
by François Fénelon

What men lack most is the knowledge of God. They know, when they have read a good deal, a certain sequence of miracles and of marks of sovereign control the deeds of history. They have seriously meditated on the corruption and the frailty of the world. They are even convinced of certain laws useful to reform their habits as touching their salvation. But this building lacks foundation. This body of religion and Christianity is without a soul. What should stir the truly faithful is the idea of a God who is all, who does all, and to whom we owe all.

He is infinite in all things: in wisdom, in power, in love. We must not be astonished if everything which comes from him has this character of infinity, and is beyond human reason. When he prepares and arranges anything, his plans and his ways are, as Scripture says, as far above our plans and our ways as heaven is above the earth. When he wants to carry out what he has resolved, his power is not shown by any effort, because there is no deed, great as it may be, which is any more difficult to him than the most ordinary one. It has cost him no more to draw heaven and earth out of nothingness, such as we see them, than it does to cause a river to run in its natural course, or to allow a stone to fall from above to below. His power is displayed entirely in his will. He has only to will, and things are at once accomplished. If Scripture represents him speaking during creation, it is not that he needed to have a single word proceed from him in order to have his will understood by the nature which he wished to create. This word, which Scripture tells of, is entirely simple and entirely inward. It is his creative thought, and the resolution which he made deep within himself. This thought was fruitful, and without going forth from him, it drew from him, as from the source of all existence, everything which composes the universe. His compassion, moreover, is nothing more than his pure will. He has loved us before the creation of the world. He has seen us. He has known us. He has prepared good things for us. He has loved us and chosen us from eternity. When some new good comes to us, it flows from this ancient source. God never has any new will for us. He does not change. It is we who change.

August 4

Knowing God (Part 2 of 4)
by François Fénelon

When we are just and good, we are being like him and are in harmony with him. When we fall away from righteousness, and when we stop being good, we stop being like him and being in harmony with him. It is an unchangeable rule, by which the changeable creature draws near or goes away successively. His rightness toward the wicked and his love for the good are merely the same thing. It is the same goodness which unites with all which is good, and which is incompatible with all that is evil. As for compassion, it is the goodness of God which, finding us evil, wishes to make us good. This compassion, which we are conscious of in time, has its source in the eternal love of God for his creature. He alone gives true goodness. Unhappy is the presumptuous soul who hopes to find it in himself. It is the love which God has for us which gives us all.

But the greatest good which he can do for us is to give us the love which we ought to have for him. When God loves us enough to make us love him, he reigns in us. He makes our life, or peace, our happiness, and we begin already to live by his abundant life. This love which he has for us bears his infinite character. He does not love as we do, with a limited and narrow love. When he loves, the dimensions of his love are infinite. He becomes man with him. He gives him his flesh to eat. It is by such wonders of love that the infinite surpasses all the affection of which men are capable. He loves as God, and this love is entirely incomprehensible. It is the height of foolishness to wish to measure infinite love by limited knowledge. O how great and agreeable he is in his mysteries! But we have not the eyes to see them, and we lack the sensitiveness to see God in everything. It is not surprising that men do so little for God, and that the little which they do for him takes such effort. They do not really know him. They hardly believe that he exists. The belief in him which they have is rather a blind submission to the power of public opinion, than a living and distinct conviction of divinity.

August 5

Knowing God (Part 3 of 4)
by François Fénelon

We only know God as some kind of marvelous being, vague and far from us. We think of him as powerful and severe, one who demands a great deal of us, who upsets our desires, who threatens us with great harm, and against whose terrible judgment we must be prepared. Thus think those who do think seriously about religion, small as their number is. We say, "There is a man who fears God." Indeed he only fears him without loving him, as children fear the teacher who uses the rod, as a bad servant fears his master's beating, when he serves him with trembling, and without caring for his interest. Would we want to be treated by a son, or even by a servant, as we treat God?

It is because we do not know him, because if we knew him we would love him. "God is love," as St. John said. He who does not love him does not know him, for how can we know love without loving him? Therefore it stands to reason that all those who only fear God do not know him. But why did you create all these things? They were all made for man, and man was made for you. That was the order which you did establish. Woe to the soul who reverses it, who wishes all for himself, and who shuts himself up in himself! This violates the fundamental law of creation. No, my God, you cannot give up your essential rights as Creator. That would be to degrade yourself. You can pardon the guilty soul who has outraged you, because you can fill it with your pure love. But you cannot stop being opposed to the soul which takes your gifts to itself, and which refuses to relate through a sincere and unselfish love to its Creator. Only to fear you is not to relate ourselves to you. On the contrary, it is only to think of you for our own sakes. To love you simply to enjoy the advantage to be found in you, this is to relate you to self, instead of relating self to you. What must we do then to relate ourselves entirely to the Creator? We must abandon ourselves, forget ourselves, lose ourselves, enter into your interests, O my God, against our own. To have no will, no glory, no peace but yours. In a word, it is to love you without loving ourselves.

August 6

Knowing God (Part 4 of 4)
by François Fénelon

How many people, leaving this life loaded with good qualities and good works, will never have this complete purity, without which we cannot see God. Alas, how many people rely on their own virtues and are not willing to make an unreserved denial of self! This saying is hard for them, and horrifies them, but it will cost them dear for having neglected it. They will pay a hundred times over for their self-centeredness and the futile consolations which they did not have the courage to give up.

Let us repeat. Such is the grandeur of God, that he can do nothing except for himself and for his own glory. It is this incommunicable glory of which he is necessarily jealous, and which he can give to no one, as he himself has said. On the other hand, such is the wickedness and the dependence of the creature, that he cannot, without raising himself to a false divinity, and without violating the unchangeable law of his creation, do anything, say anything, think anything, wish anything for himself or for his own glory.

***

There are blessings that are of a higher and purer order that will yet come from God. The good life is more valuable than life. Character is a greater prize than health. Rightness of heart and love of God are further above temporal gifts than heaven is above the earth. If then we are incapable for a single moment of possessing the inferior and common gifts without God's help, how much stronger reason must there be that he should give us the other glorious gifts of his love, of detachment from ourselves, and of all the virtues!

We are nothing by ourselves. We only exist because God causes us to exist, and only for the time which pleases him. Thus we have life and being only as the gift of God.

August 7

Holy and Wholly for Us
by Bryan L. Herde

God the Father gave His only Son
Because He knew there could be just one
Means to reconcile our sin,
One way to bring us in,
Our hearts forever win.

A perfect man would have to live,
His own life He would have to give
For salvation to be unfurled,
Freely offered to a fallen world.

So Christ came to fulfill the Law
And became sin, embodying every flaw,
To shed His blood for you and me
And to die alone upon a tree.

This He did 'til "It is finished."
His body now dead, diminished;
He took the keys to hell and death,
Then was raised to draw new breath.

Now in Him we are wholly sealed
By His Spirit to whom we yield,
The holiness of Christ to us now graced,
As in Him we are forever placed.

In our hearts He does now dwell
And now for us no fear of hell.
We live as one within and without,
Wholly, completely, no basis for doubt.

August 8

Godliness: The Perfect Heart (Part 1 of 5)
by Catherine (Mrs. William) Booth

For the eyes of the Lord run to and fro throughout the whole earth, to show himself strong in the behalf of them whose heart is perfect toward him.
2 Chronicles 16:9

What is this perfect heart? "Ah!" you say, "that is the point." Yes, that is the point, and we will try to show what kind of a heart this is. It must *be a different kind of heart to hearts in general;* all hearts are not perfect towards God, or else His eyes would not have to be running to and fro throughout the earth to find them. "Be you perfect," says the Savior, "even as your Father which is in Heaven is perfect." That means something. We will try to find out what it does mean: "Jesus said unto the rich young ruler, 'If you will be perfect, go and sell that you have, and give to the poor, and you shall have treasure in Heaven: and come and follow Me'" (Matthew 19:21). And, again, "However, we speak wisdom among them that are perfect" (1 Corinthians 2:6). And, "That the man of God may be perfect, thoroughly furnished unto all good works" (2 Timothy 3:17).

Now, what do they mean by a perfect heart? Well, the most basic rendering of all theologians and all schools is this, that it means *sincerity* and *thoroughness.* Well, that is all I want. Give me a man sincere and thorough in his love, and that is all I want; that will stretch through all the ramifications of his existence; it will go to the ends of his fingers and his toes, through his eyes, and through his tongue, to his wife, and to his family, to his shop, and to his business, and to his circle in the world. That is what I mean by *holiness!* Then, taking the lowest translation, it means that a man is wholehearted in love, and thorough out-and-out in service! Amen. For that man who is thus perfect towards God, God will indeed show Himself strong in more ways than one! This cannot mean a merely natural heart, it must mean a renewed heart, because there are no perfect hearts by nature. There is no one in this sense that does good and sins not, for every child of Adam has gone astray like a lost sheep, has done the things he ought not, and left undone the things he ought to have done, and the whole world has become guilty before God.

August 9

Godliness: The Perfect Heart (Part 2 of 5)
by Catherine (Mrs. William) Booth

For the eyes of the Lord run to and fro throughout the whole earth, to show himself strong in the behalf of them whose heart is perfect toward him.
2 Chronicles 16:9

There are no naturally perfect hearts. It must mean, then, a heart renewed by the Holy Ghost, put right with God, and then kept right. A heart cannot be kept right until it has been *put right,* and that is the secret of the failure with some of you. You are trying to bring forth fruit before the tree is planted. You are looking for the fruit of a perfect heart before you have got one. You may well be disappointed. You must get your heart renewed, and then kept right by the power of the Holy Ghost.

Then, what does this perfect heart imply? ONE: *A heart perfect in its loyalty to God,* thoroughly gives over to God's side, regardless of consequences—*loyal.* These are the hearts that God wants. This was the difference between David and Saul.

From the first calling of David from the sheepfolds, right to the end, with one or two exceptions, during the whole of his life, he was loyal to God, and, if you will carefully search his history, you will find that this was true in all his wars, and all his dealings with the nations round about, and with the leaders of affairs in his own kingdom—in everything.

David was loyal to God. It was the interests of God's kingdom that lay at David's heart—not his own honor, ease, or self-promotion—not his own fame or riches, or building himself a house—it was the house of his God that was dear to his heart. *He was loyal;* whereas Saul was loyal only as far as it served his own purposes and interests. He was never perfect towards the Lord his God, and, at last, God cast him off, and Samuel did also, and you know what his end was. Just the difference between the two—loyal and un-loyal!

August 10

Godliness: The Perfect Heart (Part 3 of 5)
by Catherine (Mrs. William) Booth

For the eyes of the Lord run to and fro throughout the whole earth, to show himself strong in the behalf of them whose heart is perfect toward him.
2 Chronicles 16:9

A heart perfect towards God! What does it mean? TWO: *Perfect in its obedience.* That man or woman who has this kind of a heart ceases to pick and choose which among the commandments of God he shall obey, and which he shall not—he ceases to have his own will, though sometimes he may have a struggle with his own will, and the path that God may call him to take may look to him as if it were a dangerous or risky way, and he may wait a little bit, to be thoroughly satisfied; but when once satisfied that it is God's way, the true child will not hesitate. He confers not with flesh and blood, but on he goes, regardless of consequences. This was Paul's kind of obedience. He conferred not with flesh and blood; he counted all things manure and trash, and he went on doing so to the end—thorough in his obedience.

People come to us and want to know what they are to do; they feel that they are only half-hearted in God's service; they have neither joy nor power, and say, "What must I do?" and we take, as God helps us, the dissecting knife, and try to find out the difficulty. We get them down under the blaze of the Holy Spirit's light, and try to probe them and find where they are wrong. Perhaps the Lord leads us to the sore spot, and we point out the difficulty, but, instead of obeying, they shrink away. They look ahead, and they see that to obey the light will involve loss of some kind—perhaps reputation, wealth, family associations, ease, or loss of friends, loss of temporal comforts, loss of good business. Loss is in the background, and they see it. They know where we are leading them, and they slip back; they do not want to see, and yet they do not want to consider themselves dishonest, so they turn their heads away, and will not look in the direction of the light. That is not a perfect heart, but a partial heart towards the Lord God.

August 11

Godliness: The Perfect Heart (Part 4 of 5)
by Catherine (Mrs. William) Booth

For the eyes of the Lord run to and fro throughout the whole earth, to show himself strong
in the behalf of them whose heart is perfect toward him.
2 Chronicles 16:9

The partial heart, so common, alas, now days, wants to serve God a little. It is willing to go a little way with God, but not all the way; so that, taking the most basic interpretation, that is not a perfect heart towards the Lord. Can it be expected that the Lord should show Himself strong in behalf of such people? Do you think you would if you were God?

Suppose you were a king, and had a prince or statesman who was serving you very valiantly and devotedly while he served himself; but, suppose the tables were turned, and you were dethroned and cast away into exile, your name being tossed about the nation where you once reigned as king, in disgrace and dishonor; suppose this statesman gave you up, and said, "Oh! I am going to be on the side of the reigning monarch. I was very devoted to this man while he reigned, but I cannot afford to be devoted to him now his interests are dragged in the dust; I must be on the winning side." What would you think of such a man? And if you were restored to your kingdom and power, would you show yourself strong on behalf of such a man? No; you would remember, as David did, the man who cursed you.

But if you had a prince or statesman who followed you into exile, who ministered to you in secret, who tried to hold up your interests, who contended for your righteousness and justice, and held up your name and tried to make the people see that you were a good and true man, who held on to you, when all the nation was calling you traitor—if you came back to your throne, would you not show yourself strong in behalf of that man? Of course you would. The Lord says He will show Himself strong in behalf of those of such a heart towards Him.

August 12

Godliness: The Perfect Heart (Part 5 of 5)
by Catherine (Mrs. William) Booth

*For the eyes of the Lord run to and fro throughout the whole earth, to show himself strong
in the behalf of them whose heart is perfect toward him.*
2 Chronicles 16:9

Why will God not show Himself strong in your behalf? Because you do not
show yourself thorough in His behalf. The moment you show yourself
thorough, that moment will He show Himself strong for you. Daniel was
one of the perfect-hearted men; he served his God when he was in
prosperity. He set his window open to pray every day. Then his enemies
persuaded the king to make a decree that no man should pray but to this
king for so many days. "Now," they said, "we shall have him." But Daniel
just did as he normally did, he went and prayed with his window open. You
say, "That was demonstrative religion, that was courting opposition. What
need was there for him to make this display; could he not have shut the
window and gone into an inner room? Why could he not have gone into an
inner chamber and prayed?" Because he would be thorough for his God in
adversity, in the face of his enemies, as he was in prosperity. So he went and
prayed with open window to the God of Heaven, and because He is the
God of Heaven, He is able to take care of His own. His heart was perfect
towards the Lord his God.

THREE: *This perfect heart is perfect in its trust;* and, perhaps, that ought to have
come first, for it is the very root of all. Oh, how beautiful Abraham was in
the eyes of God. How do I know that Abraham had a perfect heart towards
God? Because he trusted Him. I dare say he was surrounded with
weaknesses, had many erroneous views toward man and earth, but his heart
was perfect towards God. Do you think God would have failed in His
promise to Abraham? Abraham trusted Him almost to the blood of Isaac,
and God showed Himself strong in his behalf, and delivered him, and made
him the Father of the Faithful; and crowned him with everlasting honor, so
that his name, from generation to generation, has been a pillar of strength
to the Lord's people, and a crown of glory to his God.

August 13

Perfection not Destructive of Desire
by George Matheson

Perfect and entire, wanting nothing.
James 1:4

Is that desirable—to lose all sense of desire? Is not the cure worse than the disease? How can it be a joy to me to have nothing left to wish for? No, but there is no such fear. Perfection is not an absence of desire; it is an absence of want. The satisfaction of a desire is not its death, but its being unimpeded. To fill any craving of my heart is not to remove the craving; it is to remove that which hinders it. Think you that the longing of love is less warm when it has found its object? Not so. The wish of my heart is not killed in being gratified; it lives on in its joy. It is far more apt to be killed by starvation than by fullness. If I want for a long time, the appetite goes; it cannot exist without exercising it. Neither can my heart's love; it will die by long denial. To be overflowing, it must be satisfied. Its longing will never be so great as in the moment of realization. Its hunger will never be so deep as in the hour of filling. Its craving will never be so strong as in the day of fruition. I shall not cease to desire when I have ceased to be in want. My heart shall rest from its flight; but it shall rest upon its wing.

Son of Man, I do not fear to be made perfect in You; I do not fear that when I have gained my promised land I shall weep for my lost wants. The more I possess You, the more I must desire You. It is the possession of You that makes me hungry; it is the sight of You that makes me thirsty. I cry for earthly food before I have tasted it; but I must taste before I can cry for You. Nothing but the vision of beauty can create my thirst for beauty. It is from the supply of my want that my desire comes. My prayer begins, not where you are missing, but where You are present; it comes from the fullness, and not from the emptiness, of my soul. It is my want that dims my power of wishing, which is my power of prayer. My hope is impeded by fear. My faith is clogged by doubt. My love is blunted by uncertainty. Take away my wants, and You will perfect my wishes. My hope shall become boundless. My faith shall become cloudless. My love shall become flawless. I shall seek You with a perfect will when I shall want no more.

August 14

The Humility of Love
by George Matheson

Love boasts not of itself.
1 Corinthians 13:4

This is the main difference between love and duty. Duty has a sense of merit; love has none. Duty has always the feeling that it has done very well; love never admits that it has come up to the mark. Duty says, "Lord, we have prophesied in Your name, and in Your name done many wonderful works;" love cries, "When did we see You hungry and give You food?" How does this humility of love compare to duty? Is not love the higher of the two? Duty is mere talent; love is genius. Why should genius be more humble than talent? Because it really takes less trouble. It is as natural for genius to soar as for the bird to soar. It is written, "Genius does what it must; talent does what it can." Therefore, talent is always more conceited than genius; it is more conscious of its labor because it really has more labor. Love is the genius of the heart. It does its work because it cannot help it—not because it ought, but because it must. That is why it renounces merit. That is why it casts its crown in the dust. That is why it declines the winner's crown.

Lord, I should like to be among those who veil their faces before Your throne; it is the humility of genius, the humility of love. I can never have the face veiled until I have stood before Your throne; only the men with the front view are humble. When I was far back from the throne of Your beauty I was wonderfully vain; there was no veil upon my face; I marveled that the Cherubim were veiled. But as I draw near I begin to understand. It is their deep sense of love that takes away their sense of merit. Therefore they say: I have no merit in serving You, O my Christ. I cannot help it. It is no crown to me because it is no choice to me. If I served You from duty I might praise myself every morning. But where shall love find room for boasting! Can the mother boast of her devotion to her child! Can the brook boast of its reflection of the sun! My love to You must always make me feel that I am following afar off, never so far as when nearest to Yourself.

August 15

Is Life a Tragedy? (Part 1 of 5)
by George H. Morrison

When men speak of the tragedy of life, I take it that that is exactly what they mean. No one denies that life has exquisite joys. No one denies that there are days of sunshine, seasons when all the trees in the forest clap their hands. But if life is tragedy, its ultimate end is darkness; the play is progressing toward sorrow, not joy. We have to cross the sandbar into the boundless deep, but we dare not hope to see our Pilot there. No matter what the struggle and the strain, life is not tragedy if the end be happy. It is only when we believe that human life is moving towards a climax of unhappiness, that we can talk of the tragedy of life.

Now the mood or temperament which interprets the world this way goes by the familiar name of pessimism. A pessimist is one who says life is a tragedy. And I call pessimism a mood or temperament because it reveals itself in every human activity. It bursts out into poetry in Byron. It creeps into politics under the name of Nihilism. It becomes a religion in the great creed of Buddha. It has its philosophers in men like Schopenhauer. Had you asked Byron what he thought of life, he would have answered that for all its glories it was tragedy. If you travelled to the dreamy East and asked the Buddhist what he thought of life, he too would tell you that human life is tragedy, and that the great aim of life is to get rid of selfhood. Millions believe, then, that life is a tragedy, and all who believe that, we call pessimists.

And I think it is one marked feature of today that that mood has crept into our popular literature. The pessimistic spirit has been popularized in a way that the world has never seen before. I do not forget that the best masters have never accepted that gospel of despair. I do not forget the magnificent faith of Browning, nor the quiet and glowing hope of Tennyson, though even Tennyson, as his life advanced, seems to have lost some of his strong assurance. But the fact remains that the plays and novels and stories that are greedily devoured by hundreds of thousands today are largely tinged with the pessimistic temper.

August 16

Is Life a Tragedy? (Part 2 of 5)
by George H. Morrison

Once, a novel would hardly have been called a novel unless it closed with the ringing of marriage bells. But now it is quite allowable to close with the decaying of hope in a wild and stormy sunset. The belief that life for all its effort is but tragedy, that the world is hurrying forward to the dark, that man is the powerless instrument of fate, a helpless pawn on the chessboard of the universe—this thought, subtly and stealthily, is finding its way into the hearts of thousands in the leisure hours they give to lighter reading. Now I wonder if we can explain at all the prevalence of this pessimistic mindset. I think there are three things that help us to account for it.

Firstly, there is a very noble reason. It is that we take life very seriously now. We are all interested in the great social problems, and that has opened our eyes to the miseries abroad. It was all very well for the poet Pope, for instance, to pen that famous line, "Whatever is, is right." But that was the optimism of ignorance, not of knowledge, the faith of an age that shut its eyes to facts; and I think turning away from that was quite inevitable: brave hearts were bound to rise up and deny it. Depend upon it, that if one century says "Whatever is, is right," the next century will take its own revenge and say "Whatever is, is wrong." The world advances as the pendulum swings, and through extremes we come to the middle at last. I think, then, there is something noble in our pessimism. It at least means that we have begun to see and feel. We are taking life so seriously now, and we are feeling the pressure of its burden so that the shallow optimist who refuses to face facts is out of date by half a century.

But then again this is a time of contrasts, and a time of sharp contrasts is almost always pessimistic. It is when class is separated from class, that men begin to feel the hopelessness of things. In a little village you rarely find a pessimist; the lawyer and the shoemaker are too good friends for that. I mean that the rich are not so very rich, and the poor are not so very poor; they mix and mingle in a common brotherhood, and there is nothing like that for keeping the heart sweet.

August 17

Is Life a Tragedy? (Part 3 of 5)
by George H. Morrison

But it is not village life that is prominent today. It is the life of the great and crowded city. And in a city the rich are a great deal richer, and the poor in a score of senses are far poorer; and the separation and conflict inevitably produced carry the hardness into innumerable souls. Our modern pessimism is not the child of the country. There is no glory of the Highland heather in it; no music of the hills, nor any song of birds. It is the child of the city, that place of glaring contrasts, of down-crushing, of simmering discontent. It is there that men speak of the tragedy of life.

But perhaps there is a deeper reason still. I refer to the materialism that is current. There is a strong tendency abroad that meets us constantly, to explain man in terms of force and matter. In some quarters the great thought of evolution has been pushed so far, and the doctrine of heredity has been so strained, that man is practically a robot, and what we call free will is a sweet delusion. Such teaching is but fatalism in disguise. It is John Calvin without the grace of God. And Calvinism with God's grace was stern enough; but without it, it is the nursing-mother of despair. If I thought there was no reality in my free will, I should become a pessimist tomorrow. If I am only propelled towards the inevitable by the pressure of the long past that is within me, life immediately becomes a tragedy for me. And I doubt not that it is some dim sense of that, moving in what is called the spirit of the age, that gives what I have named the pessimistic note to so many books that are being widely read.

If there ever was a man in history who had ample cause to be a pessimist, I think it was our Savior Jesus Christ. Whatever life may be for you and me, life was no sweet paradise for Him; and if all experience was summed up in His experience, He had some right to talk of the tragedy of life. He was filled with the passion to love and to serve His fellows, yet they cried "Crucify Him, crucify Him! Not this man, but Barabbas." From the hour of His baptism, right along all His ministry, there lay the shadow of the cross to come. A tragedy moves with noble steps towards calamity. Christ moved with supreme nobility to Calvary.

August 18

Is Life a Tragedy? (Part 4 of 5)
by George H. Morrison

Instead of pessimism, Christ talked about His joy; He looked facts in the face and yet was joyful. Instead of that, Christ talked about His peace; a peace that passed all understanding filled His heart. But, most significant of all, He turned to men and said, "I am come that they might have life and might have it more abundantly." This, then, was the very object of Christ's coming; that men might enjoy a larger measure of life. Had life been a tragedy to Jesus Christ, I do not think He would have wished to add to it.

Buddha looked out on life and saw its sorrow; and he said, "Life is a tragedy, let us get done with it." But Jesus looked out on life, saw all its sorrow, and felt it with an intensity Buddha never knew, and yet in the face of it all He dared to say, "I am come that the world might have more abundant life." The question is, can we discover the sources of this amazing optimism of Jesus?

In the first place, Christ was supremely certain that His Father was present and working in the world. Above all sorrow and sin, and struggle and failure, Christ felt the pressure of a sovereign power, and the movement of the infinite love of heaven. In the Old Testament men had proclaimed God's sovereignty, but it was an awful and tremendous sovereignty. With Jesus it has become a much more gentle attribute; it clothes the grass and sees the sparrow fall.

You remember the famous line of Robert Browning, "God's in His heaven, all's right with the world"? That was one source of the optimism of Browning; but the optimism of Jesus went a great deal deeper. It was the fact that God was in His world so that the ravens were fed and the lilies were adorned, and so that the very hairs of a man's head are numbered—it was that which gave a radiant quietness to Christ.

August 19

Is Life a Tragedy? (Part 5 of 5)
by George H. Morrison

Jesus believed, with a faith that was magnificent, in the freedom and the worth of personality, and whenever a man comes to believe in that, it is impossible to hold that life is a tragedy. How tenderly and skillfully Jesus dealt with men! It is clear that every man was a new problem to Him. Were manhood forged and fashioned by resistless influences, Christ would have dealt with men upon the scale of the hundred; but Christ never dealt upon the scale of hundreds, Christ always dealt upon the scale of one. That means that personality is real. That means that every life is a new thing. That means that in the worst there is some possibility that can be touched by love and become conquering. And it was that faith burning in the heart of Jesus like a flame which kept Him so calm and hopeful in the world.

Then never forget that Jesus believed in heaven; He launched life out on to an endless course. There may be many tears in the first act of the play, but it is too soon yet to say it is a tragedy. Who knows but that the master brain which planned the drama may be going to lead the action into sunlight? I can understand a man being a pessimist if he really believes that death is the end of all. The pessimist would have a strong case against the Almighty if the individual perished at the grave. But if beyond that there is eternal life, with its never-ending expansion of the soul, I think it well to suspend judgment for a little.

We shall not lose our individuality in heaven: "In My Father's house are many mansions." And we shall certainly not cease to work: heaven is the joy of the Lord, and the Lord is never idle. All we have struggled to be shall become possible. All that we tried to do shall meet us there. The cravings for better things we could not achieve, the longings that stirred us though never a man knew of them, shall be the first angels to kiss us in the glory. In the mighty conception of that eternal destiny, time ceased to be a tragedy for Christ.

August 20

The Eloquent Silence of Jesus (Part 1 of 8)
by David James Burrell

"If it were not so, I would have told you."
John 14:2

It is a little thing to say of Jesus that he was an honest man. And yet there is much in that; for "an honest man's the noblest work of God." Moreover, there is nothing as rare. The rule among men is masks and disguises. Not one of us would be willing to have a window in his breast through which our neighbors might see the secret imaginations of our hearts.

An honest man is a two-sided man; that is, his silence is as honest as his speech. A lie may be told by the lifting of the eyebrows, or the pointing of a finger. It is possible "to convey a libel with a frown, or wink a reputation down." Indeed, a falsehood may be told by making no motion at all. A gossip comes to you with a scandalous story which you have reason to believe is false; in common honesty you should make an indignant denial, but you utter not a word. Speak up, man! Silence gives consent. Silence is a liar, a slanderer, a forsworn enemy to friendship and truth and righteousness. Let us say then that Jesus, the divine Teacher, was absolutely honest. There was no deceit on his lips; there was no treachery in his heart. His life was as transparent as his utterance; his silence was as candid as his speech.

There are those who insist upon having no creed but the teachings of Christ. If that statement may be accepted in its full significance, we shall not disagree with it. The teachings of our Lord had to do with all the great problems and truths of the endless life. But when we speak of his teachings, we must be permitted to include his eloquent silence. For in many ways his silence was more eloquent than his words. He found his disciples in possession of certain views regarding truth, which, had they been false, it was his simple duty as an honest Master to eliminate those views.

August 21

The Eloquent Silence of Jesus (Part 2 of 8)
by David James Burrell

"If it were not so, I would have told you."
John 14:2

First, with respect to himself. The world had been looking for the coming of Christ. This feeling of expectancy was universal, but the Jews in particular were highly expectant. The coming of Messiah was spoken of as "The Consolation of Israel." They had been led by their prophets from time immemorial to believe that in the fullness of time one would appear who should restore the glory of their nation. His nature and character were predicted in minute detail. This was "The Hope of Israel." The disciples of Jesus as Jews shared in the common expectancy. In their familiar interactions with Jesus, listening to his sermons and beholding his wonderful works, they came to believe that he was the long expected Christ. Let it be observed that he permitted them to entertain that view and uttered no word against it.

At the beginning of his ministry he was announced by John the Baptist as the Lamb of God. The term had no significance whatever, except as it pronounced Jesus to be the fulfillment of all the sacrifices which the children of Israel had been regularly offering in forgiveness of their sins. John meant, if he meant anything, that Jesus was "the Lamb of God slain from the foundation of the world." It was so understood by the disciples, though with only a dim comprehension of the manner in which that implication was to be ultimately fulfilled. And Jesus allowed his disciples to rest in that view of his office and work. As he was once journeying through Caesarea-Philippi, he asked his disciples, "Who do men say that I am?" And when they answered, "Some say one thing, and some say another," he further inquired, "But who do you say that I am?" Then Peter made his good profession, "You are the Christ, the Son of the living God." Not only did Jesus make no disavowal, but he distinctly consented in the words, "My Father which is in heaven has revealed it unto you."

August 22

The Eloquent Silence of Jesus (Part 3 of 8)
by David James Burrell

"If it were not so, I would have told you."
John 14:2

In the upper room Jesus met his disciples after his resurrection, and asked doubting Thomas to thrust his fingers into his wounds in evidence of his triumph over death. Then the skeptical disciple fell before him, crying, "My Lord and my God." Had Jesus been less than very God of very God, he must, in common honesty, have said in that very moment, like the angel in Revelation [19:10], "See you do it not." But he permitted this act of divine homage, and so by his silence distinctly avowed his equality with God.

There are moments when all believers are tempted to doubt. How could it be otherwise, when the great truths lie in the realm of the invisible, and we have only fleshly eyes? We walk by faith. Our faith as Christians rests upon the testimony of our Lord. We stand at the manger bewildered by the mystery of the incarnation. How can it be that he whom the heaven of heavens could not contain, lies here, wrapped in enveloping cloths? We stand under the cross and say, "How can it be that the Sovereign of Life should thus bow to the King of Terrors?" We stand at the open tomb and say within ourselves, "How can it be that one whose helpless hands were folded over his breast, should by his own power break these chains and take captivity captive?" At this point the silence of Jesus is as convincing as his speech. "You believe in the incarnation, you believe in the atonement, you believe in the resurrection, and you rightly believe; for if these things were not so, I would have told you."

I Would Have Told You
by Bryan L. Herde

"Hush, My child, rest and trust in Me.
If you needed to know any differently
I would have told you calmly, quietly
What to do, what to think, certainly."

234

August 23

The Eloquent Silence of Jesus (Part 4 of 8)
by David James Burrell

"If it were not so, I would have told you."
John 14:2

Second, as to Scripture. At the time of Christ, the Jewish people had the most implicit faith in their prophecies. The Scribes were an order of Biblical experts, set apart to the study of the Scriptures. They would not touch the parchment with unwashed hands; they weighed and measured the relative value of its doctrinal truths and precepts. If ever "Bibiolatry" [making an idol of the Scriptures] prevailed on earth, it was in those days. The people regarded the Scripture as the whole truth, and nothing but the truth. They taught it to their children; they committed it to memory; they bound it as frontlets between their eyes.

The disciples of Jesus, as loyal Jews, shared in the common belief as to the infallibility of holy Scripture. If they were mistaken in this opinion of Scripture, Christ as their honest teacher should have told them so.

He was accused of being opposed to the Scriptures because he had denied the traditions of the elders. In refuting this charge he repeatedly announced his loyalty to "the Law and the Prophets," that being the technical title of the Scriptures at the time. He said, "I have not come to destroy the Law, but to fulfill it"; and, "Not one jot or tittle of the Law shall pass away until all be fulfilled." He said again, "Search the Scriptures, for in them you think you have eternal life, and these are those which testify of me." In his sacramental prayer for his disciples he said, "Sanctify them by your truth, your word is truth." He referred with approval to many of those particular portions of Scripture which among some are now suspected to be too fantastic and false. He made reference to the story of Lot's wife, the destruction of the cities of Sodom and Gomorrah, and the Flood. He referred to Jonah in the whale's belly as a prophetic type of his resurrection from the dead, and, in a manner, risked the genuineness of his mission and work upon the truth of it.

August 24

The Eloquent Silence of Jesus (Part 5 of 8)
by David James Burrell

"If it were not so, I would have told you."
John 14:2

We find ourselves in a serious dilemma. If the Scriptures are not true, our Lord either knew or did not know it. In the latter case he was manifestly not qualified to be a teacher in spiritual things. To say that Jesus, in emptying himself of his divine attributes, went so far as to become ignorant in matters supremely important to spiritual life, is to rob him of all that should constitute a true Savior of men. To say that he was not so wise in his acquaintance with the great doctrines of the spiritual world, or with the oracles that reveal them, as some of our modern Biblical experts believe, is to blaspheme the incarnate Son of God. It is difficult to see how any who accept that view, should profess to receive him as Prophet, Priest or King.

But the alternative is worse. If Jesus was aware that the Scriptures were not true, as his disciples received them, but in fact largely a collection of myths and traditions in many points untrustworthy and false—this being the position which many of our destructive critics have assumed—and by his silence allowed his disciples to rest in their cultish worship, their faith in falsehood, their misapprehension of alleged truth, then it is impossible to regard him as an honest man.

The very air is full of insinuations against the book. Have we been mistaken in our confidence? Have we been affixing our faith to an editor's collection of myths and fables? It is impossible to believe that Christ who has promised to direct his people, as he led his disciples into truth, should have permitted us to rest in such a disastrous misunderstanding. We believe in the Scriptures because we believe in him. Our faith in the oracles rests upon the honesty of our great Teacher. There is infinite assurance in his word, "If it were not so, I would have told you."

August 25

The Eloquent Silence of Jesus (Part 6 of 8)
by David James Burrell

"If it were not so, I would have told you."
John 14:2

Third, as to the "Larger Hope." The Jews believed in Gehenna. Their thought of eternal punishment found its illustration in a deep ravine called Hinnom close by the temple, where the waste of the sacrifices was thrown. There the fires were always burning, and decay was a continuous process. From this came the phrase, "Their worm dies not, the fire is not quenched." The Jews believed in a future life. They believed furthermore that the present life is probationary and that the future state must be determined by character formed here and now. And they believed also in the eternity of punishment. To these views which were shared by the disciples Jesus gave the weight of his authority again and again. He spoke of the separation of the wheat from the weeds; of the goats from the sheep. He spoke of hell as a place of weeping and wailing and grinding of teeth. He used the phrase "forever and ever." He said, "If your hand offends you, cut it off: it is better for you to enter into life maimed, than, having two hands, to go into hell, into the fire that never shall be quenched; where their worm dies not, and the fire is not quenched."

It thus appears that the direct teaching of Jesus was most affirming as to the matter of eternal punishment for unforgiven sin. The suggestion that his warnings were not founded upon an actual danger, but merely intended to frighten the indifferent person, is not for a moment to be allowed. He found his disciples and the people generally believing in an awful truth, and he left them there. Had there been a "Larger Hope," a reasonable ground for the thought of another probation in the future life, he must have suggested it. He was the kindest soul that ever lived on earth, yet by his words, and still more by his silence with reference to the common belief, he taught that the only hope of salvation is in repentance in this present life. The belief of the universal church of Christ is the same; and if it were not true he would have told us.

August 26

The Eloquent Silence of Jesus (Part 7 of 8)
by David James Burrell

"If it were not so, I would have told you."
John 14:2

Fourth, as to heaven. His disciples had given up all to follow him. For their devotion to his Messianic claims, they were cast out of the synagogues and persecuted in many ways. They believed in the compensation of a blessed future. They looked forward to a delightful day, when abundant restitution should be made for all their losses and sufferings. We entertain the same hope. The teaching of Jesus with reference to heaven is most comprehensively found in his words, "In my Father's house are many mansions, if it were not so, I would have told you; I go to prepare a place for you." It is a prepared place for a prepared people. It is a home where the redeemed shall meet in joy unspeakable and full of glory.

One of the most frequent questions with reference to heaven is, Shall we know each other there? It is inconceivable, in view of the relation of the disciples to each other and Christ, that they should not have entertained that view; and they must have been greatly encouraged in that belief by the words of Jesus in this connection: "If it were not so I would have told you." I can remember when my conception of heaven was chiefly associated with the glowing descriptions in the book of Revelation. It meant gates of pearl, and golden streets, and multitudes of white-robed angels singing a perpetual song, "Holy, holy, holy Lord God Almighty!" But there came a time when a beloved sister fell asleep, and thereafter her face was always associated with every thought of that celestial city. Then the dear father went, and then the first-born of the household, and then another "with folded hands and dreamy eyes went through the gates of paradise." And now all heaven is full of faces, and there are hands beckoning and voices calling. So, more and more, as the years pass, do I realize the joyous significance of the Master's word, "My Father's house." Heaven is home.

August 27

The Eloquent Silence of Jesus (Part 8 of 8)
by David James Burrell

"If it were not so, I would have told you."
John 14:2

Heaven is the glorious hope which dwells in the hearts of God's people everywhere. We look for a jubilant day, when we shall see the familiar faces of those who have gone before us, and clasp hands in the indescribable joy of reunion, and shall remain forever. The words of the Master, so far as he spoke directly with reference to the unseen world, are all in harmony with this belief. Still more convincing, however, is his assurance, "In my Father's house are many mansions; if it were not so, I would have told you."

What then is our conclusion? Be not faithless, but believing. We are often tossed about in doubts and misgivings as the disciples were in their little boat on Galilee when Jesus came to them walking on the waves. "It is I," he said; "be not afraid." And Peter answered, "If it be you, tell me to come to you upon the water." The Lord said: "Come." Peter set forth bravely until, as the waves surged about him, he began to sink and cry, "Lord, save me or I will perish." The hand of the Master was stretched forth with this word, "O you of little faith, wherefore did you doubt?" Yes, beloved, why did we ever doubt? Our faith is strengthened by the teachings of our Lord in his word and in his silence.

The pagan Pythagoras said, "If God were ever to render himself visible among men, he would choose light for his body and truth for his soul." He has made himself visible among men in the incarnate form of Jesus, which shines ever upon us through an atmosphere of truth. Let us believe. This is the peace of Christian living, to believe in the absolute bluntness of the incarnate Son. "You believe in God," he said, "believe also in me. The things which I have taught you abide in infinite truth and wisdom. If it were not so, I would have told you."

August 28

Why Christ Must Depart (Part 1 of 8)
by Henry Drummond

"It is expedient for you that I go away."
John 16:7

It was on a night like this that the words were spoken. They fell upon the disciples like a thunderbolt startling a summer sky. Three and thirty years He had lived among them. They had lately learned to love Him. Day after day they had shared together the sunshine and the storm, and their hearts clung to Him with a strange tenderness. And just when everything was at its height, when their friendship was now pledged to be unbreakable in the first most solemn sacrament, the unexpected words come, "I must say goodbye; it is expedient for you that I go away." It was a crushing blow to the little band. They had staked their all upon that love. They had given up home, business, friends, and promised to follow Him. And now He says, "I must go!"

Let us see what He means by it. The words may help us to understand more fully our own relations with Him now that He is gone.

ONE: The first thing to strike one is the way Jesus took to break the news. It was characteristic. His sayings and doings always came about in the most natural way. Even His profoundest statements of doctrine were related to some minor circumstance happening in the day's events. So now He did not suddenly proclaim the doctrine of the Ascension. It leaked out, as it were, in the ordinary course of things.

The supper was over; but the friends had much to say to one another that night, and they lingered long around the table. They did not know it was the last supper, never dreamed of it; but there had been an unusual sweetness in their interaction, and they talked on and on. The hour grew late, but John still leaned on his Master's breast, and the others, grouped around in the twilight, drank in the solemn gladness of the first Communion.

August 29

Why Christ Must Depart (Part 2 of 8)
by Henry Drummond

"It is expedient for you that I go away."
John 16:7

Jesus and the disciples have finished their Passover meal. Suddenly a shadow falls over this scene. A sinister figure rises stealthily, takes the bag, and makes for the door unobserved. Jesus calls him: hands him the piece of bread dipped in broth. The spell is broken. A terrible revulsion comes over Him—as if a stab in the dark had struck into His heart. He cannot go on now. It is useless to try. He cannot keep up the perhaps forced spirits.

"Little children," He says very solemnly, His voice choking, "only a little while I am with you." And "Where I go you cannot come." The hour is late. They think He is getting tired. He means to retire to rest. But Peter asks straight out, "Lord, where are You going?" Into the garden? Back to Galilee? It never occurred to one of them that He meant the Unknown Land.

"Where I go," He replies a second time, "You cannot follow Me now but you shall follow Me afterward!" *Afterward!* The blow slowly falls in a dim, bewildering way as it begins to dawn upon them. It is separation.

We can judge the effect from the next sentence. "Let not your heart be troubled," He says. He sees their panic and concern, and doctrine has to stand aside until experiential religion has ministered. And then, it is only at intervals that He gets back to it; every sentence almost is interrupted.

Questionings and misgivings are started, explanations are insisted on, but the terrible truth will not hide. He always comes back to that—He will not lessen its meaning, He still insists that it is absolute, literal; and finally He states it in its most bare and naked form, "It is expedient for you that I go away."

August 30

Why Christ Must Depart (Part 3 of 8)
by Henry Drummond

"It is expedient for you that I go away."
John 16:7

Why was it expedient for Jesus to go away? TWO: Notice His reasons for going away. Why did Jesus go away? We all remember a time when we could not answer that question. We wish He had stayed, and had been here now.

***

Jesus must have had reasons for disappointing a human feeling so deep, so universal, and so sacred. We may be sure, too, that these reasons intimately concern us. He did not go away because He was tired. It was quite true that He was despised and rejected by men; it was quite true that the pitiless world hated and scorned and trod on Him. But that did not drive Him away. It was quite true that He longed for His Father's house and ached and longed for His love. But that did not draw Him away. No. He never thought of Himself. It is expedient for *you*, He says, not for Me, that I go.

Sub-Point One: The first reason is one of His own stating. "I go away *to prepare a place for you.*" And the very naming of this is a proof of Christ's considerateness. The burning question with every man who thought about his life in those days was, Where is this life leading? The present was dim and unknowable enough, but the future was a fearful and unsolved mystery. So Christ put that right before He went away. He gave this unknown future form and color. Eye has not seen, nor ear heard, nor has it entered into the heart of man what the Lord went away to prepare for those that love Him. It is better to think of this, to let our thoughts rest on this, that He prepares it, than to fancy details of our own. If Christ had not gone away, what then? We would not either. The circumstances of our future life depended upon Christ's going away to prepare them; but the fact of our going away at all depended on His going away. We could not follow Him hereafter, as He said we should, unless He led first. He had to be the Resurrection and the Life.

***

August 31

Why Christ Must Depart (Part 4 of 8)
by Henry Drummond

"It is expedient for you that I go away."
John 16:7

Why was it expedient for Jesus to go away? *Sub-Point Two:* Another reason why Jesus had to go away was to be very near. It seems a paradox, but He went away really in order to be near. Suppose, again, He had not gone away; suppose He were here now. Suppose He were still in the Holy Land, at Jerusalem. Every ship that started for the East would be crowded with Christian pilgrims. Every train flying through Europe would be packed with people going to see Jesus. Every mailbag would be full of letters from those in difficulty and trial, and gifts of reverence to show men's gratitude and love.

You yourself, let us say, are in one of those ships. The port, when you arrive after the long voyage, is blocked with vessels from every country. With much difficulty you land, and join one of the long trains starting for Jerusalem. As far as the eye can reach, the caravans move over the desert in an endless stream. You do not mind the scorching sun, the choking dust, the elbowing crowds, the burning sands. You are in the Holy Land, and you will see Jesus! Yonder, at last, in the far distance, are the glittering spires of the Holy Hill, above all the polished temple dome beneath which He sits. But what is that dark seething mass stretching for miles and miles between you and the Holy City? They have come from the north and from the south, and from the east and from the west, as you have, to look upon their Lord.

But it cannot be. You have come to see Jesus, but you will not see Him. They have been there weeks, months, years, and have not seen Him. They are a yard or two nearer, and that is all. The thing is impossible. It is an anti-climax, an absurdity. It would be a social outrage; it would be a physical impossibility.

September 1

Why Christ Must Depart (Part 5 of 8)
by Henry Drummond

"It is expedient for you that I go away."
John 16:7

Christ foresaw the difficulties of staying when He said it was expedient that He should go away. Observe, He did not say it was necessary—it was *expedient*. The objection to the opposite plan was simply that it would not have worked. So He says to you, "It is very kind and earnest of you to come so far, but you are mistaken. Go away back from the walls of the Holy City, over the sea, and you will find Me in your own home. You will find Me where the shepherds found Me, doing their ordinary work; where the woman of Samaria found Me, drawing the water for the noon meal; where Mary found Me, among the commonplace household duties of a country village." What would religion be, indeed, if the soul-sick had to take their turn like the line of patients waiting for free healthcare outside the clinic? How would it be with the old who were too frail to travel to Him, or the poor who could not afford it? It would be physically impossible for millions to obey the Lord's command, "Come unto Me, and I will give you rest."

For their sakes it was expedient that He should go away. It was a great blessing for the world that He went. Access to Him is universally complete from every corner of every home in every part of the world. For the poor can have Him always with them. The soul-sick cannot be out of reach of the Physician. The blind can see His beauty now that He has gone away. The deaf hear His voice when all others are silent, and the mute can pray when they cannot speak. Yes, the visible Incarnation must of necessity be brief. It was expedient for everyone that He went away. He would be nearer man by being apparently further away. The limitations of His earthly body confined Him while He stayed. He was subject to geography, locality, space and time. But by going away He was in a spaceless land, in a timeless eternity, able to be with all men always even unto the end of the world.

September 2

Why Christ Must Depart (Part 6 of 8)
by Henry Drummond

"It is expedient for you that I go away."
John 16:7

Sub-Point Three: Another reason why Jesus went away—although this is also a paradox—was that we might see Him better. When a friend is with us we do not really see him as well as when he is away. We only see points, details. It is like looking at a great mountain: you see it best a little way off. Climb up the sides of Mont Blanc, you see very little—a few rocks, a pine tree or two, a blinding waste of snow; but come down into the Valley of Chamounix and there the kingly mountain dawns upon you in all his majesty. Christ is the most gigantic figure of history.

***

Sub-Point Four: Still another reason. He went away that we might walk by faith. After all, if He had stayed, with all its inconveniences, we would have been walking by sight. And this is the very thing religion is continually trying to undo. The strongest temptation to every man is to guide himself by what he can see, and feel, and handle. This is the core of Ritualism, the foundation of Roman Catholicism, the essence of idolatry. Men want to see God, therefore they make images of Him. It is not so much a sin of presumption; it is a sin of mistake. It is trying to undo the going away of Christ. It is trying to make believe that He is still here. He who seeks God in tangible form misses the very thing he is seeking, for God is a Spirit. The desire burns within him to see God; the desire is given to him to make him spiritual, by giving him a spiritual exercise to do; and he cheats himself by exercising the flesh instead of the spirit. Instead of letting the spiritual appetite elevate us into the spirit, we are apt to degrade the very instrument of our spiritualization and make it minister to the flesh. It was expedient that Jesus should become a Spirit in order that the disciples should be spiritualized. Life in the body to all men is short. The mortal dies and puts on immortality. So Christ's great aim is to strengthen the after-life. Therefore He gave exercises in faith to be the education for immortality. Therefore Jesus went away to strengthen the spirit for eternity.

September 3

Why Christ Must Depart (Part 7 of 8)
by Henry Drummond

"It is expedient for you that I go away."
John 16:7

Sub-Point Five: But the greatest reason Jesus had to leave has yet to be mentioned. He went away so *that the Comforter might come.* We have seen how His going away was a provision for the future life. The absent Lord prepares a place there; the absent Object of faith educates the souls of the faithful to possess and enjoy it; But He provides for the life that now is. And His going away has to do with the present as much as with the life to come.

***

The doctrine of the Holy Ghost is very simple. Men stumble over it because they imagine it to be something very mysterious and unintelligible. But the whole matter lies here. Our verse above is the key to it. The Holy Spirit is just what Christ would have been had He been here. He ministers comfort just as Christ would have done—only without the inconveniences of circumstance, without the restriction of space, without the limitations of time. We need a personal Christ, but we cannot get Him, at least we cannot each get Him. So the only alternative is a spiritual Christ—a Holy Spirit, and then we can all get Him. He convicts the world of sin, of righteousness, and of judgment. Christ had to go away to make room for a Person of the Trinity who could deal with the world. He Himself could only reprove the individual of sin, of righteousness, and of judgment. But work on a larger scale is done now that He is gone. This is what He refers to when He said, "Greater works than these shall you do." And yet Christ did not go away that the Spirit might take His place. Christ is with us Himself. He is with us and yet He is not with us, that is, He is with us by His Spirit. The Spirit does not reveal the Spirit: He speaks not of Himself, He reveals Christ. He is the link, the connection between the absent Christ and the world—a spiritual presence which can penetrate where the present Christ could not go. It was expedient for the present Christ to go away that the universal Christ might come to all.

September 4

Why Christ Must Depart (Part 8 of 8)
by Henry Drummond

"It is expedient for you that I go away."
John 16:7

Why did Jesus have to go away? *Finally,* if all this was expedient for us, this strange relation of Jesus to His people ought to have a startling influence upon our life. Expediency is a practical thing. It was a terrible risk going away. Has the expedient which Christ adopted been worthwhile to you and me? These three great practical effects at least are obvious:

A: Christ ought to be as near to us as if He were still here. Nothing so simplifies the whole religious life as this thought. A present, personal Christ solves every difficulty, and meets every requirement of Christian experience. There is a historical Christ, a national Christ, a theological Christ—we each want Christ. So we have Him. For purposes of expediency, for a little while, He has become invisible.

B: Then consider what an incentive to honest faithfulness this is: the visible eye of the Master is off us. No one inspects our work. Wood, hay, stubble, no man knows. It is the test of the absent Christ. He is training us to a kind of faithfulness whose high quality is unachieved by any other earthly means. It was after the Lord was gone that the disciples worked. They grew quickly after this—in energy, in usefulness, in reliance, in strength of character. Before they had rested in His love. Did you ever think what a risk it was for Him to go away? It was a terrible risk—to leave us here all by ourselves. And yet this was one of His ways of elevating us.

C: Lastly, He has only gone for a little while. "Behold, I come quickly." The probation will soon be past. "Be good children until I come back," He has said, like a mother leaving her little ones, "and I will come again, and receive you unto Myself, so that where I am, you may be also." So we wait until He comes again—we wait until it is expedient for Him to come back.

September 5

God Himself Working His Will In Us (Part 1 of 3)
by Andrew Murray

Now the God of peace, that brought again from the dead our Lord Jesus, that great shepherd of the sheep, through the blood of the everlasting covenant, make you perfect in every good work to do his will, working in you that which is well-pleasing in his sight, through Jesus Christ; to whom be glory for ever and ever.
Hebrews 13:20-21

The same God who worked out His will in Christ for our redemption, is working out that will in us too. What God did in Christ is the pledge of what He will do in us too. That Christ did the will of God secures our doing that will too. Listen to the wondrous teaching.

Now the God of peace, who brought again from the dead the Great Shepherd of the sheep in the blood of the everlasting covenant, our Lord Jesus, make you perfect to do His will. All that is said about the Lord Jesus refers to the previous teaching of this Epistle. It has taught us what the covenant was, what the blood of the covenant, what the exaltation to the throne of Christ as the Priest King, the Great Shepherd of the sheep. And now it says that the God of peace, who did it all, who gave Christ to do His will and die on the Cross, and then raised Him from the dead, that same God will perfect us to do His will. As much as it was God who sent and enabled Christ to do His will, and through that perfected Him and perfected our salvation, it is God too who will perfect us in every good thing to do His will. God's will being done in us is to God of the same interest as His will done in Christ; He cares for the one as much as the other. The same Omnipotence which created for Christ a body through the Virgin Mary, and empowered Christ—who could do nothing of Himself—to do that will, even to the agony of Gethsemane, and the surrender of His Spirit into His Father's hand on Calvary, and then raised Him from the grave to His own right hand, the same Omnipotent God is working in you that you may do His will. Oh, for grace to believe this—the God who worked all in Christ, even to raising Him from the very dead, is working all in us!

September 6

God Himself Working His Will In Us (Part 2 of 3)
by Andrew Murray

Now the God of peace, that brought again from the dead our Lord Jesus, that great shepherd of the sheep, through the blood of the everlasting covenant, make you perfect in every good work to do his will, working in you that which is well-pleasing in his sight, through Jesus Christ; to whom be glory for ever and ever.
Hebrews 13:20-21

***

To remove all doubt of God working His will in us, there is more. There follows: working in us that which is pleasing in His sight, through Jesus Christ. The center words, to do His will, are welded fast between what precedes: God Himself make you perfect in every good thing; and what follows: working Himself in you that which is pleasing in His sight. How wonderful the connection between our doing and God's working. He fits us in every good thing to do His will, so that the doing of it is really our work, and yet at the same time it is His own working in us. God fits us for the work, and then works it through us. And so all is of God!

The first lesson is: The one object of the great redemption is to fit us to do God's will here on earth. For that we were created; that was God's image and likeness in us; that was our fitness for fellowship with God, and the participation in His rule of the world to which we were destined. To redeem and bring us back to this, God worked that stupendous miracle of power and of love; His Son becoming man, that as man He might show us how to do God's will, and how by doing it sin could be atoned and conquered. For this Christ lives in heaven and in our hearts, that through Him God may work in us that which is well pleasing in His heart. What the sinner needs to know when he is called to repentance, what the believer needs to be continually reminded of and encouraged in, is this: to do God's will is what I have been redeemed for. The entire failure of so much Christian life is simply owing to this, that the Church has not clearly and persistently preached the great message, that all God's wondrous grace has this one object, to restore us to the original glory of our creation, and make it our life to do His will.

249

September 7

God Himself Working His Will In Us (Part 3 of 3)
by Andrew Murray

Now the God of peace, that brought again from the dead our Lord Jesus, that great shepherd of the sheep, through the blood of the everlasting covenant, make you perfect in every good work to do his will, working in you that which is well-pleasing in his sight, through Jesus Christ; to whom be glory for ever and ever.
Hebrews 13:20-21

The second lesson of God working His will in us is of no less importance—we can do God's will because God Himself fits us for it, working in us that which is pleasing in His sight. Oh! how little this is known or believed by believers. The call to do all of God's will is made of no effect by the terrible unbelief that says: It cannot be; I cannot do it. Men say that they believe that all the mysteries of redemption, up to Christ's resurrection and exaltation to heaven, were accomplished "by the working of the strength of God's might" (Ephesians 1:20). But they do not believe what Scripture affirms just as distinctly (Ephesians 1:19), that the same exceeding greatness of His power works in those that believe. The will of God is so holy and Divine, no one can do it but God Himself. God has given you a renewed will, capable of knowing and desiring, and even delighting in His will, but not of doing it in your own strength. The work of our will is to accept His will as being indeed what He will work in you. This is indeed our highest glory, that God must work all in all, will work in us both to will and to do.

The last lesson follows naturally: Our great need and our great duty, when we have accepted our calling to live only to do His will, is to bow before God in continual humility and dependence, asking to know fully our utter impotence, and seeking to trust confidently in His power working in us. And with this, to understand that His power cannot work freely and fully in us, except as He dwells in us. Jesus said: The Father abiding in Me does the work. It is "through Jesus Christ" God works in us what is pleasing in His sight. That is, through Jesus Christ dwelling in the heart, by the power of the Holy Ghost, God by a continual secret, almighty operation works out His will in us, by shaping us to do it.

September 8

Divine Leading (Part 1 of 3)
by John R. MacDuff

He leads me in the paths of righteousness for His name's sake.
Psalm 23:3

There is a world of comfort contained in the simple words, "He leads me." It was the cloudy pillar of old which conducted the Hebrews from encampment to encampment; which marked out for them their Elims and their Marahs [resting oases].

The God of the pillar-cloud still directs the journey of His people. He still appoints the bounds of their dwellings; His leading may be to the bitter pool, but often (most frequently) to some gracious palm-grove. Whether, however, bitter or sweet, joyful or sorrowful, how comforting the assurance that our lives are no chance coincidence of events and circumstances; we are not like weeds thrown in the waters, to be tossed and whirled in the swirling pools of whimsical accident, our future a self-appointed one.

There is a Divine hand and purpose in all that befalls us. Every man's existence is a biography, written chapter by chapter, line by line, by God Himself. It is not the mere cartoon or outline sketched by the Divine Being, which we are left to fill in; but all the minute and delicate shadings are inserted by Him.

Looking no further than to our relation to Him as creatures, it is impossible for a moment to entertain the thought of our being beyond the leading of God, and to speak of a life of self-government and self-dependence. The complex machinery of the outer world, dumb inanimate nature in all its integral parts, is upheld by Him: "He counts the number of the stars." If one of these heavenly bodies were to be jostled from its place, plucked from its silent throne in the heavens, it is well known that the balancing of the material system would be fatally disturbed—anarchy and revolution would reign triumphant.

September 9

Divine Leading (Part 2 of 3)
by John R. MacDuff

He leads me in the paths of righteousness for His name's sake.
Psalm 23:3

Shall we own God as the leader of stars and planets, and ignore His sovereignty over the human spirit? Shall we acknowledge that He is Lord in the material universe, and not supreme in the empire of thought and human will? No, "His kingdom rules over all." Angel, archangel, cherub, and seraph; man, beast, worm, "these all wait upon You!" He "leads in righteousness." He has an infinite reason for all He does. It is not for us to attempt to unravel the tangled thread of sovereign control. Israel cried for deliverance from Egypt. Their cry was answered. How? By leading them at once to Canaan? No, as we have seen, by a forty years' period of probation and discipline. God often, like Jacob of old, blesses the sons of Joseph with crossed hands. We, in our half-blind, short-sighted faith, would presume to dictate to Him, and prejudge the wisdom and correctness of His procedure. We are tempted to say with Joseph, "Not so, my father." But like the old patriarch, "He guides His hands intentionally."

As the sheep of His pasture, He may not be leading you along the bright meadow or sunny slope; He may be lingering among stunted crops; He may be turning down some sticker patch—plunging into gloomy forest openings, while acres of rich sunny pasture are close by. But He sees *what you did not see.* He sees pitfalls here; He sees a cliff there. He knows you better, He loves you better, than to set you in slippery places, and cast you down to destruction. He sees, if that fortune had been unbroken, that dream of ambition realized, that clay-idol undethroned—the alienated heart would have gradually, but terribly, turned away from Him. Trust Him. "We expect," says Evans, "the blessing in our way, He chooses to bestow it in His." In the middle of perplexing dealings say, "I *know*" (you cannot say "I *see*"), but let faith say, "I know, O God, that Your judgments are right, and that You in faithfulness have afflicted me."

September 10

Divine Leading (Part 3 of 3)
by John R. MacDuff

He leads me in the paths of righteousness for His name's sake.
Psalm 23:3

What grandeur and dignity, what a safety and security it would give to life, if we sought ever to regard life as the leading of the Shepherd—God shaping our purposes and destinies, that wherever we go, or wherever our friends go, He is with us! Even in earthly journeyings if our pathway is to be the great and wide sea—"He gives to the sea His decree"—winds and waves and storms are His voice. If it is to be tearing along the highway, nothing but that tiny iron thread between us and death—He curbs the wild frenzy of the fiery steed; He puts the bit in his iron mouth.

He gives His angels charge over us to bear us up and keep us in all our ways. If it is to be our position in the world, He measures out every drop in the cup. He assigns us our niche in His temple, fills or empties our bank accounts, makes vacant the chairs of our homes. Let us seek to say, in the spirit of Galileo when he became blind, "Whatever is pleasing to God shall be pleasing to me." We can take no more than the near, the limited, the earthly view of His dealings: let us pause for the infinite disclosure of eternity.

Look at the farmer laboring in his field. All this deep plowing is for the insertion of the necessary seed. In doing the work, he may appear to act roughly. Ten thousand insects nestling quietly in their homes in the ground are rudely unhoused. All at once their covered dwellings are pulled apart. Many a happy commonwealth is scattered and overthrown in the upturned furrow—little worlds of life being demolished by the ruthless, remorseless plow blade. So, some of our earthly plans may be attacked—our worldly treasures scattered by the iron teeth of misfortune. But all is preparation of a higher good, a harvest of rich blessing crowning the soul, as He does the year with His goodness, and making its paths bountiful!

September 11

The Way Known (Part 1 of 3)
by John R. MacDuff

He knows the way I take.
Job 23:10

The Book of Job has been well defined to be "the record of an earnest soul's perplexities, where the double difficulty of life is solved, the existence of moral evil, and the question of whether suffering is a mark of wrath or not. What falls from Job's lips is the musing of a man half-stunned, half-surprised, looking out upon the darkness of life, and asking sorrowfully, 'Why are these things so?'"

In his checkered experience he loses at times the footsteps of a God of love. Through anguished tears he gives expression to his soul-trouble, "Oh, that I knew where I might find Him." "Behold, I go forward, but He is not there; and backward, but I cannot perceive Him. On the left hand, where He does work, but I cannot see Him: He hides Himself on the right hand, that I cannot see Him" (Job 23:8-9).

But though to sense and sight all is dark, faith rises to the heights, and, piercing the covering cloud, her voice is heard, "But He knows the way that I take." All that Providential drama is arranged by Him: life, with all its lights and shadows, its joys and its sorrows. It is enough for the sufferer to be assured that his path and circumstances are not the result of chance or accident. The furnace (to take the new image employed in the same verse) is lighted by the God whose hand was for the moment hidden; and that same faith can add, "When He has tried me, I shall come forth as gold."

Believer! what a glorious assurance! This way of yours—it may be a crooked, mysterious, tangled way—this way of trial and of tears, "the way of the wilderness"—"He knows it." The furnace, seven times heated—He lit it.

September 12

The Way Known (Part 2 of 3)
by John R. MacDuff

He knows the way I take.
Job 23:10

Oh! how would every sorrow and loss be aggravated and embittered if we had nothing to cling to but the theory of random selection and dreary acceptance! But we may take courage. There is an Almighty Guide knowing and directing our footsteps, whether it be to the bitter Marah pool [Exodus 15:23], or to the joy and refreshment of Elim [Exodus 15:27]. That way, dark to the Egyptians, has its pillar of cloud and fire for His own Israel.

The furnace is hot; but not only can we trust the hand that kindles it, but we have the assurance that the fires are lighted not to consume, but to refine; and that when the refining process is completed (no sooner—no later), He brings forth His people as gold. When they think Him least near, He is often nearest. "*When* my spirit was overwhelmed, *then* You knew my path."

Can we realize these truths in our everyday experience? Can we think of God, not as some mysterious essence, who, by an Almighty declaration, placed on matter certain general laws, and, retiring into the solitude of His being, left these to work out their own processes: but is there joy to us in the thought of His being ever near; enveloping our path and our lying down? Do we know of one brighter than the brightest radiance of the visible sun, visiting our bedroom with the first waking beam of the morning: an eye of infinite tenderness and compassion following us throughout the day, "knowing the way that we take;" a hand of infinite love guiding us, shielding us from danger, and guarding us from temptation—"The keeper of Israel who neither slumbers nor sleeps?" Yes, also and when the furnace is lighted, do we see Him not only kindling it, but seated nearby, as "the refiner of silver," tempering the fury of the flames?

September 13

The Way Known (Part 3 of 3)
by John R. MacDuff

He knows the way I take.
Job 23:10

***

How it would take the sting from many a provoking trial, to see what the same patriarch Job saw (in his hour of aggravated woe, when every earthly Elim-palm [tree at an oasis—Exodus 15:27] lay flat at his feet with stripped and withered branches)—no hand but the Divine. He saw that hand behind the gleaming swords of the Sabeans [Job 1:15]—he saw it behind the lightning-flash—he saw it giving wings to the uncontrolled storm—he saw it in the awful silence of his looted home—"The Lord gave, and the Lord has taken away; blessed be the name of *the Lord!*" In seeing God in everything, his faith reached its climax when this once-powerful prince of the desert, seated on his bed of ashes, could say, "Though He kills me, yet I will trust in Him!" We joyfully believe the day is coming when we shall write under every mystic sovereign action, "He has done all things well." He knows and appoints "the way" both for ourselves and for others. Oh, comforting thought! enough to dry all tears and silence all grumbling.

> If all things work together
> For ends so grand and blest,
> What need to wonder, whether
> Each in itself is blest?
>
> If some things were omitted
> Or altered as we would,
> The whole might be unfitted
> To work for perfect good.
>
> Our plans may be disjointed,
> But we may calmly rest
> What God has once appointed,
> Is better than our best.

September 14

Mistaken Magnitudes (Part 1 of 5)
by George H. Morrison

"You blind guides, who strain at a gnat, and swallow a camel."
Matthew 23:24

It was one great complaint of our Lord against the Pharisees, that they had lost the relative magnitude [significance] of things. They were very much in earnest about that Jewish law; but for all that they had sadly misinterpreted the law. They laid great stress upon the infinitely little, until the weightier matters of the law passed out of sight. They magnified trifles. It is that spirit which Jesus is rebuking in the familiar proverb of our text. You blind guides, (this is what He means) cannot you see that some things are great and some are little? If there are larger and lesser lights in the great heavens, will there not be similar differences in God's other areas? It is the evil of not seeing things in true proportion that is present to the mind of Jesus Christ.

One of the great arts of worthwhile living is to see things in their relative importance. I have known so many who failed in what was worthiest, not because they were weaker than their neighbors—for the strongest of us is pitifully weak—they failed because they never seemed able to grasp the difference between things that were really great and really little. Mr. Froude, in his Spanish story of the Armada, makes a significant remark about the Spanish king. He is showing the incompetence of Philip II, and he says: "the smallest thing and the largest seemed to occupy him equally." That was one mark of Philip the Second's incompetence. That gave the worst of all possible starts to the Armada. And for the equipping of more gallant vessels than these ships, and the fighting of severer battles than they fought, that spirit spells incompetency still. It is a great thing to know a trifle when you meet it. It is a great thing to know that cobwebs are cobwebs. It is equally great, when the decisive moment comes, to seize it and use it with every power of manhood. It is such swift distinguishing between the great and little, such vision of the relative magnitude of things; that is one secret of a quiet and conquering life.

September 15

Mistaken Magnitudes (Part 2 of 5)
by George H. Morrison

"You blind guides, who strain at a gnat, and swallow a camel."
Matthew 23:24

Now I think that this gift of seeing things in their true magnitudes [significance] is very difficult to exercise today. We live in such a hurried fashion now, that we have little leisure to take these moral measurements. When I am traveling sixty miles an hour in the express train, I have very hazy thoughts about the countryside. Villages, towns, meadows, woods go flashing by, but the speed is too fierce for accurate observing. So it is with our lives today; they hurry forward so. The morning paper has hardly been unfolded when the children are announcing the evening paper in the streets. The wide world's news comes crowding in on us; we are spectators of an endless panorama. And all this change, and movement, and variety, while it makes men more eager, more intense and responsive, is not conducive to well-balanced judgment. We are a great deal sharper now than men were once. I do not think we are a great deal deeper. It is the still waters that run deep, and stillness is hardly a characteristic of the city.

I have often been humbled, when I lived among them, at the wise judgment of a Highland shepherd. The man was not clever; he read little but his Bible; his brilliant son was home with his prizes from college, and I dare say, in the eyes of his brilliant son, the father was fifty years behind the times. But you get the shepherd on to moral questions, on to the relative magnitude of things, and in spite of all the Greek and Latin of the prizewinner—and the father is infinitely proud of these bright eyes—in spite of the Greek and Latin of the son, you recognize the father as the greater man. Something has come to him among the silent hills; the spirit of the lonely moor has touched him; he has wrestled with a few great truths, a few great sorrows, alone, in the middle of the rolling miles of heather. And it is that discipline of thoughtful quietude, controlling and purifying the moral judgment, that puts the keenest intellect to shame.

September 16

Mistaken Magnitudes (Part 3 of 5)
by George H. Morrison

"You blind guides, who strain at a gnat, and swallow a camel."
Matthew 23:24

This failure to see things in their true proportions is often seen in relation to our grievances. When a man has a grievance—and many men have them—he is almost certain to have distorted vision. You can block out the sun by the smallest coin if you hold the coin near enough to the eye. And we have a way of dwelling on our grievances, until we lose sight of the blue heaven above us. How ready we are to dwell on petty insults! How we take them home with us and nurse and fondle them! A little discourtesy, and our soul begins to fester! We are all skillful at counting up our grievances. Open a new page and count your mercies now. It is supremely important to see things in their magnitudes, and perhaps you have never learned that lesson yet. The man who suspects is always judging wrongly. If there be any virtue, if there be any praise, think on these things, says the apostle.

Of course I am aware that the failure to see things in their true proportions has sometimes got physical and not moral roots. There come days when the grasshopper proves itself a burden, and the simple reason is that we are weary. Let a man be vigorous, and strong, and well, and he can take the measurement of his worries very easily. But when he is weary with the winter toil of a great city we know what alarming proportions trifles take. Christ understood that matter thoroughly: "Come you apart," He said, "and rest awhile." The disciples were overstrung and overwrought, and the tact and tenderness of Jesus dealt with that. What the men wanted was a little rest. Never accept the verdict of your weariness. Never judge anything when you are tired. We are so apt to be resentful and think bitter things, when all that we want is a little rest and sunshine. All that will come, the birds will sing again; the dew of May mornings will sparkle on the grass. We shall see things in their true proportions then. Meantime trust in God.

September 17

Mistaken Magnitudes (Part 4 of 5)
by George H. Morrison

"You blind guides, who strain at a gnat, and swallow a camel."
Matthew 23:24

In this connection to the magnitude of things, too, I find a gleam of glory in the beneficial effects of sleep. Of all the secondary ministries of God for helping us to see things as they are, there is none quite so wonderful as sleep. We go to rest troubled, perplexed, despairing. We cannot see how we shall get through at all. But when we waken, how different things are! Sleep has knit up the raveled sleeve of care. Now Jesus loved to speak of death as sleep. He seems to have kept that word death in reserve, as the name for something darker and more terrible. Tennyson talks of "the death that cannot die," and I think that is what Jesus meant by death. Our "death," for Christ, was sleep, and sleep is the passage to a glad awaking. Shall not that sleep do for us what tonight's will do, and help us to see things truly in the morning? Then we shall know even as we are known. There will be no mistaken magnitudes in heaven. There will be no errors in proportion there. We shall no longer be blind to the relative importance of things that confused us when we fell asleep. The love at home that we despised down here, and the selfishness that made those whom we loved unhappy, and the work we tried to do with so much failure, and the exquisite joys, and the bitterness of tears—all these we shall see at last in their true magnitudes when we awaken in the eternal morning. Meanwhile we are on this side of the grave. There are heavy mists lying along the valley.

I want to ask, then, what are the gospel powers that help a man to see things as they are? First, then, remember that the gospel which we preach puts love at the very center of our life. It makes all the difference what you put first and foremost, and the gospel of Jesus Christ puts love there. That was the tragedy of these poor Pharisees. It is always a tragedy when love dies out. When anything else other than love is at the center, the gnats and the camels are certain to get mixed. For love alone sees purely, clearly, deeply.

September 18

Mistaken Magnitudes (Part 5 of 5)
by George H. Morrison

"You blind guides, who strain at a gnat, and swallow a camel."
Matthew 23:24

Love always seeks the best interpretation. Love never makes the most of petty faults. The windows of love are of the finest glass. And it is that spirit of loving interpretation that helps a Christian to see things as they are. If without love I never can know God, then without love I never can know anything. For every blackthorn [large shrub] that breaks into snow-white blossom, and every bird that is winging its way from Africa, and every human heart, however evil, has something of the Creator in its being. Take away God, and things are chaos to me. And without love, I never can know God. You understand then, the wisdom of Jesus Christ in putting love at the center of our life. It focuses everything. It links the little and the great with the Creator, and brings things to their relative importance. And then the gospel takes our seventy years and lays them against the background of eternity.

***

It is because Christ has brought immortality to light that the Christian sees things in their true proportions. The efforts and strivings of our seventy years are not adjusted to the scale of seventy, they are adjusted to the scale of immortality. This life is not the book, it is the first chapter of the book. A man must be alert to his eternal destiny if he wants to know the magnitude of things. And then the gospel brings us into fellowship with Christ, and that is our last great lesson in proportion. The heart that takes its measurements from Jesus is likely to be pretty near the truth. It is one of the hardest tasks of every earnest man quietly to scorn the measurements of the world, and in that task we are mightily helped by Christ. His friendship reinforces the true standards. Cherish that friendship. Live in that glorious presence. Take your measure of the worth of things from the Redeemer. And when the journey is over, and the hill is climbed, and you look back out of the cloudless dawn, I think you will find that in the fellowship of Christ you have been saved from many a mistaken magnitude.

September 19

The Breadth of Christ's Religion
by George Matheson

You prepare a table before me in the presence of my enemies.
Psalm 23:5

Christ's is the only religion that spreads a table in the presence of its enemies. This is very remarkable, because there is no religion which hates sin like that of Jesus. The only faith that will welcome to its table a guest with soiled robes is the faith that, of all others, desires purity. The Hindu must have the flesh crucified before the river of life joins the great sea. The Greek must have the flesh beautified before earth can be an object of interest to heaven. The Roman must have the flesh fortified before so weak a thing as man can be enrolled in the coming kingdom. But Christ accepts us for a hope, for a sigh, for a tear. He lets us sit down as we are, without one plea of present excellence. All other teachers cry, "Be cleansed and come;" He says, "Come and be cleansed." They tell me to put on the white robes that I may enter heaven; He invites me to enter heaven that I may put on the white robes. They tell the prodigal to reform, and he will be allowed back; He invites him to come back, and he will have a chance to reform. He prepares our table in the presence of our enemies.

I thank You, O Father, that I am judged, not by fact, but by faith. I thank You that I am allowed to sit down in the middle of my foes. You have accepted me, not for what I am, but for what I should like to be. In the very presence of my enemies You have seen me. Ignorant, powerless, unable to put my hand on one stroke of beauty. You have accepted my promise as a fulfilment; You have paid me in advance. You have given to me my tomorrow and ignored my yesterday. You have prepared for me a place at the feast above my position. My table is in the wilderness. My song is in the night; my road is on the sea; my peace is in the storm; my Christ is in the manger; my crown is on the Cross. I have been chosen by You in the presence of Your enemies.

September 20

Why God Hides Himself
by George Matheson

There was the hiding of his power.
Habakkuk 3:4

My Father pretends not to be omnipotent. It is the most beautiful fiction in all the world. It gives me what I call the freedom of the will. He puts me on an open plain, and tells me to walk alone. He never really lets me go, never loses hold of the fringe of my garment; but He hides the guidance of His hand, and makes it appear as if He were not there. He stands at a seeming distance, and says "Come." He makes me think that I am all by myself. He does not let me see His everlasting arms around me. He does not let me feel the encircling care lest I dash my foot against a stone. He does not let me know that I am guarded utterly, jealously, all around. He conceals His supporting arm in a mist; He leaves a margin for my own choice. If I need the fire by night, I need still more the cloud by day. So much vision would destroy my manhood; it would compel me to come in. I must not be compelled to come in; I must come of my own accord. I must not be driven from forbidden fruit by the flaming sword and the cherubim. The stars are so driven; there is compulsion into the way of light. But into the way of life there is no compulsion. I am not a star; I am a soul. I may not be driven; I must choose. God must hide himself among the trees of the garden that I may feel myself to be free.

Therefore, I am glad, oh, my Father, that You have not wholly revealed Yourself; I am glad there is a cloud as well as a rainbow. Men praise You for Your many voices; they ought to praise You for Your silence, too. Your silence is precious to me; it gives a voice to my heart. In Your silence my heart finds room; faith soars, imagination speeds, hope beckons, will longs, conscience cries. Your silence is my music; Your shadow is my revealing; Your night is my day. When I see not Your hand of retribution, I awake to the majesty of unaided virtue. When I hear not the sound of Your last trumpet, I listen to the judgment of the still, small voice. The ceasing of the thunders of Sinai has left room for the sighing of my love; I am glad that You have hidden the fullness of Your power.

September 21

Contentment
by Bryan L. Herde

It is a concept so naturally distasteful
That most find it unpleasant, even hateful.
But it is absolutely essential
And is assuredly consequential.

Without faith it is impossible to please God.
So is it really so very odd
That in all things to be content
Is such a crucial element?

No other God exists
Who graciously resists
All efforts to discount
The generous amount
Of care He does constantly bestow
On us and all those on Earth below.

So how does one's heart grow,
In spite of belief so slow,
To embrace a Sovereign so beneficent,
Possessor of a heart so magnificent?

Growing, relying upon the Lord I must,
As I am developing a willingness to trust
That God is attentive to each detail
And that His promises will never fail.

In spite of feelings too often deceptive,
One's heart should always be receptive
To believe promises forever proven
And the Promiser Who is the Solution.

September 22

Day by Day (Part 1 of 5)
by Andrew Murray

And the people shall go out and gather the portion of a day in its day.
Exodus 16:4

The day's portion in its day: Such was the rule for God's giving and man's working in the ingathering of the manna. It is still the law in all the dealings of God's grace with His children. A clear insight into the beauty and application of this arrangement is a wonderful help in understanding how one, who feels himself utterly weak, can have the confidence and the perseverance to hold on cheerfully through all the years of his earthly life. A doctor was once asked by a patient who had met with a serious accident: "Doctor, how long shall I have to lie here?" The answer, "Only a day at a time," taught the patient a precious lesson. It was the same lesson God had recorded for His people of all ages long before: The day's portion in its day.

It was, without doubt, with a view to this, and to meet man's weakness, that God graciously appointed the change of day and night. If time had been given to man in the form of one long unbroken day, it would have exhausted and overwhelmed him; the change of day and night continually recruits and recreates his powers.

As a child, who easily makes himself master of a book, when each day only the lesson for the day is given him, would be utterly hopeless if the whole book were given him at once; so also it would be with man, if there were no divisions in time. Broken small and divided into fragments, he can bear them; only the care and the work of each day have to be undertaken—the day's portion in its day. The rest of the night prepares him for making a fresh start with each new morning; the mistakes of the past can be avoided, its lessons improved. And he has only each day to be faithful for the one short day; and long years and a long life take care of themselves, without the sense of their length or their weight ever being a burden.

September 23

Day by Day (Part 2 of 5)
by Andrew Murray

And the people shall go out and gather the portion of a day in its day.
Exodus 16:4

Most sweet is the encouragement to be derived from this truth of gathering a day's portion in the life of grace. Many a soul is disquieted with the thought as to how it will be able to gather and to keep the manna needed for all its years of travel through such a barren wilderness. It has never learned what unspeakable comfort there is in the word: The day's portion for its day. That word takes away all care for the next day most completely. Only today is yours; tomorrow is the Father's.

The question: "What security do you have that during all the years in which you have to contend with the coldness, or temptations, or trials of the world, that you will always abide in Jesus?" is one you need, but, you may not ask. Manna, as your food and strength, is given only by the day; faithfully to fill the present is your only security for the future. Accept, and enjoy, and fulfill with your whole heart the part you have this day to perform. His presence and grace enjoyed today will remove all doubt whether you can entrust the next day to Him too.

How great is the value which this truth teaches us to attach to each single day! We are so easily led to look at life as a great whole, and to neglect the little today, to forget that the single days do indeed make up the whole, and that the value of each single day depends on its influence on the whole.

One day lost is a link broken in the chain, which it often takes more than another day to mend. One day lost influences the next, and makes its keeping more difficult. Yes, one day lost may be the loss of what months or years of careful labor had secured. The experience of many a believer could confirm this.

Believer! If you would abide in Jesus, let it be day by day.

September 24

Day by Day (Part 3 of 5)
by Andrew Murray

And the people shall go out and gather the portion of a day in its day.
Exodus 16:4

The lesson of day by day has something more to teach. There are many moments where there is no direct effort of the mind on your part; the abiding is in the deeper recesses of the heart, kept by the Father, to whom you entrusted yourself. But just this is the work that with each new day has to be renewed for the day—the distinct renewal of surrender and trust for the life of moment by moment. God has gathered up the moments and bound them up into a bundle, for the very purpose that we might evaluate them.

As we look forward in the morning, or look back in the evening, and weigh the moments, we learn how to value and how to use them rightly. And even as the Father, with each new morning, meets you with the promise of just sufficient manna for the day for yourself and those who have to share with you, meet Him with the bright and loving renewal of your acceptance of the position He has given you in His beloved Son.

Accustom yourself to look upon this as one of the reasons for the appointment of day and night. God thought of our weakness and provided for it. Let each day have its value from your calling to abide in Christ. As its light opens on your waking eyes, accept it on these terms: A day, just one day only, but still a day, given to abide and grow up in Jesus Christ. Whether it be a day of health or sickness, joy or sorrow, rest or work, of struggle or victory, let the chief thought with which you receive it in the morning thanksgiving be this: "A day that the Father gave; in it I may, I must, become more closely united to Jesus." As the Father asks, "Can you trust me just for this one day to keep you abiding in Jesus, and Jesus to keep you fruitful?" you cannot but give the joyful response: "I will trust and not be afraid."

September 25

Day by Day (Part 4 of 5)
by Andrew Murray

And the people shall go out and gather the portion of a day in its day.
Exodus 16:4

The day's portion of manna for its day was given to Israel in the morning very early. The portion was for use and nourishment during the whole day, but the giving and the getting of it was the morning's work. This suggests how greatly the power to spend a day correctly, to abide all day in Jesus, depends on the morning hour. If the first-fruits are holy, the lump is holy. During the day there come hours of intense occupation in the rush of business or the throng of men, when only the Father's keeping can maintain the unbroken connection with Jesus. The morning manna fed all the day; it is only when the believer in the morning secures his quiet time in secret to distinctly and effectively renew loving fellowship with his Savior, that the abiding can be kept up all the day. But what cause for thanksgiving that it may be done! In the morning, with its freshness and quiet, the believer can look out upon the day. He can consider its duties and its temptations, and pass through them beforehand, as it were, with his Savior, throwing all upon Him who has undertaken to be everything to him. Christ is his manna, his nourishment, his strength, his life: he can take the day's portion for the day, Christ as his for all the needs the day may bring, and go on in the assurance that the day will be one of blessing and of growth.

And then, as the lesson of the value and the work of the single day is being taken to heart, the student is all unconsciously being led on to get the secret of "day by day continually" (Exodus 29:38). The blessed abiding grasped by faith for each day apart is an unceasing and ever-increasing growth. Each day of faithfulness brings a blessing for the next; makes both the trust and the surrender easier and more blessed. And so the Christian life grows: as we give our whole heart to the work of each day, it becomes all the day, and from that, every day.

September 26

Day by Day (Part 5 of 5)
by Andrew Murray

And the people shall go out and gather the portion of a day in its day.
Exodus 16:4

Each day separately, all the day continually, day by day successively, we abide in Jesus. And the days make up the life: what once appeared too high and too great to attain is given to the soul that was content to take and use "every day his portion" (Ezra 3:4), "as the duty of every day required." Even here on earth the voice is heard: "Well done, good and faithful servant, you have been faithful over few, I will make you ruler over many: enter into the joy of your Lord." Our daily life becomes a wonderful interchange of God's daily grace and our daily praise: "Daily He loads us with His benefits;" "that I may daily perform my vows."

We learn to understand God's reason for daily giving, as He most certainly gives, only enough, but also fully enough, for each day. And we get into His way, the way of daily asking and expecting only enough, but most certainly fully enough, for the day. We begin to number our days not from the sun's rising over the world, nor by the work we do or the food we eat, but by the daily renewal of the miracle of the manna—the blessedness of daily fellowship with him who is the Life and the Light of the world. The heavenly life is as unbroken and continuous as the earthly; the abiding in Christ each day has for that day brought its blessing; we abide in Him every day, and all the day. Lord, make this the portion of each one of us.

The following was added by Bryan L. Herde
Ev'ry day the Lord Himself is near me, with a special mercy for each hour;
All my cares He fain would bear, and cheer me,
He whose name is Counselor and Pow'r.
The protection of His child and treasure is a charge that on Himself He laid;
"As your days, your strength shall be in measure," this the pledge to me He made.

Second verse of the hymn, *Day by Day*, lyrics by Lina Sandell Berg

September 27

Excerpts from George Müller's Objectives for
His Global Missionary Travels (Part 1 of 2)

During my pastoral labors for many years I found that numerous true children of God are without the knowledge of their standing in Christ. They do not dwell in the fact that they have passed from death unto life, that they are remade, pardoned, justified, accepted in the Beloved, and are no longer under condemnation. Now, having entered into all this experientially for more than half a century myself, I desire (with the help of God) to bring others also to an understanding of these blessings; and how greatly this service is needed is obvious from the fact that there are great numbers of preachers of the Gospel and pastors, who, being without the knowledge of their own personal salvation, are, in consequence, entirely empty of any real peace and joy in the Lord.

Another object I aim at is to bring Christians back to the Holy Scriptures; to urge them to test everything by the word of God, and to value only that which will stand this test. I endeavor therefore to lead believers to become lovers of the Bible by urging them to a daily, systematic, consecutive reading and study of it; for I know from an experience of more than half a century the blessedness of doing this myself, and also, what loss I experienced during the first three years after my conversion, from not doing it.

Further, I aim at a removal of divisions, at promoting brotherly love among true Christians; and with this object in view go among all real believers, by whatever name they are called, provided they are sound in the foundational truths of our holy faith. Though not agreeing at all with some of their opinions and practices, I nevertheless preach among all, having seen for many years how greatly the heart of the Lord Jesus must be grieved by the disunity that exists among His own true disciples. On this account, therefore, I have sought (in my feeble measure) to unite all real believers.

September 28

Excerpts from George Müller's Objectives for
His Global Missionary Travels (Part 2 of 2)

Since for more than half a century I have seen how very little real trust in
the Living God there is (generally speaking) even among true Christians, I
have sought also in my missionary tours, particularly, to strengthen their
faith; because, in the course of my pastoral labors, the blessed results of real
confidence in God on the one hand have come to my knowledge, and the
misery of distrusting Him also on the other.

Both in my public ministry of the Word, and private interaction with
Christians, I seek to lead my fellow disciples to more real separation from
the world and deadness to it, and to promote heavenly mindedness in them,
according to the Scriptures. At the same time, however, I warn them against
extravagances (such as sinless perfection in the flesh), which are not to be
found in the Word of God.

With God's blessing, other aged and experienced brethren and pastors may
be led to devote the evening of their life to similar service. God has been
pleased within the last thirty-five years to raise up thousands for evangelistic
work; but, it is well known that there are comparatively very few who labor
among the churches, and can bring the experience of a long life in the
service of the Lord to bear upon the assemblies of Christians whom they
visit.

If, through the reading of this book, God should be pleased to incline the
hearts of aged, experienced, and very godly servants of Christ, to devote
their declining years to the visiting of churches, both my dear wife and
myself shall consider ourselves abundantly repaid for our attempt to serve
Him by publishing this Narrative. Hundreds of times, both separately and
unitedly, we have asked our Heavenly Father to bless this labor for Him,
and we are sure that He will graciously answer our request.

September 29

Provision in Advance
by George Matheson

"To him the porter opens."
John 10:3

When a man approaches the right door, he does not need to open it himself; it is done for him. There is always someone behind the right door ready to let me in. I may knock for ages at the wrong one; I may beat with clubs of iron against opposing gates; if they are not the gates for me, they will not yield. But when I come to the true gate, the porter [keeper] opens it in advance. I never need to knock; the barriers recede from before me. I do not carve my openings in life; they are made before I come up—made by what men call accident. Pharaoh's daughter would have walked by the banks of the Nile even if I had not been drowning. The ram would have been caught in the thicket even if I had never climbed the steep of Moriah. The door that lets me in may have opened to let another out. "Then, it all happened quite naturally," you say; "there was no sovereign control in it." Yes, it all happened quite naturally, and, therefore, there *was* sovereign control in it. What is sovereign control? It is the weaving of my life into another life; it is the music of footsteps moving different ways.

I thank You, oh, my Father, that the doors of my life are not left to be opened by me. You have set before me, not a door to be opened, but "an open door." When I come up, I shall find it already ajar, and I shall enter easily in. It is the *distance* that appalls me. My door seems a closed one until I reach it. The struggles of my heart are struggles of anticipation. I need faith, not for the moment, but for the prospect. When the door is distant, the opening is invisible. Be it so, my Father; You have promised me my bread for each day, but not my bread for tomorrow. Yet, let me believe that tomorrow's door has been opened today. Let me believe that, while I was yet afar off, my Father saw me. Let me believe that the Mt. Ararat of my peace was prepared below the flood. Teach me that the fullness of my time is not my struggle, but my effortlessness.

September 30

The Gain of Loss
by George Matheson

Perhaps he therefore departed for a season, that you should receive him forever.
Philemon 1:15

There are possessions which only become our own when for a time we have lost them. There are joys which never abide with us until they have passed through the cloud. We, like Philemon, are enriched by our bereavements. We often hold a faith just because we have been born to it; and its value is unknown. But a cloud comes and removes it out of our sight; and suddenly it becomes precious. We awake to the knowledge that there has been a diamond in our hand. We find that we have been rich without knowing it. We would give all the world to get back what yesterday we determined to be of no price. And in that very desire we are richer, better than we were before. It is better to know the preciousness of faith, even while not having it, than to have it and not know its preciousness. It is better to cry for Christ whom you believe to be absent than to stand in His presence and count it a worthless thing. And the very cry will bring Him back; for what is your need of Him but Himself within you? The cry will bring Him back—no longer to be ignored, but to be cherished; no longer to be an appendage to life, but to be life itself; no longer to be a Sunday guest, but to abide with you forever.

My Father, help me to realize the gain of my losses. I speak of the silver lining in the cloud; teach me that the cloud itself is the silver lining of my life. My life is colorless until Your cloud comes. It is in the moment of departure that I recognize my angel; the wings are revealed in the act of disappearing. Men say You are manifested by what You give; I think You are more manifested by what You withdraw. The veil is never so torn from my heart as in the hour when You claim back Your own. Your gift becomes most glorious when You cover it with Your hand. You have trained my love by loss; You have educated my faith by shadow; You have taught me morning by night. You have hid Yourself behind the curtain, that I may learn to cry for You.

October 1

Trouble at the Thought of God (Part 1 of 6)
by John Ker

I remembered God, and was troubled.
Psalm 77:3

This man felt it. Surrounded by many and painful adversities, he turned to what men are taught to consider the great source of all comfort, the thought of God; and here is his remarkable experience: "I remembered God, and was troubled." We cannot conceal from ourselves that this is an experience repeated in many cases. The thought of God does not give them that comfort which they desire, or which they feel it ought to give. It may be very useful for us to consider such a subject: *"Trouble is not removed by the thought of God."* In doing so we shall not confine ourselves to the phase of the subject in the heart of this speaker, but take a wider view, so as to meet, through God's help, a larger range of difficulty. There are two points of view under which we wish to present the subject—the strangeness of such an experience, and some of the reasons that may account for it.

ONE: The strangeness of such an experience—that a man should remember God and yet be troubled.

Consider that such an experience is *against all that is made known to us of the nature of God.* We do not now speak of the nature of God that is made known in his works, for here we believe there might be room for very great trouble to the most thoughtful mind; the question of sin is so perplexing, and the voice of Nature is so dissonant. On the whole, perhaps, a thoughtful man would be swayed to the view of God that gives comfort. The very thought—I am a sinner, and yet I am spared by a God of justice—may suggest to us the idea of mercy in God, and of his long-suffering kindness having a gracious purpose. And yet it is so difficult to say how much of this reasoning comes from the reflected light of God's Word that we cannot tell how far it would go if left to itself, or rather we can say that left to itself it has done very little.

***

274

October 2

Trouble at the Thought of God (Part 2 of 6)
by John Ker

I remembered God, and was troubled.
Psalm 77:3

"God was in Christ, reconciling the world unto Himself, not counting their trespasses against them. For He has made Him to be sin for us, who knew no sin." It is free, infinite mercy, not obscuring any part of his character, but taking it all into its keeping, and offering Him as a reconciled and reconciling God to every child of the human race. If in the Gospel there are still warnings and threatenings and terrible views of the evil of sin, let it be remembered that the end for which the Gospel entered the world was not to present these, but to present that which saves from them. Many think the Bible is hard because it speaks this way of sin and the sinner's doom. But let it be borne in mind that the Gospel finds the disease in our world; it does not make it. The only new thing it brings is the cure, and it describes the disease and shows the danger, that the cure may be made welcome. Its great word, like that of its Lord and God, is "I have come not to destroy men's lives, but to save them."

***

Is it some heavy cross that crushes to the very earth? "Commit your burden to the Lord, and He shall sustain you." Is it some great emptiness, clear or undefined, some deep and weary longing that cannot articulate, but can only cry? "My God shall supply all your need according to his riches in glory by Christ Jesus." What about the sad changes and desolations of time, when Jesus Christ promises to be "the same yesterday, today, and forever"? What about death when we have the word, "I am the Resurrection and the Life"? Such promises offer us the possession not only of divine gifts, but of God himself; "whereby are given unto us," says the apostle, "exceedingly great and precious promises, that by these you might be partakers of the divine nature" (2 Peter 1:4). That the heart of a man who hears these words and believes that they come from the lips of God should be troubled at remembering Him, must seem very strange.

***

October 3

Trouble at the Thought of God (Part 3 of 6)
by John Ker

I remembered God, and was troubled.
Psalm 77:3

If one thing be true about man's soul it is this, that apart from God no full, satisfying end can be found for it. The soul is greater than the whole world, and the greater cannot be blessed by the less. We should not have wondered if a man had said, "I thought of life and its fleeting joys, of time and its emptiness, of earthly possessions and fame and knowledge and all the pleasant things of life—how brief they are, and how in one day they perish. I looked abroad on worldly friendships, and saw how fickle they were, how a man is wounded in the house of his friends, how death makes homes and hearts desolate, and the bitterness of death flowed in upon my own soul." But that a man should turn with his soul to God, to God for whom that soul was made, to Him who can satisfy it and who alone can, to the light of all intelligence, the life and joy of all holy spirits, and that he should say, "I remembered God, and was troubled"—this must seem extremely strange. Some account can surely be given of it that may help to clear the character of God, and ensures us of finding Him, if we have been seeking fruitlessly.

TWO: *We shall consider, then, some of the reasons that may be given for such an experience as this.*

The first reason we mention is that *many men do not make God the object of sufficient thought.* They think of Him now and then in a general way, when the fact of his existence is forced upon them by the speech of others, or when they are compelled to confront the idea of Him in some crisis of life, in a moment of conviction, or in an hour of trial. But the thought flashes across like lightning in the night, as unwelcome and almost as rapid: God is there, charged with the possibility or the probability of some dreaded calamity or painful restraint.

October 4

Trouble at the Thought of God (Part 4 of 6)
by John Ker

I remembered God, and was troubled.
Psalm 77:3

Many people do not make God the object of sufficient thought. This is the religion or irreligion of immense numbers, and of many who call themselves Christians; they "do not like to retain God in their knowledge." They feel as if they could be comfortable only when they banish Him out of mind, and enjoy his world without being troubled with Himself. Their courage or their consciousness will not let them come to the dreadful atheistic conclusion, "There is no God"; but they will not aim resolutely at the only other consistent alternative, "There is a God, and I know Him to be my friend;" and so they hang in wretched suspense, remembering God, only to be troubled. But if He is to be known He must be sought, and sought with earnest effort. There is nothing in his world worth finding that does not require diligent seeking.

***

Another reason why many are troubled at the thought of God is that *they are seeking Him with a wrong view of the way of access.* The most frequent mistake of all is that men think they cannot look God in the face unless they have something of their own in their hand: good works or good thoughts, some outward reformation or inward repentance. They are constantly putting the question, "What shall we do that we might work the works of God?" and here is the answer, so old, yet needing always to be repeated, "This is the work of God, that you believe on Him whom He has sent" (John 6:29). There is something so great and God-like, so utterly unlike the manner of men, in pardon and peace and eternal life being offered without a single condition on our part, that it is hard to realize it. Hence the many false forms of Christianity that are constantly springing up, and that put outward ceremonies and works, or inward purifications and states of mind, in the foreground ere we can reach Christ. Now, it is the whole effort of the Bible to put Christ first and before all. The Father brings Him forward with the words, "This is my beloved Son; hear Him." He steps forth with the invitation, "Come unto Me, all you that labor and are heavy laden, and I will give you rest." Rest begins and ends with "Me."

October 5

Trouble at the Thought of God (Part 5 of 6)
by John Ker

I remembered God, and was troubled.
Psalm 77:3

A third reason why some are troubled at the thought of God is that *they are seeking Him with some thought of reserved sin.* There is a class of men who have a sense of the importance of salvation, and a certain desire to obtain it, but lurking in the life there is some cherished and unholy object, some friendship with evil, some forbidden pleasure, open or secret, which they will not relinquish. Many a young man approaches Christ respectfully, with the word "good Master" on his lips and the great prize of eternal life in his eye, but the world's love in some form is there to draw him back. They go away sorrowful, for the conscience rises up to accuse the heart, and the heart itself in silent hours counts its poor gain and feels its loss. And whether a man has turned his back on Christ, or professes to be his friend, he can never think of God without trouble, if he is holding on to conscious sin. True peace can never dwell in the same heart with impurity.

Nothing can be more true than that the Gospel offers unbought pardon to every sinner, but it is equally true that it cannot save a man who resolves to continue in sin; because the Gospel is more than pardon, it is life—and only then can it be peace. It says with its author, "Neither do I condemn you;" but it adds, "go and sin no more." We say, "Open your hand to receive the free gift of God," but how can you receive it if every finger closes down on some sinful indulgence? And, if you open it far enough to let the Gospel enter among your sins, the sins must die or the Gospel cannot live. Do you complain of this? Complain that it will not save you from sin and let you live a sinner! That Christ will not quietly hold fellowship in your heart with Satan! And you, you wish to write Christ's name over the door, and will have not only men but God read the inscription, "The Lord is there;" and yet you will keep the world and the devil in the house and wonder why you should have trouble! I pray that such may have trouble and trouble evermore until they find a peace that will stand the test not only of their own consciences but of the eye of God.

October 6

Trouble at the Thought of God (Part 6 of 6)
by John Ker

I remembered God, and was troubled.
Psalm 77:3

We mention as a fourth and last reason why some think of God with trouble, that *they have a mistaken view of God's manner of dealing with us in this world.* We wish to speak here of a class of person more advanced than any we have yet referred to, comprising many sincere and enlightened Christians. They have thought very earnestly about God; they have a clear view of the way of acceptance through Christ; they are very desirous to be delivered from all that is opposed to the divine will; and yet they have trouble in thinking about God. There are so many things in the dark and dismal world which He permits—so much of difficulty in the Bible which they feel He could have made more clear—such troubles in our life, in what we may call our true life, our spiritual life, which we long to have ended, and which still go on. What volcanic outbursts of human evil; what slow progress of the only thing that can cure it; how our way is hedged in with thorns even when it seems the way of duty; how our prayers, do as we will, scarcely rise above the level of our lips and appear to bring no answer!

These questions of God's ways are still for our study, for nothing that belongs to Him can be indifferent to us, and earnest souls will thirst for light on all that concerns Him. But we shall not wait for the answer before we embrace Him; we embrace Him first that we may find rest, and from that center pursue our search, or calmly wait until God discloses it. As surely as the gloom of the cross yielded to the light of resurrection, as day follows night, as the ordinances of heaven fail not, so surely will God have his present strength for you and his coming song. The thought of God that for a while brings trouble shall be made the source of hope, the pledge that all with you and with his universe shall be ordered to a happy end, and even here among the trouble and struggle of earth He can put into the mouth some notes of the praise of heaven: "I will sing unto the Lord as long as I live: I will sing praise to my God while I have my being. My meditation of Him shall be sweet. I will be glad in the Lord."

October 7

Jesus As A Friend (Part 1 of 8)
by James Russell Miller

"Long, long centuries
Agone, One walked the earth, his life
A seeming failure;
Dying, he gave the world a gift
That will outlast eternities."

The world has always paid high honor to friendship. Some of the finest passages in all history are the stories of noble friendships—stories which are among the classics of literature. The qualities which belong to an ideal friend have been treated by many writers through all the centuries. But Jesus Christ brought into the world new standards for everything in human life. He was the one complete Man—God's ideal for humanity. "Once in the world's history was born a Man. Once in the roll of the ages, out of innumerable failures, from the stock of human nature, one bud developed itself into a faultless flower. One perfect specimen of humanity has God exhibited on earth." To Jesus, therefore, we turn for the divine ideal of everything in human life. What is friendship as interpreted by Jesus? What are the qualities of a true friend as illustrated in the life of Jesus?

It is evident that he lifted the ideal of friendship to a height to which it never before had been exalted. Duty had a new meaning after Jesus taught and lived, and died and rose again. He presented among men new conceptions of life, new standards of character, new thoughts of what is worthy and beautiful. Not one of his beatitudes had a place among the world's ideals of blessedness. They all had an unworldly, spiritual basis. The things he said that men should live for were not the things which men had been living for before he came. He showed new patterns for everything in life. In his farewell to his disciples he gave them what he called a "new commandment." The commandment was that his friends should love one another. Why was this called a new commandment? Was there no commandment before Jesus came and gave it that good men should love one another? Was this rule of love altogether new with him? In the form in which Jesus gave it, this commandment had never been given before.

October 8

Jesus As A Friend (Part 2 of 8)
by James Russell Miller

There was a precept in the Mosaic law which at first seems to be the same as that which Jesus gave, but it was not the same. It read, "You shall love your neighbor as yourself." "As yourself" was the standard. Men were to love themselves, and then love their neighbors as themselves. That was as far as the old commandment went. But the new commandment is altogether different. "As I have loved you" is its measure. How did Jesus love his disciples? As himself? Did he keep a careful balance all the while, thinking of himself, of his own comfort, his own ease, his own safety, and going just that far and no farther in his love for his disciples? No; it was a new pattern of love that Jesus introduced. He forgot himself altogether, denied himself, never saved his own life, never hesitated at any line or limit of service, of cost or sacrifice, in loving. He emptied himself, kept nothing back, spared not his own life. Thus the standard of friendship which Jesus set for his followers was indeed new. Instead of "Love your neighbor as yourself" it was "Love as Jesus loved;" and he loved unto the uttermost.

When we turn to the history of Christianity, we see that the type of friendship which Jesus introduced was indeed a new thing in the world. It was new in its motive and inspiration. The love of the Mosaic law was inspired by Sinai; the love of the Christian law got its inspiration from Calvary. The one was only cold, stern law; the other was burning passion. The one was enforced merely as a duty; the other was impressed by the wondrous love of Christ. No doubt men loved God in the Old Testament days, for there were many revealings of his goodness and his grace and love in the teachings of those who spoke for God to men. But wonderful as those revelations were, they could not for a moment be compared with the manifestation of God which was made in Jesus Christ.

The Son of God came among men in human form, and in gentle and lowly life all the blessedness of the divine affection was poured out right before men's eyes. At last there was the cross, where the heart of God broke in love.

October 9

Jesus As A Friend (Part 3 of 8)
by James Russell Miller

No wonder that, with such inspiration, a new type of friendship appeared among the followers of Jesus. We are so familiar with the life which Christianity has produced, where the fruits of the Spirit have reached their finest and best development, that it is well-nigh impossible for us to conceive of the condition of human society as it was before Christ came. Of course there was love in the world before that day. Parents loved their children. There was natural affection, which sometimes even in heathen countries was very strong and tender. Friendships existed between individuals. History has enshrined the story of some of these. There always were beautiful things in humanity—fragments of the divine image remaining among the ruins of the fall. But the mutual love of Christians which began to show itself on the day of Pentecost surpassed anything that had ever been known in even the most refined and gentle society. It was indeed divine love in new-born men. No mere natural human affection could ever produce such fellowship as we see in the Pentecostal church. It was a little of heaven's life let down upon earth. Those who so loved one another were new men; they had been born again—born from above. Jesus came to establish the kingdom of heaven upon the earth. In other words, he came to make heaven in the hearts of his believing ones. That is what the new friendship is. A creed does not make one a Christian; commandments, though spoken amid the thunders of Sinai, will never produce love in a life. The new ideal of love which Jesus came to introduce among men was the love of God shed abroad in human hearts. "As I have loved you, love one another" was the new requirement.

We may note the tenderness of the friendship of Jesus. It has been suggested by an English preacher that Christ exhibited the blended qualities of both sexes. The most kindly and affectionate men are sure sometime to reveal at least a shade of harshness, coldness, bitterness, or severity. But in Jesus there was never any failure of tenderness. We see it in his warm love for John, in his regard for little children, in his compassion for sinners who came to his feet, in his weeping over the city which had rejected him and was about to crucify him, in his thought for the poor, in his compassion for the sick.

October 10

Jesus As A Friend (Part 4 of 8)
by James Russell Miller

Another quality of the friendship of Jesus was patience. In all his life he never once failed in this quality. We see it in his treatment of his disciples. They were slow learners. He had to teach the same lesson over and over again. They could not understand his character. But he wearied not in his teaching. They were unfaithful, too, in their friendship for him. In a time of alarm they all fled, while one of them denied him, and another betrayed him. But never once was there the slightest impatience shown by him. Having loved his own, he loved them unto the uttermost, through all dullness of understanding and all unfaithfulness. He suffered unjustly, but bore all wrong in silence. He never lost his temper. He never grew discouraged, though all his work seemed to be in vain. He never despaired of making beauty out of deformity in his disciples. He never lost hope of any soul. Had it not been for this quality of unwearying patience nothing would ever have come from his interest in human lives.

The friendship of Jesus was unselfish. He did not choose those whose names would add to his influence, who would help him to rise to honor and renown; he chose lowly, unknown men, whom he could lift up to worthy character. His enemies charged against him that he was the friend of publicans and sinners. In a sense this was true. He came to be a Savior of lost men. He said he was a physician; and a physician's mission is among the sick, not among the whole and well. The friendship of Jesus was not checked or foiled by the discovery of faults or blemishes in those whom he had taken into his life. Even in our ordinary human relations we do not know what we are engaging to do when we become the friend of another. "For better for worse, for richer for poorer, in sickness and in health," runs the marriage covenant. The covenant in all true friendship is the same. We pledge our friend faithfulness, with all that faithfulness includes. We know not what demands upon us this sacred compact may make in years to come. Misfortune may befall our friend, and he may require our aid in many ways. Instead of being a help he may become a burden. But friendship must not fail, whatever its cost may be. When we become the friend of another we do not know what faults and follies in him closer acquaintance may disclose to our eyes. But here, again, ideal friendship must not fail.

October 11

Jesus As A Friend (Part 5 of 8)
by James Russell Miller

What is true in common human relations was true in a far more wonderful way of the friendship of Jesus. We have only to recall the story of his three years with his disciples. They gave him at the best a very feeble return for his great love for them. They were inconstant, weak, foolish, distrustful. They showed personal ambition, striving for first places, even at the Last Supper. They displayed jealousy, envy, narrowness, ingratitude, unbelief, cowardice. As these unlovely things appeared in the men Jesus had chosen, his friendship did not slacken or lose its hold. He had taken them as his friends, and he trusted them wholly; he committed himself to them absolutely, without reserve, without condition, without the possibility of withdrawal. No matter how they failed, he loved them still. He was patient with their weaknesses and with their slow growth, and was not afraid to wait, knowing that in the end they would justify his faith in them and his costly friendship for them. Jesus thought not of the present comfort and pleasure of his friends, but of their highest and best good. He did not pamper them. He never lowered the conditions of discipleship so that it would be easy for them to follow him. He did not carry their burdens for them, but put into their hearts courage and hope to inspire and strengthen them to carry their own loads.

He did not keep them secluded from the world in a quiet shelter so that they would not come in contact with the world's evil nor encounter its assaults; his method with them was to teach them how to live so that they should have the divine protection in the midst of spiritual danger, and then to send them forth to face the perils and fight the battles. He knew that if they would become good soldiers they must be trained in the midst of the conflict, hence he did not fight their battles for them. He did not save Peter from being sifted; it was necessary that his apostle should pass through the terrible experience, even though he should fail in it and fall. His prayer for him was not that he should not be sifted, but that his faith should not altogether fail. His aim in all his dealings with his friends was to train them into heroic courage and invincible character, and not to lead them along flowery paths through gardens of ease.

October 12

Jesus As A Friend (Part 6 of 8)
by James Russell Miller

We are in the habit of saying that the follower of Christ will always find goodness and mercy wherever he is led. This is true; but it must not be understood to mean that there will never be any hardness to endure, any cross to bear, any pain or loss to experience. We grow best under burdens. We learn most when lessons are hard. When we get through this earthly life, and stand on the other side, and can look back on the path over which we have been led, it will appear that we have found our best blessings where we thought the way was most dreary and desolate. We shall see then that what seemed sternness and severity in Christ was really truest and wisest friendship. One writes:

If you could go back to the forks of the road—
Back the long miles you have carried the load;
Back to the place where you had to decide
By this way or that through your life to abide;

Back of the sorrow and back of the care;
Back to the place where the future was fair—
If you were there now, a decision to make,
Oh, pilgrim of sorrow, which road would you take?

Then, after you'd trodden the other long track,
Suppose that again to the forks you went back,
After you found that its promises fair
Were but a delusion that led to a snare—

That the road you first travelled with sighs and unrest,
Though dreary and rough, was most graciously blest,
With a balm for each bruise and a charm for each ache.
Oh, pilgrim of sorrow, which road would you take?

October 13

Jesus As A Friend (Part 7 of 8)
by James Russell Miller

Sometimes good people are disappointed in the way their prayers are answered. Indeed, they seem not to be answered at all. They ask God to take away some trouble, to lift off some load, and their request is not granted. They continue to pray, for they read that we must be persistent, that men ought always to pray and not to faint; but still there seems no answer. Then they are perplexed. They cannot understand why God's promises have failed. But they have only misread the promises. There is no assurance given that the burdens shall be lifted off and carried for us. God would not be the wise, good, and loving Father he is, if at every cry of any of his children he ran to take away the trouble, or free them from the hardness, or make all things easy and pleasant for them. Such a course would keep us always children, untrained, undisciplined. Only in burden-bearing and in enduring can we learn to be self-reliant and strong. Jesus himself was trained on the battlefield, and in life's actual experiences of trial. He learned obedience by the things that he suffered. It was by meeting temptation and by being victorious in it that he became Master of the world, able to deliver us in all our temptations.

Not otherwise can we grow into Christ-like men. It would be unkindness in our Father to save us from the experiences by which alone we can be disciplined into robust and vigorous strength. The promises do not read that if we call upon God in our trouble he will take the trouble away. Rather the assurance is that if we call upon God he will answer us. The answer may not be relief; it may be only be cheer. We are taught to cast our burden upon the Lord, but we are not told that the Lord will take it away. The promise is that he will sustain us under the burden. We are to continue to bear it; and we are assured that we shall not faint under the load, for God will strengthen us. The assurance is not that we shall not be tempted, but that no temptation but such as man can bear shall come to us, and that the faithful God will not suffer us to be tempted above that we are able to endure. This, then, is what divine friendship does. It does not make it easy for us to live, for then we should get no blessing of strength and goodness from living.

October 14

Jesus As A Friend (Part 8 of 8)
by James Russell Miller

There was no real pain or sorrow in anyone which did not touch Jesus' heart and stir his compassion. He bore the sicknesses of his friends, and carried their sorrows, entering with wonderful love into every human experience. But he did more than feel with those who were suffering, and weep beside them. His sympathy was always for their strengthening. He never encouraged exaggerated thoughts of pain or suffering—for in many minds there is a tendency to such feelings. He never indulged in depression, self-pity, or any kind of unwholesomeness in grief. He never spoke of sorrow or trouble in a despairing way. He sought to instill hope, and to make men braver and stronger. His ministry was always toward cheer and encouragement. He gave great eternal truths on which his friends might rest in their sorrow, and then bid them to be of good cheer, assuring them that he had overcome the world. He gave them his peace and his joy; not sinking down into the depths of sad helplessness with them, but rather lifting them up to sympathy with him in his victorious life.

The wondrous hopefulness of Jesus infuses all his ministry on behalf of others. He was never discouraged. Every sorrow was to him a path to a deeper joy. Every battle was a way to the blessing of victory. Every load under which men bent was a secret of new strength. In all loss gain was enfolded. Jesus lived this life himself; it was no mere theory which he taught to his followers, and had never tried or proved himself. He never asked his friends to accept any such untested theories. He lived all his own lessons. He was not a mere teacher; he was a leader of men. Thus his strong friendship was full of magnificent inspiration. He called men to new things in life, and was ready to help them reach the highest possibilities in achievement and attainment. This friendship of Jesus is the inspiration which is lifting the world toward divine ideals. "I, if I be lifted up from the earth, will draw all men unto me," was the stupendous promise and prophecy of Jesus, as his eye fell on the shadow of the cross at his feet, and he thought of the fruits of his great sorrow and the influence of his love. Every life that is struggling to reach the beauty and perfectness of God's thought for it is feeling the power of this blessed friendship, and is being lifted up into the likeness of the Master.

October 15

Failures (Part 1 of 6)
by Hannah Whitall Smith

The very title of this chapter may perhaps startle some. "Failures," they will say, "we thought there were no failures in this life of faith!" To this I would answer that there ought not be, and need not be; but, as a fact, there sometimes are. And we have got to deal with facts and not with theories. No teacher of this interior life ever says that it becomes impossible to sin; they only insist that sin stops being inevitable, and that a possibility of uniform victory is opened before us. And there are very few who do not confess that, as to their own actual experience, they have at times been overcome by momentary temptation. Of course, in speaking of sin here, I mean conscious, known sin. I do not touch on the subject of sins of ignorance, or what is called the inevitable sin of our nature, which are all covered by the atonement, and do not disturb our fellowship with God. I have no desire nor ability to speak of the doctrines concerning sin; these I will leave with the theologians to discuss and settle, while I speak only of the believer's experience in the matter. And I wish it to be fully understood that in all I shall say, I make reference simply to that which comes within the range of our consciousness.

Misunderstanding, then, on this point of known or conscious sin, opens the way for great dangers in the higher Christian life. When a believer, who has, as he trusts, entered upon the highway of holiness, finds himself surprised into sin, he is tempted either to be utterly discouraged, and to give everything up as lost; or else, in order to leave the doctrine unharmed, he feels it necessary to cover his sin up, calling it weakness, and refusing to be honest and above-board about it. Either of these courses is equally fatal to any real growth and progress in the life of holiness. The only way is to face the sad fact at once, call the thing by its right name, and discover, if possible, the reason and the remedy. This life of union with God requires the utmost honesty with Him and with ourselves. The intimacy which the sin itself would only momentarily disturb, is sure to be lost by any dishonest dealing with it. A sudden failure is no reason for being discouraged and giving up all as lost.

October 16

Failures (Part 2 of 6)
by Hannah Whitall Smith

We are not preaching a state of being, but a walk. The highway of holiness is not a place, but a way. Sanctification is not a thing to be picked up at a certain stage of our experience, and forever after possessed, but it is a life to be lived day by day and hour by hour. We may for a moment turn aside from a path, but the path is not wiped out by our wandering, and can be instantly regained. And in this life and walk of faith, there may be momentary failures, which, although very sad and greatly to be disapproved, need not, if rightly confronted, disturb the attitude of the soul for total consecration and perfect trust, nor interrupt, for more than the passing moment, its happy fellowship with its Lord. The great point is an instant return to God. Our sin is no reason for ceasing to trust, but only an unanswerable argument why we must trust more fully than ever. From whatever cause we have been betrayed into failure, it is very certain that there is no remedy to be found in discouragement.

***

"Lie down and be discouraged" is always the enemy's temptation. Our feeling is that it is presumptuous, and even almost disrespectful, to go at once to the Lord, after having sinned against Him. It seems as if we ought to suffer the consequences of our sin first for a little while, and endure the accusations of our conscience. And we can hardly believe that the Lord can be willing at once to receive us back into loving fellowship with Himself. A little girl once expressed this feeling to me, with a child's outspoken openness. She had asked whether the Lord Jesus always forgave us for our sins as soon as we asked Him, and I had said, "Yes, of course He does." "Just as soon" she repeated, doubtingly. "Yes," I replied, "the very minute we ask, He forgives us." "Well," she said deliberately, "I cannot believe that. I should think He would make us feel sorry for two or three days first. And then I should think He would make us ask Him a great many times, and in a very pretty way too, not just in common talk." She only said what most Christians think, and, what is worse, what most Christians act on, making their discouragement and their very remorse separate them infinitely further off from God than their sin would have done.

October 17

Failures (Part 3 of 6)
by Hannah Whitall Smith

We can only walk in this path of righteousness by looking continually unto Jesus, moment by moment; and if our eyes are taken off of Him to look upon our own sin and our own weakness, we shall leave the path at once. The believer, therefore, who has, as he trusts, entered upon this highway, if he finds himself overcome by sin, must run with it instantly to the Lord. He must act on 1 John 1:9: "If we confess our sins, He is faithful and just to forgive us our sins, and to cleanse us from all unrighteousness." He must not hide his sin and seek to sooth it over with excuses, or to push it out of his memory by the lapse of time. But he must do as the children of Israel did, rise up "early in the morning," and "run" to the place where the evil thing is hidden, and take it out of its hiding place, and lay it "out before the Lord." He must confess his sin. And then he must stone it with stones, and burn it with fire, and utterly put it away from him, and raise over it a great heap of stones, that it may be forever hidden from his sight. And he must believe, then and there, that God is, according to His word, faithful and just to forgive him his sin, and that He does do it; and further, that He also cleanses him from all unrighteousness. He must claim immediate forgiveness and immediate cleansing by faith, and must go on trusting harder and more absolutely than ever.

***

Our courage must rise higher than ever, and we must abandon ourselves more completely to the Lord, that His mighty power may even more perfectly work in us all the good pleasure of His will. Moreover, we must forget our sin as soon as it is confessed and forgiven. We must not dwell on it, and examine it, and indulge in a luxury of distress and remorse. We must not put it on a pedestal, and then walk around it and view it on every side, and so magnify it into a mountain that hides our God from our eyes. We must follow the example of Paul, and "forgetting those things which are behind, and reaching for those things which are in front of us," we must "push toward the goal for the prize of the high calling of God in Christ Jesus."

October 18

Failures (Part 4 of 6)
by Hannah Whitall Smith

The truth is, the only remedy, after all in every emergency, is to trust in the Lord. And if this is all we ought to do, and all we can do, is it not better to do it at once? I have often been brought up short by the question, "Well, what can I do but trust?" And I have realized at once the foolishness of looking for deliverance in any other way, by saying to myself, "I shall have to come to simple trusting in the end, and why not come to it at once now in the beginning?" It is a life and walk of faith we have entered upon, and if we fail in it, our only recovery must lie in an increase of faith, not in a lessening of it.

***

Anything allowed in the heart which is contrary to the will of God, whether it seems ever so insignificant, or seems ever so deeply hidden, will cause us to fall before our enemies. Any bitterness held toward another, any self-seeking and harsh judgments indulged in, any slowness in obeying the voice of the Lord, any doubtful habits or surroundings, any one of these things will effectually cripple and paralyze our spiritual life. We may have hidden the evil in the most remote corner of our hearts, and may have covered it over from our sight, refusing even to recognize its existence, of which, however, we cannot help being all the time secretly aware. We may steadily ignore it, and persist in declarations of consecration and full trust, we may be more sincere than ever in our religious duties, and have the eyes of our understanding opened more and more to the truth and the beauty of the life and walk of faith. We may wonder, and question, and despair, and pray; nothing will do any good until the accursed thing is dug up from its hiding place, brought out to the light, and laid before God. And the moment a believer who is walking in this interior life meets with a defeat, he must at once seek for the cause not in the strength of that particular enemy, but in something behind, some hidden lack of surrender lying at the very center of his being. Just as a headache is not the disease itself, but only a symptom of a disease situated in some other part of the body, so the sin in such a Christian is only the symptom of an evil hidden probably in a very different part of his being.

October 19

Failures (Part 5 of 6)
by Hannah Whitall Smith

Sometimes evil may be hidden even in something, which at a brief glance, would look like good. Beneath apparent zeal for the truth, may be hidden a judging spirit, or subtle leaning on our own understanding. Beneath apparent Christian faithfulness may be hidden an absence of Christian love. Beneath an apparently rightful care for our affairs may be hidden a great want of trust in God. I believe our blessed Guide, the indwelling Holy Spirit, is always secretly showing these things to us by continual little twinges and pangs of conscience, so that we are left without excuse. But it is very easy to disregard His gentle voice, and insist to ourselves that all is right; and thus the fatal evil will continue hidden in our midst causing defeat in most unexpected areas.

An excellent illustration of this occurred to me once in my housekeeping. I had moved into a new house and, in looking it over to see if it was all ready for occupancy, I noticed in the cellar a very clean-looking cider-cask closed up at both ends. I debated with myself whether I should have it taken out of the cellar and opened to see what was in it, but concluded, as it seemed empty and looked nice, to leave it undisturbed, especially as it would have been quite a piece of work to get it up the stairs. I did not feel quite easy, but reasoned away my hesitation and left it. Every spring and fall, when house cleaning time came on, I would remember that cask, feeling that I could not quite rest in the thought of a perfectly cleaned house, while it remained unopened, for how did I know but under its attractive exterior it contained some hidden evil. Then, most unaccountably, moths began to fill my house. They increased rapidly and threatened to ruin everything I had. I suspected my carpets to be the cause, and subjected them to a thorough cleaning. I suspected my furniture, and had it newly upholstered. I suspected all sorts of impossible things. At last the thought of the cask flashed on me. At once I had it brought up out of the cellar and the end knocked in, and I think it is safe to say that thousands of moths poured out. The previous occupant of the house must have closed it up with something in it which bred moths, and this was the cause of all my trouble.

October 20

Failures (Part 6 of 6)
by Hannah Whitall Smith

I believe that some innocent-looking habit or indulgence, some apparently unimportant and safe thing, about which we have now and then little twinges of conscience, something which is not brought out into the light, and investigated under the searching eye of God, lies at the root of most of the failures in this higher life. All is not given up. Some secret corner is kept locked against the entrance of the Lord. And therefore we cannot stand before our enemies, but find ourselves struck down in their presence. In order to prevent failure, or to discover its cause if we have failed, it is necessary that we should keep continually before us this prayer, "Search me, O God, and know my heart; try me and know my thoughts; and see if there be any evil way in me, and lead me in the way everlasting." There may be something very deceptive in our sufferings over our failures. We may seem to ourselves to be wholly occupied with the glory of God, and yet in our inmost souls it may be self alone that causes all our trouble.

Our self-love is touched in a tender spot by the discovery that we are not so saintly as we thought we were; and this embarrassment is often a greater sin than the original fault itself. The only safe way to treat our failures is neither to justify nor condemn ourselves on account of them, but to lay them quietly and simply before the Lord, looking at them in peace and in the spirit of love. All the old mystic writers tell us that our progress is aided far more by a simple, peaceful turning to God, than by all our humiliation and sorrow over our lapses from Him. Only be faithful, they say, in turning quietly to Him alone, the moment you realize what you have done, and His presence will deliver you from the snares which trapped you. To look at self plunges you deeper into the swamp, for this very swamp is, after all, nothing but self, while the gentlest look towards God will calm and deliver your heart. Finally, the Lord Jesus is able, according to the declaration concerning Him, to rescue us out of the hands of our enemies, that we may "serve Him without fear, in holiness and righteousness before Him all the days of our life."

October 21

On Loneliness (Part 1 of 5)
by Joseph Parker

"I have no man, when the water is troubled, to put me into the pool;
but while I am coming another steps down before me."
John 5:7

A human being reduced to a state of helplessness! Take a man at his peak, when his system is healthy, when his word is law to those who are around him, when a call will bring servants and friends, and one would regard it as impossible that such a man would be reduced to the state of helplessness described in this text. Yet look at the impoverishing and weakening process. First of all, there is a downturn of his business, and his thousands are reduced to hundreds; then the great house is given up, and the proud head stoops under the humble roof. Presently, affliction strikes down wife and child, and the air becomes too cold even for the oldest friend. The next blow is at the man's own health; paralysis withers the limbs once so strong, and the hand which was once the sign of authority droops in pitiful weakness; the voice has now no meaning in it to anybody, its law and force are forgotten. There lies the man in pain, in weakness, quite alone, uncared for, lover and friend gone, and no counselor at hand. He is alone in the crowd; the eye sees him, but has no pity for him; his useless struggles only add torture to his pain.

There is really a good deal of this kind of thing in society, a good deal of loneliness, helplessness, unsuccessful effort, and diminished hope. Oh, those unsuccessful efforts, how they tear the heart right open, or heap upon it burdens which are too heavy! The bravest will is battered down by them. Lonely—oh, so lonely—yet within sight of the healing pools!

Alone
by Bryan L. Herde

Broken, hurting, sad, alone.
From me slips a cry, a moan.
Will someone finally notice me?
"Help me!" is my aching plea.

October 22

On Loneliness (Part 2 of 5)
by Joseph Parker

"I have no man, when the water is troubled, to put me into the pool;
but while I am coming another steps down before me."
John 5:7

Most of us know what loneliness means, for some form or other of the unhappy experience has come upon us in the working out of our life. We sometimes celebrate with recollections of this sort now that we are strong, yet the gash upon the young heart is not quite overgrown; we can still find it, and we are happy when our very failures have disclosed to us the purposes of love which God was working out. Those failures strained us much at the time; they went far towards souring our disposition forever, but we're saved from that ill fate. We have come to see how the long waiting at the edge of the pool has created in us a lingering and hopeful patience towards other sufferers, and we have learned to be more merciful in our judgment of those whose eager haste for self-recovery made them apparently cruel to feebler men. Many times, just when we were upon the point of success, a rival has overtaken us, and left us to suffer and beg by the poolside.

This reminds us that according to the text there is not only much helplessness but much selfishness in the world. Every man has a case of his own, which is right enough; the point of selfishness is that many men, having been cured, have forgotten that their cure binds them in God's law of love to see that other sufferers are aided in their attempts at recovery. Of all who had been cured at the pool not one remained to give this man the benefit of his strength. What a world this would be without social generosity—that is, without one man finding joy in helping another! Selfishness makes the world a very little place; a very cold, fruitless, gloomy corner. Love is the only ink which does not fade; love is the only memory which strengthens with time; love is the bond which never corrodes. We have only as much as we have given; by as much as we have helped other people, we have laid up reserves of strength which will give us mastery and honor in time to come.

***

October 23

On Loneliness (Part 3 of 5)
by Joseph Parker

*"I have no man, when the water is troubled, to put me into the pool;
but while I am coming another steps down before me."*
John 5:7

There is a way of doing a kindness which looks as if no kindness had been done, a gentle and delicate way which adds preciousness to the gift. I have known some men to do a kindness as if they were receiving it rather than giving it, so that the poor were not made to feel their poverty. This was Jesus Christ's method, and it will be ours as we approach His likeness.

We need not look long for opportunities of helping suffering men into the pool of healing; every day is rich with such opportunities to the man whose eyes combine the discernment of good judgment with the kindness of compassion.

This reminds us that Jesus Christ always, as in the text, went about doing good; not waiting for the lost, but seeking them; not standing still, but going after it until it was found. Sometimes Jesus Christ's help was sought, sometimes it was offered, but whether this way or that, Jesus Christ spent no idle hours. The stream of His most merciful help poured from an inexhaustible fountain, and no poor, broken-hearted humble seeker was ever excluded from the healing waters.

This case illustrates His compassionate method. To whom does He address Himself? To the loneliest and most helpless of men! Truly might that man say, "When there was no eye to pity, and when there was no arm to save, Your own eye pitied, and Your own arm brought salvation." The same field of philanthropic service lies before us all. What if we should all resolve that every day we should make a point of assisting one man towards the pool of healing?

***

October 24

On Loneliness (Part 4 of 5)
by Joseph Parker

"I have no man, when the water is troubled, to put me into the pool;
but while I am coming another steps down before me."
John 5:7

The Christian method of service compels men to go out and seek opportunities to do good; and to every man Jesus Christ says, "When you have repented, strengthen your brethren;" being healed yourself, help others to the place of recovery. It is an infallible sign that a man has not undergone Christian healing if he has no care about healing others; it is only an external cure, some poor patchwork of morality which fear of the law may have pressed upon him, not the divinely emboldened energy which warms and stirs the heart with all the impulses of far-reaching love. The philanthropy of morality goes at the command of conscience, but the philanthropy of the Cross goes at the command of love.

You know the difference between the two commands? Conscience never developed a grand nature; it has struggled with urgent persistence and many piercing stings to keep men upright and honest, but it has never worked in them any excess of good nature, or fruitfulness of generous service. Christianity never dulls the conscience, yet never seems to expect much from it; its chief hope is in Christianized human love. Conscience has but a limited effect; love has rule over the whole man. Conscience will use its plumb line and T-square, and with sharp-pointed compasses will describe the range of duty, but love will surround every straight line with flowers, and to the majesty of correctness will add all the graces and delights of beauty. Conscience is like the watchman who travels on his rounds at night time; it is enough for him that gates and doors are closed, and that bolts and bars are all in their places; but love is like the friend who watches by the sleepless pillow of sickness, and with many a kind touch smooths the hard way of the sufferer. Through all Christian service the same principle holds good: conscience may tell a man what to do, but by an almost omnipotent control love makes him do it.

***

October 25

On Loneliness (Part 5 of 5)
by Joseph Parker

"I have no man, when the water is troubled, to put me into the pool;
but while I am coming another steps down before me."
John 5:7

This brings me to say that the lost man's hope is in Jesus Christ. He who saves the sufferer at Bethesda must save all other dying men. It is the glory of Jesus Christ that He saves when others give up in despair. He seeks the lost. When a man feels that the last human hope has gone out, and left his sky without a streak or glimmer of light, Jesus Christ will come through all the darkness, and make it glow with the brightness of morning. But not until then. So long as man puts his hope in men, Jesus Christ stands off; but as soon as the dying eye turns towards Him all His heart opens in one great offering of life. This is the Gospel which we have to preach; can you wonder why now and again we are carried away in a perfect ecstasy of joy? We have felt the sad loneliness and helplessness of sin, and none can tell what gladness was brought to our hearts when Jesus Christ first spoke to us. There was a tone in His voice which was lacking in all others, a persuasive kindness which quite won us back to hope.

***

So our text has two sides—one dark, the other bright. On the one side we see what sin would bring us to, what loneliness, helplessness, and extremity of suffering; on the other we see from where comes the light of hope and the hand of unfailing power. As the poor man at Bethesda was anxious for salvation, as Jesus spoke to that poor man, so He speaks to every one of us; and now is the solemn hour in which we may return an answer to Christ's entreating love. Now we are without excuse. Jesus himself will testify against us if we complain of helplessness. His arm is our arm; his resources are ours; his divinity is our sun and shield. Don't throw away this word of hope; hide it in your troubled hearts; listen to it when the world is gloomy and silent, and even though you are depressed you shall be saved by the One Savior of helpless men. I urge you to hope in Christ.

October 26

The Unconditional, Conditional, Unconditional Love of God
(Part 1 of 3)
by Bryan L. Herde

*"For God so loved the world that He gave His only Son that whoever believes in Him
should not perish but have eternal life."*
John 3:16

One verse, three very large truths. Motivated by immeasurable and holy love for people, God's unconditional love moved Him to reconcile the separation sin created. But His unconditional love in giving His Son, Jesus, did require the fulfillment of one condition in order for it to be fully effective in each and every heart. And that one thing is being able to stand before God in perfect holiness. In order for that to happen, each person "must be born again" (John 3:7 KJV) by believing that:

- Jesus is who the Bible says He is: "Yes, Lord," Martha told Him, "I believe that you are the Christ, the Son of God, who was to come into the world" (John 11:27);
- "For all have sinned and fallen short of the glory of God" (Romans 3:23);
- Jesus did what He said He would do, which was to "give His life as a ransom for many" (Matthew 20:28);
- Consequently, "God made Him [Jesus], who had no sin to be sin for us, so that in Him we might become the righteousness of God" (2 Corinthians 5:21); and
- "Therefore, there is now no condemnation for those who are in Christ Jesus, because through Christ Jesus the law of the Spirit of life set me free from the law of sin and death" (Romans 8:1-2).

With belief, the unconditional love of God is fully engaged in the life of every believer:

For I am convinced that neither death nor life, neither angels nor demons, neither the present nor the future, nor any powers, neither height nor depth, nor anything else in all creation, will be able to separate us from the love of God that is in Christ Jesus our Lord (Romans 8:38-39).

October 27

The Unconditional, Conditional, Unconditional Love of God
(Part 2 of 3)
by Bryan L. Herde

"For God so loved the world that He gave His only Son that whoever believes in Him should not perish but have eternal life."
John 3:16

The unconditional love of God for all people was succinctly communicated by Jesus when He said, "Greater love has no one than this, that he lay down his life for his friends" (John 15:13). God did precisely that in Christ for everyone. The unconditional love and full acceptance of those who believe in Christ are clearly affirmed by the prayer of Jesus the night before He was crucified (John 17:20-26):

"My prayer is not for them alone. I pray also for those who will believe in Me through their message, that all of them may be one, Father, just as You are in Me and I am in You...Righteous Father, though the world does not know You, I know You, and they know that You have sent Me. I have made You known to them, and will continue to make You known in order that the love You have for Me may be in them and that I Myself may be in them."

It is the conditional aspect of God's love that is so easily and, dare I say, readily bypassed in our world today. Much is said about God's love, but extremely little about holiness, especially as He Himself defines it, qualifies it, and requires it. That is why it is impossible to separate the fact that "God is love" (1 John 4:16) from the fact that "God is holy" (Psalms 99:9). What many want to avoid is the inherent purity of God's love. Its pure and uncompromising holiness are the imbedded "DNA" of who He is. Being that He is both love and holy, one cannot simply ignore, or even prefer the other. Both essences are fully unified so that God is not:

Fickle	Unjust
Erratic	Unfair
Uncertain	Whimsical
Nebulous	Subject to man's desires or standards
Flawed	Capable of being defined by personal preferences

October 28

The Unconditional, Conditional, Unconditional Love of God
(Part 3 of 3)
by Bryan L. Herde

"For God so loved the world that He gave His only Son that whoever believes in Him should not perish but have eternal life."
John 3:16

God is a purity that is not subject to the definitions of society. God Himself plainly speaks about holiness and its essential reality throughout all of Scripture, including the New Testament. This vital truth is especially clear in Hebrews 12:14, "Make every effort to live in peace with all men and to be holy; without holiness *no one* will see the Lord" (emphasis added). So you see that love and holiness are inextricably intertwined. Love that isn't holy is something else, but it is definitely not God's love. And even more absolute is the fact that since God is the Creator of all, and He is love, then love itself can only be defined by the One who is love and who has created mankind in His own image with love being an inherent part of that whole. However, with the fall of Adam and Eve, love in humans has been distorted into something other than what it was intended to be. Hence, "love" often describes many things that aren't truly love, such as lustful desires, fornication (pre-marital sex), adultery, or worse. Furthermore, the only way that individual holiness can be secured is to have it granted by accepting the holiness of Jesus Christ as becoming one's own holiness (1 Corinthians 1:30).

The unconditional love of God has this as its one condition: you must be born again, for "whoever believes in the Son has eternal life, but whoever rejects the Son will not see life, for God's wrath remains on him" (John 3:36). Once a person has satisfied this one condition, the unconditional love of God is then able to flow freely and securely for that person as promised to us in Romans 8:39, "nothing in all creation will be able to separate us from the love of God that is in Christ Jesus." Unconditionally, the love of God gave His only Son for us. Conditionally, the love of God is received through belief in Jesus Christ. Unconditionally, the love of God fully encompasses us in Christ.

October 29

Instinctive Christians
by George Matheson

That you may be found of Him in peace.
2 Peter 3:14

There are two sets of minds in the Christian life—those who find Christ and those whom Christ finds. Those who find Christ are active; those who are found by Christ are passive. The one has a hard struggle; the other enters the gates "in peace." There are some whose experience is that of the wise men of the East; they search for the star, and discover it after many days. There are others like the keepers of the flock of Bethlehem: they are engaged in their own work, and the star comes to them. The men of the East are men of talent; they plan, and they succeed. But the keepers of the flock are men of genius: they never need to plan; they are illuminated in a moment. In the middle of their daily toil there is suddenly with them a multitude of the heavenly host singing "glory." They are like the great masters in music: their work costs them little trouble. They are born to love; they are made to sacrifice; they are bound to say the right thing at the right time. The garment of goodness looks good on them, it sits gracefully on them. It is a garment, not of heaviness, but of praise. The men who are found by Christ take the kingdom by violence.

Son of Man, I would like to be one of Your men of genius—one of those who are found by You. I would like Your life to be my starting point rather than my goal. I would rather fly with You than to You. I do not want to wait for Your rest until the end of the journey; I want to journey on Your wing. I would have rest before I start—rest to help my start, rest to sustain my start. It is by Your rest I would travel; I would walk by rest, run by rest, fly by rest. There is no power of motion like resting in You. The caring of Your Spirit is a rushing, mighty wind; it will carry me beyond myself—into the life of my brother. Wait not until I seek You, among the troubles of the wilderness. Bring Your message of peace, and I shall be strengthened for every war. I shall find myself when I am found by You.

October 30

The Answer to Prayer
by George Matheson

*Now know I that the Lord saves His anointed; He will hear him from His
holy heaven with the saving strength of His right hand.*
Psalm 20:6

The deepest answer to prayer is not a voice—not a "yes" or a "no"; it is the support of a hand. This is not the common view. I cry to God in the night, and strain through the silence for a message. I never doubt that the answer shall be a voice, never dream that the reply shall be nothing but a consent or a denial. I have asked for the removal of a trouble; I assume that it will either be granted or refused. Not so thinks the Psalmist. His best hope for prayer is neither the one nor the other. He says that God answers His anointed souls, not by a voice, but by a hand—not directly, but indirectly. There comes from the silent skies no ringing of music; there flashes through the outward dark no gleam of glory; but into the heart there steals a strange strength, an unaccountable peace. Perhaps it was not felt at once. You were in search of another kind of answer, and may not have recognized its coming. It seemed to grow up naturally, to be a bit of yourself, to have nothing superhuman in it. It was not like an answer to prayer at all—it was so woven with your ordinary life. Yet, it was God's own messenger, the response to your cry of yesterday. You spoke to God through one door, and He answered you by another; you opened at the front, and He came in at the back; you asked to be lifted into heaven, and He gave you more power to live on earth; you craved melody for the ear, and He sent you, instead, the saving strength of His right hand.

Son of Man, I accept the answer that was given to You. Your cup did not pass, but Your angel came. Your angel came by the back door, when You were weeping at the front. He came before Your tears were ended. The answer to Your prayer entered Your heart unseen. It was born in the hour of sorrow; it grew up while Your tears were falling; but when it was full grown, there was a great calm. When I pour forth my soul in strong crying and tears, let me believe that the answer is already come. I am looking too far to find it. I seek it in the clearing of the cloud; I expect it in the spilling of the cup; my eye is all on the front, and I forget the back door.

October 31

Frightening Things We No Longer Fear
by Bryan L. Herde

Be alert and of sober mind. Your enemy the devil prowls around like a roaring lion looking for someone to devour. Resist him, standing firm in the faith, because you know that the family of believers throughout the world is undergoing the same kind of sufferings.
1 Peter 5:8-9

For we do not wrestle against flesh and blood, but against principalities, against powers, against the rulers of the darkness of this age, against spiritual hosts of wickedness in the heavenly places.
Ephesians 6:12

In the King James Bible there are nearly one hundred instances where "fear not" and "be not afraid" are spoken, mostly directly by God, or one of His angels, or one of His prophets, or by Jesus Christ. We must remember that though our spiritual enemy is powerful, he is a defeated enemy: "And having disarmed the powers and authorities, God made a public spectacle of them, triumphing over them by the cross" (Colossians 2:15).

By the authority of Christ Himself, we have been granted the ability to "resist the devil and he will flee from you" (James 4:7). Don't you love the word "flee?" Not "slink," or "slowly walk" or "hesitatingly depart." "Flee!" However, I don't believe that many of us consciously do this nearly as often as we should. By the shout of faith and the confidence we have in Christ, we proclaim "I resist you, my enemy, in the Almighty Name of Jesus Christ!" How often do we feel the cloud of oppression settle upon us, when instead, by trusting the promise of resisting Satan, we can claim the freedom we have in Christ?

So on this day known as Halloween, if you really want to dress up in something powerful and impressive, then follow the instructions given to us in Ephesians 6:14, "Put on the full armor of God, so that when the day of evil comes, you may be able to stand your ground." Clad in the armor of Christ, and facing an already defeated enemy, we can stand fearlessly and confidently in Christ, Who is our Strength, our Shield and our Defender.

November 1

Triumph of Faith (Part 1 of 4)
by Andrew Murray

And the man believed the word that Jesus had spoken unto him.
John 4:50

***

This story [of the royal official with the sick son] has often been used to illustrate the different steps of faith in the spiritual life. Let me point out to you the three aspects of faith which we have here: first, faith seeking; then, faith finding; and then, faith enjoying. Or, still better: faith struggling; faith resting; faith triumphing. First of all, faith struggling.

Here is a man, a heathen, a nobleman, who has heard about Christ. He has a dying son at Capernaum, and in his desperation leaves his home, and walks some six or seven hours away to Cana of Galilee. He goes to Jesus, and his prayer is that the Lord will come down to Capernaum and heal his son. Christ said to him, "Except you see signs and wonders, you will not believe." He saw that the nobleman wanted Him to come and stand beside the child. This man had not the faith of the centurion—"Only speak a word." He had faith. It was faith that came from hearsay, and it was faith that did, to a certain extent, hope in Christ; but it was not the faith in Christ's power such as Christ desired. Still Christ accepted and met this faith. After the Lord had thus told him what He wished—a faith that could fully trust Him—the nobleman cried the second time, "Sir, come down before my child dies." Seeing his earnestness and his trust, Christ said, "Go your way; your son lives." And then we read that the nobleman believed. He believed, and he went his way. He believed the word that Jesus had spoken. In that he rested and was content. And he went away without having any other pledge than the word of Jesus. As he was walking homeward, the servants met him, to tell him his son lived. He asked at what hour he began to mend. And when they told him, he knew it was at the very hour that Jesus was speaking to him. He had at first a faith that was seeking, and struggling, and searching for blessing; then he had a faith that accepted the blessing simply as it was contained in the word of Jesus.

November 2

Triumph of Faith (Part 2 of 4)
by Andrew Murray

And the man believed the word that Jesus had spoken unto him.
John 4:50

Then came the third step in his faith. He believed with his whole household. That is to say, he did not only believe that Christ could do just this one thing, the healing of his son; but he believed in Christ as his Lord. He gave himself up entirely to be a disciple of Jesus. And that not only alone, but with his whole house.

Many Christians are like the nobleman. They have heard about a better life. They have met certain individuals by whose Christian lives they have been impressed, and consequently have felt that Christ can do wonderful things for a man. Many Christians say in their heart, "I am sure there is a better life for me to live; how I wish I could be brought to that blessed state!" But they have not much hope about it. And if you say, "Do you believe that He will do it for you?" they at once say, "I know He is willing, but whether He will actually do it for me I do not know. I am not sure that I am prepared. I do not know if I am advanced enough. I do not know if I have enough grace for that."

The struggling and wrestling and seeking are the beginnings of faith in you—a faith that desires and hopes. But it must go on further. And how can that faith advance? Look at the second step. There is the nobleman, and Christ speaks to him this wonderful word: "Go your way; your son lives;" and the nobleman simply rests upon that word of the living Jesus. He rests on it, and without any proof of what he is to get, and without one man in the world to encourage him, He goes away home with the thought, "I have received the blessing I sought; I have got life from the dead for my son. The living Christ promised it to me, and on that I rest." The struggling, seeking faith has become a resting faith. The man has entered into rest about his son.

November 3

Triumph of Faith (Part 3 of 4)
by Andrew Murray

And the man believed the word that Jesus had spoken unto him.
John 4:50

Dear believers, this is the one thing God asks you to do: God has said that in Christ you have eternal life, the more abundant life; Christ has said to you, "I live, and you shall live also." The Word says to us that Christ is our Peace, our Victory over every enemy, who leads us into the rest of God. These are the words of God, and His message has come to us that Christ can do for us what Moses could not have done. Moses had no Christ to live in him. But it is told to you that you can have what Moses had not; you can have a living Christ within you. And are you going to believe that, apart from any experience, and apart from any consciousness of strength? If the peace of God is to rule in your heart, it is the God of peace Himself Who must be there to do it. The peace is inseparable from God.

Take care! Do not seek the peace of God or the peace of Christ apart from God and Christ. But how does Christ come to me? He comes to me in this precious Word; and just as He said to the nobleman, "Go home; your son lives," so Christ comes to me today, and He says, "Go your way; your Savior lives." "Lo, I am with you always." "I live, and you shall live also." "I wait to take charge of your whole life. Will you let me do this? Trust to me all that is evil and feeble; your whole sinful and perverse nature—give it up to Me; that dying, sin-sick soul—give it up to Me, and I will take care of it." Will you not listen and hear Him speak to your soul? Will you not, like the nobleman, take the simple step of faith, and believe the word Jesus has spoken? Will you not say, "Lord Jesus, You have spoken: I can rest on Your Word. I have seen that Christ is willing to be more to me than I ever knew; I have seen that Christ is willing to be my life in the most actual and intense meaning of the words." All that we know about the Holy Ghost sums itself up in this one thing: The Holy Ghost comes to make Christ an actual, indwelling, always-abiding Savior.

November 4

Triumph of Faith (Part 4 of 4)
by Andrew Murray

And the man believed the word that Jesus had spoken unto him.
John 4:50

Lastly, comes the triumphant faith. The man went home holding tightly to the promise. He had only one promise, but he held it firmly. When God gives me a promise, He is just as near me as when He fulfills it. That is a great comfort. When I have the promise I have also the assurance of the fulfillment. But the whole heart of God is in His promise, just as much as in the fulfillment of it, and sometimes God, the promiser, is more precious because I am compelled to cling more to Him, and to come closer, and to live by simple faith, and to adore His love. Do not think this is a hard life, to be living upon a promise. It means depending upon the everlasting God. Who is going to say that is hard? It means depending upon the crucified, the loving Christ. Be ashamed to say that is a difficult thing. It is a blessed thing.

And if you want spiritual power in your own house, if you want power in your Bible class, if you want power in your social circle, if you want power to influence the nation and if you want power to influence the Church of Christ, see where it begins. Come into contact with Jesus in this rest of faith that accepts His life fully, that trusts Him fully, and the power will come by faith to overcome the world; by faith to bless others; by faith to live a life to the glory of God. Go your way, your soul lives; for it is Jesus Christ who lives within you. Go your way; not trembling and fearful, but *rest in the word and the power of the Son of God.* "Lo, I am with you always." Go your way, with the heart open to welcome Him, and the heart believing He has come in. Surely we have not prayed in vain. Christ has listened to the yearnings of our hearts and has entered in. Let us go our way quietly, restfully, full of praise, and joy, and trust; ever hearing the words of our Master, "Go your way, your soul lives;" and ever saying, "I have trusted Christ to reveal His abundant life in my soul."

November 5

Curiosity (Part 1 of 5)
by George H. Morrison

*And He killed the men of Bethshemesh because they had looked
into the ark of the Lord.*
1 Samuel 6:19

It was a great day for the men of Bethshemesh when the cattle came lowing along the highway, and the ark of God was restored to them again. It was like the restoration of nationality, when they saw that symbol of God upon the cart. The ark had been a prisoner with the Philistines. Now it was back again, and there was hope. I do not wonder that they rejoiced to see it, as they were reaping their wheat harvest in the valley.

But joy has got its perils as well as sorrow. To be too glad is sometimes dangerous. The heavens are all blue; the only cloud on the infinite expanse is but a speck no bigger than a man's hand; but elements of storm and thunder may be in it. So was it at Bethshemesh as they rejoiced while they were gathering their wheat harvest in the valley. They were so happy, they forgot themselves; something of reverence and awe had passed away. Here was the ark; but were the old tablets of stone inside the ark? Or had the Philistines, with their immoral hands, damaged that writing of God's finger? Oh, how they longed to know! Until at last, somewhat unhinged by joy, and it may be a little flushed with wine, their burning curiosity mastered them, and they looked into the ark of the Lord. And God was angry at that rude disrespect, and He killed the men of Bethshemesh. And the joy of harvest was turned into a funeral hymn, because the Lord had killed many of the people.

You see, then, what the sin of Bethshemesh was. It was the sin of unlawful curiosity. It was the irreverent prying of the thoughtless into the secret place of the Creator.

November 6

Curiosity (Part 2 of 5)
by George H. Morrison

*And He killed the men of Bethshemesh because they had looked
into the ark of the Lord.*
1 Samuel 6:19

O friend, although there are no golden cherubim with touching wings over the mercy-seat, although there are no poles to bear it by, no tables of grey stone from Sinai in it, remember there is still an ark of God! There is an ark of God wherever man is, for the presence of the Infinite is there. There is an ark of God wherever Christ is, for in Him dwells the fullness of the Godhead bodily. And when I peek lovelessly into my neighbor's character, and when I gaze irreverently on the heart-mysteries of Immanuel, I do not know but that in the sight of God I am as guilty as Bethshemesh was. Of course there is a curiosity which is lawful; there is a curiosity which is really noble. We would never have reached our present heights of knowledge—the race would have been stationary and stagnant—but for the fierce inquisitiveness to know. And yet the noblest curiosity is seldom wholly and solely intellectual. It has roots in the heart; it moves in a moral atmosphere; it has visions of larger life and holier conduct. Far off, it does not end in self. It concludes and finds its crown in God.

A recent writer has illustrated this well, and shown us this difference between lawful and unlawful curiosity, by distinguishing the two different kinds of knowledge that a son may wish to have of his father. One son might be intensely curious to know his father's mind, his father's heart. He is eager to learn what his father loves and hates, that he may love what takes his father's love, and hate the objects of his father's hate. He wants to be like his father in his character. That son is nobly and lawfully inquisitive. But another son is curious to know what his father is worth, and how much he will likely leave. He wants to know if he can plunge into debt, and if he can count on a life of pleasure afterwards. And there is nothing moral, nothing fine in that. It is a poor and worthless curiosity.

November 7

Curiosity (Part 3 of 5)
by George H. Morrison

*And He killed the men of Bethshemesh because they had looked
into the ark of the Lord.*
1 Samuel 6:19

Now which is your curiosity about God? That is the question, children of the King! All idle curiosity ends in self. It is myself, and my self-love, that it wants to gratify. But the curiosity that is a moral power rests in the infinite sovereign control of God; it pries not, for the mere sake of prying, in the dark; it believes that even in mystery is good news; it then asks, and seeks, and knocks, wherever God is, for it knows that love and life and power are there. In other words, it is faith that makes the difference. It is trust that determines the virtue or the sin. Had Eve but trusted God with all her heart, she had never been curious about the fatal tree. Had the men of Bethshemesh but trusted in Jehovah, and that He could guard His own among the Philistines, they would never have been so curious about the ark. O brother, we need a deeper trust: trust in the possibilities of every man, trust in the intellect that plans and guides. It is on that that the reverent, earnest curiosity is built which carries a man to his noblest and his best!

This lawful curiosity is so necessary and so useful for the enriching of humanity, that it is quite clear to any fair observer that God goes to great pains to arouse it in us. It is one of the arts of a loving and kindly God to excite the curiosity of His dull children. Think of the world, for instance. Did it ever occur to you how the wonderful beauty of the world stirs a strange curiosity in the soul about the Eternal? In the presence of some glorious sunset, the noisiest chatterer grows quiet for a moment: it is as if it cried to him, "Be still, you noisy one; this splendor is the evening garment of your God." So beauty, whatever other ends it serves, helps to awaken the mystical in man; it suggests far more than it can ever prove; it hints that beyond the logic of the creed there is something we cannot grasp and cannot utter. It is the veil of the eternal figure. It keeps us curious, eager, childlike until the end.

November 8

Curiosity (Part 4 of 5)
by George H. Morrison

*And He killed the men of Bethshemesh because they had looked
into the ark of the Lord.*
1 Samuel 6:19

Think of the great fact of personality. Is not God at pains to make us lovingly curious there? All souls are wrapped in strange disguises; there is not a heart that is not veiled and hidden somehow; all which, through the ceaseless interactions of mankind, is one of the ways of God to keep us curious.

But in every man there is an unexpected something of mystery, a veil, a problem; and just because we have been created so, we are all and always of interest to each other. It is that interest, degenerate and corrupt, that makes the busybody and the scandal-bearer. It is that same interest, touched by the spirit of God, that breaks into sympathy and brotherly kindness. Without it, we should all be indifferent to each other.

Think of the Bible. Is there any book that was ever given to man that stimulates curiosity like that? It has been read, and studied, and fed upon, and prayed through, for centuries of growth and change, and the world is curious about the Bible still. No man is curious about the Shorter Catechism. The Confession of Faith excites no curiosity. Yet the truths of the Bible are gathered up in these, and they are a noble part of our inheritance. But the Bible is so simple, yet so deep; so demanding and majestic, yet so beautiful: it has the secret of such a sweet reserve; it casts the veil of silence with such delicacy, and just at the point where we should give worlds for more; that like the beauty of nature and the fact of character, it leaves us eager, stimulated, longing, curious. O restless, curious heart, be not discouraged! That craving has been stirred by the Almighty. Do not diminish it. Consecrate it. Trust it. You shall be satisfied when you awake.

November 9

Curiosity (Part 5 of 5)
by George H. Morrison

*And He killed the men of Bethshemesh because they had looked
into the ark of the Lord.*
1 Samuel 6:19

In closing, let me speak a word about Jesus' treatment of the curious spirit. And we cannot study the gospels without seeing—and it is very important that we see it—that Jesus was fully alive to the difference between lawful and unlawful curiosity. When we remember how He hid Himself; when we think that in every miracle there is some reserve, so that there is always ample room for curiosity, and no man is absolutely compelled to believe; above all, when we recall the parables, and think how they suggested, stimulated, roused, and sent men home to question and to wonder—we see at once that Jesus recognized the place of curiosity as a religious force. But then, on the other hand, remember this. One day there came an idly-curious man to Jesus, and he asked, "Lord, are there few that are saved?" And Jesus, turning to him sharply, said, "Strive to enter in at the narrow gate." And another day, after He had risen from the grave, you remember how Peter came, all curiosity, and said, "Lord, what shall this man do?" And Jesus said to him, "What is that to you: you follow Me." In both, the curiosity was idle. In both, it was met in the same way by Christ. They were turned from questioning to quest. They were brought back to action and to duty. There was something for them to do—then let them do it. The other matters may be left to God.

So when you are tempted to be idly curious, tempted to pry into forbidden things, I ask you to remember that brief command of Jesus, "What is that to you: you follow Me." You have a soul to save. You have a life to sweeten. You have a cross to carry. You have a heaven to win. There is really no time to be idly inquisitive. Call home that utterly unworthy curiosity. Do your own work to your own music. And when this little sleep is over and we waken, we shall have such a long and steady look into the Ark, that we shall say it was worth waiting for.

November 10

Awaiting the Unfolding of God's Plans for Us
by Bryan L. Herde

The unfolding of Your words gives light; it gives understanding to the simple.
Psalm 119:130

Contentment follows trust. True, godly contentment is impossible without trust in the loving kindness and sovereign involvement of our Heavenly Father in the details of our lives. Rest follows trust. Peace follows trust. Security follows trust. In fact, every benefit and grace of God will yield its fullness when one abides in Christ and allows Him to manifest His will and desires for us and through us.

Another aspect of the secret of becoming content is to literally live Jesus' command to "take no thought for tomorrow" (Matthew 6:34). Contentment is best realized when we live within the context of moments that comprise a day. Much of our frustration and anxiety is generated when we are looking beyond now into the future. When Paul said "forgetting those things which lie behind" (Philippians 3:13), the past is also a place where we should spend no time. What we are left with, when living between tomorrow and the past, is today and this moment. Contentment only dwells in the now—it cannot survive our non-sovereign thoughts of tomorrow or the burden of our past. Letting go of the need to control our future or make up for our past will do wonders for moving us into greater contentment with our present.

Most of our discontentment has come due to future-looking and future-thinking. In the first place, the future is none of our business—it is owned by God and Him alone. We have no right to be there before our time. Certainly, we have an eternal future to look forward to but that is not what I'm talking about. It is our tendency to predict, plan and pursue a future that we want and exert a whole lot of effort to try to escape the one we don't want. That is not living in obedience to Jesus' command to "take no thought for tomorrow." We look unto the Lord and wait for the unfolding of His plans for us in His time. In the meantime, we responsibly handle what is before us at this moment and we leave the results and the possibilities up to the One who knows.

November 11

David—In His Graces (Part 1 of 5)
by Alexander Whyte

"I have found David the son of Jesse, a man after My Own heart,
who shall fulfill all My will."
Acts 13:22

I would happily begin David's shining graces by saying that faith in God is the true and real and living root of them all. I would willingly begin with David's faith, were it not that there is no word in all our tongue that carries less meaning and less vision to most people's minds and hearts than just this so frequent sound—faith. As Pascal says, we all believe in that dead word—God; but there is only one here and another there who really and truly believes in the living, ever-present, and all-present God. But this is David's shining distinction above all God's saints—unless there are two or three in the New Testament who equal and excel David. In his pure, courageous, noble youth; all through his hunted-down days; fallen and broken and full of the pains of hell; filling up his dreary gift of years— David is always the same unconquered miracle of faith in God. Take and read and hear what David says to the Philistine giant about God, and you will see somewhat of his youthful faith in God.

Then pass on to far on in his life, and open the hundred and thirty-ninth psalm; and I am safe to say that David, the author of that psalm, and Jesus of Nazareth, whom I may call the finisher of it, have been the only two saints and sons of God on the face of this earth who have ever taken up, understood, and imaginatively and unceasingly employed in their prayers that great believing psalm. And therefore it has been that they are the only two, father and son, to whom a voice came from heaven saying, You are a man after My own heart, and, This is My beloved Son, in whom I am well pleased. Jesus Christ was by far the greatest and the best believer this earth has ever seen. But the best of it is that He was indebted to David's psalms of faith, and trust, and resignation, and assurance to support and to give utterance to His faith in His Father. The psalms of David were our Lord's constant prayer-book. When, therefore, you begin to ask after and to enter on the life of faith, open and read David's life and David's psalms.

November 12

David—In His Graces (Part 2 of 5)
by Alexander Whyte

"I have found David the son of Jesse, a man after My Own heart,
who shall fulfill all My will."
Acts 13:22

"Wherever true faith is, it frames the heart to the most childlike and friend-like dispositions towards God. Faith, my brothers, is a passion; it is a strong and a commanding instinct of our hearts after Christ, and after mystical union with Christ, so that we cannot be at peace and satisfied without Him" (Dr. Thomas Goodwin).

***

Humility is the grace of graces for us sinners to learn. There is nothing like it, and we must have continual training and exercise in it. You must go to all the schools, and put yourself under all the disciplines that the great experts practice, if you would put on true humility. And the schools of God to which He puts His great saints are such as these. You will be set second to other men every day. Other men will be put over your head every day. Rude men will ride brutally over your head every day. God will set his rudest men, of whom He has whole armies, upon you every day to judge you, and to find fault with you, and to correct you, and to blame you, and to take their business away from you to a better person than you can ever be. Yes, He will take you in hand Himself, and He will set you and will keep you in a low place. He will set your sins in battle formation before your face. He will require silence, and place your mouth in the dust, and a rope on your head, and your heart in a pool of tears, long after you had thought that you were to be set in a wealthy place.

It is David who rises before me as I speak of injuries, and insults, and detractions, and depreciations, and threats, and yet sorer, and yet severer and more immediate handlings by God Himself. David might have put Joab, and Shimei, and all the rest of his tutors and governors in the front of the battle as he put Uriah. But no more will he seek to silence a single one of his many reminders and accusers; no, not the most malignant, insolent, and unceasing of them all.

November 13

David—In His Graces (Part 3 of 5)
by Alexander Whyte

"I have found David the son of Jesse, a man after My Own heart,
who shall fulfill all My will."
Acts 13:22

If once you let David, or any other man, begin to taste the heavenly sweetness of true humility over pride, and over rebellion, and over retaliation, he will become positively enamored and intoxicated with his humiliations. What once was death and hell to him will now be life and peace and salvation to him. What at one time he had almost committed murder to cover up, he will now declare from every housetop. When I was a child every Sabbath day I used to read David's challenge to the giant, and I thought I was sanctifying the Sabbath over that Scripture. But for many years now, and more and more of late years, my Bible opens of itself to me at the place where Shimei casts stones and dirt at David, until David says, "So let him curse, because the Lord has said to him, 'Curse David.'"

My children still read Goliath on Sabbath evenings, but I am on the watch to see how soon I can safely introduce them to Shimei. Shimei is the man for me and mine! Only I hope I may endure my schoolmaster to the bitter end better than even David did. Let me take insults, and injuries, and snubs, and attacks from men, and God's hand itself, as David that day took Shimei's curses. No, things that would seem to you to have nothing in the world to do either with my past sins or with my present sinfulness—let me have David's holy instinct, let me lay down David's holy rule, to look at everything of that kind that comes to me as so many divine calls and divinely opened doors to a deeper humility.

Graces also grow by what they feed on; and humility grows by deliberately dieting on such humiliations as these, both human and divine. God's true saints all see, more or less, their own repulsiveness on account of sin, and the exceedingly hateful nature of all sin.

November 14

David—In His Graces (Part 4 of 5)
by Alexander Whyte

*"I have found David the son of Jesse, a man after My Own heart,
who shall fulfill all My will."*
Acts 13:22

Like David, we sometimes master, to some degree, and at other times smother down our passions of resentment and retaliation and ill-will. But with us as with David, at our best it is only an appearance of and a surface showing of self-mastery. The bad blood is there still. Jeremiah is entirely right about us. He is divinely and entirely right about the resentment, and the hatred, and the ill-will of our hearts at all who have ever hindered us, or injured us, or detracted from us, or rebuked us, or refused to flatter us. Yes, we will say, my injured and resentful heart is desperately and deceivingly wicked. Desperately, and deceivingly, and down to death wicked. But no longer than that. No longer after death. After death we shall be done both with death and hell; and after death we shall awake in His likeness who died, not cursing Judas, and Annas, and Caiaphas, and Herod, and the soldier with the spear, but saying over them all with His last breath, Father, forgive them, for they know not what they do. For even unto this were we called.

There is one thing, so far as I remember, that David never failed or came short in. "My honest scholar," says Isaac Walton "all this is told to you to move you to thankfulness; and, to move you more, let me tell you that though the prophet David was guilty of murder and adultery, and many others of the most deadly sins, yet he was said to be a man after God's own heart, because he overflowed more and more with thankfulness than any other that is mentioned in Holy Scripture. As may appear in his book of Psalms, where there is such a mixture of his confessing of his sins and unworthiness, and such thankfulness for God's pardon and mercies as made him to be called, and that by God Himself, to be a man after His own heart. And let us, in that, labor to be as much like David as we can."

November 15

David—In His Graces (Part 5 of 5)
by Alexander Whyte

"I have found David the son of Jesse, a man after My Own heart,
who shall fulfill all My will."
Acts 13:22

"Would you like to know?" asks William Law in his beautiful chapter on singing psalms—would you like to know who is the greatest saint in the world? Well, it is not he who prays most or fasts the most; it is not he who gives the most alms, or is most eminent for temperance, chastity, or justice; but it is he who is always thankful to God, who wills everything that God wills, and who receives everything as an instance of God's goodness, and has a heart always ready to praise God for His goodness.

And then Law winds up with this, and I wish it would send you all to the golden works of that holiness-laden writer—sometimes, he adds, imagine to yourselves that you saw holy David with his hands upon his harp, and his eyes fixed upon heaven, calling in ecstasy upon all creation, sun and moon, light and darkness, day and night, men and angels, to join with his joyful soul in praising the Lord of heaven. Dwell upon this thought until you think you are singing with this divine musician; and let such a companion teach you to lift your heart unto God every new morning in his thanksgiving psalms. Or make a morning psalm suitable to your own circumstance out of David's great thanksgiving psalms. You should take the finest and the choicest parts of David's finest and choicest psalms and, adding them together, make them every morning more and more able to express your own thankful hearts. And, until you have had time to compose a psalm exactly suitable to your own standing in grace, you might meantime sing this psalm of David every morning with a spiritual mind and a thankful heart:

Bless, O my soul, the Lord your God,   For You art God that dost
And not forgetful be   To me salvation send.
Of all His gracious benefits   And I upon Thee all the day
He has bestow'd on thee.   Expecting do attend.

November 16

When Standing Is Enough (Part 1 of 2)
by Bryan L. Herde

Therefore put on the full armor of God, so that when the day of evil comes,
you may be able to stand your ground, and after you have done everything, to stand.
Ephesians 6:13

David, in Psalm 27:13-14 made a similar statement to Paul's in the verse above, "What would have become of me had I not believed that I would see the Lord's goodness in the land of the living! Wait and hope for and expect the Lord; be brave and of good courage and let your heart be stout and enduring. Yes, wait for and hope for and expect the Lord" (*Amplified Version*).

Charles Spurgeon in his devotional *Morning and Evening* wrote in his June 3 morning passage, "Our King determines our placement and our role in His kingdom, not us. We are not in a position to determine where we should be during our time upon this earth. That is not our right. Only Jesus Christ knows where, what, when, how and why we exist."

Wherever the Lord places us, we are to be content in this: He has chosen our place and we are privileged to serve Him in whatever manner He chooses. Remember, we are not our own, we are bought with a price (1 Corinthians 6:20).

If I am a janitor, then I am a janitor by royal decree. If I am a CEO, then I am a CEO by royal decree. Neither position is considered to be inferior to the other by our Eternal King. The difficulty is that we judge through the eyes of the world and our flesh, and *we* have determined respective value, not God. In God's economy, a janitor is just as valuable as a CEO. A janitor must wait upon the Lord just as a CEO must wait upon the Lord. A janitor must follow the lead of the Master to the same degree a CEO must follow the lead of the Master. Neither is to rely upon self at any level.

As John Milton said, "They also serve who only stand and wait."

November 17

When Standing Is Enough (Part 2 of 2)
by Bryan L. Herde

*Therefore put on the full armor of God, so that when the day of evil comes,
you may be able to stand your ground, and after you have done everything, to stand.*
Ephesians 6:13

All of this is precisely why we are exhorted to fix our eyes, our thoughts and our hearts upon Jesus. The very instant we move our attention off Him and onto ourselves, we will be pulled down into self-pity, judgmentalism and sin.

In this lifetime, we must learn to trust in God's choices, which can be so very contrary to the world's views, as well as those of our flesh. Ultimately, our issues boil down to self versus God. We will either evaluate our effectiveness by standards of this world or we will trust the Lord to determine our effectiveness based upon His criteria.

That is why Jesus said in John 6:29, "The work God requires is this: that you believe on the One He sent." Boiled down to its very essence, that is the source of all of our difficulties. It is the testing of our hearts by the Lord to cultivate belief in Him and to purge us of our unbelief. Self versus God, trust versus fear, belief versus unbelief—these are battles in which we are engaged.

In all the things that we find ourselves doing for God, let us never forget that believing God is *the* work He requires of us. That is why we are constantly brought face to face with so many different types and degrees of difficulties—that we may believe in Him and trust Him completely, no matter what.

Stand and believe. There is no higher duty nor is there any greater privilege. For it is the Lord of all creation we believe and it is based upon His royal will that we stand where we are. We must wait for Him to act when He has determined the right time has come. Until then, we stand and when we have done everything else, we continue to stand.

321

November 18

The Retrieving of Yesterday
by George Matheson

They joy before You according to the joy in harvest.
Isaiah 9:3

The kind of joy which I would like to have in the presence of God is the joy of harvest. What is the joy of harvest? It is a resurrection joy. It is not the gladness which comes from getting anything new; it is the satisfaction of seeing the rising of buried things—the bursting from the ground of what I believed to be dead. There is no joy to me like that. It is far more than being lifted out of my trouble; it is the lifting of my trouble itself. It is good to be taken from the fearful pit, and from the muddy dirt; but it is not the highest thing. It is much to be delivered from my past; but it is more to have my past vindicated, justified—to be able to say, "It was good for me to have been afflicted." You may tell me that the night is far spent, and the day is at hand; it is good, but it is not sufficient. I want to know that there are songs in the night itself. I want to feel that I have not been wasting time. I want to believe that even my desert moments have been a march to the promised land.

Oh! You, who have come to seek and to save lost things, buried things, I lift my eyes to You. Many have offered me a golden tomorrow; You alone have offered to retrieve my yesterday. Give me back my past, oh, Lord. Restore to me the waste places of my heart. Reveal to me the meaning of my failures. Teach me the track of the path I thought trackless. Show me the angel sitting on the tomb of my buried self. Show me that the man with whom I wrestled, like Jacob at Peniel, was a man from heaven. Show me the vision of beauty that hovered over my pillow of stone. Show me that there was manna in my desert, which even the Promised Land did not hold. Then shall I have a harvest joy, a resurrection joy, the joy of gathering the buried past. Then shall my heart be satisfied that the struggle of the soul was autumn's gain. Then shall my mountain view indeed be beautiful, for it shall be seen from the place of my former valley. The joy of harvest is the joy of redeeming love.

November 19

The Comfort of Christ's Experience
by George Matheson

"In the world you will have trouble; but be of good cheer, I have overcome the world."
John 16:33

Christ spoke the words in this verse at a time when to all appearance the world had overcome Him. He was standing on the borders of death. There were times in His life in which we could have understood such an utterance. We could have understood it in the moment of resurrection, when He had beaten down His calamities. We could have understood it in the moment of ascension, when He had left His hardships behind. But to say it in the very middle of His afflictions—that seems a strange thing. And yet, why so? When does a man overcome his enemy? Is it when he beats him down? Hardly; that is to conquer the enemy, but not the hostility. Is it when he leaves him behind and soars into other spheres? No; that is to escape rather than to overcome. The real hour of overcoming your enemy is the hour in which you find some good in him—the hour in which you stand in his presence, and are not consumed. So was it with Jesus and the trials of this life. He beat them down in His rising; He escaped them in His ascending; but only in His voluntary Cross did He overcome them. His moment of world-conquest was the moment in which He took the cup. When He tasted that cup and found it not to be absolutely bitter—that was the hour in which He truly overcame.

Son of Man, it is Your voice on the Cross that brings me good cheer. You have other voices of triumph; but they have no bearing on me. I cannot beat down my disaster; Your resurrection is beyond me. I cannot escape my disaster; Your ascension surpasses me. I can take Your cup, for it is my own cup. It is a cup without mystery and without miracle—made up of my own sorrows. And when I see it in Your hand, and hear You say, "I have tasted it and was unharmed," my heart grows light within me. If You have found rest to Your soul after taking the burden, I may well be of good cheer; I can take courage when I learn of You.

November 20

Thanksgiving
by George Matheson

In everything give thanks.
1 Thessalonians 5:18

Surely this is a hard saying! Am I to thank God for everything? Am I to thank Him for loss, for pain, for poverty, for toil? I may believe that the time will come when I *shall* thank Him; that is an act of faith. But am I to turn faith into realization? Must I celebrate the victory before the battle? Is it possible? Is it human? Is it desirable? Is it pleasing to my Father that loss should be pleasant to me? Is my heart to make no distinction between the sunshine and the cloud? Is not one half of my joy just the absence of pain? If I stop shrinking from pain, how shall I keep my joy?

***

Be still, my soul; you have misread the message. It is not to give thanks for everything, but to give thanks *in* everything. It is not to praise God for the night, but to bless Him that the night is not deeper. Think on this: you have never reached the absolute depth of any darkness, never come to the step which has no step below it. I have read of the Son of Man that He gave thanks over the symbol of His broken body. What does that prove? That He rejoiced in being sad? It tells me that even the Man of Sorrows had not reached the extremist sorrow. Not for the pain, but for the mitigation of the pain, did the Son of Man give thanks—not that His body was broken, but that it was broken for me. In your hour of sorrow, give thanks like Jesus. Look up not at the height you have lost; look down on the depth you have not fathomed. There might have been no ram caught in your thicket. There might have been no dream dreamt in your prison cell. There might have been no bush burning in your desert. Herod might have come without the wise men; Bethlehem might have come without the angels; Calvary might have come without Gethsemane. Your Father has never allowed the deepest of misery to any human spirit. It is written that He has put my tears into His bottle; the quantity of your griefs is measured; there is a boundary which they cannot pass. Thank God for that boundary, oh, my soul.

November 21

The Lord is Good (Part 1 of 5)
by Hannah Whitall Smith

O taste and see that the Lord is good; blessed is the man that trusts in him.
Psalm 34:8

Have you ever asked yourself what you honestly think of God down at the bottom of your heart, whether you believe Him to be a good God or a bad God? I dare say the question will shock you, and you will be horrified at the suggestion that you could by any possibility think that God is a bad God. I suspect some of you will be forced to acknowledge that, unconsciously perhaps, but nonetheless truly, you have, by your doubts and your fault finding, attributed to Him a character that you would be horrified to have attributed to yourself.

***

You shrink with horror, perhaps, from the suggestion that you could under any circumstances, even in the secret depths of your heart, attribute to God what was bad. And yet you do not hesitate to accuse Him of doing things, which if one of your friends should do them, you would look upon as most dishonorable and unkind. For instance, Christians get into trouble; all looks dark, and they have no sense of the Lord's presence. They begin to question whether the Lord has not deserted them, and sometimes even accuse Him of indifference and neglect. And they never realize that these accusations are the same as saying that the Lord does not keep His promises, and does not treat them as kindly and honorably as they expect all their human friends to treat them. If one of our human friends should desert us because we were in trouble, we would consider such a friend as very far from being good.

How is it, then, that we can even for one moment accuse our Lord of such actions? No, dear friend, if the Lord is good, not sincere only, but really good, it must be because He always under every circumstance acts up to the highest ideal of that which He Himself has taught us is goodness. Goodness in Him must mean, just as it does with us, the living up to the best and highest He knows.

November 22

The Lord is Good (Part 2 of 5)
by Hannah Whitall Smith

O taste and see that the Lord is good; blessed is the man that trusts in him.
Psalm 34:8

God's goodness, practically, means that He will not neglect any of His duties toward us, and that He will always treat us in the best possible way. This may sound like a cliché, and you may exclaim, "Why tell us this, for it is what we all believe?" But do you? If you did, would it be possible for you ever to think He was neglectful, or indifferent, or unkind, or self-absorbed, or inconsiderate? Do not put on a righteous air, and say, "Oh, but I never do accuse Him of any such things. I would not dare to." Do you not? Have you never laid to His charge things you would refuse to do yourself? How was it when that last terrible disappointment came? Did you not feel as if the Lord had been unkind in permitting such a thing to come upon you, when you were trying so hard to serve Him? Do you never look upon His will as a tyrannical and arbitrary will, that must be submitted to, of course, but that could not by any possibility be loved? Does it never seem to you a hard thing to say, "Your will be done"? But could it seem hard if you really believed that the Lord is good, and that He always does that which is good? Let us be honest with ourselves.

Have we never in our secret hearts accused the Lord of the characteristics that He has told us in Ezekiel are the marks of a bad shepherd. Have we not thought that He cared for His own comfort or glory more than He cared for ours? Have we not complained that He has not strengthened us when we were weak, or bandaged up our broken hearts, or sought for us when we were lost?

You shrink in horror, perhaps, at this translation of your inward mutterings and complaining, but what else, I ask you, can they in all honesty mean? It is of vital importance now and then to drag out our secret thoughts and feelings about the Lord into the full light of the Holy Spirit, that we may see what our attitude about Him really is.

November 23

The Lord is Good (Part 3 of 5)
by Hannah Whitall Smith

O taste and see that the Lord is good; blessed is the man that trusts in him.
Psalm 34:8

It is fatally easy to get into a habit of wrong thoughts about God, thoughts which will unconsciously separate us from Him by a wide gulf of doubt and unbelief. More than anything else, more even than sin, wrong thoughts about God sap the foundations of our spiritual life, and grieve His heart of love. We can understand this from ourselves. Nothing grieves us so much as to have our friends misjudge and misunderstand us, and attribute to us motives we do not have. And nothing, I believe, so grieves the Lord. It is, in fact, idolatry. For what is idolatry but creating and worshipping a false God, and what are we doing but this very thing, when we allow ourselves to misjudge Him, and attribute to Him actions and feelings that are unkind and untrustworthy?

In the Bible it is called speaking against God. "Yes, they spoke against God; they said, Can God furnish a table in the wilderness?" This seemed a very innocent question to ask. But God had promised to supply all their needs in the wilderness; and to ask this question implied a secret lack of confidence in His ability to do as He had promised; and it was therefore, in spite of its innocent appearance, a real "speaking against" Him. A good God could not have led His people into the wilderness, and then have failed to "furnish a table" for them; and to question whether He was able to do it was to imply that He was not good. In the same way we are sometimes sorely tempted to ask a similar question.

Circumstances often seem to make it so impossible for God to supply our needs, that we find ourselves tempted over and over to "speak against" Him by asking if He can. As often as He has done it before, we seem unable to believe He can do it again, and in our hearts we "limit" Him, because we do not believe His Word or trust in His goodness.

***

November 24

The Lord is Good (Part 4 of 5)
by Hannah Whitall Smith

O taste and see that the Lord is good; blessed is the man that trusts in him.
Psalm 34:8

"Why have you made me this way?" This is a question we are very likely to ask. There is, I imagine, hardly one of us who has not been tempted at one time or another to "reply against God" in reference to the matter of our own personal make-up. We do not like our peculiar temperaments or our particular characteristics, and we long to be like someone else who has, we think, greater gifts of appearance or of talent. We are discontented with our make-up, both inward and outward, and we feel sure that all our failures are because of our unfortunate temperaments; and we are inclined to blame our Creator for having "made us this way."

I remember vividly a time in my life when I was tempted to be very rebellious about my own make-up. I was a plain-spoken, energetic sort of an individual, trying to be a good Christian, but with no special air of devotion about me. But I had a sister who was so saintly in her looks, and had such a sincere manner, that she seemed to be the embodiment of purity; and I felt sure I could be a great deal better Christian if only I could get her saintly looks and manner. But all my struggles to get them were useless. My natural temperament was far too energetic and outspoken for any appearance of saintliness, and many a time I said accusingly in my heart to God, "Why have you made me this way?" But one day I came across a sentence in an old mystic book that seemed to open my eyes. It was as follows: "Be content to be what your God has made you"; and it flashed on me that it really was a fact that God had made me, and that He must know the sort of creature He wanted me to be. We are "God's workmanship," and God is good, therefore His workmanship must be good also; and we may securely trust that before He is done with us, He will make out of us something that will be to His glory, no matter how unlike this we may as yet feel ourselves to be.

November 25

The Lord is Good (Part 5 of 5)
by Hannah Whitall Smith

O taste and see that the Lord is good; blessed is the man that trusts in him.
Psalm 34:8

The psalmist seemed to delight in repeating over and over again this blessed refrain, "for the Lord is good." It would be worthwhile for you to take your concordances and see how often he says it. And he exhorted everyone to join him in saying it. "Let the redeemed of the Lord say so," was his earnest cry. We must join our voices to his—The Lord is good—The Lord is good. But we must not say it with our lips only, and then by our actions contradict it. We must "say" it with our whole being, with thought, word, and action, so that people will see we really mean it, and will be convinced that it is a tremendous fact. A great many things in God's divine and sovereign actions do not look like goodness to the eye of sense, and in reading the Psalms we wonder perhaps how the psalmist could say, after some of the things he records, "for his mercy endures forever." But faith sits down before mysteries such as these, and says, "The Lord is good, therefore all that He does must be good, no matter how it looks, and I can wait for His explanations."

***

Our Lord uses this fact to teach us the meaning of His processes with us. "Truly, truly, I say unto you, Except a grain of wheat falls into the ground and dies, it abides alone: but, if it dies, it brings forth much fruit."

The whole explanation of the apparent wreckage of the world at large, or of our own personal lives in particular, is set out here. And, looked at in this light, we can understand how it is that the Lord can be good, and yet can permit the existence of sorrow and wrong in the world He has created, and in the lives of the human beings He loves. It is His very goodness that compels Him to permit it. For He knows that, only through such apparent wreckage, can the fruition of His glorious purposes for us be brought to pass.

November 26

Bringing Heaven to Earth (Part 1 of 6)
by John Henry Jowett

"Your will be done on earth as it is in heaven."
Matthew 6:10

I suppose that to the majority of people these familiar words suggest a funeral rather than a wedding. They bring to mind experiences to which we were compelled to submit but in which we found no delight. They awaken memories of gathering clouds, and gloomy days, and blocked roads, and failing strength, and open graves. "Your will be done!" They remind us of afflictions in the presence of which we were numb and mute. And so we have a sort of negative and passive attitude toward the words. We have a feeling toward them as to some visitor we have to "put up with," rather than to a welcome friend whose coming fills the house with life and happy movement.

And so it is that the graces and virtues, which are most frequently associated with these words, are of the dull and passive type. The grace of resignation is the plant which is most prolific in this bitter soil. Even many of the hymns in which we sing about the will of God are in the minor key, and they dwell upon the gloomier aspects of sovereign control which call for the grace of resignation. I am not unmindful of the fields of sadness which often stretch around our homes like marshy fields.

Our circumstances gather about us in stormy cloud and tempest, and the rains fall, and the floods cover our circumstances in dreary desolation. And we may reverently recall one black night in the days of the Son of Man when in Gethsemane the rains descended, and the floods came, and the winds blew, and the afflicted heart of the Savior submitted itself in strong resignation, crying, "Nevertheless, not My will but Yours be done."

And yet if resignation is our only attitude to the will of God, our life will be badly lacking in delightful strength and beauty.

***

November 27

Bringing Heaven to Earth (Part 2 of 6)
by John Henry Jowett

"Your will be done on earth as it is in heaven."
Matthew 6:10

The will of God is not always a heavy burden which we have to bear; it is something glorious which we have to do. And therefore we are not to stand before it as mourners, humbly making our submission, but as ready and eager knights gladly receiving our marching orders.

The will of God is not always associated with doing without; it is more commonly associated with a trust. It is not something withheld, it is something given. There is an active aroma about it. There is a ringing challenge in it. It is a call to chivalry and crusade. And therefore the symbol of our relationship to the will of God is not that of the bowed head, but that of the lighted lamp and dressed for action, as of happy servants delighted with their tasks.

It is in this positive relationship to the will of God that the will becomes our song, the song of eager knights upon the road, riding abroad to express the will of their King in all the common communications and relationships of men. "Your will be done on earth!" That is not merely the emotional cry of mourners surrendering their treasures; it is the cry of a jubilant army, with a King in their midst, dedicating the strength of their arms to the cause of His Kingdom.

The will of God is not something to be endured, but something to be done.

Well, now, how are we to take our share in this commission? How are we to do the will of God on earth as it is done in heaven? First of all, by finding out what life is like in heaven. "As it is done in heaven!" If our privileged orders are to make earth more like heaven it must surely be our first enquiry to find out what heaven is like.

November 28

Bringing Heaven to Earth (Part 3 of 6)
by John Henry Jowett

"Your will be done on earth as it is in heaven."
Matthew 6:10

Well, what is heaven like? I will very frankly confess to you that I am in no way helped to answer our question by the so-called spiritualistic revelations of these latter days. These strange séances with the lights out, and a trumpet on the table, and the rowdy singing, bring me no authoritative word or vision. The character of the heavenly life that is revealed is so unsatisfying—the glare of it, the gaudiness of it, its furnishings are like cheap and tasteless theatre, the utter weakness and shallowness of its utterance—they tell me nothing that I want to know. Its leaders assure me that their revelations are chasing away uncertainty, that they are transforming guesswork into firm experiences, that they are proving the reality of the life beyond, that they are making immortality certain. I am waiting for a revelation of something which deserves to be immortal. I am reverently listening for some word which is both spirit and life. I am listening for something worthy of relationship with the word of the Apostle Paul; no, worthy of the risen Lord; and what is offered to me is like costume jewelry in contrast with precious stones and fine gold. Eternal life is to me not merely endless length of line; it is quality of line; it is height, and depth, and breadth; "This is life eternal, to know You and Jesus Christ whom You have sent."

I therefore turn away from the so-called modern revelations if I wish to know what life is like in heaven. What is life like as it is lived in the immediate presence and fellowship of God? What are the habits of the heavenly community? What is the manner of their affections? What is the nature of their discernments? What are their standards of values? What are their ways of looking at things? What are their quests, and their labors, and their delights? What are their relationships one to another? Is there any answer to these questions?

November 29

Bringing Heaven to Earth (Part 4 of 6)
by John Henry Jowett

"Your will be done on earth as it is in heaven."
Matthew 6:10

If I wish to learn what life is like in heaven, I turn to the One who came from heaven. He made certain tremendous claims, and the very greatness of them captivates my soul and fills me with receptive awe. Let us listen to Him: "No man has ascended into heaven but He that came down from heaven."…"He that comes from above is above all; what He has seen and heard, of that He bears witness."…"The bread of God is He which comes down out of heaven and gives life unto the world."…"I have come down from heaven to do the will of Him that sent Me."

What is that last most wonderful word? It seems to come very near to the way of my quest. I am eagerly enquiring how God's will is done in heaven, and here is One who claims that He comes down from heaven to do the will of Him that sent Him. He brings heaven with Him. His speech is full of it. He talks about "your Father in heaven," He talks about, "the treasures in heaven," and about "the Kingdom of Heaven," and He uses simile after simile, and parable after parable, to tell us what it is like. "The Kingdom of Heaven is like unto…is like unto…is like unto…" The familiar words run like some lovely and inspiring song. If I want to know what heaven is like I must listen to His word.

But the revelation in Christ Jesus is more than a revelation in words. The Word became flesh and it was not only something we can hear, it was something we can see. He not only startled men's ears, as with a music which had never before been heard in their grey, ugly streets, He startled men's eyes as with a light which had never before fallen on sea or land. He not only talked about the heavenly life, He lived it. His life on earth was just a transcript of the life in heaven.

November 30

Bringing Heaven to Earth (Part 5 of 6)
by John Henry Jowett

"Your will be done on earth as it is in heaven."
Matthew 6:10

As we reverently gaze upon Him we can watch the process of the incarnation. The heavenly is being represented in the earthly, and it is taking form in human life and story. Every movement of Jesus spells a word of the heavenly literature. Every feature in Jesus is a characteristic of the invisible life. Every gesture tells a story. Every one of His earthly relationships unfolds the nature of the heavenly communion. His habits unveil their habits, His purposes reveal their purposes. The Eternal breaks through every moment, and the light is tempered to our mortal gaze. The revelation never ends. It begins in Nazareth and it continues to Calvary, and beyond Calvary to Olivet. You can never catch our Lord in some moment when the divine impulse has been withdrawn, when the inspiration ends, and when His life drops down to dull and unsuggestive routine. Everything in Jesus is a ministry of revelation. He is revelation: "I am the Truth." His earthly life reveals the landscape of the heavenly fields. If, therefore, I want to know what heaven is like I must listen to the words of Jesus, and with eager, reverent eyes I must follow the Word made flesh.

But let me give this advice about the objective. When we set about studying the words of Jesus do not let us become entangled in the letter. It is possible to be imprisoned in the words and so miss the hidden treasure. What we are in search of is the spirit of the Kingdom of Heaven; we want to know its attitudes, its royal moods, its splendid manners, its principles, its life. We must not, therefore, be discouraged and buried in the literalism of the letter. We must seek the beating heart of a simile, the secret vitality of a parable, the holy fire which burns on the innermost altar of the word. We are in search of heavenly principles, principles which we can apply to the humdrum life of earth and so transform it into heaven.

December 1

Bringing Heaven to Earth (Part 6 of 6)
by John Henry Jowett

"Your will be done on earth as it is in heaven."
Matthew 6:10

Go in search of the principles of the heavenly life. And whenever you find a heavenly principle, something which controls and orders the life of heaven, write it down in your own words, and regard it as one of the controlling guides of monotonous life. Do the same with the Master's life. What a brief little record it is! I turn away my eyes to my book shelves and I see the life of [Abraham] Lincoln in five large volumes. I then turn to the biography of Jesus, and in the Bible which I am using it covers 107 pages, and in those 107 pages the story is told four times over! Go over it with the utmost slowness. You are in search of something more precious than gold, yes, than much fine gold. If our Savior moves, if He turns His face toward anybody, if He looks at a little child, or at someone who is near the Kingdom of Heaven, follow the movement, and watch Him, and challenge your judgment as to its significance. Is the movement a revelation? Is it an earthly segment suggesting a heavenly circle, and can you attempt to reverently complete the circle? In this way must we go in search of the heavenly principles, and when we have found one let us express it in our own words, and write it down as one of the fundamental controls of human life.

And when you have got your heavenly principles, when you have analyzed them, and have arranged them in some order, will you have many of them? I do not think so. Will your notebook be overflowing with entries? I do not think so. You will probably have just a little handful, perhaps not more than a dozen of them, perhaps only half a dozen; but they will be something you can handle, for not only are they the principles of heaven, they are the laws of heaven for our life on earth, they are the fundamental things in the ministry of transformation, and they are to make earth and heaven one. If, therefore, you want to know what life in heaven is like, study Him who came from heaven, the Son of Man who is in heaven.

December 2

Laughter and Sorrow (Part 1 of 6)
by George H. Morrison

Even in laughter the heart is sorrowful.
Proverbs 14:13

Few men have had a larger experience of life than Solomon, and few have directed a more penetrating gaze on the strange drama that was unfolding around them. The court of kings is a proverbial theatre of human nature, and Solomon was familiar with court life all his days. He had known saints of God like his own father David. He had been in touch with men and women of all nations. Our text, then, is not the expression of a recluse, but of one who had large experience of humanity. And it is notable that, for the writers of His Bible, it was such men whom God generally chose. It was not hermits, nor men who dwelt apart from the great crowd, who were honored by Heaven to be Heaven's penmen. It was men who had known the strain and stress of living, who had carried the burdens of that complex task, who had entered largely into the joy and sorrow that blend in the light and shadow of the crowd. Moses was no stranger to the rich life of Egypt. David had passed from shepherding to kingship. The prophets of Israel were inspired statesmen, intensely alive to the needs and to the trend of the national life in which they found themselves. And Paul was at home in any company.

Now do you see the reason of this choice of instruments? It is that we might catch the sound of a brother's voice, and feel the impression of a brother's hand, in the divine Word which comes to lead us heavenward. The greatest books do not speak to us as strangers. They are not voices from regions where we have never journeyed. They interpret and illuminate these inarticulate longings in us, which beg for utterance yet cannot find it. And the Bible is the greatest of the great in that sense, that it pulsates and throbs with sweet and mysterious brotherhood. It was vitally necessary, if this book were to take hold, that it should not reach the heart as something alien. And one of God's methods for making that impossible was to use Solomon and the prophets and Paul as messengers.

December 3

Laughter and Sorrow (Part 2 of 6)
by George H. Morrison

Even in laughter the heart is sorrowful.
Proverbs 14:13

There are three truths that flash on me out of our text today. The first is the difference between the outward and inward life. Even in laughter—Listen! how it rings and echoes! Is it not the sign and revelation of a cloudless heart? But even in laughter, says Solomon, the heart is sorrowful. He is thinking of the duality of life.

Now that is one of the discoveries we make with growing intimacy. It is part of the joy, and part of the pain, of friendship, that it comes to find under the outward habit a world of things it never once suspected. No men or women worthy of the name would wear their heart upon their sleeve "for crows to peck at."

There is a reserve which is inseparable from true dignity, in the common course of daily life. But as intimacy ripens the barriers are broken, glimpses are had of things we never dreamed of; there are hills that reach heavenward, and valleys strewn with boulders; there are ripening harvests, and gardens with a grave in them, all in the mystical country of the heart; and we were walking in darkness and we never saw them, until the sunrise of friendship grew in the east.

You never would have thought, when you first met him, that that rough and rude and somewhat boisterous man had a heart as tender as a little child's. And you may meet a woman casually twenty times, and she is always bright and always interested; it is only long afterwards that you discover that there was a shrouded cross and a hidden sorrow there. That, then, is one of the gains and pains of friendship: it reveals to us the duality of life.

December 4

Laughter and Sorrow (Part 3 of 6)
by George H. Morrison

Even in laughter the heart is sorrowful.
Proverbs 14:13

In all our Lord's dealing with men and women we feel that the difference between the outward and the inward was in front of Him. You will not grasp the influence of Jesus, in all its wonderful impact on mankind, unless you bear in mind this strange duality.

I do not refer to the methods of our Savior in dealing with those who were consciously insincere. Christ unmasked hypocrites instantly and terribly: the Light was far too strong for that disguise. What I mean is that under all outward manner our Lord discerned the struggle of the heart; He was never misled by laughter or by speech; He never ignored all that we cannot utter. And if the woman of Samaria felt that she had found a friend; if Zacchaeus was not despised, nor Matthew hated; if the lawless and intractable zealot was redeemed; if Peter was ransomed and rescued from himself—there was the insight of love in it, the genius of the heart; there was the knowledge that life is deeper, richer, sadder, than is ever to be gathered from a surface view.

That, then, is the first truth in our text. The second is this: Sorrow and joy are strangely knit together. Even in laughter the heart is sorrowful.

If you have ever lived in a little town or village you know how life is intermingled there. The classes are not separated as in the cities; they blend insensibly into one another. Children of all stations go to school together; the better-off have companions in very humble homes; the banker and the blacksmith will be excellent friends. All the intermingling of a more primitive life resembles the intermingling of our being. We are each of us knit together into unity by bonds too subtle for anyone to detect. See how often a man's faults are virtues in excess! How all that is darkest interweaves with what is brightest! It is that intermingling of the light and shadow that makes the moral government of life so intricate.

December 5

Laughter and Sorrow (Part 4 of 6)
by George H. Morrison

Even in laughter the heart is sorrowful.
Proverbs 14:13

And could anything be more opposed than joy to sorrow? There seems to be a broad world between the two. The one is sunshine, the other is cloud. The one is music, the other is a cry. The one is the summer time bathed in warmth and light, the other is the wailing of the wind in the late autumn. Surely there can be no kinship of these two? Ah, yes! even in laughter the heart is sorrowful. There is a mystical union between our smiles and tears. Solomon saw what you and I have seen, that sorrow and joy are strangely knit together. We see this in the lives of our greatest men, for instance. It is one of the lessons we learn from great biographies. The greatest are very seldom solemn, and certainly they are almost never joyless.

Mohammed had drunk deep of the sorrows of mankind, yet "Mohammed," says a Scottish professor in a very charming essay, "Mohammed had that indispensable requirement of a great man, he could laugh." Luther was plunged into a sea of trouble, yet the laughter of Luther was notoriously boisterous. True joy is not the mere escape from sorrow. It may be that the capacity for gladness is just the other side of the capacity for pain. In the lives of the greatest, then, we learn this lesson, that sorrow and joy are strangely knit together.

We find this in our own greatest moments, when the fire of life flashes up in some fierce intensity. When the heart throbs, and feeling is kindled, and every nerve is quivering with emotion, we scarcely know if we are sorry or glad. It is a master-touch of our master dramatist [Shakespeare] that in the very heart of his tragedies you will have some fool or jester. It means far more than a mere relief from the agony; it means that the light and the shadow are akin. Has no one, after some great hour, said this to you: "I did not know whether to laugh or cry"? It ought to have been an hour of exquisite gladness, and in the middle of the gladness came the tears.

December 6

Laughter and Sorrow (Part 5 of 6)
by George H. Morrison

Even in laughter the heart is sorrowful.
Proverbs 14:13

I see from the newspapers that this is a great time for marriages; and if there is any day in life that should be cloudless, would you not expect it to be a wedding day? Yet even in the marriage service comes the shadow, "Until death do you part." That, then, is one mark of our greatest hours. They intermingle and mix these opposites. There have come moments to every one of us, when sorrow and joy were strangely knit together.

And do you not think that is true of Jesus Christ? It is one of the mysteries of that perfect life. He was a Man of sorrows and acquainted with grief; His soul was exceedingly sorrowful, even unto death. Yet through it all, and in the middle of it, our adorable Lord is talking of His joy. Do you remember the Mount of Transfiguration? Was it not an hour of spiritual glory? Whatever else it was, and it was much else, it was the announcement and forerunner of resurrection gladness. Yet even in that hour there was the agony: they spoke of the death He should accomplish at Jerusalem. "My joy"—and yet He was the Man of sorrows. "My peace"—and yet "Why have You forsaken Me?"

Sorrow and joy are strangely knit together in the human experience of Jesus Christ. That, then, is the second truth.

Laugh or Cry
by Bryan L. Herde

Occasionally, we don't know whether to laugh or cry
About something strange, bizarre, we don't know why.
Helpless to prevent it, uncertain as to what to do,
We rest in our Sovereign, because He always knew.

December 7

Laughter and Sorrow (Part 6 of 6)
by George H. Morrison

Even in laughter the heart is sorrowful.
Proverbs 14:13

The third and the deepest is this: Sorrow lies nearer to the heart of life than joy. Even in laughter the heart is sorrowful: at the back of all there is the heart's unrest. We never talk about a heavy joy: we only talk about a heavy grief. Happiness bubbles up or ripples over; there is some suggestion of the surface in it. But sorrow is heavy, and what that implies is this, that when God casts it into the sea of life it sinks by its own weight into the deeps. Joy is most real, thank God, intensely real. It is only the pessimist who would call joy a mockery.

But underneath all laughter is a pain, a craving that gnaws, a sorrow we cannot restrain; even in our language there is the sad suggestion that sorrow lies nearer to the heart of life than joy. I sometimes think that our Lord had this in mind when He said in His sermon, "Blessed are they that mourn." The mourner is blessed because sorrow fathoms the deeps, and if rightly taken makes the surface-life impossible. For sorrow lies nearer to the heart of life than joy, and to get near life's heart is always blessed. But whether that be so or not, this one thing I see clearly. Unless this proverb of Solomon prove itself true, the cross is not life's true interpretation. In the center of history stands the cross of Calvary, and the cross is the epitome of woe.

And if life's deepest secret be gladness and not sorrow, if laughter runs deeper into the heart than tears, then the cross that professes to touch the deepest depths can be nothing but a tragic mistake. I do not think that we have found it so. I do not think that the cross has ever failed us. It is a great thing to have a man like Solomon telling us that even in laughter the heart is sorrowful. But it is greater still to have a risen Savior, who sealed that in the sorrow of the Cross.

341

December 8

Our Lord's Favorite Graces: Meekness and Lowliness of Heart
(Part 1 of 4)
by Alexander Whyte

*"Take My yoke upon you, and learn of Me; for I am meek and lowly in heart:
and you shall find rest unto your souls."*
Matthew 11:29

When our Lord says of Himself that He is meek and lowly [humble] in heart it sounds to us, at first sight, somewhat like self-praise. And indeed not here only, but all up and down the four Gospels the same personal note and the same self-appraising tone prevails until we are led to search for, and with some anxiety, the proper explanation of that so unexpected and so startling manner of speech in our Lord. And then when we enter right into that universal habit of His and fully understand it, we see that it is just another evidence and just another result of the perfect purity, perfect humility, perfect simplicity, and absolute sinlessness of our Lord. He could say with the most perfect truth and innocence and properness what no other man that ever lived could have said without presumptuous sin. He could say that He alone knew the Father, and that He alone could reveal the Father; and then He could say with the same breath that He was meek and lowly in heart, and all the time be as innocent of pride or self-praise as if He had only said how old He was, or how many feet high He stood in His stature. And to the same degree that we become like Him we also shall be able to speak about ourselves, and to describe ourselves, and even to appraise ourselves, and, all the time, to do so as truthfully and as honestly as He did.

Now, what exactly is this thing here called meekness and lowliness of heart? And when and where do we see these most excellent graces exhibited in our Lord? Just open the Four Gospels and you will meet with the meekness, and the gentleness, and the lowly-mindedness of Jesus Christ in every chapter. Lowliness best describes His birth and the household in which He was brought up. And the same word best describes His everyday life all down to His death. He filled up all His appointed days on this earth, with words and deeds of divine authority and divine power, all at the same time.

December 9

Our Lord's Favorite Graces: Meekness and Lowliness of Heart
(Part 2 of 4)
by Alexander Whyte

"Take My yoke upon you, and learn of Me; for I am meek and lowly in heart: and you shall find rest unto your souls."
Matthew 11:29

On every page of the Four Gospels you will read how our Lord turned His cheek to those who hit Him, how He blessed when He had been shamefully treated. How He was a man of sorrows and acquainted with grief. He was oppressed, and He was afflicted, yet He opened not His mouth. He is brought as a lamb to the slaughter, and as a sheep before her shearers is mute. And yet in all that, His meekness and His lowly-mindedness were such that the yoke He bore was made easy to Him, and the burden that was laid upon Him was made light to Him.

Now it would not be a thing much to be wondered at if a meek and lowly mind were to be found in you and in me. For how can we be found other than meek and lowly-minded? No man who knows himself at all can hold his head high or have his heart proud. But that will not account for the humility and meekness of the One who committed no sin. He had always washed His hands in innocence. He had nothing in His past life to make Him either afraid or ashamed. He was holy, harmless, pure, and separate from sinners. And yet never was any prostrate sinner so lowly in his own eyes as was the sinless Son of God. And how is it to be accounted for? Simply to be a creature of Almighty God was enough to make the Man Jesus of Nazareth the meekest and the most lowly-minded of men. Never did any other creature of Almighty God see down to the very bottom of all frailty, and vanity, and emptiness as did the best of the creatures. And that such a creature as man should be exalted into everlasting union with the Eternal Son of God—that finished the incomparable meekness and humility which His own creation had begun. Promotion, privilege, honor, exaltation: these things fill fallen creatures like us with pride and vanity and puffed-up hearts. But Jesus Christ was all the humbler and all the more lowly-minded because of His adorable union with the Godhead.

December 10

Our Lord's Favorite Graces: Meekness and Lowliness of Heart
(Part 3 of 4)
by Alexander Whyte

*"Take My yoke upon you, and learn of Me; for I am meek and lowly in heart:
and you shall find rest unto your souls."*
Matthew 11:29

Now, let us be sure that we clearly understand all this and take it to heart. For it is all told to us first for our learning and then for our example and our imitation. It was our Lord's meekness and lowly-mindedness that made His great burden so light. His burden was far from light; His meekness, and His lowly-mindedness, and all. But He could not have carried His burden a single step of His life's way but for His meekness under it. And it is out of His own experience that He here speaks to us. "Bring just a meek heart to your burden, as I did," He says to us. "Bring just the same mind to your yoke that I brought to my yoke, and see how easy it will feel." Now, He so impresses us with what He says here that if He were staying in this city tonight we would go to Him on the strength of this invitation of His. And we would tell Him the whole sad story of our cruel yoke and our heavy burden.

But even if He were here in the body, it is in the spirit alone that He could really assist us. Go to Him in the spirit then; tell Him that as His cross on the way to Calvary crushed Him, so your cross, your burden, and your yoke will not take long to crush you into your grave unless you get help from Him to bear all these things. He may possibly remove your burden altogether if you are persistent enough. He can wholly remove it if that seems good in His sight. On the other hand, who knows. He may have such a plan in His divine will concerning you that He may say to you that His grace is sufficient for you, and that His strength is to be made perfect in your weakness. Go to Him in any case, and whatever He sees is good to do with you and your burden, He will at any rate begin to give you another heart under it. He will begin to give you what His Father gave Him. He will give you, burden or no burden, a meek and lowly heart.

December 11

Our Lord's Favorite Graces: Meekness and Lowliness of Heart
(Part 4 of 4)
by Alexander Whyte

"Take My yoke upon you, and learn of Me; for I am meek and lowly in heart:
and you shall find rest unto your souls."
Matthew 11:29

A truly meek and lowly heart will enable you to carry ten burdens as big as yours, and ten yokes as annoying as yours, and that to the end of your days on earth. It is not your burden that so weighs you down. It is your proud, rebellious, self-seeking, self-pleasing heart. Once you get a new heart from Him—a humble, meek, lowly heart, your yoke from that day will be easy and your burden light. You have not thought enough on a thousand good reasons that God must have for the way He is yoking you and loading you. If you looked more at yourself, and at what your salvation must need at His hand and at your own hand to work it out, you would bow your head to His will continually, and would hold your peace. Had He dealt with you according to your sins, and rewarded you according to your iniquities, you would not be here to find fault with the way He is leading you to pardon and peace and everlasting life. When you begin to look at yourself in ways like these, already your yoke will have lost half its agitation, and your burden half its weightiness.

***

Take courage and come to Him, for He is as meek and lowly-minded, as accessible, and as friendly in heaven as ever He was on earth. And more so, if that were even possible. Though He is high, He is not any more high-minded than ever He was, as you will live to testify and tell, if you only take your case to Him. The truth is, this wonderful text sounds clearer and surer from heaven today; more heart-winning and more heart-commanding than ever it sounded on earth. Come unto Me—our Lord says that from heaven to us, as He was never able to say it on earth—all you that labor and are heavy laden, and I will give you rest. Take My yoke upon you and learn of Me; for I am meek and lowly in heart and you shall find rest unto your souls.

December 12

"He Calls...by Name." (Part 1 of 2)
by John Henry Jowett

"He calls His own sheep by name, and leads them out."
John 10:3

The individual is not lost in the indiscriminate crowd. The color of a personality is not merged in the monotonous grey of the multitude. The personalities are distinguished. God never mistakes one person for another. We are not so much alike that we are treated as crowds. We are not repetitions of a type, uniform articles cast in a common and unvarying mold. We are individuals, every one original and unique, and bearing individual characteristics and names. He never confuses Thomas and John, or Peter and Nathaniel, or Mary and Martha. Each name suggests its special problem, and requires specific ministry. The ministries are varied and unequal, and in their inequality are to be found their grace and justice.

In inequality is found the rarest fairness. Equal bonds may mean unequal strain. Therefore it is not similarity and equality of treatment that we require, but treatment guided by the discernment of the individual need. It is, therefore, an encouraging messenger which comes to us from the Word of God, and which tells us that the Lord is acquainted with the individual need, and that from Him we receive the inequalities of mercy and grace. "He knew what was in man." "He calls his own sheep by name." But this was said of Him in the day of His gracious struggle, when He walked the heavy road of pilgrimage and pain. This was spoken in the day of His humiliation, when He interacted with men, when He visited their lowly dwellings, and moved among their common haunts, and sympathetically knew the needs of the individual heart. Will it be true of Him when He rises again on the third day, clothed in resurrection glory? In His humiliation He knew the individual heart; will exaltation create forgetfulness and alienation? When the pilgrimage is done, and death and the grave are left behind, when the humiliation is ended, and glory has begun, will He be the same companionable, discerning, sympathetic presence? Will He any longer know the individual life?

December 13

"He Calls...by Name." (Part 2 of 2)
by John Henry Jowett

"He calls His own sheep by name, and leads them out."
John 10:3

I turn to the wonderful record, with the music of my text ringing in my heart, "He calls His own sheep by name," and half-trembling I listen to His speech on the resurrection morning. "Mary stood outside at the tomb weeping...Jesus said unto her, *Mary!*" It is the same Master. And here is Thomas, trembling with misgiving, half stunned by the grim and unforgettable reality which he had seen on Calvary, with his hope buried in a sealed tomb, and despairing of any sweet and appealing tomorrow. "Jesus said unto him, *Thomas,* put your finger here." "He calls His own sheep by name." It is the same gracious look.

And here is Peter, consumed by self-distrust, fearful of vows and confessions, wanting to proclaim his love, and yet half afraid to look at the One he loved. "Jesus said unto him, *Simon*...do you love Me?" It is the same unchanging and discerning sympathy. "Mary!" "Thomas!" "Simon!" It is the same Jesus, now clothed in the incorruptible, ministering to the individual life, applying His grace and comfort to the individual heart. "Mary!" There He is consoling a mourner. "Thomas!" There He is ministering to a doubter. "Simon!" There He is healing and restoring a denier. "I know my sheep." "Mary!" There the resurrection Lord is ministering to the pain of bereavement. "Thomas!" There the resurrection Lord is ministering to the pain of doubt. "Simon!" There the resurrection Lord is ministering to the pain of treachery and denial. Is there not something beautiful and fruitfully helpful in a record which tells us that the wealth of the resurrection ministry was given to the individual heart? The glorified Lord made His way to the three dark lanes in human life—to bereavement, to misgiving, to self-contempt. If I want to be calmed by my Lord's voice in the black crisis, I must familiarize myself with its tones in the common day. Happy the soul that is so familiar with the voice, that it cannot mistake its music when the calm sunny day has passed into a troubled and turbulent night.

December 14

The Intolerance of Jesus (Part 1 of 5)
by George H. Morrison

"He that is not with Me is against Me."
Matthew 12:30

Our Lord had just performed a notable miracle in healing a man who was possessed of a devil. It had made a profound impression on the people, and had forced the conviction that this was indeed Messiah. Unable to dispute the miracle itself, the Pharisees tried to discredit the power behind it, and in their cowardly and treacherous way they suggested that there was something demonic about Christ. With a readiness of resource which never failed Him, Christ showed in a flash the weakness of that argument. If He was the friend and comrade of the demons, was He likely to make a brother-demon homeless? Then catching fire at these insinuations, and moved to righteous anger by these slanders, He said, "He that is not with Me is against Me."

I want, then, to address the intolerance of Jesus Christ. However startling the subject may appear, and however the sound of it may jar us, I am convinced we shall never understand our Lord if we fail to take account of His intolerance.

We have heard much of the friendliness of Jesus, and of the depth and range of His compassion; nor can we ever exaggerate, in warmest language, the warm and generous aspect of His character. But it is well that the listening ear should be tuned to catch the sterner music of that life, unless, missing it, we miss the fine severity which goes to the perfecting of moral beauty. Wherever the spirit of Jesus is at work, there is found a sweet and masterful intolerance.

The one thing that the gospel cannot do, is to look with easy good-nature on the world. And if this passionate, urgent claim has ever marked the activities of Christendom, we must try to trace it to the source and find it in the character of Christ.

348

December 15

The Intolerance of Jesus (Part 2 of 5)
by George H. Morrison

"He that is not with Me is against Me."
Matthew 12:30

Of course there is an intolerance so cold and hard that it must always be foreign to the Master's spirit. All that is best in us condemns the disposition which lacks the redeeming touch of comprehension. As life advances, if we live it well, we commonly grow less rigid in our judgment. By all we have seen and suffered, all we have tried and failed, our sympathies grow broader with the years. We learn how precious is the grace of charity; how nearly alike may be the fiercest combatants; how great is the allowance we must give for those of whose hidden life we know so little. The fact remains that in all great personalities, there is a strain of what is called intolerance. There are spheres in which all compromise is treachery, and when a man must say with Luther, "Here I stand." And that intolerance, far from being the enemy of love and sympathy and generous culture, is the rock that a man needs to set his feet on if he is to cast his rope to those who cry for help. You find it in the God of the Old Testament: "You shall have no other gods before Me." He is a jealous God and permits no rival. He must be loved with heart and soul and strength and mind. You find it in the music of the psalmist, and in the message of prophet and apostle, and you find it embraced among all the love that shone in the character of Jesus Christ.

Never was a man so tender as the Lord. Never was a man so swift to sympathize. Never did sinners so feel that they were understood. Never did the lost so feel that they were loved. Yet with all that pity and grace and boundless comprehension, I say that you have never fathomed the spirit of the Master until you have recognized within its range a certain glorious and divine intolerance. Jesus loved us and He gave Himself for us. He says to every weary heart, "Come unto Me." But that same spirit which was so true and tender could be supremely unyielding and inflexible. The gentle Savior was strikingly intolerant, and because of His intolerance He died.

December 16

The Intolerance of Jesus (Part 3 of 5)
by George H. Morrison

"He that is not with Me is against Me."
Matthew 12:30

We trace the intolerance of Christ in His attitude towards hypocrisy. One thing that was unendurable to Jesus was the loud and meaningless profession of religion. You can always detect an element of pity when Jesus is face to face with other sins. There is the yearning of infinite love over the lost; the hand outstretched to welcome back the prodigal. But for the hypocrite there is no gleam of pity, only the blasting and withering of wrath. "Woe unto you, scribes and Pharisees, hypocrites." It is the intolerance of Jesus Christ.

We trace it again in those stupendous claims that Jesus Christ put forward for Himself. The Lord our God is a jealous God, and the Lord our Savior is a jealous Savior. "I am the way, I am the truth, I am the life"—"No man comes unto the Father but by Me"—"No man knows the Father except the Son, and He to whomever the Son will reveal Him." What do you make of these amazing claims, and of that splendid intolerance of any rival? Yet all these words are in the gospel record as surely as "a bruised reed He will not break."

Do you say there are many doorways to the Father? Christ Jesus stands and says, "I am the door." Do you say there are many shepherds of the sheep? Christ stands in His majesty and says, "I am the shepherd." Concerned, merciful, full of a great compassion, Christ is intolerant of any rival; either He stands alone to be worshipped and adored, or He disappears into the mists of fable. So far as I am aware that is unique; there is nothing like it in religious history.

It is Christ alone, the meek and lowly Savior, who lifts Himself up in isolated splendor. Friend of the friendless and brother of the weakest, He is intolerant of any sharing of His claims.

December 17

The Intolerance of Jesus (Part 4 of 5)
by George H. Morrison

"He that is not with Me is against Me."
Matthew 12:30

I trace this same intolerance in the allegiance which Christ demands from us. He is willing to take the lowest place upon the cross; but He will not take it in your heart and mine. He was born in a manger, reared in a lowly home, and grew to His manhood in obscurest circumstances. But the moment He enters the kingdom of the heart, where He is king by conquest and by right, there everything is changed, and with a great intolerance He refuses every place except the first. "Whoever loves father or mother more than Me is not worthy of Me"—"Let the dead bury their dead; you follow Me." That is the word of a King in His own kingdom, claiming His rightful place among His subjects. And when you speak of the meek and lowly Jesus, never forget there is that imperial note there. He is divinely intolerant of everybody who would usurp the throne that is His right.

The first thing I note in the intolerance of Jesus is that it is the child of glowing faith. The intolerance of Christ is little else than the other side of His perfect trust in God. When someone is a stranger to you, bound by no ties of love, you are little affected by what is said about him. The talk may be true, or it may not be true, but it is none of your business, and you do not know. But the moment a man becomes a hero to you, that moment you grow intolerant of anyone belittling them. If you believe in a woman, your heart is aflame with anger should anyone tarnish her name even with a breath.

***

It is easy to be infinitely tolerant, if all that Christ lived for means but little to you. An age that can tolerate every kind of creed is always an age whose faith is burning low. And just because Christ's faith burned with a perfect light, and flashed its radiance full on the heart of God, you find in Him, in all His godward life, a steady and magnificent intolerance.

December 18

The Intolerance of Jesus (Part 5 of 5)
by George H. Morrison

"He that is not with Me is against Me."
Matthew 12:30

The intolerance of Jesus is the intolerance of perfect understanding. It was because He knew so fully, and sympathized so deeply, that there were certain things He could not bear. One great complaint we make against intolerance is that it does not sympathetically understand us. It is harsh in judgment, and fails in comprehension, and has no conception of what things mean for us. We have all met with intolerance like that, but remember there is another kind. He is intolerant because He comprehends. He knows what sin is; He knows how sweet it is; He knows its havoc, its loneliness, its dust and ashes. And therefore He is stern, uncompromising, and says to us, "Choose whom you will serve." There are men who are intolerant because of ignorance; Christ is intolerant because He knows.

Lastly, the intolerance of Jesus is very distinctly the intolerance of love. Love bears all things—all things except one, and that is the harm or hurt of the beloved.

Now we all know that when our Savior came, He came at the urging and in the power of love; wonderful love, love that endured the worst, love that went up to Calvary to die. And just because that love was so intense, and burned with the passion of the heart of God, things that had been tolerable once were found to be intolerable now. That is the secret of the gospel's sternness and of its passionate protest against sin. That is why age after age it makes itself plain, and says, "He that is not with Me is against Me."

The love that bears all things cannot bear that hurt or harm should rest on the beloved. Christ is intolerant because He loves.

December 19

As Christ in the Father (Part 1 of 3)
by Andrew Murray

*"As the Father has loved me, so I have loved you. Abide in My love,
even as I abide in My Father's love."*
John 15:9-10

Christ had taught His disciples that to abide in Him was to abide in His love. The hour of His suffering is near, and He cannot speak much more to them. They would doubtless have many questions to ask as to what that abiding in Him and His love is. He anticipates and meets their wishes, and gives them His own life as the best description of His command. As the example and rule for their abiding in His love, they have to look to His abiding in the Father's love. In the light of His union with the Father, their union with Him will become clear. *His life in the Father is the law of their life in Him.* The thought is so high that we can hardly take it in, and is yet so clearly revealed, that we dare not neglect it. Do we not read in John 6:57, "As I live by the Father, *even so* he that eats me, shall live by me"? And the Savior prays so distinctly (John 17:22), "that they may be one *even as* We are one: I in them, and You in me." The blessed union of Christ with the Father and His life in Him is the only rule of our thoughts and expectations in regard to our living and abiding in Him.

Think first of *the origin* of that life of Christ in the Father. They were one— one in life and one in love. In this His abiding in the Father had its root. Though dwelling here on earth, He knew that He was One with the Father; that the Father's life was in Him, and His love on Him. Without this knowledge, abiding in the Father and His love would have been utterly impossible. And it is only this way that you can abide in Christ and His love. At His birth He became man, and took your nature that He might be one with you. By your new birth you become one with Him, and are made partaker of His Divine nature. The link that binds you to Him is as real and close as bound Him to the Father—the link of a Divine life. Your claim on Him is as sure and available as was His on the Father. Your union with Him is as close.

December 20

As Christ in the Father (Part 2 of 3)
by Andrew Murray

"As the Father has loved me, so I have loved you. Abide in My love,
even as I abide in My Father's love."
John 15:9-10

Since there is the union of a Divine life, it is one of an infinite love. In His life of humiliation on earth He tasted the blessedness and strength of knowing Himself the object of infinite love, and of dwelling in it all day; from His own example He invites you to learn that here lies the secret of rest and joy. You are one with Him: yield yourself now to be loved by Him; let your eyes and heart open to the love that shines and presses in on you on every side. Abide in His love.

Think then too of *the mode* of that abiding in the Father and His love which is to be the law of your life. "I kept my Father's commandments and abide in His love." His was a life of subjection and dependence, and yet most blessed. To our proud self-seeking nature the thought of dependence and subjection suggests the idea of humiliation and servitude; in the life of love which the Son of God lived, and to which He invites us, they are the secret of blessedness. The Son is not afraid of losing anything by giving up all to the Father, for He knows that the Father loves Him, and can have no interest apart from that of the beloved Son. He knows that as complete as is the dependence on His part is the providing on the part of the Father of all He possesses. Therefore when He had said, "The Son can do nothing of Himself, except what He sees the Father doing," He adds at once, "Whatever things the Father does, those also the Son does as well: for the Father loves the Son, and shows Him all things that He Himself does." The believer who studies this life of Christ as the pattern and the promise of what his may be, learns to understand how the "Without me you can do nothing," is but the forerunner of "I can do all things through Christ who strengthens me." We learn to glory in infirmities, to take pleasure in necessities and distresses for Christ's sake; for "when I am weak, then am I strong."

***

354

December 21

As Christ in the Father (Part 3 of 3)
by Andrew Murray

*"As the Father has loved me, so I have loved you. Abide in My love,
even as I abide in My Father's love."*
John 15:9-10

Believer! abide in the love of Christ. Take and study His relationship to the Father as promise of what your own can become. As blessed, as mighty, as glorious as was His life in the Father, can yours be in Him. Let this truth, accepted under the teaching of the Spirit in faith, remove every trace of fear, as if abiding in Christ were a burden and a work. In the light of His life in the Father, let it from now on be to you a blessed rest in the union with Him, an overflowing fountain of joy and strength. To abide in His love, His mighty, saving, keeping, satisfying love, even as He abode in the Father's love—surely the very greatness of our calling teaches us that it never can be a work we have to perform; it must be with us as with Him, the result of the spontaneous outflowing of a life from within, and the mighty in-working of the love from above. We need to have our souls still unto God, gazing upon that life of Christ in the Father until the light from heaven falls on it, and we hear the living voice of our Beloved whispering gently to us personally the teaching He gave to the disciples.

Soul, be still and listen; let every thought be hushed until the word has entered your heart too: "Child! I love you, even as the Father loved me. Abide in my love, even as I abide in the Father's love. Your life on earth in me is to be the perfect counterpart of mine in the Father." Christ was the revelation of the Father on earth. He could not be this if there was not the most perfect unity, the most complete giving of all the Father had to the Son. He could be it because the Father loved Him, and He dwelt in that love. Believers are the revelation of Christ on earth. They cannot be this unless there is perfect unity, so that the world can know that He loves them and has sent them. But they can be it if Christ loves them with the infinite love that gives itself and all it has, and if they abide in that love.

December 22

Love Revealed: Meditations on John 17 (Part 1 of 3)
by George Bowen

"And I have declared to them Your name, and will declare it, that the love with which You loved Me may be in them, and I in them."
John 17:26

If it becomes us to listen eagerly and reverentially to every word that falls from the Master's lips, we ought surely to give special heed to the last words spoken by him to his disciples before he entered upon his final sufferings. If we hang breathlessly upon the words of a believer passing into the presence of Jesus, with what spellbound attention should we drink in the farewell syllables of Him who is the great object of faith!

Believers expect that on the termination of their bodies their souls shall be translated into the presence of God and the Lamb, and clothed with glory, honor and immortality. They believe that this shall be done for them because Christ has died and ever lives to make intercession for them. The blood of Jesus Christ cleanses them from all sin, so that it is not inconsistent, but every way marvelous, that the Father should make them heirs of everlasting blessedness. The love of the Father to the Son is the guarantee of this magnificent result. As it is a pure impossibility that the Father should make light of the sacrifice offered by his well-beloved Son, so it is impossible that the trust which rests upon this sacrifice should be dishonored.

Are believers, however, sufficiently impressed with the fact that the sacrifice of the Lamb has had reference not only to the ultimate redemption of their souls, but to the present enjoyment of the things pertaining to life and godliness? What are the silver threads that run most conspicuously through these five chapters [John chapters 13-17]? Joy, peace, love, humility, faith, fruitfulness, holiness and union. And now his parting blessing is given in the words, *"that the love with which You loved Me may be in them, and I in them."*

December 23

Love Revealed: Meditations on John 17 (Part 2 of 3)
by George Bowen

"And I have declared to them Your name, and will declare it, that the love with which
You loved Me may be in them, and I in them."
John 17:26

Jesus lived, loved, suffered and died not merely that we might ascend with him to glory, but that the love of God might descend and rest on us even as it had rested on him. Why should we, in estimating the value of Christ's mediating work, think exclusively or excessively of the glory that will be revealed in us when we shall have done with earth, losing sight, or almost losing sight, of the mighty value of divine love presently accumulating? We are to honor Christ by seeking for ourselves the things prominently mentioned in his promises and in this prayer. We are to magnify the effectiveness of his blood by seeking to have his peace, his joy, his experience of the Father's love. There is nothing better in heaven than what Christ here requests for his people. About to depart out of the world, he asks that the love which had so unceasingly and mightily flowed toward him during all his pilgrimage here below might not depart with him and be lost to earth—that the same gentleness and satisfaction and tenderness and sympathy that had looked down to him from the throne of heaven might continue to look down upon the earth, even upon those that believed on his name.

We expect God someday to love us even as he loves his only-begotten. Christ does not ask this for us some day, but now. The atonement of Christ has the value now that it will have in any future day. The blood that was shed on Calvary does not begin by purchasing for us a little love, and then, like the merchandise of this world, rising in value, end by purchasing the whole. But wait: How can the Father love us as he loves his only-begotten, who was holy, harmless, undefiled and separate from sinners, the express image of his person and the brightness of his glory? Do you ask me this? I ask you in reply, How can God love us at all? The difficulties are just as great to be overcome, just the same in obtaining for us the least love from the Father as in obtaining the utmost. Those difficulties, the believer needs not to be told, are overcome by the crucified One.

357

December 24

Love Revealed: Meditations on John 17 (Part 3 of 3)
by George Bowen

"And I have declared to them Your name, and will declare it, that the love with which You loved Me may be in them, and I in them."
John 17:26

There are multitudes of semi-believers who have faith to grasp a little of love, and think it presumptuous to lift their regards to anything like the love which the Father had for Jesus, and it does not dawn upon their minds that such limitation of their faith is neither more nor less than an inexcusable limiting of the value of Christ's blood. We progress in our understanding of the great love that Christ asks here for his people just as we advance in our knowledge of the cross of Christ.

The love of the Father to Christ was not a love that refused to let sorrow touch its object—not one that quickly overwhelmed his enemies with confusion, or that defended him against the approach of temptation. And the fact that the believer is surrounded with illnesses, sustains losses, encounters reversals, seems even to be looked coldly on by the God of sovereign control, is no proof that he is not loved with the love of which Christ was the object. "I in them." This is the argument of arguments, the yes and amen of all promises. "Behold me in them, treat me in them, love me in them. Do I need to ask you, O righteous Father, to continue loving me, to ask you to extend to me the same loving consideration after the cross as before it? Nothing surely could be more inappropriate than to suppose the possibility of the opposite. Well, if your love to me can know no end, no lessening, hear me, then, while I declare that I am in my disciples who dwell upon the earth, and that your love must find me there." Do you understand, O believer, the wonderfully advantageous position given to you by this declaration of Christ? He is in you, and consequently you must encounter the full measure of the Father's love to Christ when you near the throne of grace. Only believe. To slight you is to slight Him who is in you. Christ is no more in the world, but you are in the world and Christ in you. Draw near, therefore, to the throne of grace with as true a heart and in as full assurance of faith as the holy Son of God himself did when he lived here.

December 25

Bethlehem's Little Boy
by Bryan L. Herde

Fear, anger, sadness, desperation,
Chaos, anxiety, fallen creation.

Where is the hope?
Where is the joy?
A long time ago, they were born in a Boy.

Perversion, agony, suffering, strife,
Darkness, wickedness cut like a knife.

Where is peace? Where is healing?
A long time ago, where shepherds were kneeling.

Enough! I cried, Please, no more!
When will the Boy, now God-Man King, come and reign?
When will the Boy, now God-Man King, end suffering and pain?

When will the agony and tragedy
Be replaced by harmony and melody?

Oh, my Friend, my Savior, Bethlehem's little Boy,
Please come quickly and evil forever destroy.

"I am the first and the last, and the living one. I died, and behold I am alive forevermore,
and I have the keys of Death and Hell."
Revelation 1:17-18

"I am the Alpha and the Omega, the first and the last, the beginning and the end…
I am the root and descendant of David, the bright morning star…
I am coming soon."
Revelation 22:13, 16b, 20b

December 26

Near-Cuts Not God's (Part 1 of 6)
by George H. Morrison

God led them not through the way of the land of the Philistines, although that was near.
Exodus 13:17

It is strange to think that by the straight road it was a fairly brief journey from Egypt to Palestine. Four or five days' hard marching, by the route that is now common with the traders, would have brought the children of Israel to the promised land. Four or five days would have done it comfortably; yet Israel took forty years to do it. And we know the hardships, and the sorrows, and the battles, that filled these forty years with bitterness. Yet for all that, the leadership was God's. The pillar of cloud and fire led the advance. The longest way round was the shortest way home. There was a near-cut [short-cut], certainly; but here, at any rate, the near-cut was not God's.

And it is not difficult to see with sufficient clearness some of God's reasons for this roundabout. The Bible lifts the veil a little, and we find first that there was compassion in it. That near way was through the land of the Philistines, and the Philistines were skilled and subtle in the arts of war. To have brought Israel face to face with them—Israel, fresh from the stubble-field, and with the broken spirit of the slave still in them—to have done that might have been to have spoiled everything, and to have sent them scattering headlong back to Egypt. The time was coming when the armies of Israel would be more than a match for any ranks of Philistines. The time was coming—the Almighty was hastening it; only the time for that had not come yet. So by a thousand lesser trials and combats, sharp brushes, unexpected difficulties, an all-compassionate God prepared the rabble to be a disciplined army of the Lord. And it took forty years to do that thoroughly. It was a very compassionate, drawn-out process. The road was very roundabout, granted. But it was the right road for all that.

December 27

Near-Cuts Not God's (Part 2 of 6)
by George H. Morrison

God led them not through the way of the land of the Philistines, although that was near.
Exodus 13:17

There was more than compassion in God's roundabout path to Canaan; there was education, and true compassion is generally educational. We hardly realize what we would have lost, nor how incalculably poorer the human race would have been, if Israel had been permitted the near-cut. Five days by the power of God might have brought them to Canaan, but still with Egypt and its bondage in their blood. It took one night to take Israel out of Egypt, but forty years to take Egypt out of Israel. And when I think of all that Israel learned in the storm and the shadow of that difficult journey; when I remember how it enriched and deepened their knowledge of themselves, and of their God, I feel that the purpose of the Divine was in it: they were being educated for your sake and mine. God led them not through the way of the Philistines, though that was near. And we are all debtors to that leadership.

That, then, was one feature of God's guidance. It avoided the near road, and it took the roundabout; and if you have been living with the open eye, watching the method of the Divine in things, you have seen much that is similar to this. But we forget so readily, that it is part of a preacher's job just to recall parallels at times. Let us name, then, some of the larger areas, where again the near-cut was not God's.

Think of the discovery of nature's secrets: of coal, of iron, of steam, of electricity. God formed this world to be inhabited, said the prophet; and these great powers, or instruments of power, have slumbered or flashed since the world was. And a single whisper from God would have communicated everything, and put mankind in possession of the secrets.

December 28

Near-Cuts Not God's (Part 3 of 6)
by George H. Morrison

God led them not through the way of the land of the Philistines, although that was near.
Exodus 13:17

There have been centuries of patient toil and striving; endless mistakes, long gropings in the dark; there have been suffering and sacrifices in the cause of science, as great as any of Israel in the desert; and then, and not until then, at long last, did the secrets of the world begin to dawn. It has been very roundabout, that road to power; but it has been the right road, in spite of its treacherous winding. For the powers of nature would have mastered us; we should have been their slaves and not their lords had we been faced with them, just after Egypt. And in the effort to know, to understand, and to see, we have learned so much, and have been so elevated, that the roundabout has been a priceless blessing, and we are all debtors to that leadership.

Or rising upward, think of the coming of Jesus. I detect the same leadership of God in that. I see in it the action of that Hand that took Israel to Canaan by a circuit. What is the meaning of all the old religions, of the primitive faiths that were old when Christ was born? And what is the meaning of these thousand sacrifices that smoked on the altar of Gentile and of Jew? They mean that from the first dawn of history man has been crying for a Savior-God. Yet the ages passed, and the Savior never came. And empires arose, and kingdoms passed away, and philosophies were born and flowered and perished, and the prophets prophesied and the psalmists sung: and the world was dying, and all for want of God. Surely, in response to the world's need, He might have come a thousand years before! But God had no near way to Bethlehem. He led the world around and through the desert before He brought it to the king at Nazareth. We see now that there was a fullness of time. There was kindness and education on the road. The world had to be led so to be ready, and we are all debtors to that leadership.

December 29

Near-Cuts Not God's (Part 4 of 6)
by George H. Morrison

God led them not through the way of the land of the Philistines, although that was near.
Exodus 13:17

There is one other region where a similar guidance of God is very evident. I refer to the evangelizing of the world. We talk of the difficulties men feel about foreign missions. I believe that one of the greatest of them all, when one seriously thinks about the matter, is the slow progress that missions seem to make. After the resurrection, on that glad summer morning, men bowed to the gospel like a field of corn. And Jesus Christ is still the power of God: why, then, are the nations not yielding to His love? Is there no near road to the heathen? No thrill from the Infinite that might tingle through Africa until twenty thousand cried aloud for Jesus? Ah, it would be exquisitely pleasing; but you must remember near-cuts are not God's. Slowly, along the roads that business has opened, and by the highways along which battle marched, leaving them blood-red in its own grim way; slowly, by a man here, and by a woman there, and the men are not saints, but of similar passions with ourselves—and by unceasing labor, and by unrecorded sacrifice, the world is being led to know of Jesus. And we have learned so much in that hard struggle, so much of the world, so much of human nature; we have seen such love evolved, such courage and such heroism, that we are all debtors to that leadership.

Now so far I have been dwelling on larger spheres; but I would be sorry ever to close a sermon without having a plea for individual souls. I wish to tell you, then, of one thing I have noticed in the Bible (and when a matter occurs often there, you may be sure there is need for such repetition), I have noticed that most of the high and generous souls—the gallant spirits of the two covenants, let me say—have been tempted to take the near-cut, and in the power of God have conquered it.

December 30

Near-Cuts Not God's (Part 5 of 6)
by George H. Morrison

God led them not through the way of the land of the Philistines, although that was near.
Exodus 13:17

Many have resisted the temptation of the near-cut. Take Abraham, for instance. God had made a promise to Abraham that all the land of Canaan would be his. And Abraham dwelt in Canaan, and he grew rich in it, and he owned not a foot of it, except his wife's grave. Do not you think he had counselors in his tent, and in his own mind, to whisper to him, "Abraham, arise! you have a host of followers; go out and win the land"? And Abraham could fight and conquer when he liked—take for example, his battle with the five kings for Lot's sake. But he refused that near-cut to the promise; he rejected it: he said God must fulfill, not I; and he died in a strange country, dwelling in tents, though God had pledged him Canaan for his own. Tempted by the near road, he refused it. He felt by faith that God's ways were roundabout. And when he opened his eyes on the other side of Jordan, and in the true Canaan saw the King in his beauty, I promise you he knew that God's road was best.

Or think of David. God had made a promise to David that the Kingdom of Israel would be his. And David was persecuted and hunted in the hills, until there came that never-to-be-forgotten morning by the sheep pens, when Saul went into the cave to relieve himself. And the men of David said unto him, "Behold the day of which the Lord said unto you: I will deliver your enemy into your hand." One stab and his great enemy was dead. The times were rough, and no one would have blamed him. One cut—yes, a near-cut to the throne. But "the Lord forbid that I should do this thing!" David refused it; he put the thought from him like poison. And when at last, after Mount Gilboa, he came to his throne by the way that God appointed, I promise you he felt God's ways were best.

December 31

Near-Cuts Not God's (Part 6 of 6)
by George H. Morrison

God led them not through the way of the land of the Philistines, although that was near.
Exodus 13:17

Think with all reverence of Jesus Christ, tempted in all ways like as we are, yet without sin. Why did He come to earth to live and die for us, except that the kingdoms of this world might become His? And the devil takes Him up into an exceeding high mountain, and shows Him all the kingdoms of the world, and said to Him: "All these things I will give You if You will fall down and worship me." It was the old temptation. I speak with utmost reverence—it was Jesus being tempted by near ways. There was a quicker and an easier road than Calvary. "Partner Yourself, Jesus, in Your magnificent powers—partner Yourself with the spirit of the world, and triumph is certain; there needs to be no Gethsemane; men will be quick to feel the King in You and crown You." Then said Jesus unto him: "Get away from Me, Satan, for it is written you shall worship the Lord your God." And when I think of the long road of Jesus, round by the villages, and through the Garden, and on to the cross, and into the grave, I feel, if I never felt it in my life before, that near-cuts are not God's.

Now I want you to carry out that truth. You want to be prosperous? There is no near road to that, consistent with Christian principle and God. And there is no near road to joy, nor to Christian character; you must go around by the desert to that Canaan. Be patient. Do not be showy or flashy. Hold to it, unyielding, in the dark, and go ahead. And though the way is strangely roundabout, full of mistake and struggle and secret cry, it will emerge, in the good time of God, into the land that flows with milk and honey.

Short Cuts
by Bryan L. Herde

Always in a hurry trying quickly to get something done.
Looking for a short cut, hoping hurdles there are none.
Instead of waiting patiently for something to unfold,
We strive ahead anxiously, circumstantially controlled.

February 29
BONUS FOR LEAP YEAR

The Buoyancy of Faith
by John Henry Jowett

[Peter] walked upon the waters to come to Jesus.
Matthew 14:29

Faith is always the secret of buoyancy. We can plant our footsteps in the sea when our faith is resting in the Lord. The waves can never overwhelm us. We ride upon the storm. When Mrs. Booth, the mother of the Salvation Army, was dying, she proclaimed in great triumph, "The waters are rising, but I am not sinking!" When old Mr. Honest [from John Bunyan's *Pilgrim's Progress*] reached the river he found that, in Christ Jesus, its destructiveness was broken, and he went through the waters singing, "Grace reigns!" And so it is in all the rivers and floods through which the believer has to pass; he cannot be held by them, he rises above them, he is their superior in the Lord. And thus the believer in Christ Jesus is to be distinguished by his buoyancy. This is to be his song as he confronts the most tremendous seas, "Therefore we will not fear though the waters roar and be troubled!" His fame is to be that of the man whom nothing can sink. He is to be always on the top of circumstances, their master and not their slave. Like the Apostle Paul, he is to be "always confident," knowing whom he has believed. When the spirits of others are sinking he is to be the one to encourage them, to lift them up by his own unquenchable cheer. He is to sing songs in the night.

And what times are these for the display of spiritual buoyancy! What great reasons for walking the troubled seas! What opportunities for witnessing to the power of the resurrection in lifting the soul above the floods of death and hell! Jesus walks the waters which He calls us to tread. He does not send us on a daring but lonely errand: He invites us into His fellowship. The walk on the deep is a journey with the Lord. And, therefore, by faith we share His conquests. "The works that I do you shall do also." We can walk the stormy sea! And when those who do not know the Lord look upon our power to rise above the troubled circumstance, their souls will begin to move toward the secret of our life, and by faith they also shall find the same uplifting strength in the fellowship of Christ.

Authors' Biographies

Thank you, Wikipedia, for providing nearly all of the information describing each of the authors!

Booth, Catherine (1829-1890) was co-founder of The Salvation Army, along with her husband William Booth. Because of her influence in the formation of The Salvation Army she was known as the "Mother of The Salvation Army." Catherine Booth was eloquent and compelling in speech, articulate and devastatingly logical in writing, she had for over twenty years defended the right of women to preach the gospel on the same terms as men. At first, Catherine and her husband had shared a ministry as traveling evangelists, but then she came into great demand as a preacher in her own right, especially among the well-to-do. A woman preacher was a rare phenomenon in a world where women had few civil rights, and no place in the professions. Catherine Booth was both a woman and a fine preacher, a magnetic combination that attracted large numbers to hear her and made its own statement about the validity of women's ministry. She died of breast cancer at age 61 at Crossley House.

Bowen, George H. (1816-1888) was an American missionary, newspaper man, linguist, and translator in India. He was known as "The White Saint of India" for his resemblance in manner and dress to the Hindu holy men. Like many New Englanders of his generation Bowen was a skeptic, especially after reading the works of Edward Gibbon; however at the age of 28, in 1844, he grew into an acceptance of the Christian God upon reading William Paley's *Natural Theology*. Bowen subsequently enrolled in the Union Theological Seminary in New York and graduated from there in 1847. He went to India the next year as a missionary under the auspices of the American Board of Commissioners for Foreign Missions. Bowen became assistant editor in 1851 and edited and published the *Bombay Guardian* from 1854 until his death in 1888. Bowen was the director of the Bombay Tract and Book Society. Beginning in 1871, Bowen worked with American Methodist William Taylor administering to the needs of the offspring of Indian and European unions. In 1873 he joined the Methodist church.

Brooks, Phillips (1835-1893) was an American Episcopal clergyman and author, long the Rector of Boston's Trinity Church and briefly Bishop of Massachusetts, and particularly remembered as lyricist of the Christmas hymn, "O Little Town of Bethlehem." During the American Civil War he upheld the cause of the North and opposed slavery, and his sermon on the death of Abraham Lincoln was an eloquent expression of the character of both men. His sermon at Harvard's commemoration of the Civil War dead in 1865 likewise attracted attention nationwide. In 1869 he became rector of Trinity Church, Boston; today, his statue is located on the left exterior of the church. He was for many years an overseer and preacher of Harvard University. In 1881 he declined an invitation to be the sole preacher to the university and professor of Christian ethics. On April 30, 1891 he was elected sixth Bishop of Massachusetts, and on the 14 October was consecrated to that office in Trinity Church. He died unmarried in 1893. His death was a major event in the history of Boston. One observer reported: "They buried him like a king. Harvard students carried his body on their shoulders. All barriers of denomination were down. Roman Catholics and Unitarians felt that a great man had fallen in Israel."

Burrell, David James (1844-1926) accepted the call as second Senior Minister in 1891 at Marble Collegiate Church in New York City, and oversaw the redesign of the church's interior. He was responsible for many of Marble's outreach programs, including sponsoring the Sunshine Mission in Hell's Kitchen and initiating the printed sermon booklets.

Drummond, Henry (1851-1897) was a Scottish evangelist, writer and lecturer. Drummond was born in Stirling. He was educated at Edinburgh University, where he displayed a strong inclination for physical and mathematical science. The religious element was an even more powerful factor in his nature, and disposed him to enter the Free Church of Scotland. While preparing for the ministry, he became for a time deeply interested in the evangelizing mission of Moody and Sankey, in which he actively cooperated for two years. In 1877 he became lecturer on natural science in the Free Church College, which enabled him to combine all the pursuits for which he felt a vocation. Drummond's health failed shortly (he had suffered from bone cancer for some years), and he died on 11 March 1897.

Fénelon, François de Salignac de la Mothe more commonly known as **François Fénelon** (1651-1715), was a French Roman Catholic archbishop, theologian, poet and writer. He was inducted into the Académie Française in 1693 and named Archbishop of Cambrai in 1695. During his time as the educator and teacher of the Duke, Fénelon wrote several entertaining and educational works, including the extensive novel *Les Aventures de Télémaque, fils d'Ulysse* (*The Adventures of Telemachus, son of Ulysses*), which depicted the ideal of a wise king. When this novel began circulating anonymously among the court, having been fragmentarily published in 1699 without his knowledge, Louis XIV, who saw many criticisms of his absolutistic style of rule in *Télémaque*, stopped the printing and banned Fénelon from court. Fénelon then retreated to his bishopric in Cambrai, where he remained active writing theological and political treatises until his death.

Gordon, Major-General Charles George (1833-1885), also known as Chinese Gordon, Gordon Pasha, and Gordon of Khartoum, was a British Army officer and administrator. He saw action in the Crimean War as an officer in the British Army. However, he made his military reputation in China, where he was placed in command of the "Ever Victorious Army," a force of Chinese soldiers led by European officers. In the early 1860s, Gordon and his men were instrumental in putting down the Taiping Rebellion, regularly defeating much larger forces. For these accomplishments, he was given the nickname "Chinese Gordon" and honors from both the Emperor of China and the British. He entered the service of the Khedive of Egypt in 1873 (with British government approval) and later became the Governor-General of the Sudan, where he did much to suppress revolts and the local slave trade. Exhausted, he resigned and returned to Europe in 1880. A serious revolt then broke out in the Sudan, led by a Muslim religious leader and self-proclaimed Mahdi, Muhammad Ahmad. In early 1884 Gordon was sent to Khartoum with instructions to secure the evacuation of loyal soldiers and civilians and to depart with them. In defiance of those instructions, after evacuating about 2,500 British civilians he retained a smaller group of soldiers and non-military men. In the buildup to battle, the two leaders corresponded, each attempting to convert the other to his faith, but neither would accede. Besieged by the Mahdi's forces, Gordon organized a citywide defense lasting almost a year that gained him the admiration of the British public, but not of the government, which had wished him not to become entrenched. Only when public pressure to act had become irresistible did the government, with reluctance, send a relief force. It arrived two days after the city had fallen and Gordon had been killed.

Gordon, Samuel Dickey (S.D.) (1859-1936) was a prolific author and evangelical minister active in the latter part of the 19th and early 20th centuries. Born in Philadelphia, he served as assistant secretary of the Philadelphia Young Men's Christian Association (YMCA) in 1884-86 and then became state secretary for the YMCA in Ohio, serving from 1886 to 1895. He is perhaps best known for his series of books, *Quiet Talks About...*, which have their own unique style, very much different from that of other writers of the day.

Herde, Bryan L. (1955-) was born in Enid, Oklahoma where he accepted Christ as his Savior at the age of five. Throughout his childhood and young adult years, his church was his second home. His journey with the Lord over the past decades has been one where duty has been transformed into a life of intimacy with God and whole-hearted trust in the Lord. He is happily married to his wife of 40 years, Gayle. Bryan is a full-time business management consultant, strategic and succession planner, executive coach and part-time writer and Bible teacher. Beyond the U.S., his business and ministry travels have taken him to Libya, South Sudan, Kenya, Thailand, Haiti, Peru and Belize.

Jones, John Daniel (1865-1942) was a Welsh Congregational minister. He was born in Ruthin, Denbighshire, the son of Joseph David Jones (1827–70), a schoolmaster in the town and a respected musician and composer. The family moved to Tywyn, his mother's home town. In 1877, after the early death of his father, his mother married David Morgan Bynner, a Congregational minister at Chorley. Jones became well known as the minister of Richmond Hill Church, Bournemouth. He was elected chairman of the Congregational Union of England and Wales in 1909–10, and again in 1925–6. In 1919 he was elected an honorary secretary of the union, a position which he held until his death in 1942.

Jowett, John Henry (1863-1923) was an influential British Protestant preacher at the turn of the nineteenth to the twentieth century and wrote many books on topics related to Christian living. Jowett was born August 25, 1863 at Beaumont Town, Northowram in Halifax, West Yorkshire to working-class parents who attended the Congregational church in Halifax, West Yorkshire. Jowett's father was a tailor and draper. Jowett understood the problems faced by workers and while the pastor at Carr's Lane Congregational Church in Birmingham, England founded the Digbeth Institute, now an arts center. Jowett was the author of numerous books on Christian devotion, preaching, and the Bible.

Ker, John (1819–1886) was born in Tweedmuir 1819 and was a Scottish ecclesiastical writer and minister in the United Presbyterian Church. Educated at Edinburgh University, he spent some time in Germany in post-graduate work. He became pastor of East Campbell Church, Glasgow, in 1851; and in 1876 was appointed professor of practical training in the United Presbyterian Theological Hall. He died in 1886.

Macduff, John Ross (1818-1895) was a Scottish divine and a prolific author of religious essays. He published many practical and devotional works which attained a wide circulation. Macduff was educated at the High School of Edinburgh and the University of Edinburgh, and was ordained as minister of Kettins, a parish in Forfarshire close to his maternal grandfather's estate, in 1843. He was transmitted to St Madoes. He later left to take charge of Sandyford, a new church in the affluent west end of Glasgow in 1855. He preached at Sandyford for fifteen years (until 1870), and then went to live in Chislehurst, Kent, in order to focus entirely on writing. In 1857, while in Glasgow, he was appointed by the General Assembly a member of their Hymnal Committee. His 31 hymns appeared in his *Altar Stones*, 1853, and were also included with his later poems in his *The Gates of Praise*, 1876. His hymn, "Christ is Coming, Let Creation" is still included in the Church of Scotland's *Church Hymnary 4*. Macduff died at his home, Ravensbrook, Chislehurst in 1895.

Matheson, George (1842-1906) was a Scottish minister and hymn writer. He was the eldest of eight children. Matheson was educated at Glasgow Academy and the University of Glasgow, where he graduated first in classics, logic and philosophy. In his twentieth year he became totally blind, but he held to his resolve to enter the ministry, and gave himself to theological and historical study. In 1886, he moved to Edinburgh, where he became minister of St. Bernard's Parish Church in Stockbridge for 13 years. Here his chief work as a preacher was done. He died suddenly of apoplexy (stroke) at Avenell House in North Berwick on 28 August 1906 in Edinburgh and is buried with his parents in the Glasgow Necropolis. He never married.

Miller, James Russell (1840–1912) was a popular Christian author, Editorial Superintendent of the Presbyterian Board of Publication, and pastor of several churches in Pennsylvania and Illinois. Miller was born near Frankfort Springs, Pennsylvania. In 1857, James entered Beaver Academy and in 1862 he progressed to Westminster College, Pennsylvania, which he graduated in June 1862. Then in the autumn of that year he entered the theological seminary of the United Presbyterian Church at Allegheny, Pennsylvania. Miller resumed his interrupted studies after the Civil War at the Allegheny Theological Seminary in the fall of 1865 and completed them in the spring of 1867. That summer he accepted a call from the First United Presbyterian Church of New Wilmington, Pennsylvania. He was ordained and installed on 11 September 1867. On 29 October 1899, St. Paul Church in West Philadelphia was organized with sixty-six members. Miller was chosen as the temporary pastor and became its pastor in 1906. Miller remained pastor until the year of his death, 1912. The church at that time had 1,397 members.

Morrison, George Herbert (1866-1928) was the son of a minister, born in Glasgow, Scotland. He went to the University of Glasgow in 1883 and then was offered an assistant editorship under Sir James Murray, on the staff of the New English Dictionary at Oxford. After fifteen months in Oxford he returned to Glasgow for his Divinity course. In 1893 Morrison became assistant to Alexander Whyte (see above). The fifteen months at St. George's, Edinburgh, altered his whole life. From 1898 to 1902 he was minister of St. John's, Dundee, a large city church. Morrison began his ministry at Wellington Church, Glasgow, on May 13, 1902, and remained there until his death in 1928.

Müller, George (German-born 1805-1898), a Christian evangelist and Director of the Ashley Down orphanage in Bristol, England, cared for 10,024 orphans in his life. He was well known for providing an education to the children under his care, to the point where he was accused of raising the poor above their natural station in life. He also established 117 schools which offered Christian education to over 120,000 children, many of them being orphans. From the age of 69 to 78, he travelled nearly 70,000 miles between 1874 and 1883.

Murray, Andrew (1828-1917) was a South African writer, teacher and Christian pastor. Murray considered missions to be "the chief end of the church." Through his writings, Murray was also a key Higher Life or Keswick leader, and his theology of faith-healing and belief in the continuation of the apostolic gifts made him a significant forerunner of the Pentecostal movement. Murray died on 18 January 1917, four months before his 89th birthday.

Parker, Joseph (1830-1902) was an English Congregational minister. Born in Hexham, Northumberland, Parker was the son of Teasdale Parker, a stonemason, and Elizabeth (née Dodd). He managed to pick up a fair education, which afterwards he constantly supplemented. Parker's preaching differed widely from his contemporaries like Spurgeon and Alexander Maclaren. He did not follow outlines or list his points, but spoke extemporaneously, inspired by his view of the spirit and attitude behind his Scripture text. He expressed himself frankly, with conviction and passion. His transcriber commented that he was at his best when he strayed furthest from his loose outlines. He did not often delve into detailed textual or critical debates. His preaching was neither systematic theology nor expository commentary, but sounded more like his personal meditations. Joseph Parker's chief legacy is not his theology but his gift for oratory. Alexander Whyte commented on Joseph Parker: "He is by far the ablest man now standing in the English-speaking pulpit. He stands in the pulpit of Thomas Goodwin, the Atlas of Independency. And Dr. Parker is a true and worthy successor to this great Apostolic Puritan." Among his biographers, Margaret Bywater called him "the most outstanding preacher of his time," and Angus Watson wrote that "no one had ever spoken like him."

Payson, Edward (1783-1827) was an American Congregational preacher. He was born in Rindge, New Hampshire, where his father, Rev. Seth Payson (1758-1820), was pastor of the Congregational Church. His uncle, Phillips Payson (1736-1801), pastor of a church in Chelsea, Massachusetts, was a physicist and astronomer. Edward Payson graduated at Harvard in 1803, was then principal of a school at Portland, Maine, and in 1807 became junior pastor of the Congregational Church at Portland, where he remained, after 1811, as senior pastor, until his death. Archibald Alexander suggested in 1844 that "no man in our country has left behind him a higher character for eminent piety than the Rev. Edward Payson."

Reynolds, Henry Robert (1825-1896) was an English Congregational minister, college head and writer. Educated mainly by his father, in September 1841 he entered Coward College, London to prepare for the ministry. He matriculated at London University in the same year, obtaining the university mathematical scholarship in 1844 and graduating B.A. in 1848. In April 1846 Reynolds became pastor of the congregational church at Halstead in Essex, receiving permission to curtail his course at Coward College. In 1849 Reynolds accepted a call to be minister of the East Parade chapel at Leeds, entering on the duties on 28 March. In 1855 his health gave way, and during next five years he spent time on visits to Egypt, Italy, and the south of France, being frequently ill. In May 1895 he retired to Broxbourne in Hertfordshire. He died there on 10 September 1896, and was buried in Cheshunt cemetery on 15 September.

Simpson, Albert Benjamin (1843-1919), also known as **A. B. Simpson**, was a Canadian preacher, theologian, author, and founder of the Christian and Missionary Alliance (C&MA), an evangelical Protestant denomination with an emphasis on global evangelism.

Smith, Hannah Whitall (1832-1911) was a lay speaker and author in the Holiness movement in the United States and the Higher Life movement in the United Kingdom of Great Britain and Ireland. She was also active in the Women's suffrage and the Temperance movements. Born in Philadelphia, Smith was from a long line of prominent and influential Quakers in New Jersey. Hannah Whitall Smith died in England in 1911.

Watson, Thomas (1620-1686) was an English Nonconformist, Puritan preacher and author. He was educated at Emmanuel College, Cambridge, where he was noted for remarkably intense study. In 1646 he commenced a sixteen-year pastorate at St. Stephen's, Walbrook. He showed strong Presbyterian views during the English civil war, with, however, an attachment to the king, and in 1651 he was imprisoned briefly with some other ministers for his share in Christopher Love's plot to recall Charles II of England. He was released on 30 June 1652, and was formally reinstated as vicar of St. Stephen's Walbrook. He obtained great fame and popularity as a preacher until the Restoration, when he was ejected for Nonconformity. Despite the rigor of the acts against dissenters, Watson continued to exercise his ministry privately as he found opportunity. Upon the Declaration of Indulgence in 1672 he obtained a license to preach at the great hall in Crosby House. After preaching there for several years, his health gave way, and he retired to Barnston, Essex, where he died suddenly while praying in secret. He was buried on 28 July 1686.

Whitefield, George (1714-1770), also known as George Whitfield, was an English Anglican cleric who helped spread the Great Awakening in Britain and, especially, in the American colonies. Born in Gloucester, England, he attended Pembroke College, Oxford University, where he met the Wesley brothers. He was one of the founders of Methodism and of the evangelical movement generally. In 1740, Whitefield traveled to America, where he preached a series of revivals that came to be known as the "Great Awakening." He became perhaps the best-known preacher in Great Britain and North America during the 18th century. Because he traveled throughout the American colonies and drew thousands of people with his sermons, he was one of the most widely-recognized public figures in colonial America.

Whyte, Alexander (1836-1921) was a Scottish divine. He was born at Kirriemuir in Forfarshire and educated at the University of Aberdeen and at New College, Edinburgh. He entered the ministry of the Free Church of Scotland and after serving as colleague in Free St John's, Glasgow (1866-1870) removed to Edinburgh as colleague and successor to Dr. R. S.

Candlish at Free St George's. In 1909 he succeeded Dr. Marcus Dods as principal and professor of New Testament literature, at New College, Edinburgh.

Additional Books
by
Bryan L. Herde

*Against the Stream: A Business Professional's Journey
as a Disciple and Friend of God*

Travelers on the Ancient Paths: Ageless Wisdom for an Anxious World

In the Stream—Volume One: Being a Disciple of Jesus Christ

In the Stream—Volume Two: Living in the Flow of God

These are available in both print and Kindle formats at:

www.amazon.com

If you would like to make any comments or ask any questions,
please contact me at:

bryan@sovereigngrip.com

48769980R00221

Made in the USA
Middletown, DE
16 June 2019